RIGGED

RIGGED

How the Media, Big Tech, and the Democrats Seized Our Elections

MOLLIE HEMINGWAY

Regnery Publishing
WASHINGTON, D.C.

Regnery® is a registered trademark and its colophon is a trademark of Salem Communications Holding Corporation

Cataloging-in-Publication data on file with the Library of Congress

ISBN: 978-1-68451-259-1
eISBN: 978-1-68451-263-8

Library of Congress Control Number: 2021943477

Published in the United States by
Regnery Publishing
A Division of Salem Media Group
Washington, D.C.
www.Regnery.com

Manufactured in the United States of America

10 9 8 7 6 5 4 3 2

Books are available in quantity for promotional or premium use. For information on discounts and terms, please visit our website: www.Regnery.com.

CONTENTS

PROLOGUE

You're Not Wrong

If questioning the results of a presidential election were a crime, as
many have asserted in the wake of the controversial 2020 election and
its aftermath, then much of the Democratic Party and media establishment should have been indicted for their behavior following the 2016
election. In fact, the last time Democrats fully accepted the legitimacy
of a presidential election they lost was in 1988.

After the 2000 election, which hinged on the results of a recount in
Florida, Democrats smeared President George W. Bush as "selected, not
elected."[1] When Bush won re-election against then senator John Kerry in
2004, many on the left claimed that voting machines in Ohio had been
rigged to deliver fraudulent votes to Bush.[2] HBO even produced and aired
the Emmy-nominated *Hacking Democracy*, a documentary claiming to
show that "votes can be stolen without a trace," adding fuel to the conspiracy theory fire that the results of the 2004 election were illegitimate.[3]
But nothing holds a candle to what happened in 2016 after Donald
Trump's surprising defeat of former secretary of state Hillary Clinton.

Rather than accept that Trump won and Clinton lost fair and square,
the political and media establishments desperately sought to explain

away Trump's victory. They settled on a destructive conspiracy theory that crippled the government, empowered America's adversaries, and illegally targeted innocent private citizens whose only crime was not supporting Hillary Clinton.

The Russia collusion hoax had all the elements of an election conspiracy theory, including baseless claims of hacked voting totals, illegal voter suppression, and treasonous collaboration with a foreign power. Pundits and officials speculated openly that President Trump was a foreign asset and that members of his circle were under the thumb of the Kremlin.

But despite the patent absurdity of these claims, the belief that Trump stole the 2016 election had the support of the most powerful institutions, individuals, and even government agencies in the country. To question the legitimacy of the 2016 election wasn't to undermine our democracy; it was considered by some of our most elevated public figures a patriotic duty.

"You can run the best campaign, you can even become the nominee, and you can have the election stolen from you," Clinton told her followers in 2019.[4]

"I know he's an illegitimate president," Clinton claimed of Trump a few months later.[5] She even said during an interview with *CBS Sunday Morning* that "voter suppression and voter purging and hacking" were the reasons for her defeat.[6]

Former president Jimmy Carter agreed. "[Trump] lost the election and was put into office because the Russians interfered on his behalf," he told NPR in 2019. "Trump didn't actually win the election in 2016."[7]

Their view was shared by most prominent Democrats in Congress. Representative John Lewis of Georgia, for example, said he was skipping Trump's inauguration in 2016 because he believed Trump was illegitimate: "[T]he Russians participated in helping this man get elected.... That's not right. That's not fair. That's not an open democratic process."[8] Lewis had also skipped the inauguration of President George W. Bush, claiming Bush, too, was an illegitimate president.[9]

A few members of Congress joined him in 2001. By 2017, one out of three Democrats in the U.S. House of Representatives boycotted Trump's inauguration.[10] Many said they refused to take part in the installation of an "illegitimate" president.

The corporate media didn't condemn leading Democrats' refusal to accept the results of the 2016 election. In fact, the media amplified the most speculative claims of how Trump and Russia had colluded to steal the election from Clinton. They dutifully regurgitated inaccurate leaks from corrupt intelligence officials suggesting Trump and his staff had committed treason. They ran stories arguing that Republicans who didn't support their conspiracy theory were insufficiently loyal to the country or somehow compromised themselves.[11]

It was all nonsense. Even Robert Mueller, who ran a multi-year and multi-million-dollar government investigation into claims that Trump personally colluded with Russian president Vladimir Putin to steal the election from Clinton, found no evidence to support the fevered accusations.[12]

The reporters who pushed this conspiracy theory were never held accountable by their peers for peddling leaks and lies. They received raises and promotions, honors and awards, and the applause of their colleagues. Some were given Pulitzer Prizes for "reporting" that was closer to fan fiction than an accurate description of events.[13]

From 2016 through 2020, the easiest way to achieve stardom on the political left was to loudly proclaim one's belief that the 2016 election was illegitimate—stolen by the Russians on behalf of a corrupt traitor. Conspiracy-mongering, up to and including the assertion that the president of the United States was a secret Russian spy, was the highest form of patriotism.

And then 2020 happened.

At the drop of a hat, America's electoral system went from irredeemably corrupt and broken in 2016 to unquestionably safe in 2020. Voting methods that were allegedly used to steal elections in 2004 and 2016 suddenly became sacrosanct and unquestionable in 2020. Whereas so-called election experts repeatedly warned pre-2020 about the pitfalls of electronic voting and widespread mail-in balloting, by November 2020 any discussion about the vulnerabilities of those methods was written off as the stuff of right-wing cranks and conspiracy-mongers.

Such dismissals required ignoring quite real problems with election integrity affecting hundreds of U.S. elections at the state and local levels, and even the 1960 presidential election, when John F. Kennedy won just 118,574 more votes than Richard Nixon. That Electoral College win hinged on victories in Illinois, where Chicago vote totals were suspiciously high for Kennedy, and Texas, a state where Kennedy's running mate Lyndon B. Johnson had been known to exert control over election results. Official biographers and historians have claimed one or both states would have been won by Nixon in a fair election.[14]

If concerns about election integrity were valid from at least 1960 through 2016, then surely those concerns were even more valid in 2020, an election year unlike any other in American history.

In the lead-up to the election, thanks in part to the coronavirus pandemic that gripped the world, wide-ranging electoral reforms were implemented. Across the country at the state, local, and federal levels, political actors rammed through hundreds of structural changes to the manner and oversight of elections, resulting in what *Time* magazine would later call "a revolution in how people vote."[15] Some of these changes were enacted by state legislatures, some by courts, and others by state and county election officials. Many changes, allegedly justified by the global pandemic, were broad reforms that Democrats had long desired. The crisis was their chance to sneak in contentious policies through the back door.

The bedrock of the American republic is that elections must be free, fair, accurate, and trusted. Election lawyers will tell you that fraud is almost impossible to conclusively find after the fact, and that to fight it, strong rules and regulations are needed on the front end. That's why Democrats and Republicans fight so bitterly about the rules and regulations that govern the process.

What happened during the 2020 election must be investigated and discussed, not in spite of media and political opposition to an open inquiry, but because of that opposition. The American people deserve to know what happened. They deserve answers, even if those answers are inconvenient. They deserve to know the effect flooding the system with tens of millions of mail-in ballots had on their vote. They deserve to know how and why Big Tech and the corporate political media manipulated the news to support certain political narratives while censoring stories they now admit were true. They deserve to know why courts were allowed to unilaterally rewrite the rules in the middle of the contest, often without the consent of the legislative bodies charged with writing election laws.

Republicans began to issue warnings about the new practices well before November 2020. They talked about how widespread changes in the manner the country conducts elections would create uncertainty, confusion, and delays.

They worried that widespread mail-in voting would lead to fraud. And they had good reason to worry. A 2005 bipartisan commission co-chaired by none other than Jimmy Carter found that absentee balloting was the largest source of potential fraud in American elections. Why should 2020 be any different?

They worried that universal mail-in balloting would make ballots harder to track, as some states bombarded addresses with ballots for previous residents who had moved out but hadn't been struck from the voter rolls. What would happen to all the excess ballots?

They worried that lowering, or in some cases eliminating, standards for signature verification on mail-in ballots could make it impossible to challenge those fraudulently cast. In an election that promised to be contentious, lowering the standards seemed like a recipe for undermining public faith in the results. Why not leave signature verification as it was, or strengthen it?

They worried third-party ballot harvesting would encourage voter fraud. Some states had called for unsupervised drop boxes to replace or supplement ordinary polling stations. What would stop those boxes from being tampered with, or, worse still, from being filled with fraudulent votes by bad actors?

They worried ballot management in some areas was privately funded by corporate oligarchs overtly hostile to the Republican Party. Didn't that give at least the appearance of impropriety? And they worried that failing to remove the deceased and those who moved out of state from voter rolls would cause worse problems in an election in which mail-in balloting would feature so prevalently.

Republicans also screamed bloody murder about the censorship by social media platforms of conservative voices and negative news stories about Democrats. They were horrified by a media complex that moved from extreme partisan bias to unabashed propaganda in defense of the Democratic Party. They watched as a completely legitimate story about international corruption involving the Biden family business—and implicating Joe Biden himself—was crushed by media and tech companies colluding to suppress it.

None of those problems went away after the election. If anything, the concern about them grew as tens of millions of Americans realized the problems associated with sloppy election procedure. It took days to get a handle on how many people had voted, much less how they had voted. And in an election of fine margins, the uncertainty surrounding basic questions of electoral procedure was reason to harbor doubts about the results.

Doubts only grew as citizens saw how difficult it was to maintain independent oversight of the counting process. Observers were often misled about whether counting had stopped for the evening. Some were kept so far away from the ballot counting that courts had to intervene.

As mail-in ballots came in and were accepted even when they were not properly filled out, Republicans saw the consequences of the mad rush to change the nation's voting laws. And they saw how the media dismissed all concerns about how the election was run without a lick of investigation.

The powers that be did whatever it took to prevent Trump from winning his re-election bid in 2020. They admitted as much in a victory lap masquerading as a news article in *Time* magazine that referred to the individuals and institutions behind the efforts to oust Trump as a "well-funded cabal of powerful people, ranging across industries and ideologies, working together behind the scenes to influence perceptions, change rules and laws, steer media coverage and control the flow of information."[16]

That's to say nothing of the widespread privatization of election systems in key districts thanks to the efforts of leftist outlets funded by Mark Zuckerberg and other billionaires. Multi-million-dollar grants to public election commissions, and the strings attached to them, were the means by which the left's sprawling voting activist arm took over huge parts of the 2020 election. These grants enabled the Democratic Party to run its get-out-the-vote operation through key cities and states. This private interference in the running of a national election had never before happened in the history of the country.

This book tells the story of how the political, media, and corporate establishments changed election laws and procedures, reduced or eliminated the oversight of ballots, manipulated the COVID-19 response, stoked violent racial unrest, published fake news, censored accurate news, and did everything in their power to make sure what had happened in 2016—a Trump election victory—could not happen again in 2020.

The media and other leftists learned a singular lesson from 2016: They could not let an outsider gain control of a system that so many political elites depend on ever again, democracy be damned. They were taking no chances. They would do whatever it took to make sure Trump lost.

Donald Trump certainly has a unique way of looking at the world, and a formidable personality. These traits are at once his biggest assets and the source of some of his biggest difficulties. Both have contributed to his most notable successes as well as his most notable failures. He is hardly blameless for his narrow defeat.

However, Trump's flaws must be weighed against the disturbing nature of the opposition arrayed against him—an army of corporate-funded left-wing activists who excused and encouraged violent riots across the country; technology oligarchs who made unprecedented efforts to normalize censorship; state and local officials who radically altered the way Americans vote in the middle of an election for partisan advantage; an ostensibly free press that credulously and willfully published fake news to damage the president; politicized federal law enforcement agencies that abused the federal government's surveillance and investigative powers to smear Trump as a puppet of a foreign power; and an opposition party that coordinated all these smears and spent years trying to impeach and remove a duly elected president from office.

Such extreme, and in some cases un-American, opposition explains why tens of millions of citizens believe that the election was conducted from the beginning in a manner that was unfair, riddled with integrity problems, and designed to make it difficult to catch fraud.

America's smug political elites, of course, responded by mocking a small group of Americans that believe in darker and crazier conspiracies about what happened. It's convenient to pretend that certain extreme beliefs are representative of all seventy-four million Trump voters, or even of just the tens of millions of Republican voters who are troubled about how the election was conducted.

But these same establishment figures never ask themselves how their own rank dishonesty contributed to an information climate that gaslights well-meaning voters—voters who are unwilling to abandon the cherished American ideals of equality and liberty to forces of social and economic control. In some respects, it would be much more comforting to believe a small cabal of people changed forty thousand votes and handed Biden the victory. That kind of corruption is much easier to root out and fix.

Those in control of America's most powerful institutions—business, media, academia, bureaucracies, and even the FBI—are engaged in a permanent struggle against half the country to bring about radical social and political changes. Voters have the right to reject those projects and hold politicians who advance them accountable at the ballot box in free and fair elections.

This fight is about conducting elections in a manner that is trusted by both winners and losers. But it's also about much more than that. It's about ensuring that American citizens still have a voice in determining the future of their country.

If you believe things went terribly wrong in the 2020 election, well, you're not crazy, and you're not alone.

But most of all, *you're not wrong.*

CHAPTER ONE

Over Before It Began

When the Florida results started to come in, President Donald Trump and his campaign team were flying high. President Trump was performing two points better than he had in 2016 in a crucial bellwether state. He was on track to win the election.

On the evening of November 3, 2020, campaign manager Bill Stepien, deputy campaign manager Justin Clark, and other senior members of the re-election campaign assembled in a small room in the White House where they would get updates on election returns.

Historically used as a meeting room for the president and First Lady, the "Map Room" is situated on the south side of the first floor of the White House residence, named for the maps President Franklin D. Roosevelt studied there while commanding U.S. military forces during World War II. It was a fitting place to watch the night unfold.

For Election Night, the room, which usually featured antique mahogany furniture, a red sofa, and an oriental rug, was filled with four black tables pushed together in a large rectangle on which computers were set. Four large flat-screen televisions showing cable news coverage and incoming data were placed on one long side of the room.

Top officials and Trump family members drifted in and out throughout the evening. Occasionally, when the crowd swelled with other guests, White House chief of staff Mark Meadows directed security to remove some people.

One floor up, four hundred of the top current and former Republican officials, ambassadors, donors, and journalists partied in the East Room of the White House, the largest room in the executive mansion and one frequently used to host receptions and events. The crowd spilled into some adjoining rooms. Former New York City mayor Rudy Giuliani was holding court, his entourage nearby. TV host Laura Ingraham was at the gathering, as was Judge Jeanine Pirro, also a TV host. Republican National Committee chair Ronna Romney McDaniel stopped by. The alcohol was flowing freely as guests dined on sliders and fries.

President Donald Trump and his family were stationed in the residences on the top floor, receiving regular updates from top officials and going between the floors to greet visitors and check on results.

The campaign team felt very good heading into Election Night. Their internal metrics showed that support for Trump wasn't just surging, but dramatically surging in the closing days of the race.

The previous Sunday had been a whirlwind of campaign activity for Trump, with large and exuberant rallies in Michigan, Iowa, North Carolina, Georgia, and South Florida, where he'd arrived at the Miami-Opa Locka Executive Airport for a midnight gathering on Sunday night. The next day, Monday, Trump held another five rallies in Fayetteville, North Carolina; Scranton, Pennsylvania; Traverse City, Michigan; Kenosha, Wisconsin; and, finally, Grand Rapids, Michigan, the same city in which he'd spent the final hours of the 2016 campaign.

Reporters expressed surprise at Trump's confidence, since they thought he had little to no shot at victory.[1] Then again, they hadn't given him a chance of winning an election since he first began running for the presidency in 2015. The campaign had learned to disregard most of the media's opinions. After four years of increasingly false narratives, the campaign staff felt that the media were more interested in willing Biden to victory than reflecting reality.

Trump's energetic barnstorming of the country marked a huge contrast from the Biden campaign. The former vice president rarely strayed far from his house in Delaware after he became the presumptive nominee.[2] The Trump campaign mocked Biden, saying he was "staying in the basement,"[3] while the Biden campaign said that Trump and Pence were imperiling public health.

Biden finally got on the road as the campaign came to a close. On November 2, Biden hit small events in Ohio and Pennsylvania. His final stop in Cleveland was at Burke Lakefront Airport, where masked guests in one hundred spaced-out vehicles honked in the place of polite applause.[4] In Pennsylvania, he hosted small drive-in events in Allegheny County and Pittsburgh.

The last two weeks of the 2020 election had been the most normal anyone on the campaign had experienced in months. Just as Biden locked up his nomination in March, the country locked down in response to the coronavirus outbreak, a global pandemic that had spread across the world from its origin in Wuhan, China. The pandemic crushed the thriving economy, one of Trump's major selling points as the country underwent what he liked to call a "blue-collar boom."[5] His deregulatory agenda, tax cuts, willingness to tackle illegal immigration to stop the flood of cheap labor into the country, and renegotiation of trade deals to strengthen industry had jump-started an economy that had been flagging throughout his predecessor's two terms. But now, churches were forced to close, children were banned from school, and public gatherings were declared illegal.

Well before their man won the nomination, the Biden team had decided to make the election a referendum on Trump, mostly because abject hatred of Trump was the main—and perhaps the only—unifying issue in the Democratic Party. A passionate and well-financed "resistance" had formed the moment Trump won his first election, and it had become the soul of the Democratic Party. Before he was inaugurated, there were riots and attempts to keep the Electoral College from voting for Trump.[6] Democratic operatives worked with bureaucrats inside the government to convince Americans that Trump hadn't won fairly, but by colluding with Russia to steal the election.

There was chatter about using the Twenty-Fifth Amendment to the Constitution—which gives the vice president and cabinet members the ability to remove the president if he is unable to serve—to get rid of Trump.[7] On top of the talk, there were congressional investigations, a special counsel appointment, and a failed impeachment. None of these outlandish ploys worked, so this passionate and unified resistance had only one hope—and that was to defeat him in 2020.

The other reason the Biden camp wanted the campaign to be a referendum on Trump was because Biden was seventy-seven years old and hardly a dynamic candidate. Trump wasn't too much younger, but, unlike Biden, he wasn't obviously showing the effects of his age. On the trail, Biden frequently stumbled over his words and made embarrassing gaffes. Though Biden already had a reputation for verbal gaffes and defensiveness from the early days of his career in Washington nearly fifty years prior, by 2020 it seemed worse.[8] Plus, the frequent flubs had helped derail his two previous runs for the highest office in the land.

COVID-19 provided the perfect justification to keep Biden off the trail. Everything was locked down. The only thing that even partially eased the limits on public gatherings was itself traumatic, a "summer of rage" in response to the killing of a suspected criminal by Minneapolis police. A bystander had taken video of the nearly ten minutes that a cop spent kneeling on George Floyd's neck during arrest as he begged for mercy before dying. Over ten thousand protests erupted around the country, at least a thousand of which resulted in violent incidents or riots.[9] Dozens of people were killed and billions of dollars of damages were reported.[10] Thousands of businesses were lost to fires and looting. The media and their activist allies pushed the narrative that America was and is an irredeemably racist country and that the George Floyd video was just the latest proof of that reality. Despite the nationwide violence, the media insisted that the Black Lives Matter movement, which included calls to "defund the police," was peaceful.[11]

Throughout his first campaign and during much of his presidency, Trump was known for gathering massive and exuberant crowds. He gave freewheeling speeches where he tested messages, made jokes, and pushed his policy ideas. But over the course of this campaign, he couldn't hold as many rallies, thanks in large part to the pandemic. COVID-19 hampered the Trump campaign and took the president out of his natural environment.

The few public events that the Biden campaign held didn't go well for the former vice president. At a Biden rally in Bucks County, Pennsylvania, more Trump supporters showed up than Biden supporters. When Biden left, he was forced to drive through a crowd of Trump supporters whom he had earlier called "chumps."[12]

Just a couple days later, more Trump supporters showed up than Biden supporters to a drive-in rally in Minnesota. An angry Biden yelled at them and called them "ugly" as they drowned out his speech.[13]

At an event in Toledo, Biden couldn't be heard over the chants of "Four More Years!" from Trump supporters across the street.[14] As Biden spoke to a group of people in their parked cars, enthusiastic Trump supporters blared horns and drowned him out with noise.

The same thing was happening at Biden rallies across the country. "Practically a Trump drive-in rally here now outside the Biden drive-in event," CNN's MJ Lee said of one Pennsylvania Biden stop.[15]

But now, with the Trump team assembled in the White House residence, all the campaigning was over. Election Day had finally arrived. Members of the Trump campaign thought they had left it all out on the field and were entering the contest in a strong position. They were confident that Election Day would crown them victors.

The Biden campaign saw matters differently. For them, Election Day had arrived two months prior. In fact, from their perspective, the election was over before the sun even rose on the East Coast that day. There was nothing left to play for; the election had already been won.

◆   ◆   ◆

Beginning with the election of Zachary Taylor in 1848, the presidential election was to be held on a single day nationwide. By law, all voters were to decide who would lead the country for the next four years on the "Tuesday after the first Monday in November."[16]

The change to a single day of voting occurred out of concern for election integrity. The 1844 election, which had been spread out over more than a month, was rife with fraud and practices that put the election's legitimacy into question. Voters also feared that election outcomes in states with earlier election dates were influencing how later states voted.[17]

But by 2020, the practice of Americans' voting on the same day was a thing of the past, and Americans returned to what had been rejected in the 1840s—a lengthy window of time for elections.

That's not to say that there had never been exceptions for those who needed them. States had long permitted limited absentee balloting for select citizens who could present legitimate reasons for why they were unable to go to the polls, such as military deployment.

But beginning in the late 1970s, restrictions were loosened. California was the first to allow "no excuse" absentee voting.[18] States across the country would follow suit.

"No excuse" absentee voting allows citizens to cast their ballots early. With the widespread adoption of this practice in recent years, the United States can no longer be said to have an election day in the strict sense of the term. The country has a months-long voting season.

This was already true before 2020, when reforms increased the length of time in which Americans could cast a ballot to ludicrous proportions. North Carolinians, for example, could vote in the 2020 election before Labor Day, a full two months before Election Day and nearly a month before the two candidates had met for their first debate.[19] The changes also obscured the deadline by which votes needed to be counted, a fixture of the system before 2020.

In 2016, absentee and mail-in ballots accounted for roughly 33 million of the 140 million ballots counted.[20] In 2020, more than 100 million of the 159 million ballots counted were cast prior to Election Day, including by early voting.[21]

The change was enough for former attorney general William Barr to sound the alarm about how widespread early, absentee, and mail-in voting was negatively affecting the voting public.[22] Extending voting well beyond voting day "is like telling a jury in a 2-month trial that they can vote any time they want during the trial," Barr said after the election in an interview at his home. "You can't say it's really a national consensus because people are all operating on a different set of facts."

The 2020 election would see an even more important nineteenth-century electoral reform put on the chopping block: the move to a secret ballot that occurred in the late 1800s.

During the colonial period, there were many methods of voting, from using different-colored beans or corn to cast votes to *viva voces*, or voice votes. In the latter system, each voter's name was called, and the voter was asked publicly before a judge, clerks, the candidates, and other voters whom he was voting for. The practice was abandoned in part because creditors would make their debtors vote for their preferred candidates, taking advantage of the public nature of the polls to ensure that debtors did their bidding.[23]

But, as a rule, the colonies moved to paper ballots early on. Governor John Winthrop, one of the leading figures in founding the Massachusetts Bay Colony, abolished public voting in 1634.[24] By 1706, Pennsylvania had passed a law requiring the use of paper ballots, with provisions given for the illiterate. By the end of the Revolutionary War, all states had moved to paper ballots.

Voting on paper used to mean remembering candidates' names and writing them down. But as the size and scope of government grew, so did the number of elected officials, and well-funded political parties began to print ballots with the names of their preferred candidates.

Political parties often gave their pre-printed ballots a distinctive design. Democrats in a nineteenth-century Charleston election, for example, printed red-checked backs on their tickets. In Orangeburg County, South Carolina Republicans made the backs of their tickets look like a playing card.[25] Privacy critics warned that this opened the door to bribery and intimidation, as voters could be bullied into carrying a recognizable ballot into the voting booth.

To limit voter intimidation, some states required that ballots be printed on white paper without any distinguishing marks, guidelines that were easily flouted. In 1851, Free-Soilers and Democrats passed a law requiring that votes be deposited in the ballot box in a sealed envelope. The envelopes were to be of the same size, color, and quality and to be furnished by the secretary of state to the town clerks, who would be stationed in the same room as the ballot box. Opponents of the law were later able to make it optional, which mostly meant that those who could be bribed would continue to be bribed.[26]

Bribery and intimidation were such big issues that the Forty-Sixth Congress of 1879–1881 issued a report detailing some of the problems that plagued insecure voting systems. The report found that employees might be taken to the polls by their employer and compelled to show their ballots before they were cast.[27] This was a particularly pronounced problem in northeastern cities and industrial centers.

With political parties' printing up the ballots that were to be used, coercion, intimidation, and outright fraud became common complaints. The purchasing of votes in exchange for liquor or money was common. In fact, buying votes wasn't even a federal offense until 1925.[28]

Following a model originally developed in Australia, cities and states began to print official ballots that voters could take and cast in a secure environment. This made buying votes much more difficult, as there was no proof for how one had voted.

In 1888, the first Australian ballot was used in Louisville, Kentucky. Clear rules were issued for how to get a candidate's name on the ballot. Massachusetts and New York used the system that same year.[29]

The practice spread across the country—South Carolina became the last state to adopt secret ballots, in 1950—and the states took on the cost of printing up ballots.[30] Party machines and other interested parties didn't like the new system because it made it very difficult to know whether attempted bribery had been successful or not. Verifiable instances of fraud plummeted.[31]

Many other practices were adopted to limit voter fraud and intimidation. States and municipalities began to keep voter rolls to limit precinct-hopping and double voting. Privacy curtains were added to voting areas.[32] Judges and observers from opposing parties were brought in to observe the casting of ballots to limit fraud from corrupt election commissions. The reforms greatly decreased the tumult of elections, and increased public confidence in election results.

As election rules across the country were gradually reformed to address corruption, the franchise was also being expanded. With the ratification of the Fifteenth Amendment in 1870, restricting voting rights on the basis of race was unconstitutional. Initially, there was an encouraging number of black Americans being elected to public office. However, southern states soon enacted Jim Crow laws, and black voters consequently faced repugnant measures such as poll taxes, literacy tests, and outright intimidation when they tried to vote. The Voting Rights Act of 1965 finally killed off Jim Crow laws, but earlier anti-corruption reforms such as the removal of partisan interests from controlling the voting process also helped rectify these racial injustices. There was a period after secret ballots were introduced where some questioned whether they were fair because they necessitated reading and writing at a time when much of the black population was illiterate, having been denied an education. However, reformers argued that the introduction of the secret ballot would prevent black voters from being publicly intimidated,[33] and they were almost certainly right about that in the long term. Women gained the right to vote in states and localities beginning in the latter half of the nineteenth century, culminating in the certification of the Nineteenth Amendment in 1920.

For more than a century, then, for nearly all voting Americans Election Day meant going into a voting place and identifying themselves to a poll worker. They voted privately, perhaps behind a curtain, with no one else allowed to see how they voted.

The move to early and mail-in voting took away some of that secrecy, along with the ability to detect fraud or coercion.

Deviations from in-person, Election Day voting are supposed to replicate the security and anti-fraud protocols a city or state has for in-person voting on Election Day. Early voting ideally follows a similar procedure to Election Day voting: an individual goes to a public place to identify himself, has his name checked off the voter roll, receives a ballot that he fills out in secret, and casts the ballot into a locked box that will be counted on Election Day.

Early voting hinges on public trust in the election officials who take custody of ballots. Voters must trust that election officials aren't playing games with ballots in the weeks before Election Day, or otherwise letting ballots be tampered with.

Mail-in balloting varies widely from state to state, but from an election integrity standpoint, the ideal situation requires the voter to request a ballot, much like he or she would in a polling place on Election Day. That way the state can mark to whom the ballot was handed out on its rolls. While the voter may fill out the ballot at his or her kitchen table, he or she must still attest to his or her identity and provide some evidence to back it up, such as a signature. The signature is supposed to be checked to make sure it matches an official signature kept on file by the state. The voter must also indicate that the vote was cast on a particular day, usually by dating the form. A few states provide secrecy envelopes to prevent outsiders from knowing how the voter cast his or her ballot.[34] That practice is designed to limit coercion from family members, employers, or special interest groups such as labor unions or political parties. It is also so that election judges determining the legality of a vote aren't incentivized to treat a ballot differently based on how it was marked.

Here, obviously, there are many deviations from the secret ballot system, and many opportunities for fraud. Prior to the 2020 election, the media and other partisans admitted that fact freely. France banned mail-in voting in 1975 because of concerns over voter fraud.[35] The 2005 Commission on Federal Election Reform, chaired by former president Jimmy Carter and former secretary of state James Baker, declared that "[a]bsentee ballots remain the largest source of potential voter fraud."[36] The bipartisan commission was formed to address voting and election integrity issues following the razor-thin 2000 presidential election, which was adjudicated at the United States Supreme Court. Of particular concern was how vulnerable voters might be coerced to vote in a way that more powerful people told them to. "Citizens who vote at home, at nursing homes, at the workplace, or in church are more susceptible to pressure, overt and subtle, or to intimidation. Vote buying schemes are far more difficult to detect when citizens vote by mail," the Carter–Baker report said.[37]

A 2001 report produced by the CalTech/MIT Voting Technology Project concluded that "the greatest fraud problems may lie in absentee balloting"[38] and recommended that states "restrict or abolish on-demand absentee voting in favor of in-person early voting."[39] Further, the report stated that "there is no evidence that liberalizing absentee voting laws or enacting early or vote-by-mail schemes has increased voter turnout dramatically.... [R]esearch has identified one condition under which absentee ballot laws increase turnout: when they are sufficiently ambiguous or liberal to allow partisan forces to use them to boost the turnout of party loyalists."[40]

Not that long ago, the notion that mail-in ballots were problematic was the accepted wisdom in liberal media outlets. "Voting by mail is now common enough and problematic enough that election experts say there have been multiple elections in which no one can say with confidence which candidate was the deserved winner," wrote Adam Liptak in a 2012 *New York Times* article headlined "Error and Fraud at Issue as Absentee Voting Rises," specifically citing the 2000 presidential election as an example.[41]

"Absentee ballots are not the only way to fraudulently win an election," wrote the *Washington Post*'s David Fahrenthold that same year, in an article which claimed that selling votes was "a common type of election fraud."[42]

All of these long-standing concerns were not only brushed aside in 2020, they were mocked as states used the pandemic to expand mail-in balloting dramatically. And leaders of the Democratic Party did not just push to make mail-in voting more popular; they lobbied to eliminate the rules designed to decrease coercion and fraud.

◆   ◆   ◆

One Democrat in particular had spent years coordinating the party's efforts to increase mail-in balloting and decrease measures to fight fraud.

Marc Elias has chaired the political law practice at the Democratic Party's powerful law firm Perkins Coie for years. He was John Kerry's general counsel in his 2004 run for president, as well as Hillary Clinton's general counsel in her 2016 run.[43] While much of Elias's reputation is thanks to the fact that he is an amazing self-promoter who amplifies his victories and hides his many defeats, Elias has operated on a level well beyond that of his Republican counterparts, particularly when it comes to dirty tricks that have undermined confidence in America's elections.

In 2016, it was none other than Marc Elias who hired Fusion GPS, the firm that cooked up the "Steele dossier," named after former British spy Christopher Steele.[44] Fusion had hired Steele to put together opposition research on Donald Trump. The result was page after page of unsubstantiated allegations about Trump's involvement with Russia, which were promptly planted in the media to influence 2016 voters by creating a nefarious narrative that Trump was somehow beholden to Vladimir

Putin. The dossier was also given to the FBI and bureaucrats in other agencies, who used the discredited information to launch a major investigation into Trump that would consume much of his presidency.[45]

Throughout the 2016 campaign, the media dripped out stories alleging that Trump's "America First" foreign policy was the result of his being controlled and blackmailed by Russia.[46] As soon as Clinton lost, she wanted the focus to be placed on Russia.[47] The media followed suit and made Russia's interference in an American election the biggest story of the century.

The Russia collusion hysteria made it difficult for Trump to staff his administration, and it even led to a powerful special counsel investigation before it was revealed that Elias had paid for the dossier as part of his legal work for the Democratic National Committee and the Clinton campaign. While journalists were encouraged to take the Steele dossier seriously, its origins as untrustworthy partisan opposition research had been hidden in the $5.6 million in legal fees that had been paid to Perkins Coie.[48]

Republican representative Devin Nunes of California and his House Permanent Select Committee on Intelligence were the rare investigators skeptical of the whole operation. They sought to find out who funded Fusion GPS's work. Nunes was attacked for his efforts, but they paid off when it turned out that Elias, Clinton, and the Democrats had been behind the dossier all along.[49]

What's more, Elias lied about his role in creating the dossier. *New York Times* reporter Ken Vogel said that when he tried to report the story of the DNC's involvement, Elias "pushed back vigorously, saying 'You (or your sources) are wrong.'"[50]

New York Times reporter Maggie Haberman agreed. "Folks involved in funding this lied about it, and with sanctimony, for a year," she tweeted.[51]

In fact, Elias's dirty trick against Trump was apparently a closely kept secret. When Clinton campaign chairman John Podesta was questioned by Congress in September 2017 on whether the campaign had been involved in the operation, he denied knowledge of any contractual agreement between the campaign and Fusion GPS. Elias, sitting right beside him, did nothing to correct the false information.[52]

❖   ❖   ❖

As damaging as the dossier and larger Russia collusion hoax were to foreign relations, national security, and domestic tranquility, Elias's real passion had long been helping Democrats win elections by changing voting laws.

As chair of the Perkins Coie political law group, he represented dozens of U.S. senators, governors, representatives, and their campaigns. He represented the Democratic National Committee, Democratic Senatorial Campaign Committee, Democratic Congressional Campaign Committee, National Democratic Redistricting Committee, and many political action committees. In addition to these openly partisan groups, he ran many lawsuits through what are called soft-money groups, or groups that help candidates without directly giving them cash.

Elias has been described by the media as a "Democratic power-lawyer," an "elections super-litigator," a "[l]egendary elections lawyer," and a "Democratic election mega-lawyer."[53]

The *New York Times* once described him as "one of the most formidable election lawyers in the country, and arguably one of the most influential of unelected Democrats in Washington."[54] *Politico* said he's "a dominant force in U.S. election law,"[55] while the *Washington Post* said he's "a go-to lawyer for Democrats in recount fights and redistricting battles."[56] *Esquire* was even more flowery, calling Elias "the paladin of voting-rights litigation."[57]

Elias is a large and imposing man. Arrogant, witty, and sarcastic, he's obsessed with doing whatever it takes to secure victories for his clients and the Democratic Party. He first got his reputation as a tenacious fighter in the recount business when he helped former senator

Harry Reid win a Nevada recount in 1998, holding his seat by just over four hundred votes.[58]

He further cemented his legend when he ran Al Franken's 2008 recount and legal challenges, which overturned the result of the election and led to a radical transformation of the country. The day after the election, Franken had lost the race to Republican senator Norm Coleman, but by only 727 votes.[59] In swooped Elias and his team of attorneys and experts, who systematically set out over the course of six months to turn the 727-vote loss into a 312-vote victory.[60] The ultimate decision in Franken's favor gave Democrats a supermajority in the Senate, which they used to enact the sweeping health care legislation known as Obamacare.

The Republicans never knew what hit them. In his landmark book *The Victory Lab*, Sasha Issenberg describes how Elias's team used data-driven methods to secure victory. Al Franken's lawyers began the recount not by trying to have all ten thousand challenged absentee ballots counted, but only the ones that went for the Democratic senator. In order to do that, they brought Andy Bechhoefer, a "microtargeting" expert who studies election demographics, into their strategy sessions:

> [Bechhoefer] ran each of the disputed voters through the campaign's database, which used a complex mix of personal and demographic information, along with polling, to give each voter a score of 1 to 100, predicting his or her likelihood of supporting Franken over his opponent, Norm Coleman. Armed with these scores, Bechhoefer was able not only to point lawyers to the unopened envelopes most likely to yield Franken votes but also to identify which of the secretary of state's categories for excluding votes had put them in a rejected pile. With that knowledge, Franken's attorneys drafted expansive legal arguments that covered entire categories of problems instead of merely contesting individual ballots in a piecemeal fashion.

Bechhoefer illustrated how lawyers were primed to defend absentee ballots that had been challenged for change-of-address discrepancies (which leaned Democratic) while hoping that those with witness-signature problems (tilting Republican) remained uncounted. At times, Franken's lawyers watched their adversary challenge ballots they knew were almost certain to be votes for Coleman, only because the Republicans had not used such sophisticated methods to model them.[61]

The move was so effective at changing the results that it left Democratic observers grinning "like a Cheshire cat," confident in the secret knowledge their opponents did not have.[62] Indeed, to this day the media report on that recount portrays it as if it were just as straightforward as could be.

The Republicans in Minnesota, meanwhile, were playing catch-up. More than a year later, the *Wall Street Journal* reported on a conservative group that had combed through criminal records and found that at least 341 convicted felons illegally voted in the state's largest county, and another 52 voted illegally in the second largest county.[63] Just those two counties alone had enough illegal votes to exceed the margin of Franken's eventual lead. But it was way too late.

"We aren't trying to change the result of the last election. That legally can't be done," a member of the conservative group told Fox News. "We are just trying to make sure the integrity of the next election isn't compromised."[64]

The Franken election affected the Senate monumentally, securing for President Barack Obama a sixtieth vote that made it possible to pass filibuster-proof legislation. If Elias hadn't changed the outcome of Al Franken's election, Obamacare probably would not have passed.

Not every recount went as well for Elias. Florida Republican Rick Scott narrowly defeated incumbent senator Bill Nelson in 2018. But late votes from Broward County in Florida pulled the election to within the

.25 percent margin needed for a hand recount. It had already reached the .5 percent margin required for a machine recount.

In came Elias and his team. He told the *Orlando Sentinel* that after the initial canvass, he wasn't sure which candidate would be ahead, but that "when I say Senator Nelson's going to prevail at the end, I mean that too."[65]

Elias bragged on a conference call with reporters that he would get the election overturned. He questioned the integrity of voting machines, saying that optical-scan machines might not have registered ballots that were poorly marked.[66] Elias filed several lawsuits that challenged then governor Scott's authority over the state's election division to enforce deadlines for mail-in ballots.[67] He was doing everything in his power to secure that seat for the Democratic Party.

Trump tweeted, "As soon as Democrats sent their best Election stealing lawyer, Marc Elias, to Broward County they miraculously started finding Democrat votes."[68]

Other Republicans were upset, too. Senator Marco Rubio highlighted that Broward County was a jurisdiction with a long history of trouble running elections.[69] In 2017, the county's election supervisor, Brenda Snipes, had ordered the destruction of 688 boxes of ballots while a lawsuit involving those ballots was ongoing, and the judge in the case ruled that Snipes had illegally destroyed ballots she was required by law to preserve.[70] She had also been cited for illegally opening mailed-in ballots during a primary, failing to issue absentee ballots, and illegally posting election results prior to polls' closing.

Apparently, none of these censures were enough to remove Snipes from her post. As Broward County kept counting and finding votes for Nelson, Rubio said control of a Senate seat was "potentially in the hands of an elections supervisor with a history of incompetence and of blatant violations of state and federal laws."[71]

Even former Florida governor Jeb Bush, who had appointed Snipes, weighed in, saying, "There is no question that Broward County Supervisor of Elections Brenda Snipes failed to comply with Florida law on multiple counts, undermining Floridians' confidence in our electoral process. Supervisor Snipes should be removed from her office following the recounts."[72]

And yet, when President Trump said in 2018 that "really bad things" were going on in Broward, which he said "had a horrible history," and that "they are finding votes out of nowhere," the *Orlando Sentinel* said Trump "continued to weave in multiple conspiracy theories" about election fraud.[73]

Scott ended up winning a number of court victories and securing the seat. A year and a half later, an audit by the Broward County auditor confirmed what Republican critics, including Trump, had been saying.[74] It found that half of Broward County's election precincts had reported more ballots cast than the number of voters, that the county experienced huge backlogs in the processing of ballots, and that the recount was plagued by poor quality control, all of which "compromises voter confidence."[75] The audit also found that state law doesn't provide "adequate controls over preventing ineligible non-citizens from registering to vote."[76]

Snipes, for her part, resigned shortly after the 2018 election. The usually braggadocious Elias largely kept quiet about the role he had played in the Nelson recount. And, of course, the media didn't admit they had been wrong about what was going on in Broward County.

◆   ◆   ◆

Elias's reckless abuse of the judicial process and election systems continued throughout 2020. He contested the results of a New York congressional race on the grounds that the voting machines they used were flawed, even though Democrats would fiercely defend the integrity of those machines elsewhere in the country when election results favored Democrats. The Fifth U.S. Circuit Court of Appeals even sanctioned him in March 2021 after he filed a supplemental motion challenging Texas voting laws that was nearly identical to one he'd filed months earlier. The first motion had been denied, and he didn't disclose the previous denial to the judges.[77]

But there is no question that Elias played a key role in radically altering election rules and procedures in ways that benefited Democrats. In January 2020, long before anyone knew how COVID-19 might affect voting, Elias published a piece arguing there was an "epidemic of uncounted ballots."[78] He said it was wrong not to count ballots that don't have signature matches, even though signature matches are one of the very few security measures through which mail-in ballots can be verified.

He publicly announced a four-pronged push to dramatically expand no-excuse mail-in balloting.[79] Postage must be free or prepaid by the government. Ballots that arrived well after Election Day must be counted. Scrutiny of signatures to determine if ballots are legitimate must decline. And "ballot harvesting," which allows third parties and outside groups to collect voters' ballots and deliver them to polling places, must be legalized and expanded.[80]

Elias had a few other ideas, too. He wanted to move away from staffing polling stations with political volunteers and instead pay government bureaucrats, a key constituency of Democrats, overtime to work on Election Day. He said high school and college students, also key Democratic constituencies, should get money and course credit for working at polling locations.[81] He said states should expand opportunities for people to drop off ballots curbside, whether they were elderly or disabled or not. He wanted more weekend voting. And he wanted voters who show up to the wrong precinct and don't have their names on the registry to have their votes counted.[82]

In large part thanks to the reaction to COVID-19, when the country was locked down and people were discouraged from leaving their homes for months, many of Elias's wishes were granted. Some states even began mailing absentee ballot applications, and in some cases ballots themselves, to every single name and address on their voter rolls.[83] They placed ballot drop boxes in Democratic voting areas and offered pre-paid postage on election mail.

Alabama, Arkansas, California, Connecticut, Delaware, the District of Columbia, Georgia, Illinois, Iowa, Kentucky, Maryland, Massachusetts, Michigan, Minnesota, Missouri, Montana, Nebraska, Nevada, New Hampshire, New Jersey, New York, North Carolina, Ohio, Oklahoma, Pennsylvania, Rhode Island, South Carolina, Texas, Vermont, West Virginia, and Wisconsin all made changes to expand mail-in balloting. Arizona, Colorado, Florida, Oregon, and Washington already had widespread or universal mail-in balloting.[84]

It was a sea change to the American electoral system, and Elias was the man responsible for much of it.

◆   ◆   ◆

Shockingly, the 2020 contest was the first presidential election since Reagan's first successful run in 1980 in which the Republican National Committee could play any role whatsoever in Election Day operations.

For nearly forty years, the Democratic National Committee had a massive systematic advantage over its Republican counterpart: the Republican National Committee had been prohibited by law from helping out with poll watcher efforts or nearly any litigation related to how voting is conducted.

Democrats had accused Republicans of voter intimidation in a 1981 New Jersey gubernatorial race. The case was settled, and the two parties entered into a court-ordered consent decree limiting Republican involvement with any poll watching operation. But Dickinson Debevoise, the Jimmy Carter–appointed judge who oversaw the agreement, never let them out of it, repeatedly modifying it and strengthening it at the Democrats' request. Debevoise only served as a judge for fifteen years, but he stayed twenty-one years in senior status, a form of semi-retirement that enables judges to keep serving in a limited capacity. It literally took Debevoise's dying in 2015 for Republicans to get out of the consent decree. Upon his passing, a new judge, appointed by President Obama, was assigned the case and let the agreement expire at the end of 2018.[85]

Poll watchers serve many functions. They deter voter fraud, but they also help with getting out the vote. Poll watchers can see who has voted, which means that campaigns and political parties can figure out which areas and voters to call and encourage to vote. They also can observe who was forced to vote provisionally, or who was turned away at the polls.

"Without poll watchers, the RNC would have no good way to follow up with its voters to help ensure a provisional ballot is later counted, direct confused voters to their correct polling place and document irregularities, such as voting equipment malfunctions and other incidents that are important flash points in a close election or recount," explained RNC chairwoman Ronna McDaniel.[86]

For decades, the Democratic Party built up expansive coordination efforts that the Republicans were prohibited from developing. Republican candidates and state parties could do things on their own, but not with help from the national party.

In 2012, the Obama–Biden campaign bragged about recruiting eighteen thousand lawyers to serve as poll watchers, providing more than three hundred observer trainings to ensure the observers understood election law. The volunteers would collect more than nineteen thousand problematic incidents at polling locations that were resolved with or without legal intervention.[87]

The consent decree also meant the RNC was kept out of almost any litigation related to Election Day. In fact, a main part of the RNC's legal efforts came to be training RNC staff to stay away from Election Day operations on Election Day, including recounts, and fending off litigation that arose from the consent decree. It utterly paralyzed the political operation of the RNC, as the slightest misstep would result in getting sued by Democrats.

For example, when former Trump press secretary Sean Spicer said in an interview with *GQ* magazine that he'd watched 2016 returns in an oversized utility room on the fifth floor of Trump Tower, Democrats deposed him to show he'd violated the order by being on the wrong floor, one tied to Election Day outreach.[88] The Democrats used that trivial fact to unsuccessfully try to get the new judge to extend the limitation on their political rivals for another decade.

Even though the decree was finally lifted after nearly forty years, it didn't mean that the Republicans were now on even footing with Democrats. Democrats had spent the last forty years perfecting their Election Day operations while everyone at the Republican National Committee walked on eggshells, knowing that if they so much as looked in the direction of a polling site, there could be another crackdown. As a result, there was no muscle memory about how to watch polls or communicate with a presidential campaign. They had spent decades not being able to organize or talk to presidential campaigns, the National Republican Senatorial Committee, or the National Republican Congressional Committee about any of these efforts. They hadn't been involved in Election Day legal disputes for decades.

What a change, then, when McDaniel announced in early 2020 her "intention to be the most litigious chair in history."[89] The comment was made in response to Democratic efforts to institute a national popular vote. But McDaniel would make efforts to combat Elias's attempts to change election laws in Democrats' favor nationwide.

Some of those attempts predated COVID-19. Elias worked through a soft-money group called Priorities USA to overturn a ban on third-party participation in Michigan elections, such as by ballot harvesting and paying for vehicles to transport people to the polls. The focus on Michigan was part of a larger operation to water down election security ahead of the 2020 election. Elias had sued Michigan's Democratic secretary of state Jocelyn Benson in the Democratic super PAC's name over laws that required signatures on absentee ballots to match signatures on files with the registrar.[90] He would end up dropping the lawsuit in April 2020, after Benson agreed to instruct election officials to notify voters whose signatures didn't match so they could fix the problem.

Benson also said she would water down the signature match requirement altogether.[91] Just before the November election, she instructed election clerks to "presume" signatures were valid and accurate. Allegan County clerk Robert Genetski and the Michigan Republican Party sued, eventually getting a court to agree in March 2021 that her direction had no basis in the law—but by the time the ruling against Benson came down, it was months too late to matter for the 2020 election.[92]

Justin Riemer, the chief counsel for the Republican National Committee, had returned to the RNC after the midterm elections in 2018. He had previously worked in the Trump administration as deputy general counsel at the Department of Education. Republicans had been severely restricted from involvement in Election Day lawsuits during the four long decades they were under the consent decree, but now they were eager to act. The Michigan lawsuit happened before COVID-19 struck. But when COVID-19 really got going, Elias and his affiliates used hysteria surrounding the pandemic as a pretext to achieve much of what they wanted.

"When COVID hit, we started seeing the Democrats initiate a bunch of litigation in the context of the primaries that were taking place," Riemer said, noting the flurry of lawsuits to extend deadlines, get rid of ID requirements, and otherwise relax laws and guidance designed to limit voter fraud.

The Democrats' well-funded effort enabled them to pursue radical change across the country. The Republicans, who did not have an extensive soft-money operation to fund litigation, had to pick when and where they would respond. They attempted to be strategic, but there was a rush to intervene in lawsuits everywhere. As they had done in Michigan, Democrats sometimes sued friendly secretaries of state or other authorities to give them a pretext to water down voting rules. The strategy was called "sue and settle," since many secretaries of state preferred to agree to change the rules rather than defend against a lawsuit. The RNC would intervene to defend the laws as passed by the legislature, particularly if the legislature was controlled by the Democratic Party and reluctant to fight on its own behalf for short-term political reasons. The RNC ended up in more than fifty lawsuits, mostly in a defensive posture of trying to preserve what the law said.

Though outmatched and outspent, the RNC managed to shut down Elias's efforts in Florida, New Hampshire, Maine, and other states. Republicans even filed some proactive lawsuits, such as when the RNC successfully sued some Iowa county auditors for illegally pre-filling out ballot application forms and sending them to voters.[93]

Campaign insiders agree that the Trump campaign should have been heavily involved in the legal effort long before March, when Matt Morgan moved from the vice president's office over to the campaign to watch election litigation. In most campaigns, litigation skirmishes in the months and years prior to the November election are few and far between. But the Trump campaign should have realized 2020 was going to be dramatically different.

The RNC and Trump campaign worked together for months, intervening in lawsuits and looking for opportunities to take the fight to the Democrats. By June 8, President Trump was picking up on news reports about the aggressive actions of Elias and the Democrats and was frustrated at how much ground Democrats had made. He directed his campaign to respond much more forcefully. The Trump campaign took over the Election Day operations, including the lawsuits, suing Pennsylvania, Nevada, and New Jersey.

The campaign also set up a massive legal and political operation to monitor Election Day operations. More than fifty-seven thousand people were trained and deployed around the country to observe votes and make challenges as necessary.[94] It was unlike anything that Republicans had ever done at a national level. When campaigns or parties recruit someone to make a voter contact, they train them in the same techniques in every state. But for poll watchers, the rules differ from state to state. There are fifty different sets of rules and fifty different sets of roles and responsibilities that people can be taught. In Georgia, a poll watcher can observe, but can't challenge a single vote in the polling place or in the counting room. The poll watcher records and monitors a potential infraction and makes challenges later. In Michigan, it's the opposite: election challengers are to make their objections immediately to precinct officials.

Tens of thousands of Election Day staff and volunteers were spread throughout the field. They had been trained to detect, deter, and document. They were told that the best way to deal with a problem is when it occurs. If poll watchers saw a problem, they were to talk to election officials on the ground. If that didn't work, they were told to raise a stink about it on social media. By the time lawyers get involved in Election Day disputes, it's usually too late. However, if the deterrence didn't work, the plan was to document possible wrongdoing and push it to the state-wide war room. And if the state campaign office couldn't handle it or worried that the issue was more widespread and systemic, it was to push it up to the national war room.

Seventeen states were viewed as high-priority and had at least one war room. So, for example, Pennsylvania had a Pittsburgh war room and a Philadelphia war room.

About one hundred attorneys and political people were assembled at the Eisenhower Executive Office Building right next to the White House on Election Day. Each of the high-priority states was assigned an attorney and political lead. There were also RNC lawyers and other political operatives. Everyone was crammed into the third floor of the building. They had to bring in everything for the room at their own expense, so as not to violate the Hatch Act, which bars government employees from using taxpayer resources for electioneering.

It's always difficult to track turnout from one presidential election to another, but it's a vital task. Tracking turnout shows campaigns where they can send volunteers to squeeze out more votes. Since precincts change constantly, campaign operatives usually look for single-precinct counties to keep their eyes on, as these allow campaigns to compare election years more easily.

But with the dramatic expansion of mail-in balloting, it became almost impossible to track what turnout was really like even in those counties. Mail-in ballots were segregated from the precinct totals, so campaign operatives couldn't tell whether turnout in some counties was low or whether voters had decided to cast their ballots by mail.

Experienced election observers were likely to have an idea of what voter turnout by precinct looked like, but the massive increase in mail-in ballots made it impossible to compare 2020 results to previous baselines. This made it more difficult to spot anomalies and potential fraud. It also made it nearly impossible for Republicans to determine where campaigns ought to dedicate resources to turn out voters on Election Day, whereas Democrats had closely been tracking mail-in ballots from their voters for nearly two months.

The Trump campaign was closely monitoring seventeen states. Throughout the day, campaign heads Bill Stepien and Justin Clark would receive status updates on at least four of these states every fifteen minutes. That meant each of the high-profile states was briefed to the campaign leadership once an hour. It was frankly too many to keep track of effectively.

Still, Election Day was going smoothly. Most issues that need addressing come up in the first hour and a half after polls are supposed to open. A precinct fails to open for voters, or ballots don't arrive where they're supposed to, or voter registration has a glitch. Those types of issues were dealt with quickly.

For the remainder of the day, the main issue that came up was access, as Democrats repeatedly blocked Republicans from viewing the counting of ballots in Michigan and Pennsylvania. Republicans kept suing for access, but saw limited results.

Even that issue, though, was about counting votes, not voting itself. According to Trump, "It's true that the vote counter is far more important than the candidate." This is hardly a unique political observation. Famed cartoonist Thomas Nast depicted the corrupt Boss Tweed at a polling place in 1871 saying, "As long as I count the votes, what are you going to do about it?" As long as the issue was counting in-person votes, the Trump campaign was in good shape. The real fight would be about the mail-in ballots and all the unknowns that the new, experimental voting system had introduced.

◆　　◆　　◆

When Florida results came in, Trump campaign officials were thrilled. To beat the mail-in ballot numbers racked up by the Democrats, Republicans would need to turn out their voters on Election Day. Everything had to go smoothly, and Election Day was make-or-break. In Florida and in other key states, the Trump campaign had managed to do exactly that.

The campaign had run ads in Florida suggesting Democratic nominee Joe Biden was a supporter of socialism, a message that resonated deeply with Miami's heavily Cuban population. The fact that parts of Biden's base had pushed for him to pick Representative Barbara Lee of California as his running mate had helped the Trump team with its messaging, since Lee was known for her ties to far-left groups and being openly pro-socialism.

Not only was southern Florida coming in strong for Trump, but so was the I-4 corridor, the stretch of land that encompasses Tampa, Orlando, and the mostly rural areas in between. The area has a mix of recent college graduates and senior citizens, such as those in the large retirement community The Villages. It has immigrants from different countries and migrants from the north.

Seniors were a serious worry for the Trump campaign, as polling showed them to be the most susceptible to the Biden team's focus on the approaching "dark winter" for Americans, thanks to the coronavirus pandemic. Momentum had shifted, though, and the Trump team felt confident.

Sure enough, the I-4 results came in great. Trump was doing well with seniors, with women, and with non-Cuban Hispanics, too.

In 2016, Trump had won Florida by 1.2 percent, the first of many races that went his way.[95] Republicans in Florida had won statewide in 2018, but much more narrowly. Governor Ron DeSantis eked out a win over Andrew Gillum by .4 percent. Rick Scott had only defeated Bill Nelson by .2 percent.[96]

Though Trump's 2020 polling numbers in Florida were lagging behind his 2016 figures, he performed much better in 2020. Trump won Florida by 3.3 points in 2020.[97] By Florida standards, it was a blowout. And that gave the campaign a good feeling about Georgia, a state he'd won easily in 2016 that is just north of the Florida border and surrounded by states that were going for Trump.

Back in the Map Room, the more senior members of the Trump team received reports that things were going well in other key contests. Texas was in the bag. Campaign leadership felt good about Ohio, and even good about North Carolina, a state that had given them trouble during the campaign.

Throughout the campaign, media polls gave Trump no shot at winning. And when it came to swing state polling, which gets much more attention than other polling, the results looked like downright propaganda in support of Joe Biden.

In recent elections, Wisconsin had proven to be a key swing state. President Obama won Wisconsin by fourteen points in 2008[98] and seven points in 2012.[99] Trump had eked out a narrow victory by less than one percentage point in 2016, when he ran against former secretary of state Hillary Clinton.[100]

Despite the Trump campaign's insistence that its internal data showed he would win a close race, the media told a different story. Most dramatically, ABC News and the *Washington Post* published a poll less than a week before Election Day that claimed Biden was going to win Wisconsin by seventeen points. At that margin, Trump wasn't just done in Wisconsin. He had no hope anywhere.

Seventeen points in Wisconsin meant a likely electoral blowout nationwide for Biden. It would take a miracle for Trump to win if he were down seventeen points in a swing state such as Wisconsin—a state that had been crucial to his 2016 victory.

The *New York Times*'s last poll said that Biden would take Wisconsin by eleven points.[101] Reuters/Ipsos said he would win by double digits, ten points.[102] CNN and CNBC were slightly more sober, each saying that Biden would only crush Trump by eight points,[103] akin to what Obama had done when he was decisively victorious over former Massachusetts governor Mitt Romney in 2012.

Two of the most accurate polling firms, Trafalgar and Susquehanna, predicted something far different: a too-close-to-call nail-biter of a race with Biden up by only one to three points. Despite being far more accurate, those two polling firms were regularly criticized by others in the polling industry for having a right-wing bias. The media polls and the left-wing university polls, which were consistently wrong, said that Wisconsin would be a blowout for Biden. But there were pollsters doing decent polling showing the race for what it was. While these polls received attention on high-traffic aggregators like RealClearPolitics, they received little to no attention on television or other major media.

Polls with as much as seventeen-point predicted victories for Biden shaped news coverage for months and hurt morale in the Trump team. Even if they'd learned better than most to not believe polls or other media narratives, the bad headlines were difficult to ignore.

"Polls are one of the most dishonest things," President Trump said, reflecting on the matter later from his Mar-a-Lago home. "I have never seen dishonesty like this. They're dishonest with polls. You know it's suppression to keep people home. Do you know how many people didn't vote because of that poll and Wisconsin? And probably other places too, that poll got so much publicity."

At least one pollster agrees with Trump. After the 2020 election, pollster Jim Lee of Susquehanna Polling & Research blasted the politicization of his industry and issued a statement noting that a slew of inaccurate polling results that almost universally overstated Biden's support left pollsters "vulnerable to criticisms of contributing to voter suppression."

Throughout the campaign, any time President Trump had a good moment or message, a poll would come out alleging that he still had no chance of winning. The media would caveat their message with a reminder that they'd been wrong in 2016, but all of the numbers they published alleged that Trump had no chance.

On Election Night, the top campaign staffers were looking for signs. The media had said Iowa would be very close, a claim the Trump campaign had disputed. The *New York Times*'s last poll in the state had Biden winning Iowa by three points.[104] The local *Des Moines Register* poll said it was a seven-point race for Trump, just like 2016 had been. But the corporate media polls from national outlets got all the oxygen. Early returns showed it wouldn't be close. Trump would eventually win the state by eight percentage points. The campaign also looked toward Ohio. As goes Ohio, so goes Pennsylvania, they thought. They knew if they didn't win Ohio by a similar margin as they did in 2016, Pennsylvania would be a problem. The media polls indicated it would be a nail-biter. It wasn't. As Ohio came in, they were crushing it. Trump won it by half a million votes, just as he had in 2016.

Pennsylvania was looking good. So was Michigan. They thought Wisconsin was going to be tough, but they were in the game. They were certainly not losing by seventeen points.

◆   ◆   ◆

Part of the battle on Election Night is the media battle. The Biden campaign knew this and had been telegraphing for months that the media should not call races where Trump was ahead. They said any such massive leads by Trump were a "red mirage" that would be obliterated once mail-in ballots were counted.

As the polls closed on the East Coast, the media began announcing that Biden and Trump had won in a few states. All eyes moved to Florida. The results showed Trump with a strong lead, but nobody was calling it. It was bothering some Trump fans, who felt the delay indicated the media's hostility toward President Trump.

"It's time to call FLORIDA!" White House press secretary Kayleigh McEnany tweeted at 9:33 p.m. "How long will it take for the media to acknowledge it?"[105]

"Trump is up in #Florida by 3.5 points & 381000 votes with 91% reporting & only 50000 votes left to count. It's over. So why won't they call the race?" Rubio tweeted at 9:50 p.m. "To deny Trump an early swing state win until Arizona and Nevada close."[106]

"President @realDonaldTrump is up in Florida by almost 400,000 votes with more than 90% of precincts reporting. Why haven't networks called the race? It's a done deal and the refusal to recognize the obvious speaks volumes about the (lack of) objectivity of these outlets," Florida governor Ron DeSantis tweeted at 9:57 p.m.[107]

At 11:04 p.m., the Fox News Decision Desk, the first to do so, announced that Trump had won Florida decisively. The Associated Press followed suit a few minutes later. The triumph for the Trump campaign was short-lived.

About fifteen minutes later, Fox News called Arizona, a state Trump had won in 2016, for Biden.

After the debacle in 2000 where the networks called the critical state of Florida incorrectly for Al Gore at 10:00 p.m. ET, the networks had made a big point about how they would err on the side of caution in the future, which might have explained the delayed call in Florida. (Though Republican partisans complain with some merit that Democrat-won states seem to get called more quickly than Republican states.)

Which made the rush to call a critical battleground such as Arizona less than ninety minutes after the polls closed very odd. Arizona had been a key swing state for many election cycles, though the Democrats had only managed to carry it one time in the last seventy years, and even then it was Ross Perot's 8 percent in 1996 that allowed Bill Clinton to win the state with 46.5 percent of the vote.

Campaign staff described it as "a gut punch." One staffer said it was like driving full speed down the interstate and having your car thrown in reverse. At that point, Arizona was closer than the team wanted it to be, but they still felt they would pull it off.

It was a bit of a shock at Fox as well.

Fox News, where this author is a contributor, is unique among cable networks in retaining a distinction between its opinion and news programming.[108] The news side handles Election Night and other big coverage. Its Decision Desk, a group of pollsters, statisticians, and political analysts, is independent from both the opinion and news programming. In 2018, Fox News was the first to predict that Democrats would take control of the House, saying the party would win more than the twenty-three seats needed to retake the majority after eight years as the minority party. The call was made at 9:30 p.m. on the East Coast, before polls had closed in California.

Normally, the Decision Desk would make a call and alert the hosts and reporters covering the evening, who could then prepare to make the call on air. Things went a bit differently when it came to Arizona. Just a few minutes after Florida had finally gone into Trump's column, Fox's Bill Hemmer was guiding viewers through potential paths to victory for each candidate by analyzing county results in different swing states on an interactive map. When he pulled out to give viewers a look at the entire map, Arizona was blue, a sign that the Decision Desk had called it for Biden. "Why is Arizona blue?" he asked. "Did we just call it? Did we make a call in Arizona?"

Once host Martha MacCallum confirmed the call, Hemmer began noting the headwinds Trump would face going forward.

"Time out. This is a big development," anchor Bret Baier said, confirming that the Fox News Decision Desk had called Arizona for Biden. "That is a big get for the Biden campaign." Biden's picking up Arizona "change[d] the math," as it was the first race of the night to switch from one party to another since 2016. He noted how much the Trump campaign had wanted to win Arizona and said that "Joe Biden [was] ticking closer" to the necessary number of electoral votes.

The Trump campaign was aghast.

Arizona state law permits mail-in votes to be counted up to two weeks prior to Election Day. Those votes, which leaned Democratic, were some of the first to be posted when the polls closed. The state has a reputation for counting accurately and running elections cleanly, but it's inordinately slow. It took the counters in Arizona days to count their ballots, which meant that the Election Day results that were posted were largely based on absentee ballots.

Arizona governor Doug Ducey was in constant communication with the Trump team. Ducey was tracking the race because Republican senator Martha McSally was facing a rough election for a full term of the seat to which he had appointed her. That race was also closer than the polls had said it would be, but McSally still lost. She was viewed as a lackluster candidate and a drag on the Trump effort in the state. One advisor said it would have been better for Trump if she'd been replaced by "a box of rocks."

Ducey's data analysts said that things looked good for the president. Ducey tweeted his concern publicly: "It's far too early to call the election in Arizona. Election Day votes are not fully reported, and we haven't even started to count early ballots dropped off at the polls. In AZ, we protected Election Day. Let's count the votes—all the votes—before making declarations."[109]

Trump advisor Jason Miller agreed. "WAY too soon to be calling Arizona...way too soon. We believe over 2/3 of those outstanding Election Day voters are going to be for Trump. Can't believe Fox was so anxious to pull the trigger here after taking so long to call Florida. Wow."[110]

Privately, everyone on the Trump campaign was lighting up the phones of anyone at Fox they could reach. The hosts, reporters, executives, and others were receiving angry texts and fielding livid phone calls from Kellyanne Conway, Hope Hicks, Mark Meadows, Jared Kushner, and others who agreed with Governor Ducey and others about the call being inappropriately early.

Outrage on social media was brewing, too. Baier brought Chris Stirewalt, at the time Fox News's political editor and a member of the Decision Desk, on air to explain the decision. Baier asked tough questions.

"How can you call Arizona, but we can't call Ohio?" Baier asked.

The races are very different, Stirewalt said, arguing that the margins were too wide in Arizona for Trump to make up any significant ground. As for Ohio: "There is just too much vote out, and there's too much potentially heavily Democratic mail vote that may flop in at the end to get too froggy right now with Ohio," said Stirewalt. "We're going to be careful, cautious, and earnest."

Ohio was called just moments later by the Decision Desk. Trump ended up winning Ohio by 8.2 points. At the time the Arizona call was made, the margin was 8.5 points. It would eventually shrink to .3 points, or 10,457 votes out of 3.4 million cast.

Around 12:30 a.m., with viewers and Trump campaign officials raging, Baier asked Arnon Mishkin, Fox's main statistician at the Decision Desk, who normally stays off air, "Are you 100 percent sure of that call, and when you made it? And why did you make it?"

Mishkin said that while there were outstanding votes, they were mostly mail-in from Maricopa County, which Fox predicted would mostly go for Biden. "I think what we've heard from the White House is that they are expecting to get, that they need just to get 61 percent of the outstanding vote and there are 870,000 outstanding votes and they'll be getting that. That's not true. The reality is that they're likely to get only about 44 percent of the outstanding votes that are there. We're right now sitting on a race that is Biden at 53 percent, Trump at 46 percent. I'm sorry, the president is not going to be able to take over and win enough votes to eliminate that seven-point lead that the former vice president has," he told Baier.

The Trump team didn't get 61 percent of the remaining Arizona votes when all the votes were counted more than a week later, but they did get something very near it, ending just shy of the votes needed to win. In the final Arizona tally, Biden had 49.4 percent of the vote to Trump's 49.1 percent.

The Associated Press, which joined with the Fox News Decision Desk in its elaborate alternative to exit polling that involved interviewing voters over the course of several days, called the Arizona race in the early hours the next day. The *New York Times*, CNN, ABC News, CBS News, and NBC News viewed the race as too close to call until November 12, more than a week later.[111] And as the Arizona vote inched closer and closer with each batch of ballots, Fox executives debated whether to pull back the call, a rare but occasionally necessary step.

For example, the Decision Desk made a prediction just after 9:00 p.m. on Election Night that Democrats would gain at least five seats in the House, strengthening their majority. Instead, Democrats lost a dozen seats, shrinking their majority to a razor-thin margin. That call was corrected more than a week after it was issued.

The Decision Desk, acting independently from the rest of the network, had put many of the network's anchors and journalists in an uncomfortable position. Calling battleground states early has been frowned on for decades. Rushing the call for Biden of a battleground state that has historically been won by the GOP in the midst of a razor-thin election was sure to cause problems.

In any case, on Election Night, Trump supporters saw that he had huge leads in Michigan, Wisconsin, and Pennsylvania. He had won Florida by more than three points and appeared safely ahead in North Carolina and Georgia. It seemed that he was going to pull off another massive upset. The race was certainly nothing like the Biden blowout the media had promised for months on end.

Late at night, reports circulated on social media, many of them inaccurate, that many blue areas had stopped counting votes for the evening. While it was true that the media and election observers had been told counting had stopped for the night in Atlanta, for instance, it hadn't. Combined with the Arizona call, many Trump supporters began to be concerned and suspicious. Others were confident he'd win, just as he had in 2016.

◆   ◆   ◆

Five days after Election Day, the media would call the race for Biden. The intervening days would see Trump slowly lose his majorities in

Michigan, Wisconsin, Pennsylvania, and Georgia. Arizona took a while to count, but it came down to ten thousand votes in Biden's favor.

What began as a triumph for Trump ended with Biden's declaring victory by the weekend.

How did this happen? The political class, the corporate media, and their pollsters were all dramatically wrong, and yet Biden would still eke out a presidential victory of just under 43,000 votes across three states, out of a total of nearly 160 million. Months later, *Time* magazine would run its now infamous article bragging about how it had been done.

Without irony or shame, the magazine reported that "[t]here was a conspiracy unfolding behind the scenes" creating "an extraordinary shadow effort" by a "well-funded cabal of powerful people" to oppose Trump.[112] Corporate CEOs, organized labor, left-wing activists, and Democrats all worked together in secret to secure a Biden victory. For Trump, these groups represented a powerful Washington and Democratic establishment that saw an unremarkable career politician like Biden as merely a vessel for protecting their self-interests. Accordingly, when Trump was asked whom he blames for the rigging of the 2020 election, he quickly responded, "Least of all Biden."

Time would, of course, disingenuously frame this effort as an attempt to "oppose Trump's assault on democracy," even as *Time* reporter Molly Ball noted this shadow campaign "touched every aspect of the election. They got states to change voting systems and laws and helped secure hundreds of millions in public and private funding." The funding enabled the country's sudden rush to mail-in balloting, which Ball described as "a revolution in how people vote."[113]

The funding from Democratic donors to public election administrators was revolutionary. The Democrats' network of nonprofit activist groups embedded *into* the nation's electoral structure through generous grants from Democratic donors. They helped accomplish the Democrats' vote-by-mail strategy from the inside of the election process. It was as if the Dallas Cowboys were paying the National Football League's referee staff and conducting all of their support operations. No one would feel confident in games won by the Cowboys in such a scenario.

Ball also reported that this shadowy cabal "successfully pressured social media companies to take a harder line against disinformation and used data-driven strategies to fight viral smears." And yet, *Time* magazine made this characterization months after it was revealed that the *New York Post*'s reporting on Hunter Biden's corrupt deal-making with Chinese and other foreign officials—deals that alleged direct involvement from Joe Biden, resulting in the reporting's being overtly censored by social media—was substantially true. Twitter CEO Jack Dorsey would eventually tell Congress that censoring the *New York Post* and locking it out of its Twitter account over the story was "a mistake." And the Hunter Biden story was hardly the only egregious mistake, to say nothing of the media's willful dishonesty, in the 2020 election.

Republicans read the *Time* article with horror and as an admission of guilt. It confirmed many voters' suspicions that the election wasn't entirely fair. Trump knew the article helped his case, calling it "the only good article I've read in *Time* magazine in a long time—that was actually just a piece of the truth because it was much deeper than that."

The 2020 election was far more vicious than the 2016 election, Trump said. "We got them by surprise in '16. They had no idea what was coming down the tracks. And then in '20 they were willing to do anything they could and it started from the day I took office or before I took office, from right after the election with the Russia hoax."

They had used every weapon in their arsenal to take down Trump and marginalize his supporters, and by and large they succeeded. Joe Biden would be the forty-sixth president of the United States, even though less than a year earlier Trump had looked unstoppable.

At his Mar-a-Lago home months later, Trump said, "It hurts to lose less than to win and have it taken away."

CHAPTER TWO

Taking On the Establishment

Before the 2018 mid-term elections, Trump's political advisors were thinking about the president's re-election bid and noticed a curious commonality among incumbent presidents who didn't get re-elected: they all faced challengers from within their own party.

Five U.S. presidents since 1900 have lost their bid for a second term. William Taft lost to Woodrow Wilson, Herbert Hoover lost to Franklin Roosevelt, Gerald Ford lost to Jimmy Carter, Jimmy Carter lost to Ronald Reagan, and George H. W. Bush lost to Bill Clinton. While each election is determined by unique factors, all five of these failed incumbents dealt with internal party fights or serious primary challenges.

Intraparty conflicts consumed these failed campaigns through much of the election year. This major distraction didn't allow them to run a campaign against their general election opponent until late summer. It wasn't necessarily why they lost, but it was a key issue the Trump team wanted to avoid.

A primary challenger didn't need to be that successful to cause a great deal of damage. Pat Buchanan entered the 1992 presidential primary race just ten weeks prior to the New Hampshire primary. He got

38 percent in the New Hampshire primary, which was the biggest percentage he got in any of the primaries he competed in. President George H. W. Bush didn't lose a single primary, but the fact that Buchanan and other challengers received significant support showed Bush's weakness and forced him to worry more about the challenge from his right than from the opponent to his left.

Buchanan only received 18 delegates out of 2,209,[1] but his brief campaign resonated with party voters. When he gave a rousing speech at the GOP convention in Houston about a great battle of values in the country, the crowd loved it and the speech dominated media coverage. The Trump team didn't want something similar to happen again.

The team was eager to start the general election campaign early, so they had to make sure there was no drama at the convention. To do so, they had to make sure there were no pathways to the convention for the very small but committed Never Trump contingent in the GOP. That way, they could make sure that the convention was unified.

In 2016, Trump won the primary battle by securing 44.9 percent of the vote, a plurality.[2] Even after securing the nomination, he faced incredibly strong intraparty opposition, much of it from the establishment and elected Republicans. Unlike so many Republican politicians who claim they will govern as conservative during Republican primaries but move to the left for the general campaign and in office, Trump honored his stated commitment to conservative policies. He appointed conservative judges and justices, exited from the Paris climate accord, led a massive deregulatory effort, got the economy roaring, didn't start any new wars, and aggressively defended American interests abroad. His actions earned the support of the party's voters.

Despite these policy accomplishments, or in some cases because of them, powerful elements of the Republican Party and conservative media establishment continued to resist his presidency. These groups were eager to fight him for control over the party.

The Trump campaign didn't fear a grassroots revolt à la Buchanan. His campaign staff knew that Trump had won over the support of

Republican voters. They were worried about the GOP establishment backing a primary effort against Trump. It was almost the opposite scenario to Bush's challenge by Buchanan, when party elites were completely unified behind Bush but the base was less pleased.

Bill Stepien and Justin Clark proposed the Trump campaign set up a "Delegates and Party Organization"[3] (DPO) department with dedicated staff and resources all devoted to ensuring that there were no primary challenges and that convention delegates were supportive of Trump. Launched at the end of December 2018, it was the first department headquartered over at the campaign's offices in the Rosslyn area of Arlington, Virginia. Veteran political operative Nick Trainer ran the effort. He had three regional deputies who divided up the fifty states and six territories and districts that had primaries or caucuses to send delegates to the Republican National Convention.[4] The Republican nomination path includes all states, no matter how Republican or Democratic they may vote in the general. And since the goal was to present a completely unified convention, each one mattered.

A friendly state GOP chairman would make the process much easier, so helping elect Trump-friendly chairmen was an early priority. It got going right away in January 2019 when Massachusetts Republicans picked their new leader. Charlie Baker, Republican governor of Massachusetts, strongly disliked Trump. He announced he had voted for no one for president in 2016. Trump supporters were making noise about demanding respect from him. His hand-selected candidate was the current chairman.

The DPO group worked to make sure former state representative Jim Lyons was elected state party chair. Lyons ended his speech to the convention saying he would make Massachusetts great again, a reference to President Trump's campaign slogan. "In rebuke to Charlie Baker, state GOP picks conservative to lead party," the *Boston Globe* announced.[5] Winning that fight meant the Trump team had the ability to work with Lyons and the executive committee to change the rules of the state party with respect to delegate allocation.

Previously, if a Republican candidate got a certain percentage of the vote in the Massachusetts primary, he or she would get a certain percentage of delegates. The rules were changed so that instead of delegates' being allocated according to the percentage of the vote a candidate received, candidates could only get a delegate if they got more than 50 percent of the vote.[6] And delegates to the national convention had to be approved by the winning campaign.

Monitoring and engaging state chairman races was the first phase of the operation. The Trump team managed to get forty Trump-supportive state chairmen elected or re-elected. The team worked with chairmen or legal counsel in each state, looking for someone with respect in the party to make the argument for Trump to others. The field staff went to every single one of the meetings where changes were discussed. Sometimes the most important role they served was simply to verify to the gathered that the Trump campaign supported the changes.

They also developed primary ballot access plans and established delegate selection processes.

No candidate or issue was too small. When a national committeeman opening appeared in Maine, the team worked to make sure the 2016 Trump state chairman Josh Tardy was elected. They whipped the vote, calling people to encourage them to vote for Tardy. He didn't have real opposition, but the team took the effort seriously enough that they weren't willing to court any risks.

They helped elect three new national committee members and re-elect two loyal national committee members.

The DPO team was so thorough that the leaders of the effort were getting briefed on who had won a "basic political operating unit" election in Minnesota, the term for the state party's lowest level of political organization.

Before the DPO crew got involved, candidates who wanted to get on the ballot as a presidential candidate in Florida only needed to get 125 signatures from each congressional district in the state or attend what was called a Sunshine Summit and pay a $25,000 ballot access fee. The

DPO team got rid of the former pathway and added a new one that said the incumbent president automatically qualified for the ballot.

Rules for delegate selection were changed. For instance, in Kentucky a rule was changed to say that "no person who did not support the Republican Presidential nominee during the most recent Presidential Election shall be elected to be a Delegate or Alternate to the District, State, or National Conventions, respectively."[7] It allowed the elimination of a whole class of people from the process who were Never Trump.

The team didn't work too much on the issue of when primaries were scheduled, but in one case they did. Washington, D.C., the base of the establishment, was a place they worried might flex its muscles against Trump. Usually, the D.C. contest was in March, but the group worked to delay it to May so that it would be at the tail end of the primary season, at a time when no incipient primary challengers could begin their rise.

They knew that when they succeeded with the effort, it would never be read about. They didn't care. They wanted to guarantee the convention would be a four-day pep rally for Donald Trump.

It was a lot of work. Trainer and his three regional directors traveled to every state and territory. They met with chairs and executive committees. They attended every convention and picked captains for district conventions. Their first step was to understand the process in each state, then make recommendations on how to improve processes, and then help implement them.

They never wanted to be seen as the guys from D.C. who were big-footing people. They'd make suggestions, but if they got pushback, they didn't force the issue. They estimated they got 70 percent of what they wanted, simply by building relationships and leveraging their new connections.

By late summer of 2019, most of the rules had been changed. The Republican National Committee had a deadline of October 1 for when each state had to submit its delegate selection plan, and then it was locked in stone.

Throughout the summer of 2019, former Ohio governor John Kasich was asked by the press to run for president. Both he and Maryland governor Larry Hogan had been rattling their sabers a bit, with Hogan even making a trip to New Hampshire. Kasich eventually said, "There is no path right now for me" [to run for president], and "I don't see a way to get there."[8]

The DPO team loved it. If he knew what they were doing, they thought, he would really know that there was no pathway.

A year after the Trump team had started forming relationships with New Hampshire's state officials, the preparations started to bear fruit. Those officials notified the Trump team whenever Joe Walsh, a one-term former congressman who had launched a quixotic bid for the presidency, or some other wannabe candidate called and asked about delegate selection. The Trump team wouldn't be taken by surprise.

Even though no solid candidates were making noise about running, Trainer and his team knew that, as Buchanan had done, someone could announce late. They wanted to make sure that even if an establishment favorite such as former presidential nominee Mitt Romney decided to cause a stink, it would be irrelevant.

The only two states that could have been a problem were Iowa and New Hampshire. From the campaign's perspective, they knew any changes to the rules in those states would be high-profile and might risk the secrecy of the operation. So they decided to campaign fully in those two states and achieve decisive wins in their contests. There was a giant deployment leading up to the Iowa caucuses, with the vice president and president holding rallies. They engaged with local field people and worked with the state party chair to make sure the caucuses were well-staffed. They even did a digital push in Iowa.

Former Massachusetts governor and Libertarian Party vice presidential candidate Bill Weld managed to win one delegate in Iowa, but in the end it didn't count.[9] In Iowa, a delegate has to be nominated on the floor of the convention to be bound to that person. The Weld delegate became a Trump delegate once the convention opened.

And when Weld didn't get a single delegate out of New Hampshire, the team knew their work had been worth it. They had known they would have to be perfect. Losing just five delegates to Bill Weld would have sparked a media frenzy. "The amount of think pieces that would have been done on what the Weld delegates would be doing on the floor would have been quite amazing," joked Trainer.

The entire effort cost only about $1.2 million. By comparison, the operation just to get former New Jersey governor Chris Christie on the ballot in 2016 cost a million dollars. It was clear the DPO team had done their work fending off even a whiff of a primary challenge. The Trump campaign would not be distracted by intraparty squabbles lasting through the summer. The small investment of money and large investment of time had paid off.

◆　◆　◆

The lack of intraparty squabbles wasn't just because of Trump's power as a candidate or his campaign's successful DPO operation. The hysterical left helped unify Republican voters. And despite Trump's winning both the nomination and the presidency, much of the initial resistance to Trump from the Republican Party establishment dissipated as scandals swirling around Trump proved to be manufactured by Democrats and the media.

When Hillary Clinton, other Democrats, and the media pushed the Russia lies her campaign had secretly funded, many Republican officeholders either believed them or declined to fight back against them. The Russia collusion hoax had been invented by the Clinton campaign and Democratic National Committee, fed to compliant reporters, and weaponized by Obama's Department of Justice. Following her loss, Clinton hoped that the campaign operation could become a bigger story and began pushing the narrative that the election had been stolen from her by collusion between Trump and Russia.

The operation had been so successful prior to the election that the FBI had sought and obtained the first of four secret warrants to spy on Carter Page, a Trump campaign affiliate and Naval Academy grad whom the Clinton campaign operation had falsely fingered as a high-level conduit to Russia. It would later turn out that the warrants had been sought on the basis of the false campaign information operation the Clinton campaign had secretly purchased.[10] But the Clinton campaign's involvement in the operation wasn't even known at that point.

The group Clinton and the Democrats had hired to run the Russia operation had invented a dossier of salacious gossip, unsubstantiated innuendo, and publicly available information with the help of Christopher Steele, a former British intelligence officer. They shared the dossier or information within it with media outlets throughout D.C. and New York, but nobody could verify anything in it, and so it wasn't getting the traction they'd hoped for. The people pushing the collusion story needed to provide reporters a way to report on it even though the information in it was false or couldn't be proven true.

Before Trump's inauguration, Obama-era officials plotted to "brief" the dossier to both Obama and Trump, for the sole purpose of leaking the fact of the meeting to CNN.[11] Once CNN reported on the meeting, BuzzFeed published the dossier, which told a story of massive collusion with the Trump campaign to steal the 2016 election.

In response to the information operation, Republicans in both the Senate and House began investigating Russian interference in the 2016 election, just as Democratic operatives had hoped.

To keep the Trump administration from finding out what the Department of Justice had done during the campaign, much less what it planned to do during his administration, several key officials needed to be sidelined before they got access to the information about the operation.

Trump's incoming national security advisor, Lieutenant General Mike Flynn, who would have been told about the Justice Department's secret investigation into Trump, was accused of violating the Logan Act, an obscure and never-enforced law prohibiting private citizens from negotiating with foreign governments in a dispute with the United States.[12] Not only did most legal experts agree the law unconstitutionally violated the First Amendment, but it wouldn't have applied to Flynn regardless, because he was talking to Russian ambassador Sergey Kislyak in his official capacity working for a president-elect.

The media went wild with the story anyway. As Obama-era officials continued to leak against Flynn, nearly every Republican on the Hill sat idly by. "Congressional Republicans divided on whether to support Flynn," was the headline in the *Washington Post*.[13] Senator Marco Rubio, one of the top Republicans on the Senate Intelligence Committee, said Flynn's contact with the Russian ambassador would be a part of the ongoing bipartisan investigation into alleged Russian interference in the 2016 election.[14] Under mounting political pressure, Flynn was pushed out of the administration.

The Russia operation then moved against Jeff Sessions, the Alabama senator whom Trump had appointed his attorney general. Sessions had failed to mention two routine and uneventful meetings he held with Kislyak when he was senator. For this grave sin, the media suggested Sessions was a Russian spy. And yet, rather than mock the idea, many Republicans called on him to recuse himself from oversight of the Department of Justice's Russia investigation. He did.[15]

When the Democrats were able to get Deputy Attorney General Rod Rosenstein to appoint a special counsel to probe the Russia collusion story, Republicans cheered.

"My priority has been to ensure thorough and independent investigations are allowed to follow the facts wherever they may lead. That is what we've been doing here in the House," Speaker of the House Paul Ryan said in a statement. "The addition of Robert Mueller as special counsel is consistent with this goal, and I welcome his role at the Department of Justice. The important ongoing bipartisan investigation in the House will also continue."[16]

"Mueller is a great selection. Impeccable credentials. Should be widely accepted," Representative Jason Chaffetz, the Republican head of the House Committee on Oversight and Reform, tweeted.[17]

Mueller and his team knew that there was no Russian collusion at the time of Mueller's appointment, so he and his team quickly focused on trying to show Trump had obstructed justice. Trump's offense? Complaining that he had been accused of a crime he didn't commit and being less trusting of the special counsel's propriety than most other Republicans.

Whenever he complained, Republicans would rush to defend Mueller, vocalizing their support and pushing legislation to protect him from getting fired by Trump. Mueller's team was staffed with partisan Democrats who had close ties to the Clintons, but Mueller himself was a Republican who had served as FBI director from 2001 to 2013. This was by design, as his reputation was supposed to protect the entire investigation.

A few members of Congress stood out for understanding the Russia collusion hoax for what it was early on. Representative Devin Nunes, chairman of the House Permanent Select Committee on Intelligence, was immediately suspicious of the Russia collusion charges, even though he was a longtime hawk who had been sounding the alarm about Russia and its election meddling for years. Because he fought against the hysteria, he received unending ire from the media and his colleagues across the aisle. He was even sidelined by an ethics investigation that dragged on needlessly for much of 2017 until he was finally exonerated.[18]

His dogged investigation, however, led to the finding that the dossier, far from being reliable intelligence for which the FBI could vouch, was secretly funded by Clinton and the Democratic National Committee.

A report Nunes put out concerning improprieties in the process of securing warrants to spy on the Trump campaign was vindicated years afterward when the inspector general of the Department of Justice issued a report about those failures, including the fact that one member of the special counsel's team had falsified evidence against Page to secure a warrant that was used to spy on the Trump campaign.[19]

For years, news stories were published and broadcast about Russia and Trump. The country was whipped into a frenzy, and polls showed the vast majority of Democrats believed Trump was compromised by Russia. A Quinnipiac poll in December 2017 showed that 86 percent of Democratic voters believed "the Trump campaign colluded with the Russian government to influence the 2016 presidential election." And when Quinnipiac asked Democrats the same question in July 2018, 74 percent responded they believed Trump had colluded with Russia. The 2018 mid-term elections were held at the height of the hysteria, and Democrats rode that wave to huge victories in the House.

It all fell apart in March 2019, when Mueller's expensive and expansive special counsel probe closed without a single American's being charged for colluding with Russia to steal the 2016 election, much less President Trump. It was a huge blow to the Democrats and their media allies. They tried to keep the collusion hoax going, suggesting that new attorney general William Barr had improperly downplayed the findings of the special counsel, but the conspiracy had run out of gas.

Democrats had hoped that the special counsel's Russia report would form the basis of an impeachment probe. Democrats hatched a last-ditch attempt to get Trump when they had Mueller testify before Congress about how his report was actually much worse for Trump than it seemed. But his testimony was disjointed, and Mueller seemed confused about the conclusions of the probe he had ostensibly led. As a result, the effort failed, and impeachment was dead in its tracks.

The day after Mueller testified, President Trump had a phone call with Ukraine's president, Volodymyr Zelensky, in which he discussed the Biden family's business dealings in the notoriously corrupt former Soviet Republic. The call reportedly worried a National Security Council staffer tasked with listening in, who soon began discussing it with others. The contents of the call were leaked, albeit quite inaccurately, to the media, and operatives began working with Representative Adam Schiff, the new chairman of the House Permanent Select Committee on Intelligence. An impeachment effort was soon launched.

But unlike the Russia hoax, Republicans didn't fall for it. In fact, not a single Republican in the House, no matter how much he or she disliked Trump or was nervous about taking on the media or Democrats, fell for the operation. The only senator to fall for it would be Mitt Romney, the senator from Utah and former Republican nominee for president whose distaste for Trump ran deep.

On February 4, 2020, the day before his acquittal in the Senate, President Donald J. Trump strode confidently into the House Chamber to deliver his State of the Union speech. His survival in the face of Democrats' politicized attacks had clearly reinvigorated him. He had beaten the attempt to get him out of office and had solidified his grasp over the Republican Party.

It took three minutes for Trump to make it from the back of the chamber to the speaker's podium, shaking hands with State of the Union attendees as he went. The audience for his fourth address before a joint session of Congress was comprised of members of the House of Representatives, members of the Senate, most of his cabinet, the Joint Chiefs of Staff, the chief justice of the United States and associate justices of the Supreme Court, and members of the diplomatic corps. The politicians and assorted dignitaries were packed on top of one another. The visitor and press galleries above the floor of the chamber were also full to the brim.

Guests, including President Trump's personal guests, such as Ivanka Trump, Jared Kushner, and Lara Trump, were seated in the gallery above the chamber, looking down on the crowd. Some members of the White House staff, such as the legislative staff, crowded in at the back of the room to listen to the speech.

The walnut-paneled House Chamber, where the State of the Union is delivered, is in the Capitol's south wing. At the southernmost edge of the chamber sits the speaker's rostrum, behind which are Ionic columns made from black Italian marble with white Alabama marble capitals at the top. An American flag is hung from the center of the back wall, with bronze fasces and Roman insignias at each side.

There was an electricity in the air. Unlike before his previous speeches in the same room, he didn't shake the Speaker's hand when he gave her a copy of his speech. Nancy Pelosi fans would make a big deal of what they perceived as a snub. But he didn't shake Vice President Mike Pence's hand either.

It was the fourth time President Trump would address a joint session of Congress, and the last of his time in office.

"Members of Congress, the President of the United States," said Pelosi, a few weeks shy of her eightieth birthday, wearing a sharp white suit. Pence, in a dark suit and blue tie, smiled as he stood behind the president. The room, or at least the Republican side of the room, erupted in more cheers and exuberant hoots and hollers. "Four more years! Four more years!" the Republicans clamored.

◆　　　◆　　　◆

So much had changed in the four years that Trump had been president—but Trump had not changed so much as the Republican Party was different. By the time Trump began his final State of the Union speech, he had triumphed in the face of considerable opposition—and he was ready to seize his moment.

The 2020 State of the Union address was a celebration of Trump's victory over the Republican establishment and obstructionist Democrats alike. Trump had proved that he could lead the country capably and implement his agenda. The speech was perhaps the high-water mark of his presidency.

Trump tended to shine at his State of the Union addresses. The speech was an opportunity to tell the American people directly all that his administration had accomplished. But more important, it was a chance to offer his vision for the country going forward.

"Three years ago, we launched the great American comeback. Tonight, I stand before you to share the incredible results. Jobs are booming, incomes are soaring, poverty is plummeting, crime is falling, confidence is surging, and our country is thriving and highly respected again."[20]

Pence smiled, as did all the Republicans in the room. Pelosi grimaced and looked down at the speech.

"America's enemies are on the run. America's fortunes are on the rise, and America's future is blazing bright. The years of economic decay are over," he said.[21]

"The days of our country being used, taken advantage of, and even scorned by other nations are long behind us. Gone too are the broken promises, jobless recoveries, tired platitudes, and constant excuses for the depletion of American wealth, power, and prestige. In just three short years, we have shattered the mentality of American decline and we have rejected the downsizing of Americans' destiny. We have totally rejected the downsizing. We are moving forward at a pace that was unimaginable just a short time ago, and we are never, ever going back!"[22]

Senator Kamala Harris, wearing a gray suit with a black turtleneck, sat expressionless. Pelosi paged through the papers and looked into the distance. James Clyburn, assistant Democratic leader, who had served in Congress since 1993, shook his head, upset.

Trump talked about slashing regulations that prevent economic growth, enacting tax cuts, and reforming trade agreements.

"Our agenda is relentlessly pro-worker, pro-family, pro-growth, and, most of all, pro-American," he said to a standing ovation, with Secretary of Labor Eugene Scalia and Secretary of Commerce Wilbur Ross smiling broadly.[23] Debbie Wasserman Schultz, a Democrat from Florida who used to chair the Democratic National Committee, looked on stone-faced from her seat.

Trump talked about the "unbridled optimism" that comes with improved economic conditions for all citizens. Seven million new jobs had been created on his watch, and the country could boast the lowest unemployment rate in over half a century.

"The unemployment rate for African Americans, Hispanic Americans, and Asian Americans has reached the lowest levels in history. African American youth unemployment has reached an all-time low. African American poverty has declined to the lowest rate ever recorded," he said.[24]

Remarkably, only Republicans applauded. The refusal of Democrats to applaud the lowest poverty rate for black Americans shocked observers, a sign of the deep-seated hatred that had marked their approach to the entire administration. Several of Trump's most vociferous critics refused even to show up.[25]

Those that did attend kept hearing more and more good economic news. Veterans, disabled Americans, workers without high school diplomas, and young Americans had record employment. "Under the last administration, more than 10 million people were added to the food stamp rolls. Under my administration, 7 million Americans have come off food stamps, and 10 million people have been lifted off of welfare," Trump said to huge cheers.[26]

Trump talked about 3.5 million working-age people joining the workforce. The net worth of the bottom half of wage earners increased by 47 percent, three times faster than the increase for the top 1 percent. The Trump economy was providing for working Americans, an accomplishment that economists had long written off as impossible.

"After decades of flat and falling incomes, wages are rising fast—and, wonderfully, they are rising fastest for low-income workers, who have seen a 16 percent pay increase since my election. This is a blue-collar boom," he said, as Senator Tim Kaine (D-Virginia), who was Hillary Clinton's vice presidential candidate in 2016, literally twiddled his thumbs. Meanwhile, Republicans erupted in jubilation.[27]

Real median household income was at the highest level ever recorded. Stock markets had soared 70 percent, adding more than $12 trillion in wealth and bolstering 401(k)s and pensions. Consumer confidence had reached new highs.[28]

Trump didn't shy away from talking about issues where he had bucked Washington orthodoxy. His opinions on "free trade" departed radically from the consensus that had dominated both the right and the left in Washington for decades. Rethinking trade, especially trade with China, was an important part of Trump's agenda, and he was keen to highlight it in his address to the nation.

"For decades, China has taken advantage of the United States. Now we have changed that," Trump said.[29] Taking on the challenge of China had been a big part of his 2016 campaign. It was no small task, and particularly roiled the establishment and the Republican Party.

China's privileged status as a trading partner had been considered untouchable ever since Bill Clinton lobbied for the accession of the communist nation to the World Trade Organization in 2000. Clinton thought the United States was getting a good deal. "Economically, this agreement is the equivalent of a one-way street," he said while in office. "It requires China to open its markets—with a fifth of the world's population, potentially the biggest markets in the world—to both our products and services in unprecedented new ways. All we do is to agree to maintain the present access which China enjoys."[30]

But since then, increased trade with the United States hasn't influenced China so much as China has influenced the United States. And China benefited more from the new arrangement than the United States did. Investors found the westernization of China's economy a tantalizing reward for massive investments in China that gutted manufacturing and other vital American industries. China skillfully managed the growth of its booming capitalistic economy while its communist government maintained centralized control.[31] The approach raised China to the world's second largest economy, with tremendous expectations of future growth.

When Trump came along in 2016, talking about "Chy-na" and the need to impose tariffs against the country, Republicans were skeptical. Republican orthodoxy had required lip service, if not actual service, in favor of lowered tariffs.

Trump's position was also somewhat misunderstood. Trump supported free trade in principle, but in a world of complex trade agreements what was presented to voters as "free trade" was often not that simple. He wanted to update trade agreements and make them more bilateral than the expert preference for multilateral deals.

Over the course of his administration, however, he received begrudging respect for his focus on China and his attempts to limit that country's rise vis-à-vis the United States. He changed the focus of America's foreign policy and single-handedly made the China threat the number one priority among experts and elected officials alike. It was another area where Trump had won over the Republican Party. And it was an important accomplishment to highlight before the nation in his address.

◆   ◆   ◆

Unlike the Republican establishment that had preceded him, Trump made it clear in his State of the Union speech that, while a thrice-married New York celebrity was an unlikely champion of conservatism, he was proud of the policy actions he had taken to promote conservative values. He was also proud of conservative culture and grassroots heroes, a rare trait among Washington Republicans.

Rush Limbaugh, the beloved radio host, had received applause when he entered the gallery and sat next to Melania Trump. Now, Trump delivered the news that in recognition of his charity work and the inspiration he had provided millions of listeners over the years, Rush would be receiving the country's highest civilian honor, the Presidential Medal of Freedom. And he'd be receiving it right then, with Melania Trump presenting the honor in the gallery.

It was a remarkable moment, and Rush was overcome with emotion.

Democratic presidents are very good at awarding the folk heroes of their constituents, regardless of whether they work in Hollywood or politics. Obama had given the Presidential Medal of Freedom to such politically polarizing figures as Ted Kennedy and Gloria Steinem.

But Republicans had for years internalized that they were second-class citizens, people whose folk heroes did not deserve recognition.

Rush Limbaugh was indisputably the best radio show host in history, something even liberals in the medium admit. He had popularized conservatism throughout the 1990s and greatly expanded its reach.

Of course Limbaugh deserved an award. But no other Republican president would have done it. And it electrified both the room and the people watching at home.

Trump used the State of the Union address to highlight his commitment to social conservatives. He had fought for the pro-life movement and wanted the American people to know.

Trump was the last person anyone in the Republican Party had expected to be a pro-life leader. In fact, much of the opposition to him in the 2016 primary was due to concern he wouldn't be. He had rarely talked about the issue except to say, as he did on *Meet the Press* in 1999, "I am very pro-choice."[32]

The pro-life movement pledged its support, however reluctantly. In return it got a leader who put up a better fight during debates against abortion than any other presidential nominee in history. In the final debate against Hillary Clinton, Trump left her struggling to respond when he said of her opposition to any restriction on abortion, "Well, I think it's terrible. If you go with what Hillary is saying, in the ninth month, you can take the baby and rip the baby out of the womb of the mother just prior to the birth of the baby."[33]

Trump continued, "Now, you can say that that's OK and Hillary can say that that's OK. But it's not OK with me, because based on what she's saying, and based on where she's going, and where she's been, you can take the baby and rip the baby out of the womb in the ninth month on the final day. And that's not acceptable."[34]

As improbable as it had once seemed, by the 2020 State of the Union address Trump had proven himself to be a thoroughly pro-life president. He had taken swift and decisive action to limit access to abortion, preventing tax dollars from funding abortions overseas and allowing states to cut federal funds to Planned Parenthood.

"Now I realize he's maybe the only person that could actually accomplish what we needed to accomplish, meaning the work that he's doing now. He's maybe the only one who'd have the backbone to do it," Susan B. Anthony List president Marjorie Dannenfelser said in a 2019 interview.

Another decisive issue that separated Trump from the Republican establishment in 2016 was border security. Despite pledging to protect the border, Republicans often lost the courage of their convictions once they made it to Washington. The Republican establishment was at best mealymouthed when it came to fighting illegal immigration, and at worst two-faced.

Trump blew all that up by running aggressively on the border issue, pledging to build a wall to keep illegal immigrants out. Trump ended up building over 450 miles of border wall, leading to a decline of illegal crossings in those areas of 90 percent. Customs and Border Protection and Immigration and Customs Enforcement seized over two million pounds of fentanyl, heroin, meth, and other narcotics. He entered into an agreement with Mexico to have asylum seekers wait safely there for their asylum hearings to gain entry to the United States.[35]

For the first time in decades, the border seemed to be getting under control.

Finally, Trump ended his address by underlining his commitment to a realist foreign policy after two decades of adventurism and interventionism—another area in which he had challenged the Republican Party and won.

When Trump ran for president, he scandalized the foreign policy establishment by speaking against the North Atlantic Treaty Organization (NATO), the military alliance that was set up after the Second World War and had expanded to thirty European and North American countries.[36] He kept the rhetoric up throughout the 2016 campaign, saying on July 20, 2016, in an interview with the *New York Times* at the Republican National Convention, "If we cannot be properly reimbursed for the tremendous cost of our military protecting other countries, and in many cases the countries I'm talking about are extremely rich...we have many NATO members that aren't paying their bills."[37]

Now, at the State of the Union, Trump drew attention to the efforts he had made in getting NATO members to live up to their commitments. "We are also getting our allies, finally, to help pay their fair share," he bragged. "I have raised contributions from other NATO members by more than $400 billion, and the number of Allies meeting their minimum obligations has more than doubled."[38]

But crucially, Trump's opposition to the failed foreign policy thinking of the previous decades didn't mean he opposed using military force when necessary.

In fact, just three months prior to the State of the Union, Trump had approved a military operation to kill Abu Bakr al-Baghdadi, the nom de guerre for the leader of the Islamic State of Iraq and Syria. When Trump took office, ISIS held over twenty thousand square miles of territory. Three years later, the caliphate was destroyed, and al-Baghdadi was dead.[39]

During his speech, Trump introduced Carl and Marcia Mueller, parents of a humanitarian aid worker named Kayla who went to Syria to care for civilians there. She was kidnapped, tortured, enslaved, and raped by al-Baghdadi himself.

After more than five hundred days in captivity, al-Baghdadi murdered her. The elite special forces who carried out the operation nicknamed their mission "Task Force 814," a reference to Kayla's birthday. "America's warriors never forgot Kayla—and neither will we," Trump said as the chamber applauded the Muellers. Her parents held up a picture while others in the gallery comforted them.[40]

When Trump talked about ending wars, he focused on the costs borne by American troops. During his speech, he highlighted an army staff sergeant named Christopher Hake who had written a letter to his one-year-old son Gage on his second deployment in 2008. But on Easter Sunday that year, Hake was killed by a roadside bomb. Trump recognized Gage and his mother Kelli as she choked back tears.[41]

The terrorist who provided the deadly roadside bombs that killed Hake and so many other U.S. soldiers was an Iranian general named Qasem Soleimani. A month prior to the State of the Union, Trump had authorized a precision strike to kill Soleimani.

"Our message to the terrorists is clear. You will never escape American justice. If you attack our citizens, you forfeit your life," Trump said.[42]

Trump reiterated his desire to end the Afghanistan war, saying it was "not our function to serve other nations as law enforcement agencies. These are war fighters that we have—the best in the world—and they either want to fight to win or not fight at all."[43]

He mentioned the heavy burden placed on U.S. families by troops' serving in America's longest war in Afghanistan. He featured Amy Williams and her children Elliana and Rowan. He highlighted her full-time work and heavy volunteer schedule while her husband, Sergeant First Class Townsend Williams, was on his fourth deployment. "[Y]our family's sacrifice makes it possible for all of our families to live in safety and in peace, and we want to thank you," Trump said. "But, Amy, there is one more thing. Tonight, we have a very special surprise. I am thrilled to inform you that your husband is back from deployment. He is here with us tonight and we couldn't keep him waiting any longer."[44]

The chamber nearly erupted in jubilation as onlookers watched, breaking out into lengthy chants of "USA! USA!"

With that, Trump ended his speech with a rousing and unifying call:

> We are Americans. We are pioneers. We are the pathfinders. We settled the New World, we built the modern world, and we changed history forever by embracing the eternal truth that everyone is made equal by the hand of Almighty God. America is the place where anything can happen. America is the place where anyone can rise. And here, on this land,

on this soil, on this continent, the most incredible dreams come true. This nation is our canvas, and this country is our masterpiece. We look at tomorrow and see unlimited frontiers just waiting to be explored. Our brightest discoveries are not yet known. Our most thrilling stories are not yet told. Our grandest journeys are not yet made. The American Age, the American Epic, the American adventure has only just begun.

Our spirit is still young, the sun is still rising, God's grace is still shining, and, my fellow Americans, the best is yet to come. Thank you. God bless you. And God bless America. Thank you very much.[45]

With the Russia collusion hoax and the failed impeachment in the rearview mirror, Trump was back on track for victory in November, and all the Democrats in the chamber that evening knew it. Trump had solidified his grip over the Republican Party, had ushered in a record-breaking economy, and had a long record of achievement that he could boast of. Trump offered a compelling vision of the American future based in civic pride and shared identity, while Democrats were more intent on denigrating the nation's past. He had grown his support and looked robust and dynamic. Immediately after it ended, Pelosi's anger and frustration boiled over. She stood up and began tearing the pages of his speech in half, the first time a Speaker of the House had so visibly violated norms of respect toward the president.

Trump's opponents would need a miracle to stop him. He was at the peak of his powers and was leading the country to new heights. But Democrats would soon get their lucky break when news of a novel coronavirus reached American shores. It was a crisis that they wouldn't let go to waste.

CHAPTER THREE

Designed in a Lab

The COVID-19 pandemic was so perfectly suited to damaging President Trump's re-election effort that it almost seemed designed in a laboratory.

In the first few months of 2020, President Trump was doing better than at any other point in his presidency.[1] As Trump would tell it, "I was winning by so much prior to the Chinese virus that George Washington with a running mate of Abraham Lincoln couldn't have won."

The hysterical predictions from elites about the troubles his administration would bring weren't just overwrought—they were embarrassingly false.

When Trump was elected, *New York Times* columnist and Nobel Prize–winner Paul Krugman wrote, "[I]f the question is when the markets will recover, a first-pass answer is never."[2] By the opening of 2020, the stock market was up more than ten thousand points and the economy was thriving, with particularly impressive gains in working-class wages and minority employment.[3]

Instead of the nuclear war that political opponents and pundits had predicted, Trump ushered in a period of relative peace. Trump was the first president in forty years who hadn't invaded a country or launched a new war.[4] He brought peace to the Middle East, brokering a series of historic deals between Arab nations and Israel.[5] And he shifted the nation's foreign policy focus to China, a nation that much of the country had come to view as a serious adversary.

The spread of the COVID-19 virus from China changed everything. The global pandemic squelched the thriving economy that was Trump's best argument for re-election. In fact, it shut down the country entirely.[6] Children were banned from school. Religious adherents were prevented from worship. Restaurants and gathering places were shuttered. It gave the media massive reserves of fuel for their unhinged anti-Trump operation. And it gave Democrats the pretext needed to radically alter voting systems in their favor across the country.[7]

As Rahm Emanuel, former Chicago mayor and chief of staff to President Barack Obama, famously said, "Never let a crisis go to waste."[8] When the COVID-19 pandemic broke out, Democrats immediately recognized that it would give them a once-in-a-generation opportunity to radically alter America's voting laws and procedures to benefit their party.

There were more than five hundred election law cases and appeals by the year's close.[9] But the "relief" plaintiffs sought in many of these cases were changes to election policy that the Democratic Party had wanted for years, such as the expansion of mail-in voting and the relaxation or removal of scrutiny of mail-in ballots.[10] And for all their rhetoric invoking principles of justice and equality, any ideological reasons Democrats had for advocating a broader system coincided with their self-interest as a party. Studies show that early voting benefits Democratic candidates and harms Republicans.[11] The concerns about public health wrought by the global pandemic gave them the perfect cover to advance their self-interested agenda.

◆　　◆　　◆

At first, COVID-19 didn't have much of an impact on the 2020 election. The Democrats were in the midst of a heated primary, and each of the remaining candidates was holding rallies and drawing crowds.[12]

But by Wednesday, March 11, a series of events dramatically altered the nation's approach. Actors Tom Hanks and Rita Wilson announced that they had caught the virus, the National Basketball Association canceled its season after a player tested positive, and the stock market was in free fall. COVID-19 had arrived, and Trump addressed the nation from the Oval Office about the pandemic.[13] From that point forward, the government response to the pandemic would be much more aggressive.[14]

Elections were an early casualty of the new approach. Ohio's Republican governor Mike DeWine canceled his state's March 17 primary election just hours before it was to be held, even though many questioned whether he had the legal authority to do so.[15] A few weeks later, Wisconsin governor Tony Evers, a Democrat, tried to do the same right before his state's April 7 general election.[16] He had previously said of canceling elections, "We certainly would not wait until the night before the election to make an historic decision like that."[17]

Evers had insisted for weeks that the election go on, even as he was locking down the state. He emphasized that even though it was a primary election, it was also a general election where local and state officers needed to be selected. "How long do we potentially leave offices not filled because we're into July or August and we haven't held a general election?" he asked rhetorically.[18]

Evers's answer was to expand mail-in voting. When Evers announced stay-at-home orders, he said, "Having as many absentee ballots as possible is absolutely a top priority [and] always has been given the emergency that we're in."[19] And with Wisconsin considered a swing state, Evers was sure to meet resistance from Republicans in his state and across the country.

The debate over how the Wisconsin election would be conducted soon became a proxy for wider debates of election protocol. Both Republicans and Democrats saw the relatively small election as relevant to November's contest and a forerunner of what was to come. The fight was on to set the rules for one of the first elections in COVID times.

On March 26, an alliance of Democratic Party–aligned groups such as Souls to the Polls, American Federation of Teachers, AFL–CIO, SEIU, and the League of Women Voters sued Wisconsin in federal court, seeking to delay the election.[20] They combined their lawsuit with others seeking to expand mail-in balloting and to allow the counting of votes past election day.

The judge didn't move the election, but he extended the deadline to request absentee ballots and gave voters an extra six days after election day to return them.[21] Democrats didn't think that was sufficient. *Politico* ran an article saying that "more than a dozen Democratic officials" thought the rule of law should be no barrier to taking action, and that Evers should unilaterally announce a delay and force someone to stop him "even in the face of an adverse court ruling."[22]

The *New York Times* applied pressure by publishing a story claiming that scared voters would be disenfranchised unless the election were delayed.[23] Governor Evers quickly called a special legislative session to get the legislature to delay the election, but they closed the session immediately without taking action.[24]

On April 6, Evers issued an executive order delaying the election, even though he acknowledged he didn't have the legal authority to do so. It was appealed to the Wisconsin Supreme Court, which overturned his order.[25] That same day, the United States Supreme Court issued a ruling on absentee ballots in Wisconsin stating that only ballots postmarked by election day and arriving within six days afterwards would be counted.[26]

Having exhausted their attempts to delay the election, Democrats and the media began claiming that the Wisconsin election would be a "super spreader" of the virus. "[W]ith voters' very lives at stake," the

New York Times wrote, "the legitimacy of the election" would be in question.[27]

"They will kill people to stay in power, literally," said Democratic strategist James Carville on election night.[28] In the end, there was no spike of cases from voting, despite hundreds of thousands of people's showing up to the polls.[29]

The Wisconsin Elections Commission would later report severe problems with ballot custody for mail-in ballots during that election. For example, one United States Postal Service official reported that workers had found "three tubs" of absentee ballots for an area covering Appleton and Oshkosh, totaling some 1,600 ballots.[30] None were ever counted.[31] In Milwaukee, nearly 2,700 ballots were never sent to voters because of a production problem.[32] Only 52.5 percent of the affected voters ended up voting, either with a replacement absentee ballot or at the polls. And hundreds of absentee ballots a day that were supposed to be mailed to Fox Point residents failed to make it to their destinations.[33]

The handling of the April election led to problems in the presidential election, too. As of 2019, Wisconsin voter rolls included more than 234,000 names of people who had moved either out of state or to a new address in Wisconsin. By law, a notice was supposed to be sent to those names and addresses and, if they didn't reply, they were supposed to be flagged by election officials as ineligible. The notice was sent, but the voters who failed to reply weren't removed from the rolls. The Wisconsin Institute for Law and Liberty sued, and a county judge ordered them removed.[34] When the Wisconsin Elections Board still refused to clean up its voter rolls, it was fined.[35] Wisconsin election officials appealed the ruling, and an appeals court allowed the names to stay.[36]

The presence of ineligible voters on voter rolls is never ideal from a voting integrity standpoint, but in-person voting limits the ability of bad actors to exploit the situation. Voters usually have to show identification to vote. It's more difficult to catch fraudulent mail-in voting because of the lack of oversight and ballot custody. Still, voters in Wisconsin were supposed to show identification the first time they voted by mail. It was the one election protection Wisconsin had maintained after refusing to clean up the rolls.

However, Wisconsin law had an exception to ID requirements for those who say they are "indefinitely" confined because of age, illness, infirmity, or disability. The highly partisan clerks of Wisconsin's two biggest and most Democratic counties told their residents to claim that they were "indefinitely confined" even if they weren't.[37] The clerks served Dane County, the state's second most populous county and home to the ultra-liberal University of Wisconsin in Madison, and Milwaukee County, the state's most populous and dense county.

Once such claims were registered, the state would send absentee ballots for all future elections, unless the recipients changed their designation or didn't return an absentee ballot.

About 195,000 of the nearly 1 million people who voted by mail in April claimed they were indefinitely confined, according to the Wisconsin Elections Commission.[38] An additional 50,000 "indefinitely confined" claims were made prior to the November election.[39] That meant that up to a quarter of a million votes were cast in Wisconsin's presidential election without any identification check at all.

"Fraudulently voting by mail by assuming the identity of any of the 234,000 phantom voters still on the state's rolls could not possibly have been easier," said Dan O'Donnell, in an examination of voting problems for the Wisconsin think tank the MacIver Institute.[40]

◆   ◆   ◆

It was around the time of the April election that Republicans and Democrats really began to notice what a dramatic difference mail-in balloting made in elections. With early voting and mail-in balloting rising in recent years, operatives had learned how to anticipate final results by incorporating early voting returns. But in the spring of 2020, thanks to an increase in mail-in voting, everything was different.

In Wisconsin's overwhelmingly Republican Seventh Congressional District, Republican Tom Tiffany was running to replace Sean Duffy in a special election in May.[41] Based on early voting returns, the Republicans were worried he might only win by five or six points, well short of what his performance should be. Duffy had won his last election in 2018 by more than twenty points.[42] If Tiffany only won by single digits, the result would embolden Democrats nationwide and demoralize Republicans, affecting both parties' fundraising and get-out-the-vote operations. The team scrambled and did one of their first Tele-Town Halls, a large conference call with voters featuring President Trump, Duffy, and RNC chairwoman Ronna McDaniel, to make sure Tiffany did well.[43]

Tiffany ended up winning by fifteen percentage points. Republican strategists realized what had happened: Democrats were more likely to vote absentee, early, and by mail, while Republicans were more likely to vote on election day.[44]

Another special election in June was also informative. On election night, Republican nominee Chris Jacobs was up by as much as forty-two points over his Democratic opponent in a race to represent New York's Twenty-Seventh District.[45] The seat had been held by Republicans, but they were expecting a much closer race. The final result after mail-in ballots were counted was *much* closer, with only five points separating Jacobs from his opponent.[46]

Both Democrats and Republicans were enthusiastic and energized, but the pattern was clear. Republicans tend to vote in person.[47] RNC surveys of voters showed that many of their voters had complete distrust of voting by mail. In some states, such as Georgia, some 80 percent of Republicans said they wouldn't vote by mail.[48]

Democrats, on the other hand, strongly preferred to vote by mail, and the vote-by-mail system was becoming a major part of the Democratic Party's get-out-the-vote operation. Regardless of fraud and other concerns, the press saw the success of the mail-in ballot effort in Wisconsin for what it was: an effort to turn out more Democratic voters.

Following the Wisconsin primaries, the *New York Times* reported, "Wisconsin Democrats are working to export their template for success—intense digital outreach and a well-coordinated vote-by-mail operation—to other states in the hope that it will improve the party's chances in local and statewide elections and in the quest to unseat President Trump in November."[49]

These primary and special election days were viewed by Democratic operatives as "an exercise in training volunteers and voters in how to vote by mail," as the *New York Times* put it.[50] Democratic voters and operatives learned how to use the system. The 110,000 people who requested absentee ballots for the Tiffany race, for instance, would also automatically be sent ballots in the fall.[51]

Democrats had figured out how to get what they wanted from existing rules. The only thing that could have been better was if they could import their "intense digital outreach and a well-coordinated vote-by-mail operation" into the official government election offices in heavily Democratic areas.[52] As will be explained in subsequent chapters, grants from liberal billionaires allowed them to do just that in five cities in Wisconsin, Democrat-heavy counties in Georgia, and overwhelmingly Democratic Philadelphia, among others. Democrats would essentially run their vote-by-mail operation through official government offices, and Republicans wouldn't find out until months after the election had passed.

Primaries and special elections with mail-in balloting also gave Democrats practice in challenging elections. Democratic organizations such as Fair Fight Action, a group founded by Stacey Abrams, a failed gubernatorial candidate in Georgia, said that the early races "provided us a template" for how to handle November.[53] Her group collected hundreds of legal affidavits from Democratic voters who said they had trouble acquiring and casting ballots. The affidavits would have been used to overturn results of the Wisconsin Supreme Court race had the conservative candidate prevailed, as the *New York Times* reported.[54]

Losing candidates and parties regularly litigate elections, whether Republican or Democrat. Abrams, who had lost to Brian Kemp in Georgia's 2018 gubernatorial race by sixty thousand votes, took election results to court.[55] Her obstinance may not have helped her become governor, but it gave her valuable experience that she would pass on to her fellow Democrats come 2020.

◆   ◆   ◆

Abrams's efforts to change elections in Georgia were relentless, and they didn't stop once her 2018 loss to Kemp was certified. Her fight laid the groundwork for an overhaul of election procedure in Georgia that would have untold effects on the 2020 election results.

A *Politico* article in November 2020 claimed that Biden's eventual win in Georgia was related to Democrats' massive efforts to fight so-called "voter suppression tactics," the left's terminology for ensuring that election fraud is limited by removing ineligible voters from polling books, having voters submit identification, and limiting the participation of outside parties in the secret voting process.[56] Democrats did invest in the project, spending tens of millions of dollars to challenge and change voter integrity laws.

"If America were a house, they'd be the termites. It's that bad," said Georgia Republican and voter database expert Mark Davis about the lawfare engaged in fighting against voting integrity laws.

Long before COVID-19, the Democratic Party of Georgia, Democratic Senatorial Campaign Committee, and Democratic Congressional Campaign Committee sued Georgia secretary of state Brad Raffensperger in November 2019 to get him to water down the state's requirements for checking signatures on mail-in ballots.[57] Governor Kemp, under pressure from Democratic groups alleging voter suppression, had already signed a law earlier in 2019 that relaxed signature requirements and made it more difficult to reject ballots for signature mismatch or other ballot problems. Elias, who was leading the lawsuits, wanted the requirements relaxed even more.[58]

On March 6, Raffensperger, with the advice and counsel of much of the state and national Republican establishment, entered a "consent decree" conceding to Elias's and the Democratic Party's demands, including a new procedure for reviewing signatures on mail-in ballots.[59] When other Republicans learned what Raffensperger had done, they were shocked. Democrats' high-powered attorneys introduced several significant changes defining how Georgia law regarding the "curing" of ballots should be interpreted. That meant that when an absentee ballot came in with problems that would typically lead it to be discounted, the voter was instead given a chance to "cure," or correct, the ballot.[60] Raffensperger's legal counsel would later testify that Republicans agreed to some of these provisions because they were eager to keep Democrats from extending election day by delaying ballot deadlines, and failure to be generous with curing procedures would encourage judges to intervene more in altering the election.[61] The decree also said Democrats would offer training and guidance material on signature verification to county registrars and absentee ballot clerks.[62]

Most important, the settlement got rid of any meaningful signature match for mail-in ballots. The law had previously required signatures to match the signatures on file with the Georgia voter registration database. But the settlement allowed the signature to match any signature on file, including the one on the absentee ballot application that Raffensperger would soon decide to send to every address on file.[63] That meant a fraudulently obtained ballot would easily have a signature match, leaving no way to detect fraud.

The consent agreement also made it more difficult to reject mail-in ballots. Under the new rules, a ballot could only be rejected if a majority of registrars, deputy registrars, and ballot clerks assigned to the task agreed to it, another burden that made it easier to just let all ballots through without scrutiny. What's more, many counties used minimum-wage temporary workers to sort through ballots, not skilled analysts of what constitutes a signature match.

The change to the law, combined with the consent decree, did exactly what the Democrats had hoped: it made it more difficult for election officials to reject absentee ballots. Critics would later note that the absentee ballot rejection rate in Georgia had plummeted since 2016, when 6.4 percent of mail-in ballots were rejected, and 2018, when 3.6 percent of mail-in ballots were rejected. In 2020, just .4 percent of absentee ballots in the general election were rejected.[64]

When Raffensperger consented to Elias's demands, few people expected there would be such a dramatic and sudden rise in mail-in balloting in 2020. Election officials are reluctant to check signatures in any election, much less scrutinize them, even when the mail-in ballots are a small percentage of the ballots cast. When dealing with hundreds of thousands or millions of such ballots, it's a practical impossibility. Even if overwhelmed election workers bother to look at iffy signatures, they often just decide to let them pass, especially since drawing attention to a problem will only bring them additional work.

But problems began to arise well before Election Day 2020. In fact, the changes agreed to in the consent decree caused problems in Georgia from the start. The first signs of trouble would emerge in the Peach State's presidential primary.

◆   ◆   ◆

On March 14, 2020, Raffensperger announced that the looming presidential primary would be moved to May 19.[65] On April 9, he postponed it again to June 9.[66] The extra time didn't keep Georgia's primary election from turning into a disaster.

"Georgia's Election Mess: Many Problems, Plenty of Blame, Few Solutions for November," read the June 10, 2020, *New York Times* headline about the "disastrous primary election" in June that was "plagued by glitches.... Democrats also saw a systemic effort to disenfranchise voters."[67]

The primary election was the first time Georgia's precincts would use the new Dominion voting machines that the state had purchased the year prior. While most counties made the adjustment with minimal problems, Fulton County, which is the largest of Georgia's 159 counties and has more than one million people, experienced long lines and technical difficulties.[68]

Citing irregularities with absentee ballots and peculiarities at polling sites, the *New York Times* said Georgia's "embattled election officials" were dealing with a voting system that suffered a "spectacular collapse."[69] The *Times* said it was unclear whether the problems were caused by "mere bungling, or an intentional effort"[70] by Raffensperger and his fellow Republicans in the secretary of state's office. The "trouble that plunged Georgia's voting system into chaos" was related to Dominion Voting Systems, the *Times* claimed, "which some elections experts had been sounding alarm bells about for months."[71]

A few months later, any complaint about a voting machine would be treated by the media as a conspiracy theory. But in 2019 and the first half of 2020, the same journalists and experts who would defend Dominion to the hilt were rabidly opposed to Georgia's voting machines, claiming they were insecure.

"Georgia likely to plow ahead with buying insecure voting machines," wrote *Politico* in March 2019 about the plan to replace voting machines, saying cybersecurity experts, election integrity advocates, and Georgia Democrats had all warned about the security problems of the new machines, which were electronic but also spit out a marked paper ballot.[72]

"Security experts warn that an intruder can corrupt the machines and alter the barcode-based ballots without voters or election officials realizing it," the article claimed.[73] It was alleged that a "meaningful audit" was "impossible."[74] When Georgia picked Dominion Voting Systems in August 2019, the *Atlanta Journal-Constitution* warned that "critics say the system will still be vulnerable to hacking," citing high-profile hacks of Capital One and Equifax, as well as the online attacks on Atlanta and Georgia courts.[75] "Election officials will have to be on guard against malware, viruses, stolen passwords and Russian interference," the article continued.[76] Again, just over a year later, saying the same thing the *Atlanta-Journal Constitution* had would become grounds for being removed from social media.

"Georgia in Uproar Over Voting Meltdown," the *New York Times* proclaimed in a June 9, 2020, story, citing problems with Dominion Voting Systems and Raffensperger's management of the election.[77] "The machines bought by the state last year were instantly controversial. Security experts said they were insecure. Privacy experts worried that the screens could be seen from nearly 30 feet away. Budget hawks balked at the price tag. And one of Dominion Voting Systems' lobbyists, Jared Samuel Thomas, has deep connections to Gov. Brian Kemp, the Republican who defeated Ms. Abrams in 2018," the article read.[78]

The *Washington Post* piled on. "As Georgia rolls out new voting machines for 2020, worries about election security persist," the *Post* reported.[79] Further, "election security experts said the state's newest voting machines also remain vulnerable to potential intrusions or malfunctions—and some view the paper records they produce as insufficient if a verified audit of the vote is needed."[80]

Again, all of these claims would be memory-holed a few months later when it was Republicans, not Democrats, expressing concerns about the security of Georgia's voting systems.

The outrage Democrats directed at Raffensperger was somewhat unfair. In Georgia, counties, not the secretary of state, are responsible for managing their own elections. The problems with the Georgia primary were focused in blue counties, particularly Fulton County, where lines stretched for hours, machines were improperly run, and volunteers were insufficiently trained.

Fulton County officials so mismanaged their handling of the primary in June that they were fined and forced into a settlement agreement that included a requirement that they be independently monitored.[81] According to the *Atlanta Journal-Constitution*:

> To avoid the fine, Fulton must maintain verifiable levels of operational competence by properly processing absentee ballots; keeping a force of 2,200 properly trained poll workers; providing at least 24 early voting sites; striving to process 100 voters per hour at any site; having a technical support staff member at every site; and creating a post-election audit. The consent order also requires Fulton to regularly update the Board on its pool of poll workers. The issue in the consent order requiring the most negotiation was over an independent elections monitor. They agreed on Carter Jones, who spent time in Africa helping countries improve their elections....[82]

The U.S. Department of Justice would also send an election monitor to Fulton County.[83]

Raffensperger also requested and received a $5,591,800 grant from the privately funded Center for Election Innovation and Research (CEIR), a group funded by Facebook founder Mark Zuckerberg and his wife Priscilla Chan.[84] The group reported Georgia used the funds to push mail-in balloting and to counteract negative messaging about mail-in voting. The secretary of state's office focused the spending in Democratic counties, hoping to avoid the negative media attention that had greeted them after the Democratic counties botched the June primary.[85] Particularly with Democrats' strategy being to drive up mail-in voting, the millions of dollars in advertising and support of Democratic counties acted as a state-run complement to Democrats' get-out-the-vote operation.

CEIR reported that it contacted all fifty states and invited them to apply for grants to help push mail-in voting. Twenty-three applied for and received money. In a report after the election, CEIR tried to downplay its work helping Democrats, saying "there was a fairly even partisan and geographic balance" in the awards. It noted that eleven of the states that received funds had voted for Trump in 2016, while twelve voted for Hillary Clinton.

Left unsaid was that Biden states received 88.4 percent of the funding and an average award of more than $3.5 million—3.34 times as large as the amount Trump states received. Four states that received funds switched from Trump states in 2016 to Biden states in 2020. Arizona, Georgia, Michigan, and Pennsylvania received $35,579,609—more than half of all funds. By contrast, Florida, a state that became more firmly Trump-supporting in 2020, received only $287,000 in CEIR funding.[86]

◆   ◆   ◆

Republicans had very good reason to be wary of Democrats' attempts to significantly change how elections were conducted in the middle of the election. Some horror stories in the run-up to November 3 would confirm their reservations.

After the vote counting in the Iowa caucus turned into a complete fiasco, even members of the Democratic Party were raising questions about whether Democrats were conducting elections fairly.

Right before the Iowa caucuses, something ominous happened. Pollster Ann Selzer, who was legendary in the polling world for producing the most accurate polls of her home state, withheld the results of her final Iowa poll because an interviewee complained that former South Bend mayor Pete Buttigieg was not given as an option. Vermont senator Bernie Sanders's supporters speculated that the poll had been killed because it showed him ahead.

The results were later leaked to Twitter, showing Sanders in the lead with 22 percent, followed by Warren with 18 percent, Buttigieg with 16 percent, and Biden with 13 percent.

The last days of campaigning in Iowa were intense. Biden had the support of the establishment, but the excitement of the grass roots seemed to be elsewhere.

Iowans went to caucus on the evening of February 3. Interest in the result was very high—but the results didn't come through for days.

The evening was a disaster, in fact. The cutting-edge electronic app used to count the votes in Iowa crashed as results were being reported, leading to a week-long delay in reporting the final tally as Democrats fought viciously.

Instead of having a chance to declare victory the morning after the caucuses, the candidates had to wait, losing out on the publicity that comes with having their first- or second-place finish plastered on major papers across the country.

Democratic National Committee chairman Tom Perez demanded a recanvassing of the Iowa caucuses three days after Iowa Democrats cast the first votes in the 2020 election without full results.

"Enough is enough," Perez wrote on Twitter. "In light of the problems that have emerged in the implementation of the delegate selection plan and in order to assure public confidence in the results, I am calling on the Iowa Democratic Party to immediately begin a recanvass."

Eventually, the results were released. More than 176,000 Democrats participated, slightly higher than in 2016 but lower than in 2008. Warren and Klobuchar came in third and fifth, respectively, with Biden tucked between them.

Fortunately for Biden, his failure as a front-runner was overshadowed by the fact that the entire Iowa caucus process had proven to be such a goat rodeo that even the winner of the Iowa caucus was unhappy. Sanders won the popular vote on both the initial and final alignments of caucus-goers, but due to arcane party rules, second-place finisher Buttigieg was given a slightly higher number of delegate equivalents, a move that outraged Sanders's fierce and numerous supporters.

It was generally acknowledged by everyone that the institutional Democratic Party viewed the Vermont socialist as unelectable and had manipulated the primary process to impede Sanders's chances of capturing the nomination in 2016, via the use of "superdelegates"—where hand-picked party insiders are given a chance to vote for the nominee—along with other procedural roadblocks the party created for Sanders. This led to outrage among grassroots party voters, and several rule changes were made that would allegedly make the 2020 Democratic primary more representative of the will of voters than it was in 2016.

But despite these promises, it appeared that Sanders was getting screwed by the Democratic establishment once again. Revelations about how the counting in Iowa in 2020 was done did not inspire confidence, to put it mildly. The vote-counting app used by the Democratic Party that crashed as they were counting votes was the product of two politically connected firms called Acronym and Shadow. One of Acronym's founders, Tara McGowan, was married to Buttigieg strategist Michael Halle. Further, Shadow had recently been paid to do work for both the Biden and Buttigieg campaigns.

Even setting aside these suspicious relationships and the vote-counting failures, the undeniable fact was that Bernie Sanders had emerged from Iowa with the most votes and somehow ended up with fewer delegates that would count toward securing the nomination. Sanders's supporters were understandably grumbling that the fix was in.

"It was like we were back in 2016," one of Sanders's Iowa campaign volunteers told *Rolling Stone*. "Except this was worse."[87]

Even Trump would look back on what happened and say, "[Sanders] is the most disrespected candidate I've ever seen. He would lose and just go on with his life like nothing ever happened." Had Sanders become the Democratic nominee, Trump thought the general election would have had a different outcome. "I don't know that the establishment would have cheated as much for him. I don't think they would have cheated because they didn't like him," he said.

And while the debacle over the inability to count the votes in Iowa's Democratic caucus garnered the most attention, another controversy about voting in Iowa was playing out in the media. That controversy would come to define how concerns about mail-in ballots would be handled for the rest of the election. Members of the media would prove either obtuse or willfully deceptive to the point they would misinform the public and prod social media companies to censor accurate information about the problems created by mail-in ballots.

What happened was this: On Monday, February 3—the day of the Iowa caucuses—the conservative group Judicial Watch put out a press release headlined, "Eight Iowa Counties Have Total Registration Rates Larger Than Eligible Voter Population—at Least 18,658 Extra Names on Iowa Voting Rolls."[88] The fact that Iowa had problems with voter rolls wasn't surprising news to anyone who had been paying attention. Judicial Watch was seizing on the news of the day to highlight an issue it had been working on long before the Iowa caucuses.

In 2019, a Judicial Watch lawsuit forced Los Angeles County to settle out of court and clean up its voter rolls—the county had a staggering 1.5 million more voter registrations on file than voting-age citizens who lived there.

That same year, Judicial Watch produced data showing that eight states and the District of Columbia have voter registration rates exceeding 100 percent, meaning they had more active voter registrations on file than eligible voters. And Judicial Watch was hardly alone in highlighting this problem—a 2012 Pew study found that 24 million voter registrations in America are "no longer valid or significantly inaccurate." That's about one out of every eight voter registrations, a number greater than the population of Florida. Pew's total also included 1.8 million dead people and another 2.75 million registered to vote in more than one state.

In 1993, Congress passed the National Voter Registration Act (NVRA)—better known as the "Motor Voter Act" because its best-known provisions enabled voter registration through the DMV. However, making it much easier to register voters has a significant downside in that it increases the likelihood of bloated and inaccurate voter rolls. The Census Bureau reports that 11 percent of Americans move every year, and while people dutifully register to vote at their new addresses, they rarely call the county clerks at their previous residences to inform them to strike their old registrations from the rolls.

Accordingly, Section 8 of the NVRA requires states to maintain accurate voter rolls. States have some discretion, but the law lays out a specific mandatory procedure to remove voters from the rolls. Essentially, what's supposed to happen is this: If the state suspects that a voter registration is no longer valid, it sends a notice requesting verification. If voters don't respond to the letter, they are listed as "inactive." Being designated as inactive presents no obstacles to voting. In fact, casting a vote automatically removes someone from the list of inactive voters. Per the law, the only people who can be removed from the rolls are those who fail to respond to the letter and do not vote in the next two federal elections.

Since passage of the NVRA, many states have simply ignored the maintenance requirements, while others have sought legal work-arounds. Robert Popper, a former deputy chief of the Voting Section in the Civil Rights Division of the Department of Justice who now works on voting issues for Judicial Watch, said the most aggressive efforts have been led by Democrats.

"The willingness of Democratic administrations to just make war on the NVRA is appalling," said Popper, whose group sued California over its voter roll failures. California in particular got a special dispensation from Clinton attorney general Janet Reno to operate under an esoteric and erroneous interpretation of the NVRA, leading the state to ignore voter roll maintenance for decades.

In 2018, the Supreme Court handed down a ruling in *Husted v. A. Philip Randolph Institute* that made it clear not voting in successive elections was an acceptable trigger for removing inactive voter registrations. States that had willfully ignored cleaning up their voter rolls would have to follow the procedures for removing inactive voters in the NVRA. Within days of the Supreme Court ruling, a federal judge issued a consent decree forcing Kentucky's Democratic secretary of state, Alison Lundergan Grimes, to remove an excess of 250,000 voter registrations from the rolls in response to an ongoing lawsuit from Judicial Watch.

And while Democratic officials may have willfully avoided cleaning up voter rolls in some cases, electoral procedures and administration are generally underfunded across the country. Even red states have done a poor job of maintaining voter rolls, so it was not surprising to anyone who was paying attention that Judicial Watch had identified eight counties in Iowa with more voter registrations on file than voters—in total it had identified thirty-eight states that had counties where the number of voter registrations exceeded the number of voting-age adults who lived there.

Suffice to say, the *Washington Post* was not only broadly ignorant of the ongoing problems with voter registrations in America, but the paper reacted to Judicial Watch's press release with an unseemly mixture of ignorance and fury. "Conservatives Spread False Claims on Twitter about Electoral Fraud as Iowans Prepare to Caucus," was the headline. The paper used the episode to suggest Judicial Watch's press release, rather than highlighting a well-established problem with American elections, was the harbinger of something sinister: "The episode showcases social media's hands-off approach to disinformation and the possible perils ahead in a divisive election season."

The *Post* contacted Iowa's Republican secretary of state, who disputed Judicial Watch's claim, pointing to voter registration data on the state's website that was allegedly more current. "Of the eight Iowa counties listed by Judicial Watch, a single one—Lyon County—has more registered voters (8,490) than adult residents (8,430), based on five-year estimates released by the Census Bureau in 2018," the newspaper reported.

Verifying the *Post*'s own reporting proved difficult. The Iowa secretary of state's own press release didn't say how many counties had more registrations than voters. "Iowa's voter registration statistics are publicly available on the Secretary of State's website. They are updated monthly," reads the release. "These numbers show that the ones claimed by Judicial Watch in their news release today are patently false." The Iowa secretary of state's office declined requests to comment further.[89]

Then there's the fact that the *Washington Post*'s own reporting was contradicted by...the *Washington Post*. *Post* blogger Phillip Bump reported on the story and produced different numbers than either Iowa or Judicial Watch. "There are, however, five counties (Dallas, Dickinson, Johnson, Lyon and Scott) where there are more people registered to vote than there were voting-age citizens counted in the vintage 2018 county population data," he wrote.[90]

Back in the real world, the issue was complicated. Judicial Watch arrived at its figures using the latest data from the federal Election Assistance Commission, which came out in July 2019. The organization hired a team of professional demographers to interpret that data. While the Iowa secretary of state has slightly more recent monthly data for voter registrations, the *Post* compared these registration numbers against census data from 2018, which is a simple and less sophisticated analysis than would be done by a demographer. Judicial Watch's methodology had previously been upheld in federal courts, and Iowa's secretary of state would likely have plenty of political or selfish motivations to insist he had not failed to adequately clean up the state's voter rolls.

Despite displaying its ignorance of the issues involved, the *Post*'s reporting was an arrogant caricature of liberal media bias. "[Judicial Watch president] Fitton also responded to [Iowa secretary of state Paul] Pate, insisting that his organization's data is accurate," Bump wrote. "It isn't."

But the *Washington Post* went even further in its mischaracterization of Judicial Watch's press release by asserting that Judicial Watch was making "claims of electoral fraud." It's absolutely true that having bloated voter rolls makes states and localities more susceptible to voter fraud. For example, people who vote twice in the same election because they are registered in two places at once are occasionally charged with voter fraud, and this is clearly enabled by failing to remove inaccurate voter registrations in a timely manner. However, pointing out the existence of inaccurate voter rolls is not the same thing as proving that voter fraud is occurring.

The *Post* was warned about this obvious distinction but ignored it. "But please be sure you are accurate and stop falsely reporting that we have alleged voter fraud, and put out false information etc.," Fitton asked *Post* reporter Isaac Stanley-Becker in an email exchange. "Please share my concerns with your editor and, in the least, fix your headline." Stanley-Becker responded with a one-sentence email saying, "My editor says dirty voter rolls are a form of electoral fraud." (This is in reference to Judicial Watch's calling inaccurate voter rolls "dirty.") Throughout the exchange Fitton repeats that Judicial Watch had not claimed specific instances of voter fraud had occurred in Iowa.

Elsewhere in the exchange, Stanley-Becker tried to rebut Fitton by noting another Judicial Watch press release that said excess voter registrations were a "red flag for voter fraud," which, as a semantic matter, is accurate and does not assert voter fraud is definitively occurring, unlike how the *Post* was characterizing Judicial Watch's work. Stanley-Becker did not respond to a request to comment on the criticisms of his story from RealClearPolitics.

Despite the fact the *Post*'s reporting was contradictory and deeply flawed, its reporting had an impact—Judicial Watch's posts on Facebook and Instagram were taken down. Such is the power of Facebook that when the site claims a story is inaccurate and blocks it, it kills 80 percent of the global internet traffic to that story.

"The data they're pointing to is actually consistent with our concerns and Facebook deletes our posts and suppresses our Instagram? Because a government official disputes our numbers?" Fitton told RealClearPolitics, adding, "It's a terrible example of the government pressuring private so-called independent media to suppress something a government official doesn't like."

If the goal of the *Washington Post* is to report the truth, there's no question its attempt to dispute Judicial Watch's press release was an enormous journalism failure that misinformed readers about the extent of the problems in America's electoral system. But if its goal was to set a precedent for social media censorship of inconvenient news and to otherwise put a partisan thumb on the scale to affect the outcome of a close election, the *Post* succeeded spectacularly.

◆   ◆   ◆

Despite the media's best efforts, a few months later, in June, it would become impossible to deny there was a link between mail-in ballots and election fraud. Following accusations of widespread fraud, voter intimidation, and ballot theft in the May 12 municipal elections in Paterson, New Jersey, state attorney general Gurbir S. Grewal charged four men with voter fraud—including the vice president of the city council, who was running for reelection.[91]

The election for Paterson, New Jersey's third largest city, would decide the fate of a municipal budget in excess of $300 million, in addition to hundreds of millions more in education spending and state aid.[92]

Due to the pandemic, voting in the Paterson City Council election was done by mail. A full 19 percent of the total ballots cast were disqualified by the board of elections. The election was such a disaster that community organizations, such as the city's NAACP chapter, called for the entire election to be invalidated. In August, a New Jersey judge did just that and ordered that a new election be held.[93]

Over eight hundred ballots in Paterson were invalidated for appearing in mailboxes improperly bundled together—including one mailbox in which hundreds of ballots were in a single packet. The bundles were turned over to law enforcement to investigate potential criminal activity in the collection of the ballots.[94]

The board of elections disqualified another 2,300 ballots after concluding that the signatures on them did not match the signatures on voter records.[95]

Further reporting by NBC uncovered citizens of Paterson who were listed as having voted but who told the news outlet that they never received a ballot and did not vote. One woman, Ramona Javier, after being shown the list of people on her block who allegedly voted, told the outlet she knew of eight family members and neighbors who were wrongly listed. "We did not receive vote-by-mail ballots and thus we did not vote," she said.[96] "This is corruption. This is fraud."[97]

There were multiple reports that large numbers of mail-in ballots were left on the lobby floors of apartment buildings and were not delivered to residents' individual mailboxes, casting further doubt on the integrity of the election.[98]

Two of the election results in Paterson were particularly close. Initially, challenger Shahin Khalique defeated incumbent Mohammed Akhtaruzzaman by 1,729 votes to 1,721. After a second recount on June 19, the race was tied 1,730 to 1,730.[99] In that race, a video posted to Snapchat surfaced that appeared to show a man named Abu Razyen unlawfully handling a large stack of ballots he indicated were votes for Khalique.[100] Khalique's brother, Shelim, and Razyen were charged by the state attorney general for crimes including fraud in casting mail-in votes, tampering, and unauthorized possession of ballots.[101]

Incumbent council member William McKoy lost by 240 votes to challenger Alex Mendez after a recount on June 1. However, the McKoy–Mendez race was far from over—in the Third Ward of the city where the race was decided, over 24 percent of all ballots were disqualified by the board of elections. Mendez was later charged with six different crimes related to voter fraud.[102] (Michael Jackson, Paterson's incumbent First Ward city councilman and council vice president, was also charged, and faced four counts related to voter fraud.)[103]

In a legal complaint, the McKoy campaign alleged outright fraud on the part of the Mendez campaign. "At least one individual, YaYa Luis Mendez, has confessed to investigators working on behalf of the [New Jersey attorney general's] office to having stolen ballots out of mailboxes, both completed and uncompleted, on behalf of and at the direction of the [Alex] Mendez campaign," according to the complaint prepared by McKoy attorney Scott Salmon.[104]

While Paterson has a reputation for civic corruption that stands out even in New Jersey, it was just one of thirty-one municipalities in New

Jersey that held vote-by-mail elections on May 12. The average disqualification rate for mail-in ballots in all thirty-one elections across the state was an alarming 9.6 percent.[105]

While other states had already demonstrated that the rapid move to mail-in balloting was disrupting elections, events in New Jersey clearly demonstrated that fraud was a concern that could not be ignored. And yet, despite the warnings, Republicans and the Trump campaign failed to fight back against the bevy of changes that Marc Elias and the Democrats had ushered in. Across the country, mail-in voting would become the norm—and, presumably, so would the opportunity for fraud.

◆   ◆   ◆

Even before anyone began voting, COVID-19 was already having a major impact on the election—the virus became the media's primary line of attack on Trump. A once-in-a-century pandemic presented an enormous number of uncertainties and challenges for the press as it was, but the media's obsession with taking down Trump meant the media adopted and discarded contradictory narratives on an almost weekly basis.

Instead of honestly reporting the biggest story of an election year, the media used the COVID-19 crisis as a cudgel against Donald Trump. They were aided and encouraged by liberal political operatives and government officials who wanted to score political points. Their bad-faith journalism was part of the broader effort to throw the election for Biden, and it had an immeasurably large effect.

When the virus first came on the global scene, the Washington, D.C., establishment could not have cared less. The Democratic Party and the media were obsessively focused on the impeachment. Trump's attention was divided between defending himself and fulfilling his duties as commander in chief.

The global pandemic loomed in the background. High-level officials in the administration, including CDC director Robert Redfield and Deputy National Security Advisor Matthew Pottinger, were hearing early on from counterparts and associates in China and Hong Kong about how quickly the illness was spreading.[106]

The CDC quickly issued guidance urging Americans to "practice usual precautions" if traveling to Wuhan.[107] The CDC began screening visitors from Wuhan for symptoms at the three airports most likely to receive flights from the region: San Francisco, JFK, and LAX. By January 20, the National Institutes of Health had started work on a vaccine.[108] The CDC's Emergency Operations Center was activated the next day.[109] On January 29, President Trump announced the formation of the "President's Coronavirus Task Force" to lead the response.[110]

On January 31, Trump banned travel for all foreign nationals who had visited China in the past fourteen days, and Health and Human Services secretary Alex Azar declared a Public Health Emergency.[111]

The Trump administration's aggressive response to the virus of instituting a travel ban was strongly opposed by the media and Democrats.

"Who Says It's Not Safe to Travel to China?" asked the *New York Times*.[112] "The coronavirus travel ban is unjust and doesn't work anyway."[113] Author Rosie Spinks suggested racism was the cause of the ban. "The coronavirus outbreak seems defined by two opposing forces: the astonishing efficiency with which the travel industry connects the world and a political moment dominated by xenophobic rhetoric and the building of walls."[114]

STAT, a health and medicine news site, ran a piece headlined, "Health Experts Warn China Travel Ban Will Hinder Coronavirus Response," and said the ban was desired by "conservative lawmakers and far-right supporters of the president," even as "public health experts...warn that the move could do more harm than good."[115] Others emphasized that Trump's policies "contradict advice from the World Health Organization (WHO), which said yesterday that countries should not restrict travel or trade in their response to the new virus."[116]

Later, when it became apparent that the restrictions were wise and the narrative needed to be changed from Trump was doing too much to that he was doing too little, members of the media tried to rewrite recent history. *Politico*'s Dan Diamond retroactively claimed, "[I]n late January, Trump's initial coronavirus moves were widely hailed as [a] strong and appropriate response."[117]

Early on, though, the conventional wisdom was that there was no need to panic over the novel coronavirus.

The media urged calm, settling on the claim that the American public had far more to worry about from the seasonal flu than from the coronavirus. "Don't worry about the coronavirus," BuzzFeed told its readers. "Worry about the flu." The *Washington Post* quoted Ian Lipkin, a U.S. epidemiologist who helped China respond to the 2003 SARS virus, as saying, "It is very unlikely that this will ever reach the level that we annually lose to flu."[118]

"Is this going to be a deadly pandemic? No," Vox told readers.[119] The *Washington Post* ran an article headlined, "Get a Grippe, America. The Flu Is a Much Bigger Threat Than Coronavirus, for Now." Another article said, "Past epidemics prove fighting coronavirus with travel bans is a mistake."[120]

The media weren't entirely to blame, as they were following the lead of public health experts in many cases. Anthony Fauci, director of the National Institute of Allergy and Infectious Diseases (NIAID), said the American public shouldn't worry about the coronavirus outbreak in China. "It's a very, very low risk to the United States," Fauci said, just before Trump shut down travel from China.[121]

As Trump expressed concern about the virus from China, Pelosi went shopping in crowded shops in San Francisco's Chinatown in late February and encouraged everyone to follow her lead. "We do want to say to people. Come to Chinatown, here we are," she said.[122]

On March 10, New York City mayor Bill de Blasio was on MSNBC's *Morning Joe* program downplaying the threat. "If you're under 50 and you're healthy, there is very little threat here. This disease even if you were to get it basically acts like a common cold and flu. And transmission is not that easy. I think there's been a misperception that coronavirus hangs in the air waiting to catch you. No, it takes direct person to person contact, direct transmission of fluids." He talked about the need to keep schools open, keep the economy going. "We cannot shut down because of undue fear."

For his part, Trump went from shutting down travel from China and Europe to downplaying real concerns to overly optimistic predictions about treating the disease. Trump started holding daily press briefings. They were initially well received, but as time went on, his off-the-cuff and erratic messaging started to play into a hostile media's hands.

In retrospect, the proper response was to urge calm—but in proportion to the threat. COVID-19 was, in fact, a significantly larger threat than the flu, and by March Democratic politicians knew enough to know that what they were saying was unhelpful, even dangerous. But with the right messaging and precautions, the pandemic could have been managed without shutting down the entire country for a year.

◆   ◆   ◆

Until the pandemic, Democrats had been very worried about Trump's being re-elected on the strength of the economy. "Dems Sweat Trump's Economy: 'We Don't Really Have a Robust National Message Right Now.' One Top Democrat Fears That Could Be 'a Recipe for Disaster in 2020,'" read one *Politico* headline in 2019.[123] "Warning to Democrats: Economy Points to a Trump Win," read another 2019 headline, pointing to a Moody's Analytics model that showed him a strong favorite to win.[124]

By March, the realization among Democrats and their media allies that the coronavirus outbreak was much more serious than they had previously thought coincided with the realization that they could benefit politically from a pandemic. Once Trump opponents realized that the shutdown was going to happen, they began to say that the real problem was that he wasn't shutting down enough.

By April, even though the economy had been shut down, Democrats began to fear that a quick recovery could spell their political doom. To beat Trump, the country had to stay shut down—and they were willing to use every weapon in their arsenal to make that happen.[125]

The media narrative soon flipped from "the flu is worse" to apocalyptic speculation. Imperial College London released a headline-grabbing paper predicting 2.2 million Americans would die from the virus.[126] According to the paper's projections, 268 million Americans would get the virus, and .9 percent of them would die.[127]

Nancy Pelosi, who just weeks earlier had been urging people to get out into the streets en masse, signaled the switch in the Democrats' posture on Trump on March 29. "As the president fiddles, people are dying," she said.[128]

But the Trump administration wasn't "fiddling"—they'd been making major policy interventions and preparing for months while Democrats and the media were downplaying the threat. Six weeks before Imperial College London warned of impending doom, Trump had shut down travel and set up the President's Coronavirus Task Force to evaluate and implement measures to combat the coronavirus, eventually assigning Mike Pence to lead it. Trump was taking the threat seriously and supported a two-week shutdown to "slow the spread," the theory being that two weeks of a shutdown would give hospitals the time they needed to keep from being overcrowded and overextended.

In mid-March, the administration brought key political appointees from different agencies into a White House working group. They were tasked with solving problems, such as setting up a testing system that could be deployed to states, securing protective personal equipment for frontline workers, building up the reserve of ventilators, and developing a vaccine. They worked with private companies each step of the way.

While the Trump team was working on the important behind-the-scenes logistics efforts, government health bureaucrats were making a hash of the public messaging surrounding the virus. Anthony Fauci, director of the U.S. National Institute of Allergy and Infectious Diseases and America's highest paid federal employee, told a Senate committee in March that people should not wear masks "because right now, there isn't anything going around right now in the community, certainly not coronavirus, that is calling for the broad use of masks."[129]

The media were already dutifully amplifying the anti-mask message. It was one of many issues on which they'd make a major about-face.

"Masks may actually increase your coronavirus risk if worn improperly, surgeon general warns," CNN reported.[130] "How to Prepare for Coronavirus in the U.S. (Spoiler: Not Sick? No Need to Buy Any Masks)," wrote the *Washington Post* in February.[131] CNN said, "There's been a run of surgical masks in the US because of the coronavirus scare. You don't need them, physicians say."[132] A later story said, "Masks can't stop the coronavirus in the US, but hysteria has led to bulk-buying and price-gouging."[133] NBC News added, "Frequent hand-washing, not wearing a face mask, is the most important step the public can take to prevent the spread of the coronavirus, the World Health Organization said."[134]

Naturally, the bureaucrats' anti-mask message was contrasted with Trump's willingness to cast about for a wide variety of possible responses to confronting the pandemic. NBC reported that Trump had become "fixated" on masks: "At the end of February and early March, Trump had become fixated on masks. He was annoyed that the government was telling people not to wear them and would angrily ask scientists and health officials in private why—if they don't help—why do doctors wear them?"[135]

The CDC changed its position in April, saying that masks should be worn. Later, Fauci would admit that the "mixed message" on masks had hampered public health by sowing distrust.[136]

Still, the Democrat–media complex threw the car into reverse yet again. During public appearances Trump rarely wore a mask, prompting outrage from the media and Democrats who were just weeks ago berating Americans for wearing masks.

In an interview with NPR, Pelosi said, "I totally agree with Joe Biden. As long as we're faced with this crisis, masks should be mandatory." She continued, "In fact, the reason the CDC hasn't made it mandatory is because they don't want to embarrass the president, or insult the president, whatever it is." Then she called him "cowardly."[137] Earlier, Biden had called Trump a "fool" for not wearing a mask, saying he was being "falsely masculine" by refusing to.[138]

The media were obsessed. "[White House press secretary] McEnany's husband attends White House press briefing without mask: Sean Gilmartin declined to cover his face after being asked to do so by a journalist," read one article.[139] "Kayleigh McEnany conducted Thursday's briefing without a mask. Are White House reporters concerned?" asked *The Washingtonian*.[140]

◆   ◆   ◆

Perhaps the craziest media coverage had to do with the drug hydroxychloroquine, which has long been used to prevent malaria and is one of the few drugs available that is used to help combat viruses.

Trump said the FDA would be "slashing all the red tape" to review new therapies that were showing encouraging results. However, unlike vaccine trials that were operated under a special presidential initiative, the trials for therapies were handled by Fauci and the National Institutes of Health, following a more typical bureaucratic pace.

In addition to the anti-malarial drug hydroxychloroquine, Trump also drew attention to an antiviral drug used to treat Ebola, known as remdesivir. Following a promising French study, he said hydroxychloroquine had "very, very encouraging early results." Of remdesivir, he said, "I think it could be, based on what I see, it could be a game changer."

USA Today's editorial board was apoplectic. "It will take more than a year to produce a vaccine to finally quell COVID-19," they wrote in March 21. "Trump's promises about quick cures…place everyone more at risk."

"Trump peddles unsubstantiated hope in dark times,"[141] and "Trump says this drug has 'tremendous promise,' but Fauci's not spending money on it," CNN wrote.[142] "Trump is spreading false hope for a virus cure—and that's not the only damage," the *Washington Post* opined.[143]

"Trump is spreading misinformation about the coronavirus—time to take away his microphone. Cable news networks should stop airing the president's COVID-19 press conferences live," argued the *Boston Globe*.[144]

"If you are in a risky population here, and you are taking this as a preventative treatment to ward off the virus or in a worst-case scenario you are dealing with the virus, and you are in this vulnerable population, it will kill you. I cannot stress enough: This will kill you," said Neil Cavuto of Fox News.[145]

The anti-Trump media hysteria regarding hydroxychloroquine culminated in three troubling developments. First, Twitter started censoring tweets that contained messages supporting hydroxychloroquine. It even took down videos from doctors praising it. Citing expert testimony, social media companies started to put their thumb on the scales of the information war. They would only weigh in more forcefully as the year went on.

Then the media tried to blame a bizarre death on Trump. An Arizona man died and his wife was injured when they allegedly drank fish tank cleaner to protect themselves from COVID, thinking it was like hydroxychloroquine.

"The man's wife told NBC News she'd watched televised briefings during which President Trump talked about the potential benefits of chloroquine. Even though no drugs are approved to prevent or treat COVID-19, the disease caused by the coronavirus, some early research suggests it may be useful as a therapy," NBC News reported.[146]

The story went viral, with media figures and left-wing activists all over social media angrily blaming Trump for the man's death. Later, the Mesa City, Arizona, police announced they had opened up a homicide investigation into the death.[147] An investigative report said friends described the victim as "a levelheaded retired engineer and recounted a troubled marital relationship that included a previous domestic assault charge against his wife," and said that the wife was a Democratic donor whose latest contribution had gone to a "pro-science super PAC."[148]

Finally, the politicized reaction started to impact the medical community's ability to objectively assess coronavirus treatments. A study that had concluded hydroxychloroquine was dangerous to patients received much media coverage. Then the journal *The Lancet* pulled it because the authors could not verify the data on which the results depended.[149] CNN had given more than ninety minutes to the study by the time it was retracted.[150]

The hydroxychloroquine saga showed that the media were out for Trump's scalp, eager to turn any action he took into a scandal. They wanted to turn the unforeseeable crisis into an irrecoverable blow to Trump's political fortunes, no matter how much collateral damage the country incurred along the way.

◆　◆　◆

Throughout the crisis, Trump would face great criticism for saying things that later turned out to be true. The media wanted to humiliate Trump and make him look like a bad leader. And their attempts to make Trump appear as a buffoon led them to elevate an old face to the national stage: New York governor Andrew Cuomo.

The media saw Cuomo as a foil against Trump, someone whom they could turn into a hero of the COVID crisis. With Joe Biden out of the picture, they wanted to make Cuomo a yardstick against which voters could assess Trump—and they were desperate to show that Trump didn't measure up.

The Trump–Cuomo showdown would display the true extent of the media's perfidy. Journalists were willing to interfere with good-faith efforts to save lives to advance the narrative that Trump was dropping the ball. When Trump recommended a course of action, the media would frame it as disastrously misinformed; when Cuomo recommended the same course of action, sometimes just hours later, they would praise his resolute decision-making. The hypocrisy reached unprecedented levels.

The first salvoes were fired when Trump told Sean Hannity on air that he doubted New York would actually need 30,000 additional ventilators or 40,000 ventilators total as claimed by New York governor Andrew Cuomo in late March.[151] Cuomo, for his part, was upset that the Trump administration had not acquiesced to his request and asked them to "pick the 26,000 people who are going to die." He said, "[T]he number of ventilators we need is so astronomical."

Cuomo also claimed the state would need 140,000 hospital beds. Yet, the Institute for Health Metrics and Evaluation, a group funded by Bill Gates, projected peak bed use would be reached on April 8, with fewer than 23,000 beds needed. Cuomo's projection was apparently off by a factor of more than six.

Despite Cuomo's requests for beds and ventilators being at odds with reality, CBS News highlighted Cuomo's quote as evidence-based, contrary to Trump's: "[E]verybody's entitled to their own opinion, but I don't operate here on opinion. I operate on facts, and on data, and on numbers, and on projections." CBS News's Audrey McNamara wrote: "The president did not echo the same tone of urgency about ventilators when he called into Sean Hannity's show on Fox News Thursday evening."

Yet little media coverage was devoted to the fact that President Trump wasn't just right about New York's exaggerated needs, but that he and his administration were even more right than they probably imagined. The Institute for Health Metrics and Evaluation said New York had already reached its peak projected ventilator usage on April 8, with a projected need of five thousand, though the actual use may have been lower.

Trump campaign official Jason Miller joked that the administration had gone so overboard in producing ventilators that they were giving them away in other countries like preprinted world champion T-shirts for the losing Super Bowl team.

Despite being wrong about key pandemic issues right from the start, Cuomo quickly rose to the top of the media favorite list. In particular, the media were obsessed with the daily press conferences held by Cuomo, leader of the state hit hardest by the coronavirus.

Anyone paying attention would have noticed that Cuomo frequently agreed with the president. After harshly criticizing Trump for saying hydroxychloroquine had promise, the media didn't mind when Cuomo said some patients would be treated with it.[152] On March 6, Cuomo said people were stealing masks and medical equipment from New York hospitals, CNBC reported.[153] When Trump made the exact same claim later that month, Vox accused Trump of "making baseless attacks on New York nurses" and "making up conspiracy theories."[154]

When Trump criticized the World Health Organization in April, the *Washington Post* wondered, "Why exactly is Trump lashing out at the World Health Organization? And do his criticisms have any merit?" The *Post* clearly thought Trump's concerns were baseless, but when Cuomo said Trump was right to question the organization two days later, Cuomo's remarks were treated as accepted wisdom.[155]

When Trump and his education secretary Betsy DeVos talked about the importance of opening schools in the fall, left-wing activist, Hollywood director, and occasional cable news pundit Rob Reiner said, "Donald Trump is actively trying to kill our children."[156] When Cuomo urged New York State schools to open in the fall just three weeks after Trump's call for kids to return to school, the *New York Times* article on his call to open schools treated it as a reasonable step and noted the governor had "received accolades for his management of the crisis."[157]

More than anything, Cuomo's daily press briefings gave the media license to heap embarrassingly obsequious praise on the governor. Puff pieces from journalists were an almost daily occurrence. And it wasn't just the news media. Popular culture also got in on the act. Comedians such as Ellen DeGeneres, Trevor Noah, and Stephen Colbert all called themselves "Cuomosexuals," gushing about his performance.[158]

Governor Cuomo's brother, CNN host Chris Cuomo, even brought him on his prime-time cable news show to joke about their childhood and discuss the crisis. Fawning over his own brother in prime time was a blatant violation of basic journalistic ethics, but CNN executives had no trouble with Chris Cuomo's asking embarrassing questions such as,

"With all this adulation that you're getting for doing your job, are you thinking about running for president?"

Cuomo eventually cashed in on all the media hype. He was paid more than $5 million for a book that was published in October and written at the height of the crisis, bragging about his performance.[159]

But as time went on, it became increasingly clear Cuomo's performance wasn't worthy of praise. In fact, his "leadership" was horrific.

At a time when very little was known about the coronavirus except that the elderly were at a dramatically higher risk of dying from it, Cuomo issued a mandate requiring nursing homes to accept residents who had tested positive. The directive stayed in place for two months. Within a year, some fifteen thousand people died from the spread of COVID-19 in long-term care facilities. Worse, Cuomo hid from the public how many people died in nursing homes out of fear that Trump would make a big deal of his failure.

His report had grossly undercounted the deaths, as his office altered the death toll of 9,844 detailed in the first draft and released a lower number of 6,432 to the public. An aide said officials "froze" when Trump's Department of Justice asked for data on the nursing home deaths.

The governors whom the media viciously opposed would end up looking far better, even if the media coverage they endured was horrific.

When Florida governor Ron DeSantis opened his state, he was mocked and attacked by the press. CNN ran headlines accusing DeSantis of putting "politics in front of lives" and saying DeSantis's "bravado fuels Florida's pandemic crisis." *Politico* barely stopped itself from putting actual profanity in a headline: "'Dumbest S—': DeSantis Takes Heat as He Goes His Own Way on Coronavirus."

Unlike Cuomo, DeSantis not only made the correct call not to return COVID-19 patients to nursing homes, but Florida significantly outperformed New York in both per capita coronavirus cases and deaths in the state.

◆   ◆   ◆

Even though the evidence showed China's communist government, aided by an incompetent and credulous World Health Organization, had lied to the world about the threat the virus posed—lies that almost certainly added to the monumental death toll—the media consensus was that any description of the virus that reflected its origins in Wuhan, China, was racist and xenophobic.

Viruses and illnesses are commonly referred to by what is believed to be their point of origin. Lyme disease, transmitted to humans by the bites of infected ticks, is so named because it was first diagnosed as a separate condition in Lyme, Connecticut. Another tick-spread bacterial disease, Rocky Mountain spotted fever, is named for similar reasons. Zika was named after the forest in Uganda where it was first isolated. Guinea worm was named after the country where the parasitic infection was observed. Norovirus was named after Norwalk, Ohio, following an outbreak there in 1968. Japanese encephalitis, West Nile, Ebola, the Marburg virus, and Lassa fever are all named for regions where they were first encountered.

It's not even that the regions are always right. The Spanish flu was probably misnamed. But no one is confused about where SARS-CoV-2 came from. It came from Wuhan. And "Wuhan flu" or "Chinese virus" is much easier on the tongue than SARS-CoV-2.

When the media collectively decided by March that calling it a "China virus" or "Wuhan virus" was xenophobic, it represented yet another shameless about-face. Media outlets had already spent months referring to the "Wuhan coronavirus" and various other names that clearly reflected the virus's foreign origin. On March 12, the conservative Media Research Center put together a video showing CNN anchor Chris Cuomo declaring that "we're starting to see a message shift here because you're starting to hear the Republicans, especially Trump, call it the 'Wuhan' or 'Chinese coronavirus.' They're looking for someone to blame." Cuomo's insipid observation was then followed by nearly two minutes of clips from media figures, including several CNN journalists, referring over the previous two months to the "Wuhan" or "Chinese coronavirus."[160] But the media's shamelessness persisted.

Instead of focusing on public health questions during daily White House press briefings, the press feigned outrage over Trump's referring to COVID-19 as the "Chinese virus."

"Why do you keep calling this the Chinese virus?" asked ABC News reporter Cecilia Vega. "Why do you keep using this? A lot of people say it's racist."[161]

"Because it comes from China, it's not racist at all. No, not at all. It comes from China. That's why. I want to be accurate," Trump said.

Vega was aghast. "To aides behind you, are you comfortable with this term?" Trump talked about how China had tried to blame the virus on American soldiers. Yamiche Alcindor, a supposed reporter with PBS, asked, "Do you think using the term Chinese virus puts Asian Americans at risk?"[162]

The media and Democrats were, as always, on the same page. Senator Kamala Harris had tweeted outrage at Representative Kevin McCarthy, House minority leader, for tweeting out a link to the CDC website with the note, "Everything you need to know about the Chinese coronavirus can be found on one, regularly-updated website." She was outraged. "Calling it the 'Chinese coronavirus' isn't just racist, it's dangerous and incites discrimination against Asian Americans and Asian immigrants."[163]

The *New York Times* responded with what it thought was a clever solution to the problem, coming up with an informal name for the virus. "Let's Call It Trumpvirus: If You're Feeling Awful, You Know Who to Blame," read one of its headlines on February 26.[164]

For Trump, the spread of a global pandemic out of Wuhan, China, furthered his long-standing contention that China is a bad actor. But rather than concede that China's role in creating the pandemic merited serious scrutiny and condemnation, the media focused obsessively on Trump's alleged racism, and gave very friendly coverage to a communist country that holds ethnic minorities in concentration camps.[165]

"How China Controlled the Coronavirus," enthused the *New Yorker*.[166] "'They Know How to Keep People Alive': Why China's Coronavirus Response Is Better Than You Think," wrote radical reporter Alexander Nazaryan at Yahoo.[167] "Its Coronavirus Cases Dwindling, China Turns Focus Outward: Beijing is mounting a humanitarian aid blitz in countries struggling with their own outbreaks. In doing so, it's stepping into a role the West once dominated," said the *New York Times* on March 18, 2020, as if it were officially doing China's public relations.[168]

Far from the hero that the media had made China out to be, the country had caused major problems through its delayed response to COVID-19 and its failure to notify the international community of the danger in a timely manner. Instead of being forthright about the outbreak, the Chinese silenced and imprisoned those who raised the alarm about it, misled the world about its severity, and then hoarded the supplies needed to combat it.

"China did not just stop selling masks—it also bought up much of the rest of the world's supply.... On Jan. 30, the last day for which data is available, China managed to import 20 million respirators and surgical masks in just 24 hours," one report said.[169]

When China finally told the World Health Organization about the virus that it had been dealing with since, it turned out, at least mid-November,[170] it blamed the origin of the virus on a "wet market"—open-air stalls selling fresh seafood and meat where animals are sometimes slaughtered.[171] This, too, was yet another piece of propaganda that an honest media would have questioned. But the media had no interest in reporting the truth. They wanted to get Donald Trump out of office.

◆   ◆   ◆

A more likely origin for the outbreak is the Wuhan Institute of Virology, a lab that studies dangerous pathogens just nine miles away from the wet market that China blamed for the illness. But the media and bureaucrats accused those who drew attention to this possibility of fomenting conspiracy theories, in another effort to weaponize the pandemic against Trump and his Republican allies.

There was reason to be suspicious, as China had been secretive from the get-go. Dr. Li Wenliang, an ophthalmologist in Wuhan, China, sent a private message to fellow doctors on December 30, 2019, warning of a strange new illness he'd seen that reminded him of severe acute respiratory syndrome. He encouraged them to protect themselves.

A few days later, the Public Security Bureau in Wuhan made him recant his message and confess he'd made false statements that had disturbed the public order. Just over a month later, he was dead after contracting the novel coronavirus that came to be known as COVID-19.

The World Health Organization, which is very close with China, supported the country in its public messaging. On January 10, it advised against any travel restrictions being placed on China. On January 14, it claimed there was "no clear evidence" of "human-to-human" transmission.

On January 23, WHO's director-general Dr. Tedros Adhanom Ghebreyesus said, "Once again, I'd like to thank the Government of China for its cooperation and transparency. The government has been successful in isolating and sequencing the virus very quickly and has shared that genetic sequence with WHO and the international community."[172]

A week later, Tedros made a fawning statement in support of the Chinese government: "We would have seen many more cases outside China by now—and probably deaths—if it were not for the government's efforts, and the progress they have made to protect the people of the world."

Many media outlets praised China for its self-proclaimed transparency and aggressive response, which allegedly included inhumanely welding people into their apartment buildings to enforce quarantine. They deployed China as a counter to make the Trump administration seem incompetent, advancing the overly optimistic view that the Chinese government was prepared for another pandemic following its battle against SARS in 2003.[173] *USA Today*,[174] Business Insider,[175] and more stories at CNN all took the same approach of giving China undue credit.[176]

But none of it was true. As the *Wall Street Journal* would later report, "China's errors, dating back to the very first patients, were compounded by political leaders who dragged their feet to inform the public of the risks and to take decisive control measures."[177]

Republican senator Marco Rubio accused the Chinese government of having "intimidated" the World Health Organization, saying China didn't share information, best practices, or data on infections among health care workers. Critics started sounding the alarm about China's and WHO's "covering up or downplaying the severity of an infectious disease outbreak."[178]

Still, the White House press corps and Democrats wanted Trump to take the blame, not China. Arkansas senator Tom Cotton went on Fox News in February and took credit for his early call to quarantine anybody coming from China's Wuhan region. He also pointed out that Wuhan contains a laboratory that studies dangerous pathogens, and that this laboratory can't be ruled out as the source of the virus. The *Washington Post* responded to the interview by accusing Cotton of fanning "the embers of a theory that has been repeatedly disputed by experts."[179]

Worse than that, the *Post* excoriated Cotton for something he never asserted, claiming that Cotton had said the virus was a bioweapon engineered and deliberately released by the Chinese. This is not what Cotton said, and one of the experts quoted by the *Post* to "debunk" Cotton would later acknowledge on Twitter that Cotton had been clear in his remarks and that Cotton was correct to suggest the possibility of a lab leak in Wuhan "cannot—and should not—be dismissed."[180]

Even though the virus caused millions of deaths and catastrophic damage to the global economy, Trump said at his home in Mar-a-Lago in May, "I never thought China did it on purpose. I thought it was done out of incompetence and I may be wrong because they were the biggest beneficiaries. Someone said, one of the greatest things I did as president was, I convinced people that China was hurting us."

When Secretary of State Mike Pompeo backed President Trump's suggestion that the coronavirus originated in a lab in Wuhan, the *New York Times* was upset and said that "intelligence agencies say they have reached no conclusion on the issue."[181] But despite a growing pattern of evidence that China needed to be held to account for unleashing a deadly virus on the world, Democrats remained laser-focused on blaming the Trump administration. Bernie Sanders made it clear: "There are legitimate questions we must ask about the Chinese government's inability to contain the virus. But Pompeo's incitement is a blatant effort to distract us from questions about Trump's own disastrous failure."[182]

◆   ◆   ◆

Unlike the Chinese government's unduly praised pandemic response, the Trump administration's effort to produce a vaccine was already evaluating mRNA technology that looked promising. Preliminary research had started in January, and Operation Warp Speed was launched in March.

And Trump wasn't shy about the hopeful prospects. "We're looking to get it by the end of the year if we can, maybe before," he said in May.

Again, the media scoffed at this prediction.

"Fact check: A coronavirus vaccine could come this year, President Trump says. Experts say he needs a 'miracle' to be right," said NBC News.[183]

"Note: Experts and officials say that is likely faster than what is possible," tweeted PBS's Yamiche Alcindor.[184] However, these "experts" had no idea what the Trump administration was doing or what break-throughs the heroic doctors and scientists were making as part of the vaccine effort.

Before COVID-19, the average amount of time it took to develop a vaccine was ten years, and it had never been done in less than four.[185] Operation Warp Speed was designed to shrink the amount of time needed by throwing money at the problem and by letting all three clinical phases of the vaccine trials proceed at the same time, instead of requiring one to be finished before starting the next. It tested safety, effectiveness, and whether inoculations affected different parts of the population differently. The government also paid for millions of vaccine doses before it even knew if they would work, incentivizing pharmaceutical companies to invest heavily in research and development.

Later in the year, when President Trump said at the second presidential debate in October that the vaccine was ready and would be announced within weeks, fact-checkers said it wasn't true. "This lacks evidence," said NPR. "None of the large trials have been completed. Top health officials say a vaccine likely won't be widely available until mid-2021."[186]

ABC said, "FACT CHECK: Most prominent public health experts have said that a vaccine will not be widely available until mid-2021."[187]

Once again, facts undercut the fact-checkers. Less than one week after Election Day, on November 9, Pfizer and BioNTech issued a press release stating that their vaccine was showing to be more than 90 percent effective in preventing COVID-19. The timing immediately raised eyebrows: Had the pharmaceutical giants delayed the release of their findings to prevent Trump from receiving a boost on the back of the good news?

The FDA issued its Emergency Use Authorization (EUA) for the Pfizer-BioNTech COVID-19 vaccine on December 11, 2020. One week later, the Moderna vaccine was approved. And as remarkable as that achievement was, the vaccine might have been approved and released to the public sooner if one self-described "activist" doctor hadn't intervened.

Throughout the pandemic, Dr. Eric Topol, an expert in molecular medicine, had styled himself as a whistleblower sounding the alarm about how the White House was handling the pandemic, building a large social media following. There was plenty of fair criticism to be had, but when Trump was admitted to Walter Reed to be treated for contracting COVID-19 in early October, *MIT Technology Review* noted that Topol's Twitter feed "questioned the president's health, his doctors' actions, and even his mental status."

The October 19 *MIT Technology Review* profile of Topol was an otherwise glowing evaluation of his efforts—specifically it was about "one doctor's campaign to stop a COVID-19 vaccine being rushed through before Election Day." *Politico* had reported ten days earlier that Pfizer was sounding out health experts about the reaction to having their vaccine approved before Election Day.[188]

After disagreeing strongly with the contents of an FDA press release, Topol had launched a public crusade urging FDA commissioner Steve Hahn to resign over his "complete subservience to Trump." In addition to his four hundred thousand Twitter followers, Topol's reputation in the medical community was such that Hahn felt obligated to respond. Hahn confessed the FDA was "sensitive to external pressure" and began having private conversations with Topol. "What they said is confidential, but all signs indicate that Topol urged Hahn to defy the White House effort to deliver a vaccine by Election Day," reported *MIT Technology Review*. "I came to respect him," said Topol of the conversations. "I was convinced he'd do the right thing."

Pfizer announced it had a vaccine that was 90 percent effective against COVID on November 9, just six days after the election. The health policy publication STAT reported that Pfizer had actually paused its testing protocol in October, "leaving samples in storage.... [I]f Pfizer had held to the original plan, the data would likely have been available in October, as its CEO, Albert Bourla, had initially predicted."[189] The FDA was also aware of Pfizer's curious decision to stop testing.

But if the Pfizer vaccine was, in fact, ready before the election—and contemporaneous reporting on Pfizer, as well as the vaccine's successful track record since being approved just a few weeks later in December, suggests it was—it's worth asking why the FDA waited to approve it. Was the FDA unduly pressured by Topol and other politicized elements of the medical community to withhold this vital information? And how many more lives could have been saved if it had been approved over a month earlier?

Reflecting on his presidency months later, Trump said, "Nobody ever pushed the FDA like I did, and I had no choice because people were dying by the millions all over the world. And I found them to be not incompetent, but unbelievably bureaucratic. It would take them 12 years to get a medication approved.... I was very nasty to them because if I wasn't, you wouldn't have a vaccine yet. I was really almost bad to them, but I wasn't bad because I'm trying to save lives, but nobody ever talked to them the way I talked to them and I got it done. That's the bottom line: I got it done."

But the fact that Trump got it done was ultimately irrelevant, given the hostility he faced. "The new vaccine coming out was a huge story, a game changer, except for one thing: If they would have reported it before the election, the fake news media would have made it a tiny story. It would not have been a big deal," he said.

Ultimately, Trump was forgiving about the handling of the vaccine. "Everybody knew the vaccine was right around the corner. It was happening. People knew that we had the vaccine, but because it came out after the election, the press made it a massive story. I knew that if it happened earlier, they would have made it into a nothing story, so I don't feel badly about that," he said.

◆   ◆   ◆

While there are still many unknowns, a year later the consensus of both American intelligence agencies and the broader medical community is that it's very likely COVID-19 originated not at a wet market, but at the Wuhan Institute of Virology.

Soon after President Biden came into office, the Trump administration's investigation into whether the Wuhan lab leaked the virus was shut down. But by May 2021, Biden announced with great fanfare he was ordering America's intelligence agencies to investigate the lab leak theory.

The same day Biden relaunched the investigation, Facebook announced it would no longer censor posts discussing whether the COVID-19 virus leaked from a lab, as it had been doing for a year. PolitiFact, which had sanctimoniously made "coronavirus disinformation" its lie of the year, ended up retracting it's harsh "pants on fire" fact-check on Dr. Li-Meng Yan, a virologist and former postdoctoral fellow at the University of Hong Kong who said there was "solid scientific evidence" COVID-19 came from a lab.

"I think a lot of people have egg on their face," said ABC News's Jonathan Karl in May 2021. "This was an idea that was first put forward by Mike Pompeo, secretary of state, Donald Trump. And look, some things may be true even if Donald Trump said them."

Other journalists still couldn't bring themselves to consider the possibility that Trump had been vindicated. Apoorva Mandavilli, one of the *New York Times* reporters on the COVID beat, was not happy the truth was coming out. "Someday we will stop talking about the lab leak theory and maybe admit its racist roots. But alas, that day is not yet here," she tweeted that same week Karl begrudgingly credited Trump.

The final indignity came in June, when BuzzFeed obtained over three thousand pages of emails from Dr. Fauci through a Freedom of Information Act request. The emails detailed the country's top infectious diseases bureaucrat's thoughts on the handling of the pandemic, and the emails revealed top government officials had been disingenuous in their messaging to the public, as had been long suspected. One email showed Peter Daszak, president of EcoHealth Alliance, thanking Fauci for publicly dismissing concerns that the coronavirus was created in a lab. EcoHealth Alliance has worked with the Wuhan Institute of Virology.

In an email, Fauci also dismissed the idea that the scientists at the laboratory were compromised by the Chinese government. "We're not talking about the Communist Chinese Party. We're not talking about the Chinese military," he said. "We're talking about scientists that we've had relationships [*sic*] for years."

When asked about Fauci's emails, Biden's press secretary declared, "[I]t's obviously not advantageous for me to re-litigate the substance of emails from 17 months ago." It was, however, advantageous to suppress the truth about COVID-19 when Biden was working to get elected.[190]

When all was said and done, Trump shared his own thoughts on how America's top public health official had handled things. "Well, who knew that he knew so little? Anthony Fauci is a good promoter—he's a great promoter. He is a better baseball pitcher than he is predicting what to do with people's health," Trump said, needling him about the wild first pitch he threw at a Major League Baseball game during his 2020 COVID publicity tour.

The pandemic was unlike anything America had experienced in the modern era, and like every other big national challenge faced in the country's history, the Trump administration had to work through the problem, making errors along the way. But unlike previous major national endeavors where the whole country had to pull together, such as World War II and the space race, this time partisan forces and the media actively worked against the country's elected leadership for partisan advantage. And, in the process, they got several major issues wrong that the Trump administration got right.

The Trump administration's Operation Warp Speed was a success that has no equal in the history of public health. That is a fact. Their early decision to go all-in on a vaccine was strategically correct, and since 2020, the evidence continues to mount that Chinese authorities told countless lies that left the world unprepared to manage a global pandemic that would kill millions. By the time Biden was sworn in in January 2021, the Trump administration had managed in one year to build public–private partnerships to handle the needs of the pandemic, had developed multiple vaccines, and had figured out how to distribute them. Nearly a million Americans a day were already being vaccinated. The media had deliberately buried this important story for the sake of harming the president's political prospects.

"They used COVID to rig an election. There was nothing I could do," said Trump.

CHAPTER FOUR

Summer of Violence

D emocrats have deployed spurious accusations of racism against Republicans for decades, but rarely with the deliberate malice they used to attack Donald Trump and his supporters. In 2020, aggravating racial tensions became a key part of the Democrats' electoral strategy, and their allies in the media and the bureaucracy were eager to fabricate and exaggerate stories to deliver the narrative that Democrats demanded.

In the year before the election, Trump was fighting for the black vote and looked like he might have some success. In 2016, he received 8 percent of the black vote.[1] Trump boasted that he'd get 95 percent of the black vote after his first term, on the strength of his economic programs that did so much to lift black wages and job growth. In reality, his campaign was hoping to get something close to 20 percent of the black male vote.

Trump had telegraphed his desire to get more support from black Americans, and his policies showed an aggressive attempt to court them, whether through criminal justice reform, expanding funding for historically black colleges and universities, or the continued deregulatory agenda that led to improved wages and job numbers for black men and women.

Black Americans began trending away from the Republican Party—the party of Lincoln and emancipation—during the Great Depression. In 1964, the Civil Rights Act passed with a higher percentage of Republicans than Democrats voting for the landmark legislation. Many southern Democrats still supported Jim Crow, and some prominent Republicans expressed concern about the legislation's constitutionality.

While Republicans' 1964 nominee for president Senator Barry Goldwater articulated his opposition to the Civil Rights Act on a strictly constitutional basis, his opponents portrayed his principled stand as racist. When Goldwater announced his vote, he objected to the public accommodation and employment parts of the bill, saying they were an unconstitutional usurpation of power by the federal government. He pointed out that he had voted for the 1957 and 1960 civil rights legislation and opposed discrimination of any kind.

Lyndon Johnson's reasons for supporting the Civil Rights Act weren't nearly as principled. According to an Air Force One steward, Johnson reportedly said of his support for the bill, "I'll have those [racial epithet] voting Democratic for 200 years."[2] The sentiment was perfectly in keeping with LBJ's racist attitudes. While in the Senate, he summed up his civil rights efforts, saying, "These Negroes, they're getting pretty uppity these days and that's a problem for us.... [W]e've got to give them a little something, just enough to quiet them down, not enough to make a difference."[3]

Following the Civil Rights Act, Lyndon Johnson and congressional Democrats aggressively pursued federal welfare programs to attract black voters. Republicans naturally objected to this rapid expansion of the federal government, and even some Democrats at the time, such as future New York senator Daniel Patrick Moynihan, warned that the "steady expansion of this welfare program" would undermine black family structures and make black poverty worse.[4] Regardless of the debates over the long-term consequences, Johnson's "Great Society" agenda provided immediate assistance to struggling black communities and was successful in further cleaving black voters from their historical affiliation with the Party of Lincoln.

By the time of Barack Obama's election as the first black president a few decades later, Democrats had a complete stranglehold on black voters. The process that began with Lyndon Johnson was complete, and Republicans now struggled to win even modest support among the black community.

Undoing the work of half a century would always be difficult, but Trump was eager to grow the Republican Party by upending the status quo on key issues, such as trade and immigration—the policy areas the party establishment was most reluctant to engage. Yet, as Trump's immigration and economic policies helped black men and women with job, wage, and business growth, the narrative that Republicans were hostile to black voters grew harder to control.

Democrats were also keenly aware there was evidence that Michigan, Wisconsin, and Pennsylvania had gone to Trump in 2016 in part because many black voters had been unenthused and stayed home rather than vote for Hillary Clinton. Mobilizing black voters was key to the left's electoral prospects, and so Democrats spent considerable effort portraying Trump as a bigot—willing to embrace any falsehood to further their political ambitions.

◆　　◆　　◆

With a looming election and Trump's making modest but politically significant inroads with black voters, Democrats made it clear they intended to exploit any and every example of racial tension.

Joe Biden had launched his campaign by repeating the Charlottesville hoax, a clear and obvious fabrication by the media intended to paint Trump—and, by proxy, Trump voters—as a supporter of racist groups. Despite Trump's clear and repeated denunciations of white nationalism and white supremacy,[5] the media ripped some remarks out of context to falsely claim that Trump had called neo-Nazis "very fine people" in the wake of demonstrations in Charlottesville.[6] Biden's commitment to this lie, a lie that he claimed was the reason he was running for president, showed how deeply committed the Democrats were to inciting racial hatred for their political gain.

This was the political context in which the nation learned of the police killing of George Floyd on May 25. Floyd, who was under suspicion of passing counterfeit bills, was killed when a police officer named Derek Chauvin restrained him by putting a knee on his neck for nearly ten minutes.

The incident was filmed by a bystander, part of a growing crowd that was pleading with the officer to back off. Floyd could be heard repeatedly begging for mercy and saying he couldn't breathe. Two other police officers helped restrain Floyd while a fourth prevented anyone from intervening to help him. Floyd was black. Chauvin was white. The other police were white, black, and Asian.

The death was immediately framed by activists and the media as an example of the pervasive racism in America, and specifically in law enforcement. Riots erupted in Minneapolis and news spread quickly across the country, dominating media coverage.

There was very little political disagreement about the event itself. Republicans and Democrats, black and white, all expressed sadness and horror at the killing.

President Trump weighed in on the event, calling Floyd's death "very sad and tragic" and saying that "justice will be served" in the case. He also told a reporter asking about Floyd's death, "I'm very sad about that. Very, very sad event."[7]

The protests of Floyd's killing led to deadly riots, dozens of fires, and extensive looting in Minneapolis over the next few days. They then spread like wildfire over the entire country. In Minneapolis, rioters even forced police to abandon their Third Precinct, where Chauvin had worked, on May 28, after which they burned it down. Some 1,300 properties in Minneapolis were damaged by the violence, at a total cost of $350 million, and of these properties nearly 100 were destroyed entirely.[8]

Uncle Hugo's, one of the country's most beloved independent bookstores and the oldest science fiction bookstore in the country, was burned down.[9] The owner of a manufacturing plant that had been burned down announced he would be moving the factory out of the city.

"They don't care about my business," 7-Sigma Inc. owner Kris Wyrobek told a local reporter, noting that law enforcement was nowhere to be found as fires were set around the factory. "They didn't protect our people. We were all on our own.... The fire engine was just sitting there, but they wouldn't do anything."[10]

In neighboring St. Paul, 330 buildings were destroyed, and the city suffered $82 million in damages. One man was shot, and another died when his building was set on fire.[11]

The nation watched the unchecked violence in horror as the deadly riots began spreading to other cities. President Trump tweeted on May 29, "These THUGS are dishonoring the memory of George Floyd, and I won't let that happen." He added, "Just spoke to Governor Tim Walz and told him that the Military is with him all the way. Any difficulty and we will assume control but, when the looting starts, the shooting starts. Thank you!"

Twitter immediately took the unprecedented step of censoring the post, saying it glorified violence, as Democrats claimed that the "looting and shooting" phrase encouraged police brutality.[12] Apparently, it had previously been uttered by Miami police chief Walter Headley in 1967, who credited police brutality with preventing riots.

In response to the criticism, Trump claimed that he didn't know of the phrase's background.

"I've heard that phrase for a long time. I don't know where it came from or where it originated," Trump said in response. "Frankly, it means when there's looting, people get shot and they die. And if you look at what happened last night and the night before, you see that, it's very common. And that's the way that's meant."[13]

He also told the media that Floyd "was in tremendous pain, obviously, and couldn't breathe. It was very obvious to anybody that watched it. It was a very, very sad thing for me to see that. We also know that most policemen, you see the great job they do; they do a fantastic job. But this was a terrible insult to police and to policemen," he said.[14]

By Friday, Chauvin was charged with murder. The medical examiner found that Floyd's heart had stopped, caused by "cardiopulmonary arrest complicating law enforcement subdual, restraint, and neck compression," though the fact that Floyd tested positive for COVID-19 and had fentanyl and methamphetamine in his system was not considered related to his cause of death.[15]

◆   ◆   ◆

If the media weren't invested in fomenting the violence, they did not seem to care that their irresponsible handling of the fraught racial dynamics involved in Floyd's death added fuel to the fire of the ongoing riots. In fact, they seemed to relish the role they played in contributing to the mounting disorder.

The media and other activists constantly alleged that Chauvin's excessive use of force was caused by racism. No evidence was provided to support these claims, which was made more difficult to believe by the fact that Floyd's arrest had been carried out by four ethnically diverse police officers.

When Chauvin was later convicted at trial of murder, prosecutors did not allege racism had any role in the killing. Asked by journalists if the killing was a "hate crime," meaning a crime committed with an additional element of bias, Minnesota attorney general Keith Ellison, a Democratic politician with past ties to the black nationalist and anti-Semitic Nation of Islam, said it wasn't.

"I wouldn't call it that because hate crimes are crimes where there's an explicit motive, and of bias," Ellison said. "We don't have any evidence that Derek Chauvin factored in George Floyd's race as he did what he did."[16]

But the facts of the case didn't matter. The media and Democratic leadership were fully invested in the narrative that the killing was proof of America's irredeemable racism. If they couldn't prove that Chauvin was racist, they would argue that police departments as institutions were examples of "systemic racism," and that there was a plot among law enforcement officers to target black people.

"It was a murder in the full light of day, and it ripped the blinders off for the whole world to see the systemic racism the Vice President just referred to—the systemic racism that is a stain [on] our nation's soul; the knee on the neck of justice for Black Americans; the profound fear and trauma, the pain, the exhaustion that Black and brown Americans experience every single day," Biden would say after Chauvin was convicted.

Even those more abstract claims couldn't stand up to reality, no matter how widely they were shared. While homicide is the leading cause of death for young black men, the lion's share of black murder victims are killed by other black men, not the police. According to a *Washington Post* database, just seventeen unarmed black men were shot and killed by police in 2020.[17] Though every unjustified death at the hands of law enforcement is a crime that should be investigated, the numbers hardly indicate the widespread problem that the left insists upon.

The media narratives had their intended effect. A survey in the fall of 2020 "found that 8 in 10 African Americans believe black men are more likely to be killed by police than die in an auto accident, as did 53% of white Biden voters but only 15% of white Trump voters."[18] America's alleged racism would be an animating issue, just like the Democrats had wanted.

In response to the media coverage ginning up racial conflict, Trump tweeted on May 31, "The Lamestream Media is doing everything within their power to foment hatred and anarchy. As long as everybody understands what they are doing, that they are FAKE NEWS and truly bad people with a sick agenda, we can easily work through them to GREATNESS!"[19]

The riots and protests were not limited to a small group of people. They were massive and orchestrated—the culmination of toxic ideas that had been injected into American discourse for years.

There's no doubt that slavery, which has often been called America's "original sin," has left an indelible mark on the country and that problems related to racism continue to this day. Many Americans alive today can still recall the horrors of state-sanctioned racism under Jim Crow laws. However, most Americans have always believed that the way to overcome these problems is to live up to American ideals and rhetoric about equality and the inherent dignity and rights afforded to everyone, regardless of race, color, or creed. Racial progress in this country was made because an unbroken line of champions of racial equality, from Abraham Lincoln to Martin Luther King Jr., argued slavery and discrimination were at odds with the country's founding ideals. While cultural and racial distinctions might be celebrated to some degree in civil society, the goal was that socially, legally, and politically America should be a colorblind society.

But in the 1960s, left-wing radicals began their long march to undermine the ideas that had driven racial progress in this country for more than a century. By the time George Floyd was killed, identity politics had become the dominant prism through which the media and all other elite institutions—but not ordinary Americans—had come to understand the world. And perhaps the most extreme version of identity politics, what Marxist academics would label critical race theory, had gained purchase in the national conversation. Robin DiAngelo, for example, the white female author of *White Fragility*, a book that explicitly dismisses Martin Luther King Jr.'s "I Have a Dream Speech" as wrongheaded, had become a celebrity author.[20]

Unlike the previous American belief that all people are created equal and endowed with inalienable rights, identity politics teaches people to look at themselves through the lens of race, sex, sexual orientation, and gender identity. People can be separated into the groups of oppressor and victim. The more white, male, and straight a group is, the more it is categorized as an oppressor. The greater a group's victimhood, the greater moral claims its members have over others.

"Identity politics should be rejected not because it demands justice for those who have been unjustly treated, but because it poses a threat to republican self-government by corroding patriotic ties, fostering hatred, promoting cultural separatism, and demanding special treatment rather than equality under the law," writes Dr. David Azerrad, an assistant professor at Hillsdale College's Van Andel Graduate School of Government.[21]

According to Azerrad, at the core of the identitarian worldview is the claim that America is, at its heart, an oppressive regime. Different groups deride America for different reasons, but the central accusations are that America is rooted in white supremacy, the patriarchy, or homophobia.[22] These beliefs have led many people to a wholesale rejection of American society and institutions.

Identity politics had been feeding into media coverage for years, but by the time of the Floyd incident it had become the dominant view of the corporate press. Dean Baquet, editor in chief of the *New York Times*, said in a staff town hall in August 2019 that the paper would be shifting the focus of its coverage of the Trump presidency from Russian collusion to race relations. At the same time, the paper published its 1619 Project, a revisionist history that argues that the nation's true founding was when the first enslaved Africans were brought to the country in 1619. The 1619 Project was founded by journalist Nikole Hannah-Jones, who asserted without evidence that the Revolutionary War was actually fought to preserve slavery.[23]

Several of America's most eminent historians, many of whom were decidedly leftist in their politics, denounced the project as riddled with factual errors and tendentious arguments, such as that slavery made America rich, that all white Americans benefited equally from slavery, that slavery was a uniquely American sin, that black people had to fight racism on their own, and that systemic racism keeps non-white Americans down.[24]

Hannah-Jones was open about her goals in pushing the 1619 Project. "If you read the whole project, I don't think you can come away from it without understanding the project is an argument for reparations," she said.[25]

After Professor Charles Kesler wrote of the violent riots hitting the nation in an essay titled "Call Them the 1619 Riots,"[26] Hannah-Jones responded, "It would be an honor. Thank you."[27] She had earlier told CBS News, "Destroying property, which can be replaced, is not violence."[28]

The *New York Times* stood by the error-riddled project, and even pushed out a curriculum for schools based on it. The 1619 Project won a Pulitzer Prize in 2020.[29]

It was no coincidence that both the *New York Times* and the Biden campaign used race as part of their anti-Trump efforts. The left knew that turning out black voters for the Democrats and preventing Trump from making gains with them would be essential to victory in 2020. Perhaps even more important, it was a good way to increase votes of young people and white women who were sensitive to accusations of racist associations. Calling Trump a racist was electorally advantageous, and the response to the George Floyd killing was another effort to sacrifice the good of the country for the good of the Democratic Party.

◆   ◆   ◆

When George Floyd was killed by Derek Chauvin, extremist groups such as Black Lives Matter sprang into action to help coordinate more than 10,330 demonstrations across more than 2,730 locations in all 50 states, plus the District of Columbia, through the latter part of 2020.

"One of the reasons there have been protests in so many places in the United States is the backing of organizations like Black Lives

Matter," wrote the *New York Times*, calling it "the largest movement in history."[30]

The scenes that came out of the riots around the country the first weekend in June were apocalyptic, although the media did their best to downplay the carnage. In one memorable image, MSNBC's Ali Velshi stood in front of a massive burning building in Minneapolis one night and said, "I want to be clear on how I characterize this. This is mostly a protest. It is not, generally speaking, unruly."[31] At a protest a couple of months later, CNN was mocked for describing a Kenosha riot as a "fiery but mostly peaceful protest" as fires and chaos raged in the background.[32]

At least twenty-five Americans were killed in the riots, which cost insurers more than $2 billion, but the media relentlessly referred to them as "peaceful" or "mostly peaceful."[33]

One of those killed was David Dorn, a black man who had spent four decades as a police officer in St. Louis before serving as a police chief. Looters shot him in the torso while he was out protecting a friend's business. He died bleeding on the sidewalk.[34]

Most major media did not care about or cover those killed in the violence. It was at odds with their "mostly peaceful" narrative. It was part of a plan.

◆　　◆　　◆

Racial exploitation has long been a part of politics, and recent years were no exception. After steady progress, perceived levels of racism had increased dramatically since 2014, during President Barack Obama's second term in office.

Gallup polling shows that from 2001 to 2014, strong majorities of Americans said race relations were either very good or somewhat good. Beginning in 2014, however, things changed. Whereas only 17 percent of polled Americans told Gallup they personally worried about race relations a great deal that year, by 2021 it had gone up to 48 percent.

Only 11 percent were "very dissatisfied" with the state of race relations in 2011. By 2021, that number had skyrocketed to 46 percent.[35]

Obama, the nation's first president of African descent, was elected in 2008 and re-elected in 2012. With racial progress in America so profound and widespread, the left had to escalate racial tensions to maintain an electorally advantageous level of outrage.

Political analyst Scott Walter highlighted how the Black Lives Matter movement contributed to the change in perceptions. The movement arose following the highly publicized deaths of Trayvon Martin and Michael Brown in 2012 and 2014, respectively. Three self-described "radical black organizers" formed the Black Lives Matter movement because they were outraged at the handling of the Martin case.[36]

One of the organizers was a woman named Alicia Garza. She was sent by the National Domestic Workers Alliance—a group underwritten by the Service Employees International Union, the Ford Foundation, the MacArthur Foundation, and the Open Society Foundation—to Ferguson to organize. That led to six hundred black activists' going on "freedom rides" to Ferguson for protests. Garza, who wrote the forward to *Revolution in the Air: Sixties Radicals Turn to Lenin, Mao, and Che*, studied Marxism and Leninism. She openly embraces radical action in support of socialism.[37]

Patrisse Cullors was the executive director of the Black Lives Movement Global Network Foundation, which initially received support through Thousand Currents, a nonprofit co-chaired by Susan Rosenberg. Rosenberg was a co-founder of the May 19th Communist Organization, which was a domestic terrorist group in the 1980s. Rosenberg had at one time been sentenced to 58 years in prison for possession "of 740 pounds of explosives, an Uzi submachine gun, an M-14 rifle, another rifle with a telescopic sight, a sawed-off shotgun, three 9-millimeter handguns in purses and boxes of ammunition" before her sentence was commuted by President Bill Clinton.[38]

Despite its radical extremism, Black Lives Matter received a tremendous amount of support from corporations and other elite groups.

Its website even proclaimed the movement wanted to "disrupt the Western-prescribed nuclear family structure" and sought to "defund the police."[39]

The affiliated Movement for Black Lives, which claimed to be made up of over 150 organizations, called for an end to all policing and criminal justice, an end to capital punishment, and an end to cash bail. It called for reparations in the form of a minimum income for black people, with mandated "curriculums" that "critically examine the political, economic, and social impacts of colonialism and slavery." It sought retroactive decriminalization of drug offenses and prostitution. It wanted divestment from fossil fuels, a cut in military spending, universal health care, and redistribution of wealth. It sought a ban on any laws protecting voter integrity, and the immediate release of all political prisoners.[40]

Among the affiliated groups were anarcho-socialist militias that glorify martyr narratives, authoritarian narratives, and revolutionary narratives. "ACAB," code for "all cops are bastards," is listed in the hate symbol database of the Anti-Defamation League. The code started appearing at BLM protests across the country.

For instance, when Portland rioters toppled a statue of George Washington in June 2020, they lit a fire on its head and tagged the statue with graffiti that said "genocidal colonist," "BLM," "ACAB," "Fuck Cops," and "1619."[41]

Iconoclasm was a major part of the movement. President Trump was roundly mocked and derided for worrying in August 2017—in a speech that the media would spin into the Charlottesville hoax—that statue destroyers would move on from statues of Confederate general Robert E. Lee to statues of former presidents and founding fathers George Washington and Thomas Jefferson. Major media accused Trump of making inappropriate and even ridiculous comments.

During the summer of violence, however, iconoclastic mobs did just that, moving on from toppling Confederate statues to defacing, damaging, and destroying statues of and memorials to Admiral David Farragut, abolitionist Matthias Baldwin, American Revolutionary War general Philip Schuyler, a Texas ranger, president and commanding general of the Union Army Ulysses S. Grant, Frances Scott Key, Abraham Lincoln, George Washington, and Thomas Jefferson.[42]

Not only was the slippery slope real, it was a race to the bottom. The iconic Equestrian Statue of Theodore Roosevelt located on public parkland at New York's Museum of Natural History was removed by the city in 2020, citing concerns that the statue was racist. In June 2020, the speaker of the New York City Council and other council members called for the removal of a Thomas Jefferson statue from city hall.

The statue of "America's most noted slave holder" is "a constant reminder of the injustices that have plagued communities of color since the inception of our country," they wrote in a letter to Mayor Bill de Blasio.[43]

Across the country, protesters tore down statues while authorities stood by. Protesters tried to tear down a statue in a park in Washington, D.C., of Abraham Lincoln and a freed slave with broken shackles rising to his feet, even though the statue had been commissioned and paid for by former slaves and Frederick Douglass had spoken at the statue's dedication.[44] A Lincoln statue identical to the one in D.C. was eventually removed in Boston because, according to Mayor Marty Walsh, the absence of a statue honoring the Great Emancipator would create a "more equitable and just city."[45]

When President Trump worried that statue removers wouldn't stop with Confederate figures, the media roundly mocked and derided him. Yet all their experts, fact checks, and smug assurances were completely wrong. Trump was right.

◆　　◆　　◆

Social media played a huge role in spreading the riots and protests across the country. The leftist tactic of requiring a show of fealty to the movement reared its head with "Blackout Tuesday," a call for all to signal their virtue by posting a black box on their Instagram accounts.[46]

Elites immediately supported the Marxist BLM movement. The 100 largest U.S. companies pledged more than $1.63 billion to BLM and related organizations. Among the corporate donors to BLM were Uggs, Amazon, Gatorade, Microsoft, Warner Records, Intel, Bungie (maker of Xbox and Microsoft games), and Nabisco. Spanx, Lululemon, AirBnB, Axe, Degree, Dropbox, Fitbit, Tinder, and many more did the same.[47]

Companies that supported non-leftist movements, by contrast, were harassed and targeted. When Goya supported President Trump's Hispanic Prosperity Initiative, the company faced cancellation. When someone erroneously claimed the CEO of Wendy's had donated to Trump, the fast-food chain faced an immediate social media backlash.[48]

Meanwhile, social media activists stirred up mobs that portrayed even benign declarations of patriotism as racist. When NFL quarterback Drew Brees said, "I will never agree with anybody disrespecting the flag of the United States of America or our country," he was widely condemned for his support of patriotism and forced to ritualistically apologize.[49]

"I acknowledge that we as Americans, including myself, have not done enough to fight for that equality or to truly understand the struggles and plight of the black community," Brees wrote on Instagram. "I recognize that I should do less talking and more listening…and when the black community is talking about their pain, we all need to listen. For that, I am very sorry and I ask your forgiveness."[50]

That wasn't good enough. He had to apologize again. Then Brees's wife had to apologize. Her apology began, "We are the problem."[51]

Sports franchises became primary pushers of the BLM movement. Perhaps most notably, the NFL's Washington Redskins dropped their name and became the Washington Football Team.[52]

The National Basketball Association painted "Black Lives Matter" courtside. The Women's National Basketball Association followed suit. Then senator Kelly Loeffler, who owned 49 percent of the Atlanta Dream, said subscribing to a "particular political agenda undermines the potential of the sport and sends a message of exclusion." She added, "The truth is, we need less—not more—politics in sports."[53]

She suggested players display an American flag on their uniforms instead. WNBA commissioner Cathy Engelbert disavowed Loeffler, and the players' union called for her to be ousted from league ownership.

Loeffler was undeterred. "[T]hey threatened to burn the system down, literally and figuratively if they don't get what they want," she said in an interview with Fox News. "This is an organization that looks to destroy American principles and I had to draw the line."[54] (She would eventually sell her stake in the team.)

In offering so much support to Black Lives Matter, corporate America showed that it was in the tank for Biden. Moderate views defending the United States against the most obscene charges were now fireable offenses, never mind publicly stating support for President Trump.

By contrast, celebrities and Democratic politicians also worked to bail out rioters who were being arrested for violent action in Minneapolis and other cities.

As Minneapolis businesses and police precincts were being fire-bombed, businesses were being looted, and people were being attacked by rioters, then senator Kamala Harris tweeted, "If you're able to, chip in now to the @MNFreedomFund to help post bail for those protesting on the ground in Minnesota."[55]

Seth Rogen, Steve Carell, Patton Oswalt, Cynthia Nixon, Jameela Jamil, Chrissy Teigen, and other celebrities all publicly announced their support of the fund to bail out rioters. The fund raised a whopping $35 million, thanks to Harris and other prominent supporters. The previous year it had only raised $100,000 total.[56] Only about 10 protesters were bailed out by the Minnesota Freedom Fund, because most of those arrested were just given citations or immediately released. So the money went to help those accused of rape, murder, and other violent felonies.

The fund paid $100,000 cash bail to spring a woman who was charged with second-degree murder for stabbing a friend to death. A twice-convicted rapist charged with kidnapping, assault, and sexual assault in two separate cases received $350,000 in cash for his release.[57]

Greg Lewin, the interim executive director of the fund, explained it wasn't about the crime but the system. "I often don't even look at a charge when I bail someone out," Lewin told a local reporter. "I will see it after I pay the bill because it is not the point. The point is the system we are fighting."[58]

◆   ◆   ◆

Trump saw the damage the rioters could do up close. Since the beginning of the George Floyd riots, protesters had been amassing in Lafayette Park across Pennsylvania Avenue, in front of the White House.

The downtown area around the White House was wracked with violence as a result of these protests, which got out of control on May 31 as authorities were trying to enforce an 11:00 p.m. curfew. Multiple fires broke out in Lafayette Park, and firefighters had trouble getting through the protest to put out a blaze that had been set at St. John's Episcopal Church, one block from the White House. The church is a national historic landmark and has been visited by every president since it was constructed in 1816.[59] The violence spilled out onto the streets surrounding the White House and across the city.

Aerial shots of the fires on cable news made it look like the White House was in the middle of a war zone. Protesters clashed with law enforcement at the barriers set up around the White House, and at least sixty members of the Secret Service were injured in the chaos, including injuries sustained from the crowd's throwing projectiles and Molotov cocktails.[60] A report emerged that Trump had been moved to a secure location to protect him from the protesters.

In the week between the death of George Floyd and the assault on the White House, at least twelve statues and memorials were defaced by vandals, including the World War II Memorial and Lincoln Memorial

on the National Mall.⁶¹ Even a statue of the nonviolent revolutionary
Mahatma Gandhi in front of the Indian Embassy was vandalized by
BLM protesters.⁶²

Following days of violent riots, Washington, D.C., announced a 7:00
p.m. curfew on Monday night. U.S. Park Police cleared the protesters in
front of the White House so a stronger security fence could be put at the
edge of Lafayette Park. About the same time, President Donald Trump
addressed the nation from the Rose Garden, announcing that the country
would restore the rule of law and protection of civil liberties to jurisdictions where anarchy had prevailed.

Afterward, he walked through Lafayette Park to St. John's Episcopal
Church, which had been set on fire the night before. Standing before a
church sign which read "All are welcome," President Trump, who had
previously said he'd be paying his respects to a very special place, held
up a Bible.

The visit to the vandalized historic church where every president
since James Madison has worshiped reassured many in the country.⁶³
The move communicated President Trump's commitment to setting order
to the chaos that had enveloped the nation.

For the media, however, these actions were nothing less than criminal abuse of peaceful protesters—despite the fact many in the same
crowd had been violent just hours previously, had been warned hours in
advance that the park was to be cleared, and that all the protestors were
violating a city-wide curfew.

The media spun a tale of violent, jackbooted cops running rampant
through the streets over innocent docile protesters. They first ran with tales
that the Park Police had used tear gas to clear the area, which the Park Police
denied, saying far less potent "pepper balls" had been deployed. And even
then, police only used the pepper balls because the crowd was throwing
"bricks, frozen water bottles, and caustic liquids" at Park Police.⁶⁴

The media were aghast that Trump would clear the park for a "photo
op"—even if it sent an important message that lawmakers must enforce
law and order and not yield to threats of violence. But the pressure to

denounce Trump in response to their sensationalist reporting was intense. Defense Secretary Mark Esper, who attended the Rose Garden speech in the Rose Garden, withered in the face of criticism and claimed that he had been misinformed about what was happening at the event. Anti-Trump Republicans in Congress, such as Nebraska senator Ben Sasse, issued statements condemning the clearing of Lafayette Park.[65]

D.C. mayor Muriel Bowser would be honored as the first speaker at the Democratic National Convention a few months later for her handling of the incident. "When peaceful protesters were teargassed across from the White House, our next speaker stood up, stood strong and turned that place into the Black Lives Matter Plaza in their honor," Eva Longoria said. Bowser had painted the words on a two-block-long section of Sixteenth Street leading to Lafayette Park.

The move attracted throngs of people to the area near the ongoing White House protest, but the carefully framed tourist selfies were belied by the fact that the windows of just about every business on or around the plaza had been bashed in by rioters. And many other parts of the capital weren't in any better shape.

More than a year after the Lafayette Park incident, the inspector general of the Interior Department released a report confirming that the area had been cleared not for a photo op, but in order to build a security fence to protect the nation's Executive Residence from rioters. Further, it was actually Bowser's D.C. police, not Trump's Park Police, who had used the tear gas a few blocks away in response to violence from a crowd breaking curfew. But the damage was done. The hysterical media reaction would scare mayors and governors throughout the country away from restoring law and order. The long summer of violence destroying American businesses and city centers had just begun.

◆   ◆   ◆

As the summer dragged on, it grew hard to deny that the violent riots were completely unmoored from any notion of social justice. According to data from the Armed Conflict Location and Event Data Project (ACLED), from May 24 through August 29 there were 11,541 "civil-society incidents," which encompass Black Lives Matter protests. Of those events, 1,101 devolved into some form of violence or rioting, and 933 of the violent incidents directly involved events affiliated with BLM.[66]

The media's spin on ACLED's report on the summer of violence was predictable, if still insulting. "The vast majority of Black Lives Matter protests—more than 93%—have been peaceful, according to a new report," wrote *Time*.[67] There really is no denying that, whatever its stated intentions, Black Lives Matter was an especially violent social movement.

Further, the statistics didn't begin to give a full sense of the tragedy—at least twenty-five people were killed as a result of the violence. Occasionally, one of the deaths, such as the tragic killing of retired black police captain David Dorn in downtown St. Louis in the midst of rioting, would merit a few human-interest stories. But by and large, the violence was downplayed in service of the broader political agenda behind Black Lives Matter, which often had little to do with improving things for black Americans—many of whom suffered the brunt of the damage done in inner-city riots.

This out-of-control violence was aided and abetted by Democratic city governments who willingly abandoned their duties to maintain law and order during the riots, and the media did their best to pretend that major urban centers hadn't descended into literal anarchy.

During MSNBC's coverage of the Republican National Convention, Rachel Maddow broke away from South Dakota governor Kristi Noem's speech to do an urgent "fact check" on the governor for noticing that several cities were overrun with violent crime as a result of the riots. To rebut Noem, Maddow brought Seattle mayor Jenny Durkan on the show, who declared Noem was "purposefully wrong" and blamed "the president and Fox News" for creating a false impression of violence in her city.[68] However, it was Durkan who was being willfully dishonest.

Earlier in the summer, Durkan had ordered Seattle police to abandon a precinct building and to cede to protester demands that they set up an "autonomous zone" in the middle of downtown where police were not allowed to enter. Almost immediately, the area became a haven for crime and drugs. To the extent that order was being maintained, there were gun-toting armed warlords wandering the streets of the Capitol Hill Autonomous Zone (CHAZ). Durkan went on Chris Cuomo's show on June 11 and said what was happening in the CHAZ was "a block party atmosphere." "We could have the summer of love," she told the world.[69]

Major media engaged in a total information blackout on the insanity in Seattle. A search of the ABC News, NBC News, CBS News, and Associated Press websites on June 11 showed not a single mention of the occupation. The *New York Times* published a piece touting the CHAZ as a haven of "free food [and] free speech" that had become a "homeland of racial justice."[70]

The day after Durkan's June 11 CNN appearance and the *New York Times*'s tourism brochure, Seattle's black female police chief confirmed that "rapes, robberies, and all sorts of violent acts have been occurring in the area and we're not able to get to [them]."[71] Eventually, two young black men were murdered in the CHAZ.

The creation of so-called "autonomous zones" also happened in Minneapolis and Portland, Oregon. These were not spontaneous hippie gatherings. They were the direct outgrowth of the ideology of hard-left groups. Autonomous zones are part of a strategy, however ill-conceived, to challenge and overthrow the elected authorities.

"For the most part, you're looking at an ideology of autonomism which is bottom-up Marxist organizing.... This was an ideology that came out of...Italy and Germany in the late 60s, early 70s," Kyle Shideler, director and senior analyst for Homeland Security and Counterterrorism at the Center for Security Policy, observed. "It was influential with the [terrorist groups] Red Brigades and the Red Army Faction, and you still see this in their language. When [American protesters] talk about autonomous action or setting up an autonomous zone, that's what they're referring to."[72]

But the media and Democratic politicians were unwilling to admit that anarchist and Marxist groups such as Antifa and BLM were exploiting racial unrest to launch a full-blown insurrection in major American cities. South of Seattle, Portland had an even more acute insurrection problem. The city is the national hub of Antifa, and violent activists spent much of July laying siege to the Mark O. Hatfield federal courthouse. By the time they focused their efforts on the courthouse, rioters had already burned the Multnomah County Justice Center jail and the Portland Police Bureau headquarters just a few blocks away.[73]

Once again, protesters exploited the media's willingness to cover for their violence. At one point, Portland's insurrectionists created the group "Wall of Moms"—a group that also included "nonbinary and people who consider themselves mothers"—to stand between the violent radicals assaulting the courthouse and the federal marshals protecting it. Columnist Jonathan Alter called the Wall of Moms a "brilliant tactic that may forever change social protest," as if he were unaware that terrorist groups such as Hamas have cynically used human shields for decades.[74]

In this media environment, it was almost shocking to read the account of an Associated Press reporter who embedded with federal law enforcement protecting the Mark O. Hatfield courthouse in downtown Portland in July. "I watched as injured officers were hauled inside. In one case, the commercial firework came over so fast the officer didn't have time to respond. It burned through his sleeves and he had bloody gashes on both forearms. Another had a concussion from being hit in the head with a mortar," Mike Balsamo reported. "The lights inside the courthouse have to be turned off for safety and the light from high-powered lasers bounced across the lobby almost all night. The fear is palpable. Three officers were struck in the last few weeks and still haven't regained their vision."[75]

Despite this, Oregon governor Kate Brown declared that additional federal troops that had been sent in to protect the courthouse had "acted as an occupying force and brought violence." Portland mayor Ted Wheeler blamed Trump for "creat[ing] the hate and the division."[76] But the Portland police union had given the city council a vote of "no confidence" that summer, and the city had been a law-and-order basket case for years under Wheeler's leadership.

In 2017, Portland canceled its annual Rose Parade after violent threats from Antifa, which objected to the Multnomah County Republican Party's being included as one of the many civic groups marching in the parade. Forget Trump; it was unsafe for even an ordinary Republican to walk down the streets of Portland. And in canceling the parade, Wheeler effectively conceded that Antifa ruled the streets. "You have seen how much power we have downtown and that the police cannot stop us from shutting down roads so please consider your decision wisely," read the threat.[77]

But in spite of the disingenuous attempts to blame the president for the inability of Democratic leaders such as Durkan and Wheeler to maintain law and order, the true nature of what was happening was not lost on Donald Trump from the outset.

"Does anyone notice how little the Radical Left takeover of Seattle is being discussed in the Fake News Media. That is very much on purpose because they know how badly this weakness & ineptitude play politically," Trump tweeted on June 14. "The Mayor & Governor should be ashamed of themselves. Easily fixed!"[78] Later, the president took aim at their hypocritical approach of enabling these protests during a pandemic: "Interesting how ANTIFA and other Far Left militant groups can take over a city without barely a whimper from soft Do Nothing Democrat leadership, yet these same weak leaders become RADICAL when it comes to shutting down a state or city and its hard working, tax paying citizens!"[79]

❖   ❖   ❖

The Trump team knew something had to be done. The fact that American cities had become hotbeds of violent chaos wasn't just another opportunity for his campaign to exploit; it was an urgent problem that needed to be solved for the good of the country. The president has a big bully pulpit, and speaking out against the radical ideology that was fomenting violent unrest was the right thing to do.

At an event celebrating the Fourth of July, the president gave an elaborately staged speech right in front of Mount Rushmore. Given the occasion, the speech was predictably heavy on patriotic themes—but with a twist. Throughout the speech, Trump acknowledged that the traditional understanding of America—a great and powerful nation whose flaws are a result of failing to live up to its founding ideals, not in spite of them—was being grossly distorted. And those dishonest distortions were being used to pit Americans against one another for political gain:

> Our nation is witnessing a merciless campaign to wipe out our history, defame our heroes, erase our values, and indoctrinate our children. Angry mobs are trying to tear down statues of our Founders, deface our most sacred memorials, and unleash a wave of violent crime in our cities. Many of these people have no idea why they are doing this, but some know exactly what they are doing. They think the American people are weak and soft and submissive. But no, the American people are strong and proud, and they will not allow our country, and all of its values, history, and culture, to be taken from them....
>
> This attack on our liberty, our magnificent liberty must be stopped, and it will be stopped very quickly. We will expose this dangerous movement, protect our nation's children, end this radical assault, and preserve our beloved American way of life. In our schools, our newsrooms, even our corporate boardrooms, there is a new far-left fascism that demands absolute allegiance. If you do not speak its language, perform its rituals, recite its mantras, and follow its commandments,

then you will be censored, banished, blacklisted, persecuted, and punished. It's not going to happen to us.

Make no mistake: this left-wing cultural revolution is designed to overthrow the American Revolution. In so doing, they would destroy the very civilization that rescued billions from poverty, disease, violence, and hunger, and that lifted humanity to new heights of achievement, discovery, and progress. To make this possible, they are determined to tear down every statue, symbol, and memory of our national heritage.[80]

This was bracing stuff and left no doubt that those encouraging violence as a means of forcing political change had to be rebuffed. The speech was a plea for unity. "We are one family and one nation...[which] belongs to every citizen, young and old, first-generation American and tenth-generation American," said the president, adding, "No matter our race, color, religion, or creed, we are one America."[81] Trump went on to speak at length about the accomplishments of Americans as diverse as Ulysses S. Grant, Frederick Douglass, the Wright Brothers, the Tuskegee Airmen, Harriet Tubman, Clara Barton, Jesse Owens, George Patton, Louie Armstrong, Alan Shepard, Elvis Presley, Muhammad Ali, Walt Whitman, Mark Twain, Irving Berlin, Ella Fitzgerald, Frank Sinatra, and Bob Hope.[82]

Trump also discussed Martin Luther King and celebrated American values as being antithetical to racism and division. "We believe in equal opportunity, equal justice, and equal treatment for citizens of every race, background, religion, and creed," he said. "Every child, of every color—born and unborn—is made in the holy image of God. We want free and open debate, not speech codes and cancel culture. We embrace tolerance, not prejudice."[83]

The media, which had trouble responding fairly to Trump in the best of circumstances, heard this speech and simply broke. Nearly every media outlet decried the speech as "dark" and, in defiance of all comprehension, racist. Robert Costa and Philip Rucker of the *Washington Post* opined in a piece falsely labeled as "news" that Trump gave "a dystopian speech in which he excoriated racial justice protesters," and that this was a continuation of Trump's "race baiting and, at times, outright racism."[84] On Twitter, Costa proclaimed that the speech was part of Trump's "unyielding push to preserve Confederate symbols and the legacy of white domination."[85]

Washington Examiner reporter Byron York noted, "To the Post, apparently, tearing down statues, or threatening to tear down statues, of George Washington, not to mention Jefferson, Lincoln, Ulysses S. Grant, and others, is 'racial justice protest.'"[86]

The press was simply in willful denial about what was happening across the country. CNN's Chris Cillizza ran a column headlined, "The 28 Most Outrageous Lines from Donald Trump's Mount Rushmore Speech."[87] In response to Trump's pronouncement that he would never allow Mount Rushmore to be desecrated, Cillizza sarcastically responded, "Uh, was there some sort of movement to tear down Mt. Rushmore I was unaware of...?" The answer was yes. On July 3, the day before Trump's speech, the *Los Angeles Times* had published an article asking, "Could the racist past of Mt. Rushmore's creator bring down the monument?"[88]

There was no question that Trump was right to be worried about the attempts not just to deface Mount Rushmore but, more broadly, the attempts to erase the "extraordinary legacies of George Washington, Thomas Jefferson, Abraham Lincoln, and Teddy Roosevelt." And yet Illinois senator Tammy Duckworth went on CNN and summed up Trump's speech by saying, "He spent all his time talking about dead traitors."[89]

◆   ◆   ◆

The entire summer amounted to the widespread gaslighting of the country by Democrats and the media. How long could liberals possibly get away with saying it was racist to demand that authorities put an end to ongoing, nationwide violent riots that had killed dozens of people?

And was the country really supposed to pretend that *New York Times* op-eds headlined "Yes, We Mean Literally Abolish the Police," demanding readers text their family members and tell them they wouldn't visit or speak to them until they make financial contributions to support "black lives," were responsible commentary?[90]

Their apologetics came to a halt in late August when the riots came to Kenosha, which happens to be one of the most important swing districts in the swing state of Wisconsin. Kenosha marked a turning point for no other reason than it made the establishment realize that the riots had the potential to damage Biden's electoral chances. Making matters worse, the riots broke out during the Republican National Convention, reinforcing Trump's law-and-order message. The Kenosha riots would dominate news coverage after two people were killed while attacking an armed seventeen-year-old who was running away from a mob.

In July, CNN's Don Lemon had blamed conservative media for creating a false impression that the violence was out of control. "Whenever Trump's poll numbers go south, they kick in with...'Democratic cities in chaos!'" Lemon said.[91]

But a month later, on August 26, Lemon had done a 180. "The rioting has to stop.... It's showing up in the polling, it's showing up in focus groups. It is the only thing right now that is sticking [for Republicans]," Lemon told his CNN colleague Chris Cuomo, who nodded along in agreement[92]—a change from Cuomo's tone in June when he had asked viewers to "please, show me where it says protesters are supposed to be polite and peaceful."[93] (Cuomo, a graduate of Fordham Law School, must have momentarily forgotten about the First Amendment, enshrining the right to "peaceably" assemble.)

Lemon went on to demand that Biden step up to give a speech condemning the riots—which is exactly what Biden did on August 31. "I want to make it absolutely clear rioting is not protesting, looting is not protesting,"[94] Biden said, using language almost identical to Vice President

Mike Pence's speech days earlier. "It's lawlessness, plain and simple, and those that do it should be prosecuted."[95] The campaign was now worried enough that it made a $45 million ad buy in swing states, airing clips of Biden's speech condemning the violence.[96]

It was remarkable that Biden had taken so long to denounce anarchy. And his disavowal was also insincere. A month later, when standing on the debate stage with Trump, Biden was in complete denial about who was responsible for the violent behavior.

"I'll tell you what, somebody's got to do something about Antifa and the left because this is not a right-wing problem, this is a left-wing—" Trump said, before being interrupted by Biden.

"His own FBI director said unlike white supremacists, Antifa is an idea, not an organization, not a militia. That's what his FBI director said," said Biden.[97]

So while cities burned, Joe Biden apologized for Antifa—instead trying to pin the blame for violence on white supremacists.

FBI director Chris Wray had, in fact, told Congress in September that Antifa is "not a group or an organization. It's a movement or an ideology."[98] Describing Antifa this way is a matter of semantics, and an insulting one at that. There are regional chapters of Antifa and Antifa organizations that have websites. Antifa's political, moral, and legal claims to violence define it as a terrorist group. And to the extent that Antifa is extremely secretive about its "leaderless resistance" tactics, this same phantom cell structure makes it similar to how more commonly understood terrorist groups, such as al-Qaeda, commonly operate.

During protests, members of Antifa carry weapons and coordinate their actions in order to evade law enforcement. "They communicate in large Signal chat rooms, an encrypted peer-to-peer app," according to reporter Andy Ngo. "They also use hand signals, they have walkie-talkie devices, and scouts who watch where the police are and provide real time updates." Antifa spent much of the year sharing tactical intelligence to help rioters do maximum damage.[99] During the riots in Minneapolis, the Antifa-friendly website CrimethInc. published an anonymously written detailed report on "how a combination of different tactics compelled the police to abandon the Third Precinct."[100]

Despite the undeniable evidence of Antifa's ongoing violence, the Trump administration faced serious obstacles trying to bring its members to justice. "[Antifa members] have very good street tactics and conflict doctrine as to how to do this work at the seams of the First Amendment—they use legitimate demonstrations as a host body," observed Trump attorney general Bill Barr. Further, they operated in liberal cities in blue states where local authorities were both reluctant to stop them and unwilling to help federal law enforcement go after them. And finally, the bureaucratic inertia within the FBI was such that the agency had long focused its attention on right-wing extremists and was ill-equipped to deal with threats from the left.

Still, Barr pushed cities to deal with the problem, at one point convening a meeting for local law enforcement to exchange intelligence on Antifa. "Every chief going around the table was saying these are left-wing Marxist extremists," said Barr. "But the FBI, I think there are people in the intelligence operation there basically saying there is no such thing as Antifa. There were others there who agree Antifa is real, but institutionally the FBI has never gotten in trouble for going after the right, they have always gotten in trouble for going after the left." Even though decades had passed, the FBI was still skittish about the criticism it had received for infiltrating radical left-wing groups in the '60s and '70s.

The inaction in response to Antifa certainly helped take the pressure off Biden, who never had to answer for the bricks flying through windows, rampant looting, toppling of statues, and assaults on innocent business owners that defined urban life throughout the summer of 2020. To do so would have been to confront an uncomfortable truth—the Democratic Party and its allies have been tolerating, encouraging, and mainstreaming political violence for decades.[101]

In 1966, Columbia University sociologists Richard Cloward and his wife Frances Piven wrote an article about the need for "cadres of aggressive organizers" to spark "demonstrations to create a climate of militancy" in cities throughout the country.[102] The plan was to disrupt law and order so thoroughly that America's politicians would impose a socialist economic system to quell the violence. Cloward and Piven were explicit about exploiting racial tensions to incite mass protests. Their inspiration for the "Cloward-Piven strategy," as it came to be known, were the Watts riots in 1965, which occurred after Los Angeles police used excessive force while arresting a black man for drunk driving.[103]

The Cloward-Piven strategy was hugely influential among the American left in the 1960s and has never really gone away. In a 2010 leaked audio recording, Stephen Lerner—who according to the *Washington Post* is "considered one of the smartest organizers, if not the smartest organizer, working in the labor movement"—solemnly invoked the Cloward-Piven strategy and urged the American left and labor movement to destabilize the country.[104] He approvingly cited fatal and destructive riots in Greece over austerity measures as a model for achieving political change in the United States.

Looking back at the way so many tolerated and defended the iconoclasm and violent riots that swept America, perhaps it's worth asking whether elements of the political and media establishment embraced a Cloward–Piven strategy to oust Trump from office and bring about radical political changes that voters would have otherwise resisted. After all, policy proposals sound different when they contain the implied threat of wanton violence.

Trump was constrained from doing anything to stop the riots, but he was also held responsible for them. Any action he took led the establishment media and political class to blame him for the destruction, while restraint caused those same people to accuse him of failing to lead. And even if voters didn't blame Trump for cities' being burned, the events made people think that things were not moving in the right direction. If you're an incumbent president running on a platform of peace and prosperity, widespread riots and unrest simply aren't good.

On August 27, 2020, Joe Biden tweeted the quiet part out loud: "Remember: every example of violence Donald Trump decries has happened on his watch. Under his leadership. During his presidency."[105] That's why the Democrats wanted to foment violence and chaos. And in the summer of 2020, they got exactly what they wanted.

CHAPTER FIVE

The Revenge of
Fake News

"I am very proud to be the nominee of the Republican Party. I love you all. God bless you, and God bless America," Trump said, turning away from the podium in the closing moments of the Republican National Convention.[1] The crowd assembled at the convention's unusual venue—the White House lawn—was on their feet. And then heads turned 180 degrees in unison as perhaps the most spectacular fireworks display Washington, D.C., has ever seen kicked off, set before the backdrop of the Washington Monument.[2]

Where the Democratic Party conventions, especially in the Obama years, had acquired a reputation for glamour and elaborate staging, Republicans endured bare-bones conventions where the speakers gamely tried to elevate otherwise drab surroundings. In 2016, Trump had made the convention in Cleveland a hub of international attention and no small amount of interparty drama.[3] But in 2020, with Trump firmly in charge of the party, the celebrity president hadn't just delivered an expertly staged convention full of showmanship—it was also an exemplar of focused and effective messaging aimed at key voting blocs. And the Trump campaign and RNC had somehow pulled this off in the most difficult of circumstances—in the face of opposition efforts to sabotage the convention.[4]

Originally, the Republican National Committee had picked Charlotte, North Carolina, to host its 2020 convention. The selection was made in July 2018, more than two years out.[5]

North Carolina was an important swing state. President Obama had won it in 2008, Mitt Romney won it in 2012, and Trump won it by a larger margin in 2016.[6]

When the coronavirus hit, Democrats postponed their convention from July to August, and quickly decided to make theirs a mostly virtual convention.[7]

The horrific nature of the coronavirus—and President Trump's handling of the pandemic—was a major theme of Joe Biden's presidential campaign. Moving to a virtual event helped support that message. Whether it was the cause or effect of the messaging focus, polls showed that Democrats were much more terrified of the coronavirus than Republicans were.[8]

As important as a virtual convention was to Democratic messaging, an in-person convention was for Republicans.

Trump repeatedly emphasized that the convention would be in person. But things began to break down when the Democratic governor of North Carolina, Roy Cooper, had other ideas. Mandy Cohen, North Carolina's Human Health and Services secretary, said that Republicans should "plan for the worst" when it came to whether they could hold their convention.[9]

Trump insisted on a full event, but Cooper and Cohen opposed him. The convention and North Carolina's Democratic political leadership discussed the possibility of daily testing for the tens of thousands of Republicans who would descend on Charlotte. Cohen said she didn't trust the testing they would use, even though it was the standard testing used at the White House. After one such phone call to hammer out an agreement, the details were immediately leaked to the press. Republicans began to realize that hostile Democratic North Carolina officials were never going to work with them, and began to look for other cities to host.[10]

In the eighteen months leading up to the 2020 convention, the RNC had been raising and spending money, hiring event staff, and even had employees living in Charlotte. But now North Carolina wouldn't let the Republicans hold the convention there, nor would they let them out of their contracts, which had been signed years ago.[11] Preparing for a convention takes a long time, and much of the money already given to the state, such as for expensive security fencing, had already been spent. Much of the $50 million security grant provided by Congress for the two conventions had already been spent as well.[12]

With Charlotte no longer a possibility, several other cities were considered to host the convention. Jacksonville was always at the top of the list. The convention center, sports arena, and associated facilities are owned by the city, and Mayor Lenny Curry was not just a Republican, but the former chair of the Republican Party of Florida and a former RNC member.[13] Unlike North Carolina's governor, Florida governor Ron DeSantis wasn't hostile, but downright supportive of the plan.[14] Not too many cities in the country had such a combination of helpful traits. The RNC announced the move to Jacksonville on June 11, but also kept a small portion of the convention events in Charlotte, knowing that if they didn't, there would be unnecessary legal issues that could drag on for years.[15]

Then Tulsa happened. On June 10, President Trump announced he'd be holding a massive rally in Tulsa, Oklahoma. It would be his first big event since the pandemic had hit three months prior and shut campaigning down. While the media openly supported the mass BLM protests that were being held across the nation, they strongly opposed Trump's plan and said it would be bad for public health.[16]

A week before the rally, expectations were sky-high. Brad Parscale, Trump's campaign manager at the time, said that nearly one million people had requested tickets for the rally.[17] They set up an overflow area to handle the crowds. In the end, the crowd size was somewhere between six thousand and twelve thousand—the two official estimates that were given. That was fewer than the arena's capacity of nineteen thousand. The ticket request issue may have been a result of political opponents' running an operation to request tickets they never intended to utilize.[18]

The rally did set a record of a different kind. More than 7.7 million Americans watched the speech on Fox News, the highest Saturday prime-time viewership in the network's history.[19] But attendance at the event was a dud. It suggested that even Republicans might be scared off by media hysteria regarding COVID-19. It also precipitated a change in the leadership of the campaign. Parscale had been named the 2020 campaign manager in February 2018. Starting in 2016, he had risen to prominence on Trump's campaign operation for his work overseeing digital advertising, TV advertising, small-dollar fundraising, direct mail, and the political and advertising budget.[20] When not even everyone on the Trump campaign thought Trump could win in 2016, Parscale did, feeling confident in his targeting of specific populations in swing states using social media advertising tools.[21]

When it came to the 2020 campaign, however, concern was growing that something wasn't quite working. Trump was frustrated with poll numbers, and others were worried about Parscale's handling of the nuts and bolts of running a campaign, including managing finances. Trump announced that Parscale was being demoted and Bill Stepien would be named campaign manager on July 16.[22]

At the same time, Jacksonville started to see increasing cases of COVID-19, and the officials there were getting cold feet. The sheriff announced he had "significant concerns" about the event and that the current plans in place were not going to work.[23] Dr. Deborah Birx had worked out an elaborate plan for testing convention-goers, but it was going to be a tremendous hassle.[24]

It was beginning to look like a convention in Jacksonville might not happen. Trump had been adamant that the convention take place in person, but when Ronna McDaniel called the president from Massachusetts and told him it was looking bad, he said they should just pull the plug. He announced it during an unrelated press conference on July 23.[25]

It was a huge shock to Republicans, even highly placed ones, that the convention was off. Holding an in-person convention was important to the messaging, vital to the vision that Trump was trying to convey to the American people. Without much time, and as the Democrats prepared for an extravagant outing, the Trump campaign would have to find a way to bring that vision home in a new setting.

◆   ◆   ◆

There was much anticipation for the Democratic convention. The team putting it on had made the strategically wise decision to go virtual early, giving them five months to plan the event.

Biden had largely laid low for the summer. His campaign was allowing the media to run both Biden's positive messaging and all the negative messages against Trump. With all that cover, they didn't feel like they had to do much. In fact, the campaign thought the less the people saw of Biden, the better.

Expectations were still high for the convention, though. Reports suggested that the event would have live components from different iconic locations. Production assistance from friends in Hollywood and celebrity appearances were all in the cards. The Democrats had been planning their virtual convention for months and looked set to make the most of the change in format.

Despite having every advantage, the Democrats couldn't deliver on the high hopes they had set for the gathering. People expected glitz and glamour but got vacuous politician-speak, technical mishaps, and a very dark message. And there was something wrong with the production quality. To many, it seemed like a "Zoom call gone wrong." One GOP aide said, "We thought the Democratic Convention was going to be like Steven Spielberg mates with George Lucas. It was going to be the best thing in the history [of] civilization. It sucked, it was terrible."

Each day of the convention felt a bit like a grind, but viewership was high and the media could still be counted on to gild the lily. "Barack Obama just delivered the finest convention speech in modern history (again). Spell-binding, chilling, optimistic, beautifully written, and expertly delivered. Incredible moment," *Politico* writer Ryan Lizza enthused.[26]

While top Trump campaign aides had publicly predicted that Biden's speech on the closing night would be a dud, it was not. It was authentic and well-received. It was twenty minutes long and delivered well. He wrapped it up and finished the convention by appearing on stage outside, in front of honking cars in a parking lot.

Democrats and the media breathed a sigh of relief. Despite a general sense of disappointment with how the convention had gone, the Democrats could count their gathering a success thanks to Biden's solid performance. That alone provided a week of good coverage from a fawning press. As the *Washington Post*'s theater critic gushed, "This convention isn't just efficient. It's award-worthy television." But after Biden's speech, the media went even more over the top. "Joe Biden delivered the speech of a lifetime," wrote *Politico*.

"Really, this might be the most confident and energetic and forceful Biden we've seen this entire election cycle," said *Politico*'s Tim Alberta.

If expectations were high for the Democratic convention, they couldn't have been lower for the Republican convention. Nothing had gone well with convention planning prior to July. In fact, nothing had even been planned. Campaign manager Brad Parscale thought the RNC was planning the convention. RNC chair Ronna McDaniel had to explain that it was the campaign's job. Nothing had been done when the convention was less than two months away.

The campaign assembled a team, combining veteran Trump operatives and family members to produce the event. Lara Trump, Tony Sayegh, Hope Hicks, and Justin Clark led the way. When they built out their timetable of what needed to be done, they had just shy of seven weeks until the convention started on August 24. They were in a race against time.

Right away, the team moved to program the event against what they expected the Democrats would be doing. They knew that Democrats were good at glitz and glamour. The Democrats would have celebrities, both from Hollywood and politics. They'd have actors, the Clintons, the Obamas, and even Republicans who had turned their backs on Trump.

Thinking they'd be unable to compete with what was certainly going to be an amazing show, the Trump team decided to go with a traditional convention look. They'd have a large hall and a podium and wouldn't go head-to-head with the Democrats on a Hollywood production. Instead of lining up celebrities, the Republicans decided to turn the convention over to the forgotten men and women to whom the president had dedicated his administration. These people would explain to their fellow Americans why the president and vice president deserved four more years.

Trump's speechwriters told the team that the president loved giving State of the Union addresses. He shined in those speeches, even more than at his rallies. And so the team decided that every night would be like a State of the Union, with the bonus that the people who normally sit in the gallery and are mentioned in the president's speech would instead be incorporated into speaking roles for the program.

They went through the list of all the people whom the president had invited to previous State of the Union addresses and tried to figure out ways to incorporate them into speaking roles on the program. Trump had kept tabs on all the individuals. When they'd read off a list of potential names to him, he'd respond with personal details. "Did you know her father just died?" he asked of one potential speaker.

"He was personally invested in the people and their stories, and they were personally invested in him," Sayegh said.

Knowing that Democrats would paint a bleak picture of America, saying the country was racist, unfair, and its history shameful, the

Trump team decided to do the opposite. The convention would celebrate America and America's story, the great Americans who wrote that story in the past, and the Americans who write that story today.

In a typical convention, each night has a theme. You might have speeches built around foreign policy one night, domestic policy another, cultural issues another. Sayegh and Lara Trump came from television, in which each hour is broken up into segments called "blocks," which are listed alphabetically.

The A block is at the top of the hour. After the commercial break comes the B block, and so on and so forth. They decided to produce the convention like a weekly TV show, with blocks, and the same theme would appear on multiple nights.

Taxes and trade; foreign policy; retail economic policies like paid family leave, childcare tax credits, and retraining the American worker; social issues such as criminal justice reform and abortion; and cancel culture—these were all potent electoral issues that the team intended to hit repeatedly.

One night featured Nicholas Sandmann, a young man who had been defamed by the media after he attended a pro-life march in Washington, D.C. Using deceptive snips of videos, the media had told the nation he'd mocked and disparaged a U.S. veteran who was Native American. When the full story came out, it turned out that he had merely stood quietly while he was besieged by a group of men trying to taunt him. At the end of his convention speech, he put on a Make America Great Again hat, the one that had led the media to attack him in the first place.

To talk about gun control, the campaign brought on the McCloskeys, a St. Louis couple who had held their weapons outside their home as an unruly group of protesters crashed through their gate. The McCloskeys had been vilified by the media for defending themselves.

The idea wasn't just to animate the base, but to grow the group of people who agreed with the Trump campaign. A politician talking about gun control was much less effective than people who had a story.

Similarly, a politician talking about cancel culture was less important than Sandmann.

In perhaps the most effective speech of the convention, South Florida businessman Maximo Alvarez talked about the horrors of totalitarianism and communism. He said his family had first fled Spain for Cuba, and then Cuba for the United States.

"I'm speaking to you today because my family is done leaving places. There is nowhere left to go. I'm speaking to you today because President Trump may not always care about being polite—but all the far left cares about is power. Power for them—not for us. I'm speaking to you today because I've seen people like this before. I've seen movements like this before. I've seen ideas like this before and I'm here to tell you, we cannot let them take over our country," he said.

When planning the event, the team also understood that there was no better showman than Donald Trump. They decided to include the president in every night of the convention, and in a meaningful way. They carved out "presidential surprises," such as his meeting with a group of hostages that he had brought back home during his presidency. He had negotiated the release and rescue of more than fifty hostages from twenty-two different countries, some of whom had been held for more than a decade.

He hosted a naturalization ceremony on air, held a meeting with frontline workers responding to the COVID-19 pandemic, and went out to Fort McHenry following Vice President Mike Pence's speech, where they met with wounded soldiers who had special prosthetics enabling them to stand for the national anthem.

Senator Tim Scott of South Carolina anchored the keynote on the first night. Melania Trump's speech from the Rose Garden went well, with Kellyanne Conway helping her manage her messaging. That night Secretary of State Mike Pompeo spoke from Jerusalem, and Kentucky attorney general Daniel Cameron spoke as well. Ambassador Ric Grenell, the country's first gay cabinet member, spoke before Pence at McHenry.

Trump's decision to accept the nomination from the White House received tremendous pushback. He'd long wanted to just accept the nomination there, after all the troubles getting Charlotte or Jacksonville to host the event. In response to those who said it was inappropriate, the campaign argued that if Biden could stay in his basement all summer, certainly Trump could accept from his back yard, even if that back yard happened to be at the White House. Besides, anytime Trump went anywhere else to give a speech, he was condemned. So he would stay home.

Trump was introduced by his daughter Ivanka. But before she spoke was another powerful moment. The parents of slain hostage Kayla Mueller talked about the difference between the Obama and Trump administrations in dealing with their plight.

"What a difference a president makes.... Let me just say this, Kayla should be here. If Donald Trump had been president when Kayla was captured, she would be here today," Marsha Mueller said, standing next to her husband Carl. You could hear a pin drop among the crowd gathered at the White House waiting for President Trump to speak.

Trump gave a long and winding speech, enjoying himself and clearly not wanting the moment to end. He advanced the message of civic pride and American unity that would define his campaign. The only thing that could outdo him was the massive firework display that closed the event—a display that only received government approval moments before it happened. As attendees left the White House grounds, many were viciously attacked by leftist mobs, a demonstration of the competing visions the two parties offered.

Aides say that the convention's success turned the campaign around. The polls in August were horrible, much like they'd been in 2016. But after the convention, everyone was on message and ready to surge towards November.

◆   ◆   ◆

The convention was so important because it helped the Trump campaign break through the media narratives and make its case directly to the American people. It served as a four-day fact check on nearly four years of false media reports about the Trump administration's accomplishments. Throughout the summer Biden was barely making public appearances, so the Biden team used the media to campaign for him. One of their tried-and-true methods was to continue with the publishing of information operations, news stories based on information from anonymous intelligence officials to create a false narrative. When it came to covering Trump, there was no story too outlandish for the media to run with, much less dare to question.

In warfare, information operations and influence operations frequently include the dissemination of propaganda in pursuit of a competitive advantage over an opponent. In campaign warfare, it's no different. One of the key structural advantages the Democratic Party has over Republicans is near-complete control of the media.

The media have long been biased in favor of Democratic politicians and policy proposals, but prior to the 2016 election, a dam broke. In a front-page *New York Times* piece on August 7, 2016, headlined "The Challenge Trump Poses to Objectivity," media reporter Jim Rutenberg said that normal journalistic standards don't apply to Trump and that reporters must be oppositional.[27]

By 2020, the media were practically campaigning for Joe Biden, acting as the primary messaging vehicle for the candidate—a level of collusion between the media and a candidate never seen before, even during the Obama era.

The media's all-out support for Biden was the logical conclusion of their coverage of the Trump presidency. For years, the media took part in an information operation that had originally been financed by Hillary Clinton's campaign and the Democratic National Committee. The information operation alleged that Trump was a tool of Russia and was colluding with the adversary to steal the 2016 election and threaten national security.[28] The bulk of the operation was the creation of the fraudulent "dossier" alleging any manner of unsavory things about President Trump, including a salacious story about Trump's hiring prostitutes to micturate on a bed previously used by President Obama in Moscow, as well as corrupt financial dealings.[29]

To help spread the lie, the groups working on the false story used anonymous sources who either currently or formerly worked in the U.S. intelligence apparatus to strongly suggest that the story was true. Intelligence operatives, who almost certainly knew that the dossier was laughable, instead treated it like it was serious. They briefed it to President Barack Obama and President-Elect Donald Trump, and then leaked the briefing on the dossier to CNN.[30] That made the dossier legitimate in the eyes of the media, who proceeded to run wild with its claims without being able to verify any of them.

It worked like a charm. For years, lies about Trump and Russia dominated the American news environment. The *New York Times* and *Washington Post* were awarded Pulitzer Prizes for stories suggesting that the leader of the country was in the employ of Vladimir Putin.[31] The damage to the Republican Party and its political officials was astronomical. They were crushed in the mid-term elections of 2018, losing more than forty House seats.[32] And the political operation was so effective that many of the weaker Republicans in the Senate were bullied into believing the lie and lobbied to protect invasive probes that ground the president's serious work of enacting his agenda to a halt.

"The information they peddle is often sensational. It can also be impossible to verify or be untrue," Barry Meier, author of *Spooked: The Trump Dossier, Black Cube and the Rise of Private Spies*, said of these information operations.[33]

The propaganda operation had succeeded in limiting Trump's ability to work, hire or maintain good staff, get cooperation with Congress, and assert authority over executive branch bureaucrats, and it had hurt his approval ratings heading into re-election.

When it turned out that the stories about Trump's colluding with Russia were lies, it should have been the press scandal of the century. Pulitzers were awarded for regurgitating falsehoods from political operatives who knowingly lied to reporters. But rather than confront their culpability in misleading the public, the media embraced one new information operation after another.

In late June 2020, three *New York Times* reporters wrote an explosive story: "American intelligence officials have concluded that a Russian military intelligence unit secretly offered bounties to Taliban-linked militants for killing coalition forces in Afghanistan—including targeting American troops—amid the peace talks to end the long-running war there, according to officials briefed on the matter."[34]

This allegedly airtight intelligence was "briefed to President Trump," and "officials" came up with ideas for potential responses, including a diplomatic complaint and sanctions, but the White House had yet to authorize anything.[35] The intelligence, the reporters claimed, had been shared with the British government.[36]

The anonymous leakers of the information, the reporters claimed, were certain that "Russian operatives" offered and paid bounties, but they had "greater uncertainty" about who authorized the plan.[37] The reporters included some speculation about why such a bounty operation would be done. There was no speculation about the motivation of the leaking "officials,"[38] but the timing of the report seemed designed to damage Trump, who had just announced a plan to fulfill his 2016 campaign promise to bring the troops home from Afghanistan.

It is worth noting that the three *New York Times* reporters—Charlie Savage, Eric Schmitt, and Michael Schwirtz—also played key roles in disseminating the Russia collusion hoax, in which anonymous intelligence officials worked with co-conspirators in the media for years to put out a false and defamatory narrative that President Donald Trump had colluded with Russia to steal the 2016 election or was otherwise compromised.[39]

Literally nothing about the political media's use of anonymous sources to spread republic-damaging disinformation in recent years should have led anyone to treat further anonymously sourced reports with any deference. Yet the entire corporate media establishment immediately circulated the story and used it to suggest Trump's advocating for a withdrawal from Afghanistan was further evidence that he was an agent of Russian president Vladimir Putin. The story dominated cable news over the weekend and into the following week.[40]

Republicans who supported continuing the war in Afghanistan indefinitely, even though it had been going on for nineteen years at that point, expressed grave concern about the report's allegations. Republican representative Liz Cheney, whose father had authoritatively claimed in August 2002 there was "no doubt" Iraq had weapons of mass destruction, demanded White House action.[41] Cheney's work against Trump would become more public after his election loss, but she was known in Washington, D.C., for working to undermine him from her position of Republican leadership in the House of Representatives.

It turned out that key details of the story were disputed by on-the-record sources. When the White House press secretary said neither Trump nor Vice President Mike Pence had even been briefed on this intelligence, reporters tried a new line of attack.

"This raises the obvious and very serious question: The US had intelligence that Russia was paying militants to kill US & allied troops, and officials decided NOT to tell the president or VP about it?" intoned NBC News's Josh Lederman.[42]

Director of National Intelligence John Ratcliffe added, "I have confirmed that neither the President nor the Vice President were ever briefed on any intelligence alleged by the New York Times in its reporting yesterday. The White House statement addressing this issue earlier today, which denied such a briefing occurred, was accurate. The New York Times reporting, and all other subsequent news reports about such an alleged briefing, are inaccurate."[43]

White House Director of Strategic Communications Alyssa Farah disputed that the intelligence was as airtight as the *New York Times* reporters had claimed, based on their anonymous and unaccountable sources: "POTUS wasn't briefed on the reports related to Afghanistan because there is no consensus within the intelligence community on the allegations at this point. The veracity of the underlying allegations continues to be evaluated."[44]

The truth of the matter was far murkier than journalists cared to let on. One of the many intelligence agencies in the government had heard from a detainee about the alleged bounties. But the other sixteen intelligence agencies didn't have the same confidence in the story that the original agency did, as intel gathered from human sources under duress is notoriously unreliable.[45] A detainee might be in a position to know something, but that doesn't mean he is telling the truth.

Uncritically spreading information like this can have deadly consequences. Much of the case for the Iraq War was based on the Bush administration's claim that Saddam Hussein possessed weapons of mass destruction. When the United States declared an end to the war late in 2011, more than 4,400 American military members had been killed and nearly 32,000 wounded. No weapons of mass destruction had been found.

It's one of the most significant and catastrophic intelligence errors in U.S. history. A bipartisan commission found that U.S. intelligence agencies "seriously misjudged" Iraq's weapons program because of their "heavy reliance on a human source—codenamed 'Curveball'—whose information later proved to be unreliable."[46] The commission wrote, "Even more misleading was the river of intelligence that flowed from the CIA to top policymakers over long periods of time—in the President's Daily Brief (PDB)" and other reports that were "more alarmist" and "less nuanced."[47]

Curveball was Germany's codename for Rafid Ahmed Alwan al-Janabi, an Iraqi defector who claimed to have built mobile weapons laboratories. President George W. Bush highlighted the claims in his 2003 State of the Union address.[48]

Secretary of State Colin Powell's speech to the United Nations on February 5, 2003, relied heavily on Curveball's claims. "My colleagues, every statement I make today is backed up by sources, solid sources.

These are not assertions. What we're giving you are facts and conclusions based on solid intelligence. I will cite some examples, and these are from human sources."[49]

Powell went on to describe Janabi's claims at length, concluding, "This defector is currently hiding in another country with the certain knowledge that Saddam Hussein will kill him if he finds him. His eyewitness account of these mobile production facilities has been corroborated by other sources."[50]

Years later, Curveball admitted he had completely fabricated his claims out of a desire to oust Saddam Hussein from power.[51]

In this case, while the intelligence agencies all agreed to investigate and look out for corroborating information, they didn't feel it was credible enough to act on. They prepared a few possible responses, but that was the end.

In any case, following the *New York Times* report, other media outlets ran with stories on the matter also based on anonymous sources. Frequently, this was described as "independent confirmation."[52]

As the story spiraled out of control, Trump called it "fake news" and a "[h]oax started to slander me & the Republican Party." He tweeted, "Probably just another phony Times hit job, just like their failed Russia Hoax. Who is their 'source'?"[53]

It was a good question. Anonymous sources can't "confirm" anything for a reader on account of being anonymous. And because they're anonymous, there is no way to tell if one media outlets' sources are independent from another's. In the Russia collusion propaganda operation, for example, anonymous sources cited to confirm a story for one news outlet were often the same source of the initial story for another.[54] Needless to say, asking the same person to repeat himself can hardly count as "confirmation."

Reporters certainly knew to be on the lookout for this and should have been careful when dealing with anonymous sources. Yet anonymous sources were all they had in their many stories.

The goal of those pushing the story may have been to fight the Trump administration's efforts to end the nineteen-year-war in Afghanistan, damage international relations, distract from the Russia collusion hoax currently under investigation, or any number of other reasons. Sometimes leaks are about internal bureaucratic wars involving people who don't care about the damage their leaking caused. One goal seemed to be to paint Trump as someone who did not care about American soldiers.

Most exasperatingly, the media and other partisans seemed eager to use the Afghan bounties story to run back into the comforting arms of the Russia collusion hoax they had perpetrated against the country for years.

CNN's Jake Tapper, for example, asked Trump's former national security advisor John Bolton, "Do you think it's possible that Putin has information on President Trump?"[55] The *New York Times* reporters also dredged up the debunked Russia collusion theories.[56] And, not coincidentally, Speaker of the House Nancy Pelosi spent several minutes pushing the debunked Russiagate conspiracy theory in an interview with ABC News's George Stephanopoulos.[57]

"With him, all roads lead to Putin. I don't know what the Russians have on the president politically, personally, financially, or whatever it is. But he wants to ignore, he wants to bring [Russia] back into the G8 despite the annexation of Crimea and the invasion of Ukraine...despite what they yielded to him in Syria, despite his intervention into our elections which is well documented by our intelligence community and despite possibly this allegation which we should have been briefed on," Pelosi said.[58]

Pelosi's pushing of the conspiracy theory met virtually no pushback from the former press secretary to President Bill Clinton. In fact, there was no accountability for any of the actors who spread the false and damaging conspiracy theory about Russia. None of the criminal leakers were ever held accountable. Neither were the reporters who conspired with them to harm the country, damage the Trump administration, hurt foreign relations, and destroy the lives of conservatives who allied them-selves with Trump.

The media were invested in this story not because they believed it was true, but because they thought it was helping Biden's campaign. In September, Joe Biden held a "Veterans Roundtable" campaign event in Tampa, Florida, where the focus was on making the Russian bounties story a political liability for Trump.[59] The night before the event, the Biden campaign's director of rapid response was on Twitter, unloading on Trump for "giving Russia a pass for putting bounties on the heads of American service members."[60]

The whole episode was an appalling example of how the media advances disingenuous campaign talking points with no pushback, more interested in acting as a partisan lapdog than in reporting the truth. Make no mistake: the Russian bounties story was almost certainly a coordinated misinformation operation. It eventually came out that Democrats on the House Intelligence Committee were briefed on reports of Russian bounties, however reliable those reports may have been, in February.[61] It's probably not a coincidence that the Intelligence Committee is led by Representative Adam Schiff, who was already notorious for leaking false stories damaging Trump to the press.[62]

And to add insult to injury, the press was fully comfortable with admitting the truth once Biden had secured his victory. In April 2021, a senior Biden official told reporters the administration had "low to moderate confidence" in the intelligence behind the reports of Russian bounties.[63] The media didn't throw a fit, as they had when Trump officials said the same thing; they accepted the Biden administration's characterization, proud that they could help their man attain the nation's highest office.

◆   ◆   ◆

The fake Afghan bounty story was just the first part of the campaign operation to make Trump seem like he didn't care about the troops.

Despite ludicrous claims during the 2016 campaign that Trump would lead the world into nuclear annihilation, he was instead creating peace. Because of the success of his foreign policy, there weren't many ways to go after Trump and the military. The Trump administration had negotiated a series of historic peace deals in the Middle East and was fighting a powerful military industrial complex to end America's longest war in Afghanistan.[64]

So the media ran another fake news story about dead soldiers. *The Atlantic*'s editor in chief, Jeffrey Goldberg, pushed out an "exclusive" story based entirely on anonymous sources alleging that "[w]hen President Donald Trump canceled a visit to the Aisne-Marne American Cemetery near Paris in 2018, he blamed rain for the last-minute decision, saying that 'the helicopter couldn't fly' and that the Secret Service wouldn't drive him there. Neither claim was true."[65]

In fact, both claims were true. A visit by helicopter was deemed unsafe by military officials because of low cloud cover, and so was a drive through crowded Paris streets and the winding country roads from Paris to the site of the cemetery about fifty miles outside of the city.[66]

Goldberg claimed that "four people with firsthand knowledge of the discussion that day" said "Trump rejected the idea of the visit because he feared his hair would become disheveled in the rain, and because he did not believe it important to honor American war dead."[67]

The article used utterly preposterous quotes and claimed they were said by the president, such as, "Why should I go to that cemetery? It's filled with losers."[68]

Trump, well known for enjoying the pomp and circumstance of military visits, toured the Suresnes American Cemetery and Memorial, a World War I cemetery, the next day.[69]

While the anonymous sources, if they existed, made outlandish claims, actual sources who were part of the discussion spoke on the record.[70]

Former White House press secretary Sarah Huckabee Sanders said the story was "BS," adding, "I was actually there and one of the people part of the discussion—this never happened."[71] Outspoken Trump critic John Bolton had already written in his book about how weather had grounded the helicopter and that it was a "straightforward decision to cancel the visit."[72] He was with Trump on his visit to France as his national security advisor.

Randolph "Tex" Alles, who was serving as director of the United States Secret Service at the time of the Paris trip, confirmed the visit to the Aisne-Marne cemetery "was definitely canceled due to weather for HMX-1. Driving was not a possibility due to Paris traffic. I was in Paris on the POTUS trip when it happened and consulted with the head of the Presidential Protective Division," he said.[73]

In addition to more than twenty on-the-record accounts from people who witnessed or were involved in the decision to cancel the visit, there were weather reports and government emails that completely eviscerated Goldberg's tale.[74]

Nevertheless, a flurry of other reporters claimed they had "confirmed" the reporting with...anonymous sources.

Goldberg, who had been on the receiving end of serious criticism for bad reporting that helped launch the Iraq War, never provided a scintilla of evidence to buttress his claims. And when pressed, he botched more claims.[75] He said French president Emmanuel Macron and German chancellor Angela Merkel had made it to the cemetery that day without a problem.[76] In fact, they hadn't. They had visited a non-American site in a different part of the country, and their security concerns were much lower than those for the United States president.[77]

When confronted with Bolton's words, Goldberg said, "I'm sure all of those things are true," and yet insisted his story was somehow also true.[78]

Trump seemed pained upon hearing the allegation, saying, "I would be willing to swear on anything that I never said that about our fallen heroes. There is nobody that respects them more. It's a horrible, horrible thing. No animal, nobody—what animal would say such a thing?"[79]

Despite the fact that there was no evidence the story was true, the Biden campaign quickly put out an ad showing pictures of the markers at Aisne-Marne with the made-up Trump quotes on top of them.[80]

"Why should I go to that cemetery? It's filled with losers," the script on the ad read over images of Aisne-Marne. "Suckers," read one quote, with the attribution line reading, "President Donald J. Trump on fallen Marines."[81]

Of all the unsubstantiated claims based on anonymous sources that he'd had to deal with, Trump said in a May 2021 conversation at his Mar-a-Lago home that the Aisne-Marne story was the worst. "That was the story that angered me the most. Think of it. They said I was in Paris in front of generals and soldiers saying these guys were suckers and losers? It was made up by *The Atlantic* and it was proven to be," he said, citing the contemporary witnesses who strongly disputed it.

He reminisced about when he first heard of the unsubstantiated story, coming out of a rally, saying, "[T]hey came out of the blue with this. I said, 'That's crazy.'"

"Of all the things that were said—and they were mostly lies—that one was the most egregious. And it was the most unfair. I demanded a retraction," he said, clearly still bothered by the unsubstantiated allegations.

Trump campaign lawyers took the rare step of demanding the Biden campaign yank their false ad based on Goldberg's unsubstantiated claims.[82]

"We sent them a legal letter. I've never done that during a campaign because during a campaign, a lot of things are said," he said. "It was the most unfair. I demanded a retraction."

Visibly pained, he said that if he'd ever said anything like that in front of members of the military, there would have been a fight. "Think of it. I'm standing there with generals and people in the military. Just from a commonsense standpoint, we're all smart people," he said.

"If I said that in front of generals, I would say, despite the fact that I'm president of the United States, there would be fisticuffs. You understand that?" he said. As further proof it never happened, he said that if he had said such a thing, "within one hour, it would have been broadcast and not years later."

There was speculation that the story had been planted by his chief of staff at the time, General John Kelly, but Trump didn't think so, even with their differences. He believed that stories with anonymous sources don't have a real source about 80 percent of the time. "I don't think they had a source. I think that they made it up," he said.

Not many days went by during the Trump administration without the major corporate media's running information operations against the president. The story of "Anonymous" makes a particularly instructive example, if only for how glaring it was.

Two years after the *New York Times* published an op-ed from what it described as an anonymous, principled conservative "senior administration official," it turned out to have been written by a low-level bureaucrat who later worked for tech giant Google and gave money to far-left Democrats.[83]

Miles Taylor revealed he was the author of the much-hyped op-ed headlined "I Am Part of the Resistance inside the Trump Administration." In the op-ed, he claimed to secretly work to thwart Trump's policy goals as the elected president of the United States.[84]

While constitutional scholars worried about implications of such unaccountable thwarting of the will of the people, most media focused instead on identifying "Anonymous." The *New York Times* assured readers that when it said "senior administration official," it meant someone "in the upper echelon of an administration."[85]

People took the *New York Times*'s claim that the anonymous writer was in the upper echelon of an administration very seriously. CNN published a column, "13 People Who Might Be the Author of the New York Times Op-Ed,"[86] that speculated about actual senior administration officials, such as Don McGahn, Dan Coats, Kellyanne Conway, Kirstjen Nielsen, John Kelly, Jeff Sessions, Fiona Hill, James Mattis, and Nikki Haley. CNN's Chris Cillizza also suggested it might even be Trump's wife Melania, his son-in-law Jared Kushner, or his daughter Ivanka.[87]

Cillizza was convinced that the august *New York Times* wouldn't risk its credibility to let an insignificant federal turnspit attack Trump. "They aren't publishing an anonymous op-ed from just anyone in the Trump administration," he said. "They especially aren't publishing one that alleges a near-coup." He added, "If some midlevel bureaucrat in the Trump administration comes to the *Times*—or has an intermediary reach out to the *Times*—asking to write a piece like this one without their name attached to it, the answer would be an immediate 'no.'"[88]

He continued, confident in the *Times*'s judgment. "Given all of that, it's telling that the Times was willing to extend the cloak of anonymity to this author—especially, again, because of the stakes and the target. This is not a decision made lightly. That the decision was made to publish it should tell you that this isn't some disgruntled mid-to-upper manager buried in the bureaucracy," he said.[89] "This is a genuine high-ranking official. A name most people who follow politics—and maybe some who don't—would recognize. The Times simply wouldn't do what it did for anything short of a major figure in Trump world."[90]

But it turned out the paper was, in fact, meretricious enough to sacrifice its institutional reputation for a low-level political appointee with an anti-Trump axe to grind. Taylor had been billed as "chief of staff at the Department of Homeland Security," but he didn't have even that position when he wrote the op-ed and was described as a senior administration official.[91]

Even if you take a very generous reading of the term "senior administration official," the Department of Homeland Security actually listed sixty-four individuals it considered "senior" at the department on the day the op-ed was published.[92] Taylor was not one of them. He was described as a policy advisor, not anything close to a senior administration official.[93]

Taylor went on to write a book as Anonymous, and to "come out" as a Trump-hating Joe Biden supporter in the summer of 2020, with the help of CNN and the *Washington Post*.[94] CNN even hired Taylor as a contributor, and the revelation of his identity still landed with a dud.[95]

While Taylor attempted to position himself as a principled conservative, he left the administration to work for Google. His former boss at the Department of Homeland Security said that if Taylor ever opposed anything about the Trump administration, it was news to his colleagues.[96]

"Having worked with Mr. Taylor on the President's immigration and counter-terrorism policy agenda, I can attest that [Miles Taylor] never vocalized disagreement with the President's policies—and in fact expressed strong support," Acting Secretary Chad Wolf said in a statement.[97]

That's a problem for Taylor, since BuzzFeed noted that after the op-ed was published, he became the chief of staff who sold the administration's "child separation policy"—a very controversial policy on the left—and never publicly or privately disagreed with it, as Wolf noted.[98]

Taylor was neither a senior administration official nor a principled conservative. He was just a willing political operative capable of lying, as he did on air when asked by Anderson Cooper if he was "Anonymous." "I wear a mask for two things, Anderson. Halloween and pandemics. So, no," Taylor said.[99]

If the *New York Times* was willing to lie about how high-level its anonymous source was for its very high-profile September 2018 information operation, what lies was it willing to tell about all the other anonymous sources it used? And if this is how one of America's biggest newsrooms operates, readers are right to ask how much other papers and media outlets were willing to lie in support of their anti-Republican narratives.

"Who's worse, the *Washington Post* or the *New York Times*, because that's been my most interesting question. You can't get worse than either, but who's the worst?" Trump liked to ask.

The media didn't just attack Trump personally; they floated convoluted conspiracy theories that were embraced by the highest levels of

Democrats. A particularly bizarre one stated that the Trump administration had declared war on the post office in order to throw the election in his favor. Pictures that showed mailboxes being moved and mail trucks being repaired went viral—definitive proof that the Trump administration was undermining the U.S. Postal Service for the president's own electoral gain.

"They're going around literally with tractor trailers picking up mailboxes. You oughta go online and check out what they're doing in Oregon. I mean, it's bizarre!" Biden said at a virtual fundraiser.[100]

As far as conspiracies go, this one was especially stupid. A total of thirty mailboxes had been removed in Portland and Eugene, Oregon. They were all located in places where the post office says there were multiple mailboxes.[101] The post office said that removing boxes is standard procedure when they become rusted, require paint, get vandalized, or simply need to be replaced.[102] Removing a few mailboxes in a state where every vote has been cast by mail for decades, a state Trump lost by eleven points in 2016 and was certain to lose again, was hardly going to swing the election.

Further, the volume of mail has been declining for decades, and that necessitates removing mailboxes.[103] In 2016, while Joe Biden was vice president, the United States Postal Service announced it had removed 14,000 mailboxes around the country in the previous five years.[104] But even with the USPS's downsizing, there was no reason to believe it would be a problem. In 2019, the USPS delivered an average of 471 million pieces of mail a day.[105] Even if every one of America's 155 million voters cast their ballot by mail, the post office wouldn't miss a beat.

But to leading Democrats, random photos of a few mailboxes being moved was evidence of an elaborate plan to suppress mail-in voting.

Obama said of what he described as "attempts to undermine the election" that the Postal Service "can't be collateral damage for an administration more concerned with suppressing the vote than suppressing a virus."[106]

Nancy Pelosi said that the Postmaster General was "an accomplice in the President's effort to cheat the election and manipulate the Postal Service to deny eligible voters access to the ballot in pursuit of his own re-election."[107]

Even Taylor Swift talked about "Trump's calculated dismantling of USPS," which she said proved that "he's chosen to blatantly cheat."[108]

The Lincoln Project's Rick Wilson said, "The biggest investigative story of this election—on par with Watergate—will be the reporter who run downs [sic] the White House and Trump campaign connection to the USPS shutdown. This is just too sweeping and organized to just be some random play."[109]

Jane Mayer, a writer at the *New Yorker* best known for white-washing leftist conspiracy theories, said that "Trump's assault on the postal service" was not just a "rogue move" but part of a calculated operation involving Mitch McConnell, too.[110]

Even Montana senator Jon Tester got in on the act, getting the USPS to cease maintenance operations in his state.[111]

While Twitter had been censoring Trump's tweets raising concerns about mail-in voting, astonishingly none of the tweets spreading the conspiracy theories about the Postal Service were censored.[112] Indeed, the entire justification for censoring Trump was that making unverifiable claims about election security undermined public confidence in the democratic process. Yet, Democratic politicians from Joe Biden on down made elaborate and easily debunked claims about the post office—and this was not deemed misinformation that had to be stopped, even as it was spread far and wide.

And worse, while there were any number of reasonable concerns about voting by mail, there was never really a question about whether the volume of mail could be handled appropriately by the Postal Service. The concern about universal mail-in balloting was that ballots would be sent to people and places they shouldn't be, where anyone could return a ballot and where it was impossible to guarantee integrity.

It was one of the dozens of fake news stories that the media ran to hamstring the Trump campaign and tilt the election in Biden's favor. And with the assistance of Big Tech, the media could exert more influence on censoring conservative opinion than ever.

CHAPTER SIX

Stifling Debates

I t was a scene straight out of a movie.

President Trump was walking to Air Force One, having just finished a ninety-minute rally in Bemidji, Minnesota, on September 18. His oft-repeated campaign event playlist was on the Village People's "Y.M.C.A." The reporters were shouting something about "RBG" at him.[1]

The Supreme Court had just announced that Associate Justice Ruth Bader Ginsburg, the oldest member of the court, had died that evening of complications from metastatic pancreatic cancer. She was eighty-seven.

The liberal justice had announced in July she was being treated for cancer again. She'd previously had colorectal cancer in 1999 and pancreatic cancer in 2009, and she had received a heart stent in her right coronary artery. In 2018, she was hospitalized for fracturing three ribs, and when she was being treated for that, her doctors found cancerous nodules in her left lung. She had surgery to remove them.

Court watchers had been wondering for years how long she would make it. While they were pretty sure this last cancer announcement would be her final, they'd made the mistake of prematurely preparing for her departure previously.

"Ruth Bader Ginsburg has died," a reporter told the president as he stood under the wing of Air Force One.[2]

"She just died? Wow. I didn't know that. She led an amazing life. What else can you say? She was an amazing woman, whether you agree or not. She was an amazing woman who led an amazing life. I'm actually sad to hear that. I am saddened to hear that."[3]

Trump's staff had contemplated having someone notify him about her death during the rally, but quickly decided against it, worried about how the crowd might react to the news of the liberal icon's death. By the time Trump got around to responding to the media questions about RBG, the playlist had moved on to the next song. Elton John's somber and uplifting "Tiny Dancer" played in the background as a slight breeze wafted across the tarmac.

The scene had a cinematic quality to it, pitch-perfect for lowering the temperature at the outset of what was predicted to be an apocalyptic confirmation process for the justice replacing RBG.

President Trump was elected in 2016 thanks in part to his promise to nominate conservative justices to the Supreme Court. To counter accusations that he wasn't sufficiently conservative, Trump drafted a list of judges approved of by leaders in the conservative legal movement, promising to nominate justices from that list. Since becoming president, Trump had updated that list a few times.[4]

Now, in 2020, just weeks before Election Day, Trump was faced with a third confirmation fight. His previous two had been notably bloody. Early in 2017, Democrats responded to his nomination of Neil Gorsuch to fill the vacated Antonin Scalia seat by refusing to consider the nomination. Their behavior gave Senate Majority Leader Mitch McConnell the fuel he needed to end the filibuster on Supreme Court nominations. The previous Senate majority leader, Democrat Harry Reid, had led Democrats to end the filibuster for all other federal judicial nominees and other executive office appointments.[5]

When a second vacancy on the court arose, Trump's nomination of Brett Kavanaugh to fill Anthony Kennedy's seat threatened to split the country in half. Democrats in Congress and the media waged a campaign of personal destruction against a man who had already passed multiple background checks and who boasted a sterling reputation. Democrats upheld the eleventh-hour testimony of Christine Blasey Ford, who accused the judge of sexually assaulting her over thirty years before, when they were both teenagers. She offered no substantiation for the allegation and couldn't even remember the date or location of where the purported assault had taken place. Every one of the four witnesses Blasey Ford said were present at the party where the assault had happened declined to substantiate her story, including her lifelong female friend and partisan Democrat, Leland Keyser.

Nonetheless, Senate Democrats and the media encouraged wild speculation that Kavanaugh was a monster. This culminated in NBC's airing an interview with a woman who accused Kavanaugh of drugging multiple women and participating in gang rapes, despite the fact that the woman kept changing her story and had a long history of restraining orders and other legal troubles that put her credibility into question.[6]

Two years later, Republicans were still angry about how shamelessly Democrats and the media had treated their nominee. Worse yet, no one had been held accountable, despite multiple criminal referrals for some of the people who had made up the lies about him.[7]

Upon Ruth Bader Ginsburg's death, Trump already knew whom he was going to nominate: Judge Amy Coney Barrett of the Seventh Circuit Court of Appeals. Trump had strongly considered nominating her when Kennedy stepped down, but he was headed off at the pass by Senators Lisa Murkowski of Alaska and Susan Collins of Maine. They told him they wouldn't support her nomination.

At that time, the Republicans barely had control of the Senate and couldn't afford to lose two votes. Thanks in part to the Kavanaugh battle, Republicans had since gained seats in the Senate, so they didn't need those votes this time around.

Upon Ginsburg's death, McConnell had told his members not to say anything. But Susan Collins had already told a *New York Times* reporter a month prior to Ginsburg's death that it was too close to the election to have a confirmation process. "I think that's too close. I really do."[8] Democrats had specifically targeted Collins for being the deciding vote on Kavanaugh's nomination. The polls all showed Collins was running behind her well-funded challenger in the impending election, and she was fighting for her electoral future. Collins said she'd vote against any nominee, no matter who it was.[9]

Everyone knowledgeable had predicted that if the replacing of moderate Kennedy with moderately conservative Kavanaugh had been a death match, certainly the replacing of liberal icon Ginsburg with a Trump appointee would be almost unimaginably worse.

Instead, the confirmation was surprisingly calm.

While the White House did its due diligence and considered Barbara Lagoa of the Eleventh Circuit and several other judges as potential replacements for RBG, it was always Barrett's race to lose.

When she flew out to meet with Trump a couple of days after Ginsburg died, she was told to start preparing for the confirmation process.

Usually, the media stake out the homes of all the contenders for a Supreme Court nomination. All movement is strictly monitored by the press for indications of who will be nominated. The Kavanaugh family had to hide luggage in a neighbor's treehouse to be retrieved later by a third party and escape out their back yard.[10] But Barrett, who has seven children with her husband Jesse, lived in a regular neighborhood in South Bend. There would be no way to subtly get seven children of ages ranging from eight to nineteen years old out to D.C. for the announcement of her nomination. They didn't even try. They just walked out the front door, cameras rolling.

Barrett's nomination was announced at a Rose Garden ceremony that Saturday, September 26, in front of about 150 people.[11]

The media immediately declared the event dangerous, returning to their on-again, off-again concern about crowds and COVID-19. And several people who had been at the event later tested positive, though it was unclear if the event had led to their diagnosis. Dr. Anthony Fauci claimed weeks later that it was a "superspreader event."[12]

Senator Mike Lee of Utah was the first to announce his positive test.[13] Democrats hoped it might delay or derail the confirmation process, but it didn't. It helped that Barrett had previously contracted and recovered from COVID-19, so she emerged from the event with no real worry that she had contracted the virus. The media, which had zealously run the campaign against Kavanaugh by publishing dubious, unsubstantiated, and increasingly ridiculous claims of impropriety, tried to go after Barrett repeatedly, but nothing took off.[14]

Articles that so much as referenced her children were poorly received, including one that tried to blame two completely unrelated COVID cases at her children's school on the Barrett children.[15] Another *New York Times* story examined details of the Barretts' adoption of two children from Haiti. The story found nothing improper, but the story raised eyebrows, since the paper was clearly on a fishing expedition to use her children against her.[16]

Media darling Ibram X. Kendi, who had received millions in corporate largesse for his disingenuous "anti-racism" efforts, called her a "white colonizer" for having a multi-racial family.[17] Conservative pundits retorted that Barrett had more black children than Ginsburg had ever had black law clerks. They further noted that RBG had been dodging accusations of racism ever since she defended legal abortion as reducing "populations that we don't want to have too many of" in an interview with the *New York Times* in 2009.

The confirmation hearings were also fairly calm. The media's nascent attempts to turn the process into scandal fell on deaf ears. The Barrett confirmation was notable for how normal it was by any standard, let alone the standards that the Kavanaugh confirmation had set.

When Barrett cited judges, cases, and laws during the second day of her confirmation hearings, she did it all from memory. Senator John Cornyn asked her what notes she was working from, and she held up the blank notepad that sat in front of her. She was widely viewed as extremely intelligent and prepared.[18]

It was a testament to how judicial confirmations should proceed. What a surprise, given the timing and the political climate.

Senate Democrats had already been burned by attacks on Barrett. When she had been nominated to the Seventh Circuit in 2017, Senator Dianne Feinstein of California had grilled Barrett on her strongly held religious views, suggesting that they would overwhelm her principles when it came to interpreting statutes and the law. "The dogma lives loudly within you," she told Barrett. The clear suggestion was that being religious was a disqualifier for being a federal judge, and regular Americans were outraged. The comment went viral, with retailers selling mugs with the slogan, and religious youth groups printing up T-shirts that took the insult as an aspiration.[19]

The Barrett nomination was noteworthy for its lack of foul play. Perhaps Democrats understood that Republicans incensed by the Kavanaugh show trials would not cave to their theatrics. The Republicans offered the Democrats no weak link to pressure and break. Their resolve prevented the Democrats from acting out of line.

That in itself contains an important lesson for Republicans, who faced blistering attacks from all sides over the course of President Trump's re-election bid. The dirty tricks and foul play that characterized the Democrats' behavior in the Kavanaugh hearing and in the 2020 election were enabled by Republican weakness. Democrats acted like toddlers because they knew their tantrums might sway a naïve Republican who craved their love.

Democrats act out in the hopes of creating enough controversy they can peel off a small handful of skittish Republicans to make their political position seem bipartisan, giving Democrats a tactical advantage. When the GOP stays united, such antics backfire, and they're forced to retreat. Democratic leaders likely made a calculated decision that they wanted to win the presidency more than they wanted to go on an ill-fated mission to stop a Supreme Court nominee they didn't have the cards to stop. It would have been political suicide for Senate Republicans not to confirm Barrett, and that fact had as much as anything to do with why Democrats pulled their punches.

In the end, Barrett was confirmed without incident, eight days before Election Day. Even Murkowski, who had once told Trump she wouldn't vote for Barrett, did so. The vote was partisan, with not even so-called moderate Democrats voting to confirm the well-respected judge. But it was still civil. ACB had replaced RBG.

◆   ◆   ◆

If managing a successful Supreme Court nomination weren't enough for the White House, the first presidential debate was just a few days after Amy Coney Barrett's Rose Garden ceremony.

Since 1988, the Commission on Presidential Debates, a nonprofit established under the joint sponsorship of the Republican and Democratic political parties, has sponsored and produced every presidential debate.[20]

In October 2019, the commission announced that it would host four debates, three presidential and one vice presidential. Trump advisors sat down with the commission that December, concerned about the commission's bias against Republicans and Trump in particular. They threatened to not take part in debates with the commission, on account of a history of bias.[21]

The debate commission used journalists as moderators, which usually, but not always, meant that Democrats had an advantage, given the extreme bias of most journalists.

In recent elections, the prime example that rankled Republicans was the second debate between President Obama and Massachusetts governor Mitt Romney in 2012. CNN's Candy Crowley repeatedly interrupted Romney and refused to allow him to answer claims made by the sitting president. When Romney said it took President Obama fourteen days before he called the attack in Benghazi an act of terror, Crowley claimed Obama had actually done so the next day in the Rose Garden.[22] In fact, Crowley was wrong. While Obama had obliquely referenced acts of terror in his remarks that day, his administration spent the next few weeks publicly blaming the attack on the U.S. consulate on a YouTube video made by an American, a dishonest attempt to shirk responsibility for a major terror attack less than two months before the election.[23]

While Republicans, including Trump, frequently performed well in debates, they often claimed that they had to battle the moderators as well as their opponents. The Candy Crowley case was instructive: Even if Crowley had been factually correct (which she wasn't), was it the place of the moderator to defend a candidate?

In December 2019, in response to reports he was frustrated with the debate commission, Trump said on Twitter that the commission was "stacked with Trump Haters & Never Trumpers" and "very biased."[24]

The Trump campaign was also disappointed that the first debate wasn't scheduled to occur until late September, despite the fact that Democrats had used COVID-19 to open mail-in balloting as early as September 4.[25] There was the prospect that millions of voters would cast ballots before seeing the two candidates, a prospect the Trump campaign very much opposed. And so they pressed the bipartisan commission to add a fourth debate earlier in the cycle, so that mail-in voters could hear the candidates debate before they voted.

"How can voters be sending in Ballots starting, in some cases, one month before the First Presidential Debate. Move the First Debate up," Trump tweeted. "A debate, to me, is a Public Service. Joe Biden and I owe it to the American People!"[26]

The commission flatly refused, saying that the dates for the debates were well known and that voters could just wait to send their ballots.[27]

To Trump's request that the debate be moderated by someone from a list of journalists less liberal than the type usually asked to host debates, the commission said it would exercise "great care, as always, to ensure that the selected moderators are qualified and fair." In other words, the commission politely refused Trump's request.

Fox News's Chris Wallace would host the first debate in Cleveland, which meant that three septuagenarians were on the stage that night.

Both candidates came out swinging. If Trump had a good line, Biden would retort, "Would you shut up, man?" or "Keep yappin', man."[28] Both candidates did an excellent job at tearing each other down, but Trump in particular missed opportunities to talk about his agenda and record.

Wallace also confronted Trump about his remarks numerous times and played defense for Biden, a decision that contributed to the debate's spiraling out of control.[29] When Biden said of a question he was supposed to answer, "I can't remember with all of his rantings," Wallace chuckled and remarked, "I'm having a little trouble myself."[30]

At one point during the debate, Wallace's repeated interruptions prompted Trump to say, "I guess I'm debating you, not him."[31]

Several times, Trump tried to talk about scandals related to Biden's family business dealings, particularly those involving his son Hunter while Biden was vice president. Biden repeatedly said it was "simply not true" that Hunter had received $3.5 million from the wife of the ex-mayor of Moscow. However, a documented wire transfer and a Senate report revealed it was.[32] "We've already been through this," Wallace said. "I think the American people would rather hear about more substantial subjects.... I'd like to talk about climate change." "So would I," Biden replied.[33]

Earlier in September, Trump had drafted an executive order directing federal agencies to halt any diversity training that included controversial topics such as "white fragility" and "critical race theory," which have their origins in Marxism.[34] According to these new "anti-racist" ideologies, virtually every institution and norm in American life was now defined as racist, and if you disagreed, proponents of critical race theory insisted your denial was proof of your own racism. This radicalism had gained currency in liberal institutions in recent years.

Yet, at the debate, Wallace pointedly asked Trump why he was against "racial sensitivity training," a question framed using Democratic talking points. Trump had taken action to reject an un-American vision of racial essentialism that quite explicitly rejects Martin Luther King Jr.'s hope that Americans be not "judged by the color of their skin but by the content of their character."[35]

Wallace's remarks were no doubt helpful to the Biden campaign, which had been falsely accusing Trump of cozying up to white supremacists for months.[36] In fact, Biden repeated the "very fine people" lie during the debate, without objection from Wallace.

Wallace also didn't ask Biden to criticize Antifa or any of the left-wing groups that were wreaking havoc all over the country. Instead, he asked Trump to "condemn white supremacists and militia groups and to say that they need to stand down and not add to the violence in a number of these cities as we saw in Kenosha and as we've seen in Portland."

Trump says he agreed to Wallace as a debate moderator in the hopes that Wallace would be mindful of the fact Trump had appeared on his Fox show, while Biden had snubbed him and previously forgotten his name. But his performance as debate moderator left Trump frustrated. "The problem was Biden would speak and it was lie after lie, after lie. Everything he said was a lie, this guy, and then Chris Wallace wouldn't let you respond. Chris Wallace was terrible," Trump said. "He wouldn't let us talk about the mayor of Moscow's wife giving three and a half million dollars to [Hunter] Biden. He protected him from the Ukraine questions, Chris Wallace protected [Biden]. He was unable to protect himself. I had Biden and Chris Wallace would not let those questions be asked."

Overall, though, Trump and Biden, as well as Wallace, were all seriously criticized for their behavior at the debate. Trump admitted that even his youngest son Barron, then fourteen, had criticized his performance.

"People thought I was too belligerent.... I will say my own son Barron said, 'Dad, you were too tough. You didn't have to keep interrupting him,'" he said.

On the other hand, the aggressiveness of the debate played well with some key audiences. A Telemundo poll of the network's Spanish-speaking viewers found that two-thirds thought President Donald Trump had won the debate.[37] An NBC/Marist poll earlier in the month showed Biden was dramatically underperforming with Latino voters in Florida.[38]

And Trump had done well enough that some in the commentariat were scared. "For the Sake of Democracy, Cancel the Trump-Biden Debates," pleaded *New York Times* columnist Frank Bruni following the first debate.[39] Their pleas would not fall on deaf ears. Going forward, the commission would intervene to take unprecedented control over the debate stage.

◆   ◆   ◆

On Thursday night, just two days after the debate, it was announced that Hope Hicks, who had traveled with the president at least three times in the previous week and participated in debate prep, had tested positive for the coronavirus.[40] After midnight, Trump tweeted that he and Melania had tested positive and would begin their quarantine and recovery process immediately.[41]

It was a serious blow, albeit one celebrated by some of Trump's political opponents. Rick Wilson, a political consultant known for dirty tricks who was affiliated with the anti-Republican political action committee the Lincoln Project, hoped that Trump's diagnosis would not have "a happy ending." Another Lincoln Project activist suggested that Trump and Hicks were in an inappropriate relationship. Yet another said Trump had failed to "protect the country" and "himself."[42]

One poll found that 40 percent of Democrats were "happy" about Trump's diagnosis. Another 41 percent were "indifferent."[43] Twitter warned users that they would be suspended if they were to "wish or hope for death, serious bodily harm or fatal disease" against Trump.[44] And yet the *Washington Post* claimed that conservatives disappointed by those reactions had "imagined" them.[45]

On Friday afternoon, the White House announced that President Trump would be headed to Walter Reed National Military Medical Center for treatment. He walked to Marine One.[46]

The media were enraged. "Totally unacceptable we have not heard from a doctor. Has the 25th Amendment been invoked???" wrote the *Washington Post*'s Jennifer Rubin on Twitter.[47]

Most of the media analysis suggested that the race was over. An NBC/WSJ poll came out alleging that Biden's lead was now fourteen points.[48] Josh Kraushaar of *National Journal* penned a column titled "The October of Doom for Republicans."[49]

But something curious happened while Trump was hospitalized. Even in the very liberal area of Bethesda, Maryland, where Walter Reed is located, crowds began dropping by to leave flowers and signs and to mingle with other supporters. Cars slowed down and honked their horns, trying to give the president support. The crowds ebbed and flowed the entire time he was there. Some liberal neighbors that dominated the area drove by and flipped off the gathered, but there was overwhelming support.[50]

During his hospitalization, doctors gave updates. The media were so hostile that when one doctor said that "the president has been a phenomenal patient," MSNBC host Rachel Maddow responded, "[T]his is absolutely ridiculous."[51]

CNN contributor Juliette Kayyem said that doctors lie and also that "[i]t is very likely that Russian intelligence agencies—through signal and human intel sources at Walter Reed, etc—have more information about the President's condition than we do (though I think we all know how the president is doing.)"[52]

Jake Tapper monologued, "Sick and in isolation, Mr. President, you have become a symbol of your own failures. Failures of recklessness, ignorance, arrogance. The same failures you have been inflicting on the rest of us."[53]

Trump affiliates went out to the crowds to hand out swag and cookies. And Trump even drove in his armored vehicle up and down the street to wave at his supporters. The media said the drive was irresponsible.[54]

President Trump wrote on Twitter. "Don't be afraid of COVID. Don't let it dominate your life."[55] Rubin responded to the note by saying, "[Y]ou are a menace to everyone around you."[56]

CNN's Wolf Blitzer called it an "outrageous tweet."[57] Carl Bernstein, former Watergate reporter, called it "heartless and cruel." Sanjay Gupta said, "This is so disrespectful. I'm not even sure I can, I can speak about this. It's incredibly, incredibly disrespectful." Gloria Borger said, "It is insulting to the people who have lost loved ones. It is insulting to every American who wears a mask. I mean, it's disgraceful, Wolf. It's absurd." Jake Tapper said, "It's okay to be afraid of COVID and it's okay that it's dominating your life because it has dominated your life!"[58]

That evening, Trump returned to the White House.[59] It was a beautiful scene for tens of millions of Americans who had spent days in prayer for their president. But the media reaction was beyond hysterical. The *Washington Post*'s Jennifer Rubin even attacked the hospital that had treated Trump because it had done its job. "Congress might want to defund Walter Reed. It is a public health hazard," she said.[60]

Angered by his quick recovery, commentators sought to recast the triumphant scene of his return to the White House. When Trump appeared on the White House balcony after his return from Walter Reed, NBC News's presidential historian Michael Beschloss tweeted, "In America, our Presidents have generally avoided strongman balcony scenes—that's for other countries with authoritarian systems."[61]

While the tweet was amplified by Beschloss's fellow Resistance members, Americans with better knowledge of presidential history responded with pictures of every other president pictured at the balcony, be it President Barack Obama (many, many times—once with communist dictator Xi Jinping, no less), President George W. Bush, President George H. W. Bush, President Ronald Reagan, President Jimmy Carter, President Richard Nixon, on back to President Dwight D. Eisenhower and President Franklin Delano Roosevelt.[62]

◆   ◆   ◆

While President Trump was still recovering, the vice-presidential debate between Senator Kamala Harris and Vice President Mike Pence took place on October 7. Though more traditional and less raucous than the previous week's debate, the event would show how committed the commission was to throwing the debates to the Biden campaign.

The vice-presidential debate was hosted by Susan Page, the Washington Bureau chief of *USA Today*, at the University of Utah in Salt Lake City.[63] Page, Nancy Pelosi's biographer, managed to draw less criticism than Wallace. But her questions still left a good deal to be desired from Republican viewers and the Trump campaign.

Mike Pence, a former congressman and talk radio host, started off strong and got stronger as the night went on. He had clearly come prepared for the debate. He had a ready recall of facts and figures to bolster his points. He nailed the questions he wanted to answer and deflected the questions he preferred not to answer.

While he let several zingers fly, he stayed calm and steady, pushing back at what he perceived as unduly false statements, but without the constant interruptions that characterized the previous Trump–Biden debate. He spoke slowly and left few cards on the table unplayed. He was nice, firm, decent, and likable.

Pence's weakest points were when he was on defense about the global pandemic gripping the country. However, he came into the debate ready to lay out how a Trump–Pence vision for America was better than the one put forth by Biden and Harris. He succeeded in conveying that vision throughout the debate.

Heading into the debate, the experts had agreed that Harris, a former prosecutor, would perform well against Pence. "Harris can rely on her prosecutorial skills—which have made more than one Republican squirm at congressional hearings—and her wattage as a rising star in the Democratic Party and first woman of color on a major party's presidential ticket," observed a *USA Today* pre-debate analysis. "Her gender brings an extra element of interest because of the Trump campaign's struggles with female voters."[64]

Harris had a very strong start to the vice-presidential debate, with a rehearsed but very effective answer criticizing the Trump administration for its failure to bring the coronavirus epidemic to heel. But when pressed for details on what she'd do differently, she struggled and never quite regained a strong footing.

She also lied frequently. At one point she attacked Pence for supporting the nomination of Amy Coney Barrett to the Supreme Court by claiming that Abraham Lincoln refused to nominate a Supreme Court justice in October 1864 because, as she put it, "Honest Abe said, it's not the right thing to do" and thought the voters should weigh in on the election first.[65] But the reason Lincoln didn't send a nominee to the Senate was because it was out of session until December, and when he submitted Salmon P. Chase's nomination on the first day of the legislative session, he was confirmed on the same day.[66]

Unsurprisingly, Harris repeated the lie that Trump had called white supremacists "very fine people," and she falsely claimed Trump had called COVID-19 a "hoax," a claim that had been made by a *Washington Post* columnist and had to be corrected.[67] Of course, the so-called fact-checkers showed no interest in correcting her deliberate mischaracterizations.

In another example of bias, Page couched a discussion of the economy in a claim that it was was not recovering. "Vice President Pence, your administration has been predicting a rapid and robust recovery, but the latest economic report suggests that's not happening." But as a matter of fact, the United States was already dramatically bouncing back from the COVID-induced shutdowns at the time of the debate. GDP increased an astounding 33 percent in the third quarter of 2020, consistent with what economists had predicted.[68]

While Page asked hard questions of Pence, Page refused to ask Harris about the issues that made her so controversial. Page didn't ask Harris about her imposition of religious tests on a nominee to the federal judiciary. She didn't ask about Harris's statement that she wouldn't trust a vaccine authorized by the Trump administration. Page didn't ask Harris about her urging people to donate money to funds meant to bail out violent rioters as dozens of American cities burned.[69]

Perhaps most incredibly, Page didn't ask Harris about the singular moment of the Democratic primary, when Harris had accused Biden of praising racist politicians and supporting racist policy. "It was actually very hurtful to hear you talk about the reputations of two United States senators who built their reputation and career on the segregation of race in this country. And it was not only that, but you also worked with them to oppose busing. And you know, there was a little girl in California who was a part of the second class to integrate her public schools, and she was bused to school every day. And that little girl was me," Harris said. Page didn't mention it, even though the opportunity was right there.

As Ari Fleischer tweeted, "Page asked [questions regarding] some of Pres. Trump's most controversial statements. Fair enough. But she didn't ask about Biden's you ain't black statement; blacks aren't diverse; [Biden's false story about] getting arrested in So. Africa; flip-flopping on fracking; packing the court or Harris comparing ICE [Immigration and Customs Enforcement] to the KKK."[70]

The Biden campaign appeared to try to explain Harris's lackluster debate performance by claiming that Pence had "mansplained" to her, a weak retort under the best of circumstances. Media certainly tried to make an issue of Pence's asserting himself at the debate. According to CBS News, Harris "uttered the first meme-worthy sentence of the debate: 'Mr. Vice President, I'm speaking'" as she "rebuke[d] Pence's interruptions during debate."[71] However, Rick Klein of ABC News noted that she was given ample opportunity to speak—Pence spoke for just over thirty-five minutes at the debate, compared to Harris's speaking time of nearly thirty-nine minutes.[72]

Pence is a deceptively strong debater who would have been tough to beat even on a good night, but Harris's comparatively weaker substance combined with a frankly awful style did not help her out.

Out of twenty-six post-debate analysts across five panels on cable and broadcast news, there were only two open Trump supporters. But even with an obviously unfriendly media, as soon as the debate was over everyone knew that Pence had done well, because all of the pundits essentially said vice-presidential debates "don't matter."[73] Obama's former campaign manager said, "Nothing changed the race,"[74] and according to the *New York Times*'s news analysis, "[T]here was no clear winner or loser."[75] While it's true that the vice-presidential slot isn't the most important thing on people's minds in a presidential election, these debates frequently matter.

One of the undervalued contributors to Trump's stunning 2016 victory was the masterful performance Pence gave in his debate against Hillary Clinton's running mate Tim Kaine. In that debate, which was focused on, what else, Trump, Pence explained why Republican voters supported him, forcing a debate on policy and staying away from the personality questions that so riled journalists.

In many respects, Pence was the yin to Trump's yang. Many pundits have never understood how the traditional Republican voter could ever vote for Trump, much less be so unfailingly loyal to him. Pence is the embodiment of the answer to that question. He articulated a Trump-supporting traditional Republicanism that many voters hold, even as he fit the mold of a more typical GOP candidate who, for better and for worse, is not a political and cultural lightning rod like Trump.

◆   ◆   ◆

Pence had injected some momentum back into the Trump campaign at a time when it was sorely needed, and as a result there was an effort to stop it. On October 8, the day after the vice-presidential debate, the debate commission announced additional restrictions to constrain the candidates. The debate commission announced that it had unilaterally decided to make the second debate virtual. It was widely viewed as a way to further control Trump. And Trump, viewing it as another in-kind contribution to Biden, said he'd skip it.

"I'm not going to waste my time at a virtual debate," he said.[76]

"President Trump won the first debate despite a terrible and biased moderator in Chris Wallace, and everybody knows it. For the swamp creatures at the Presidential Debate Commission to now rush to Joe Biden's defense by unilaterally canceling an in-person debate is pathetic. That's not what debates are about or how they're done," said Trump campaign manager Bill Stepien in a statement.[77] "Here are the facts: President Trump will have posted multiple negative tests prior to the debate, so there is no need for this unilateral declaration. The safety of all involved can easily be achieved without canceling a chance for voters to see both candidates go head to head. We'll pass on this sad excuse to bail out Joe Biden and do a rally instead."

The same day that the debate commission found its ad hoc rule changes rejected, the organization had to deal with an embarrassing situation that seemed to confirm its bias against Trump. Steve Scully, a former Biden intern and Ted Kennedy staffer turned C-SPAN host, had been chosen to moderate the second presidential debate. Scully tweeted "should I respond to Trump" in a note to Anthony Scaramucci, who had become a shrill anti-Trump activist after losing his job as Trump's White House communications director after just ten days.[78]

The next morning, debate commission chairman Frank Fahrenkopf said it was nothing. He told Fox News's Brian Kilmeade, "[Scully] was hacked, it didn't happen." The commission said authorities were investigating who had been behind the hack. C-SPAN also released a statement saying Scully "did not originate the tweet and believes his account has been hacked."

Trump supporters were outraged by this unbelievable claim. How could the commission choose a moderator who clearly had an axe to grind against the president and who had once worked for the rival candidate? The commission's ultimate decision to stick by Scully despite such a clear display of partisanship demonstratively proved that though the commission may have nominal Republicans on its board, it was hardly interested in putting on a fair contest.

Former senator Bob Dole, who was the Republican nominee for president in 1996, would confirm those fears, tweeting, "The Commission on Presidential Debates is supposedly bipartisan w/ an equal number of Rs and Ds. I know all of the Republicans and most are friends of mine. I am concerned that none of them support @realDonaldTrump. A biased Debate Commission is unfair."[79]

Former Speaker of the House Newt Gingrich said it was time to abolish the commission. "The time has come to recognize how arrogant, biased, and obsolete the Commission on Presidential Debates has become. It is an engine of insider Washington establishment domination of the political process. Its moderators all represent the Washington establishment—and the norm is hostility to Republican candidates," he said.[80] The *Wall Street Journal* editorial page said it was time to abolish both moderators and the Presidential Debate Commission.[81]

A week later, Scully, who had a history of claiming that a hacker had tweeted things on his account, admitted he had lied. He really had been soliciting guidance for how to handle Trump from a vocal Trump opponent.[82]

"I was right again!" Trump tweeted with glee. "Steve Scully just admitted he was lying about his Twitter being hacked. The Debate was Rigged! He was suspended from @cspan indefinitely. The Trump Campaign was not treated fairly by the 'Commission.' Did I show good instincts in being the first to know?"[83]

With the second debate canceled, the two candidates held town halls, ostensibly with undecided voters in attendance, on October 15. But those events would be rife with media attempts to place thumbs on the scales. NBC News's town hall with Trump featured "undecided" voters who had previously declared their disdain for Trump in MSNBC segments that had aired in the summer.[84]

Savannah Guthrie hosted the town hall with Trump, which went very well for him despite Guthrie's best efforts. Guthrie peppered Trump with questions that were extremely harsh, and she interrupted Trump regularly—but he was able to brush off her jabs and advance his message. "I'm glad Trump agreed to another debate. Didn't realize it would be with Savannah Guthrie," joked Fox News host Greg Gutfeld.

Biden's town hall, moderated by former Clinton White House communications director George Stephanopoulos, would also have fake "undecided" voters. But, predictably, they weren't covert Trump supporters: they were Democrats who had worked in the Obama administration or who had long-standing affiliations with the Democratic Party. By this point, such underhanded attempts to manipulate public opinion were par for the course.

On October 16, the debate commission announced that foreign policy—a topic that surely redounded to Trump's benefit, given his long string of successes in that domain—would no longer be a topic of the final debate.[85] However, even with the shift away from foreign policy to more general topics, there was one foreign policy issue that Biden couldn't quite avoid: the corruption of his son Hunter. On October 14, a raft of information about Biden family business dealings with China and Ukraine became public, albeit heavily suppressed by media and tech companies.[86]

At the final debate, Biden was asked about his son's work in China and the Ukraine and if "anything about those relationships [was] inappropriate or unethical." Biden responded by saying, "Nothing was unethical." However, having a son who got paid $1 million a year to serve on the board of a Ukrainian oil company, and who got that job within weeks of Biden's being appointed to oversee Ukraine policy, was by definition inappropriate and unethical. As for the recent accusations about Hunter's dealings in China, Biden's vague and rambling response speaks for itself: "My son has not made money in terms of this thing about, uh—what are you talking about? China. I have not had—the only guy who made money from China is this guy [Trump]. He's the only one. Nobody else has made money from China."

Biden was not pressed on any specifics regarding recent revelations about Hunter's deals. The moderator, NBC's Kristen Welker, quickly shifted to press Trump on the fact that Trump International Hotels Management had had a relatively small bank account in China open for two years between 2013 and 2015. It was an absurd false equivalence. "Unlike him, where he's vice president, and he does business, I then decided to run for president after that. That was before. So I closed [the bank account] before I even ran for president, let alone became president. Big difference," retorted Trump. "He is the vice president of the United States and his son, his brother, and his other brother are getting rich. They're like a vacuum cleaner. They're sucking the money every place he goes."

Despite the questionable moderation, Trump had a number of exchanges in which the campaign felt he bested Biden. Overall, the debate was a strong performance for Trump, who, unlike in the first debate, seemed to have found a balance between aggression and composure. His performance energized supporters heading into Election Day.

And though a string of final debate performances wasn't enough to carry Trump to victory, one of 2020's biggest losers appeared to be the Commission on Presidential Debates, which may not exist in 2024, absent major reforms.

"After repeated missteps and partisan actions that underscored its biases last cycle, it's clear that the Commission on Presidential Debates (CPD) is no longer providing the fair and impartial forum for presidential debates which the law requires and the American people deserve," said Republican National Committee chair Ronna McDaniel in a statement released in June 2021. "With the CPD failing in 2020 to host a single debate before the start of early voting, making unilateral changes without informing the candidates, and allowing Members of its Board of Directors to make biased and partisan statements against the Republican nominee, the Republican Party needs assurances that the CPD will make meaningful reforms to the debate process by working with stakeholders to restore the faith and legitimacy it has lost. If not, as RNC Chairman, I will have no choice but to advise future Republican candidates against participating in CPD-hosted debates."[87]

The Republican Party was waking up to the fact that the system was rigged against it, and its members were finally willing to stand up against the media and Democrats who insisted on setting the terms of the debate.

CHAPTER SEVEN

"Zuckerberg Should Be in Jail"

Donald Trump's 2016 victory was a shock to much of the country, but Silicon Valley took it especially hard. The progressive bastion of San Francisco had turned tech companies from libertarian idealists into liberal crusaders. The industry as a whole felt complicit in Donald Trump's rise and was intent on doing everything in its power to suppress his voice and those of his supporters.

Not long after the 2016 election, Google held a company-wide meeting. "As an immigrant and a refugee, I certainly find this election deeply offensive, and I know many of you do too," Google founder Sergey Brin told his employees in a meeting, a video of which was leaked to Breitbart News.[1]

Kent Walker, Google's senior vice president for global affairs, said Trump's win was a result of "xenophobia, hatred, and a desire for answers that may or may not be there." Google's CFO, Ruth Porat, started crying.[2]

Given the awesome power Silicon Valley wields in shaping American discourse, it was unlikely it was just going to accept the will of voters. From the beginning, the tech overlords were plotting how to strike back.

In the meeting, Brin suggested that "Jigsaw," a project Google had developed to combat Islamic terror propaganda, could be used to shape the opinions of Trump voters. By the time Trump was inaugurated, a former Google engineer had told Breitbart reporter Allum Bokhari that activists within the company had formed a working group to brainstorm ways to use Google's resources to undermine the Trump administration.[3]

Another Google engineer wanted to sabotage Trump's phone, which ran on Google's Android operating system, as well as ban the Gmail accounts of senior Trump administration officials. An employee in Google's advertising department personally referred purchasers of Google ads to the website of Sleeping Giants, an activist group that encourages boycotts of conservative news outlets.[4]

It wasn't any better over at Facebook, where some employees literally took a week off to grieve. "Managers sent out wistful emails pontificating about how the election was a devastating setback for women and minorities, and that we should keep their struggle at the forefront of our minds," a Facebook employee told Bokhari, author of #DELETED: Big Tech's Battle to Erase the Trump Movement and Steal the Election. "There were numerous cases of employees sending anti-Trump propaganda, invitations to protests, and solicitations for progressive charities straight to their work mailing lists."

Soon after the election, BuzzFeed was reporting, "Facebook employees have formed an unofficial task force to question the role their company played in promoting fake news in the lead-up to Donald Trump's victory in the US election last week."[5] The group was operating in open defiance of CEO Mark Zuckerberg, who said the idea that Facebook had unfairly tilted the election in Trump's favor was "crazy."[6] Zuckerberg had already faced criticism earlier, in May 2016, when Gizmodo reported, "Facebook workers routinely suppressed news stories of interest to conservative readers from the social network's influential 'trending' news section, according to a former journalist who worked on the project."[7]

By December 2016, Zuckerberg had caved. Facebook adopted a new policy of trying to combat the alleged "fake news" that troubled

Facebook's left-wing employees. The tech giant would start paying media outlets to "fact-check" news on the site. With media revenue steadily declining—in no small part because Facebook had radically disrupted the traditional journalistic business models—once reputable news organizations signed up to participate in the fact-checking program. Media outlets that were supposed to be objectively covering Facebook were now on Facebook's payroll, given the power to determine all the news that was fit to print.

Whether or not the tech companies wanted to admit it, much of Silicon Valley's anger over Trump's victory was about their inability to control American opinion. In the past two elections, the tech industry had loudly and publicly taken credit for helping Obama's two victorious campaigns.

For years, the dreamers that built Silicon Valley had prided themselves on the potential of the internet to become a digital libertarian oasis that offered people a way of opting out of the institutions that had historically sought to control what they thought and did. This was always a bit of a pipe dream, but when a Twitter executive famously referred to the social media platform as the "free speech wing of the free speech party"[8] in 2012, Americans still largely believed the internet was a force for good.[9]

But Silicon Valley's Orwellian reaction to 2016 proved once and for all that the visionaries at America's tech companies were oppressors, not liberators. In 2018, a whistleblower at Google sent Bokhari another internal document. The document was titled "The Good Censor," and it summed up Google's role in mediating America's discourse this way: "Free speech has become a social, economic, and political weapon."[10]

◆　　◆　　◆

In 2008, Obama ran the first real "online" campaign, which wasn't just important as a matter of innovation—it was at least as important as a cultural signifier. Obama was all over YouTube, Facebook, and the other still nascent social networks. Meanwhile, his campaign ran ads attacking his septuagenarian opponent for not knowing how to use a computer or his cell phone.[11]

It wasn't until Obama's reelection in 2012 that the press became obsessed with stories on the impact of social media and new technologies on political campaigns. Even for a politician used to a tsunami of adoring press, the coverage on his tech-savvy campaign was a high-water mark. A not atypical *Guardian* headline in 2012 read, "Obama, Facebook and the Power of Friendship: The 2012 Data Election."[12] (Four years later, *The Guardian* declared, "2016: The Year Facebook Became the Bad Guy.")[13]

Facebook had grown exponentially since Obama's first election in 2008, and in 2012 *The Guardian* was eager to report that a "unified computer database that gathers and refines information on millions of potential voters is at the forefront of campaign technology—and could be the key to an Obama win."[14]

The Obama campaign opened a Silicon Valley field office to tap into all the tech expertise that was rushing to help his campaign.[15] Carol Davidsen, the analytics director for Obama's campaign, would later admit that the campaign had access to all of Facebook's data, saying, "[Facebook] allowed us to do things they wouldn't have allowed someone else to do because they were on our side."[16]

For years, programmers and videogame designers had been finding creative ways to exploit peer pressure and dopamine spikes to get people to open their wallets. Getting them to the voting booth seemed like a comparatively easy task.

Facebook data was just the starting point. In 2012, Sasha Issenberg wrote *The Victory Lab: The Secret Science of Winning Campaigns*, which discusses in detail "cutting edge persuasion experiments, innovative ways to mobilize voters, and statistical models predicting the behavior of every voter in the country."[17] It soon became clear that campaigns were engaged in much more concerning behavior than merely adapting to the smartphone era.

The Obama campaign released an app to the public to help Obama volunteers canvass their neighborhoods. The app contained detailed and intimate information about people's political tendencies, such as partisan affiliation. That an anonymous volunteer could download the app just to be encouraged to knock on his neighbors' doors and instantly record his feelings about the president into an electronic database didn't seem to be cause for concern. The *New York Times* called the app the "the science-fiction dream of political operatives" and said, "The campaign is betting that the technology will vastly expand the number of supporters who will beat the pavement for Mr. Obama."[18]

Republicans had no choice but to get good at using technology and exploiting social media networks. And the Trump campaign did just that—which caused people to lose their minds.

In 2012, the Obama campaign sucked up all the data on Facebook and was greeted with a chorus of hosannas celebrating tech-savvy electioneering. In 2016, when the Trump campaign did the exact same thing, the media started yelling that the sky was falling. Throw in the fact that the Russians bought a few hundred thousand dollars' worth of election ads on Facebook, and all of a sudden social media was to blame for the election of Donald Trump to the nation's highest office.

For Trump's entire presidency, the hysteria never died down. In March 2020, *The Atlantic*'s McKay Coppins published an eight-thousand-word deep dive into the president's 2020 digital campaign operation titled "The Billion-Dollar Disinformation Campaign to Reelect the President."[19] The tone of Coppins's article was alarmist—and lots of liberal voters agreed with it. Among them was former president Obama. Obama, who felt no compunction about urging Americans to interrogate their neighbors about their political views and record their responses on his campaign's app, tweeted out a link to Coppins's article accompanied by a typically grandiose and hypocritical judgment of the Trump campaign: "Even if the methods are new, sowing the seeds of doubt, division, and discord to turn Americans against each other is an old trick."[20]

◆   ◆   ◆

If there were any technological "tricks" in the Trump years, it was abundantly obvious that they were being pulled on the president and his voters. In January 2018, Project Veritas, a journalism outlet that specializes in undercover investigations, released a video of a former "content review agent" at Twitter. The agent admitted that the platform was biased against conservatives, while Twitter employees reviewing questionable content "let a lot of the left-leaning or liberal stuff go through unchecked." Veritas's investigation also featured a former software engineer at Twitter who admitted that the company "shadow-banned" users—a term for when social media companies employ algorithms to decrease the visibility of certain users without telling them. Numerous prominent conservatives had seen sudden decreases in engagement on social media and had long suspected that this was happening.[21] In January 2020, Twitter updated its terms of service to formally assert the right to "limit distribution or visibility of any Content on the service."[22]

And Twitter was hardly an outlier. In December 2018, Google CEO Sundar Pichai testified under oath before Congress that the company doesn't "manually intervene" in search results.[23] The next month, a Google employee leaked internal discussions to Breitbart showing that the company did, in fact, interfere with search results. Google-owned YouTube, the world's second most popular search engine after Google itself, had a "blacklist"—Google's term—related to a number of political topics. If you searched YouTube for abortion, Democratic congresswoman Maxine Waters, gun control activist David Hogg, or other political topics, Google was rigging the results.[24]

But that was just the tip of the iceberg. "We have tons of white- and blacklists that humans manually curate," said one Google employee. "Hopefully this isn't surprising or particularly controversial."[25] Another employee noted that the YouTube intervention on abortion search results happened shortly after left-wing publication Slate asked Google to comment on the prominence of pro-life videos on the platform.

Google also appears to have intentionally reduced the search engine rankings and visibility of conservative media. A September 2020 report in RealClearPolitics by Maxim Lott sifted through the data of the consulting firm Sistrix, which tracks data related to search engine optimization. The data clearly show that, starting in 2017, "conservative news sites including Breitbart, the Daily Caller, and the Federalist have seen their Google search listings dramatically reduced."[26] And Google was making it absurdly difficult to find specific information on conservative outlets.

Googling the name "Breitbart" still pulls up the website, but it is nearly eliminated from any searches that don't explicitly name it. For example, Googling the names of Breitbart's reporters sometimes forces users to click through page after page of less-relevant results before hitting a Breitbart link. In the case of Joel Pollak, the first Breitbart link appears on the bottom of page seven of Google Search results. In comparison, a search on the small Google competitor DuckDuckGo returns multiple links to Pollak's Breitbart work on the first page.[27]

The decision to blackball conservative websites was almost certainly intentional. In 2018, The Daily Caller obtained more leaked internal communications showing that Google workers had debated burying conservative news sites. An employee described Breitbart and The Daily Caller specifically as "opinion blogs" that should not be elevated next to corporate media in search results, even though both websites do vital reporting and regularly break major political news, while major corporate media outlets have become hyper-partisan and routinely push fake news.[28]

It's undeniable Google is rigging results on politically sensitive topics, and that the results of this are politically disadvantageous to conservatives. The effect of this on elections appears to be far more significant than most realize. Starting in 2012, psychologist Robert Epstein, the former editor in chief of *Psychology Today*, conducted a series of experiments to ascertain the degree to which biased search engine results can shape political opinion. Most people wrongly view search engine results as the product of mechanical neutrality, merely the ranking and ordering of results, and are easily influenced by them.

Epstein, a politically liberal Harvard Ph.D., would later report that during 2016 "all 10 positions on the first page of [Google] search results in both blue states and red states" were biased toward Hillary Clinton. Based on conclusions from his previous experiments, Epstein estimated that Google alone may have swayed 2.6 million Americans to vote for Hillary Clinton.[29] In 2019, Epstein would tell the Senate Judiciary Committee that search engine manipulation is "one of the most powerful forms of influence ever discovered in the behavioral sciences."[30]

In 2020, Epstein monitored Google results using over seven hundred volunteers in three swing states and concluded, "Google search results were strongly biased in favor of liberals and Democrats. This was not true on Bing or Yahoo.... The bottom line at the moment is that these manipulations, the ones that we've so far quantified, could easily have shifted at least six million votes in just one direction."[31]

Further, Epstein observed what he claimed was overt manipulation by Google. "We also found what seems to be a smoking gun. That is, we found a period of days when the vote reminder on Google's homepage was being sent only to liberals—not one of our conservative field agents received a vote reminder during those days," he said.[32]

But the outcomes of social science experiments are debatable, and the effects of bias are difficult to measure. The overt targeting of Trump supporters across the tech and social media landscape, however, is undeniable. In July 2020, Reddit banned "r/The_Donald," a popular online community for Trump supporters that had more than 790,000 subscribers. It was a raucous and edgy community, but that hardly made it unique on a site such as Reddit, which bills itself as "the best place online to have truly authentic conversations." The ban was more likely a consequence of the personal and political animosity by Reddit's CEO Steve Huffman. In 2016, shortly after Trump's election, Huffman was so angered that he used his database privileges to edit comments from r/The_Donald members making fun of him. When evidence surfaced showing what he'd done, Huffman issued an apology.[33]

After 2016, numerous other sites were scrubbed from the web, hidden from Google searches, banned from social media, or otherwise de-platformed. Popular conservative social media accounts were banned for their political views, cutting them off from access to their users. Carpe Donktum, the internet handle for a prominent pro-Trump meme maker with 270,000 followers, was kicked off Twitter for copyright violations in June 2020.[34] For anyone who's spent any time on Twitter, where millions of memes using preexisting images are floating around constantly, it was an absurd excuse. Just over a year after Carpe Donktum was booted from Twitter, the New York Supreme Court tossed the copyright complaint Twitter had specifically cited in its decision for the ban.[35]

It's more likely that meme makers such as Carpe Donktum were so effective at disseminating a pro-Trump message that biased social media platforms found them threatening and moved to shut them down. On May 15, 2020, the month before Carpe Donktum's ban, Trump had tweeted, "Thank you to all of my great Keyboard Warriors. You are better, and far more brilliant, than anyone on Madison Avenue (Ad Agencies). There is nobody like you!"[36]

The witch hunts didn't just take place online. You could get no more dramatic illustration of how intolerant and hostile Silicon Valley was to Trump supporters than the story of Palmer Luckey—a true tech visionary who brought virtual reality to the masses as the founder of Oculus VR, the company that created the popular Oculus Rift goggles. In 2014, Facebook bought Oculus for $3 billion and brought Luckey on board to work at the company. In September 2016, it was revealed that Luckey had donated $10,000 to a pro-Trump group.[37] The company went into crisis mode and pressured Luckey to sign a letter stating that he would be voting for the Libertarian Party candidate, Gary Johnson. Luckey never signed the letter and left Facebook in March 2017.[38]

The next year, Senator Ted Cruz asked Facebook CEO Mark Zuckerberg in a Senate hearing why Luckey was fired. Zuckerberg assured the senator that "it was not because of a political view."[39] After he left, Luckey threatened to sue Facebook and negotiated an astounding settlement of $100 million over his termination, which seems like an implausible amount if he didn't have an ironclad case for wrongful termination.[40]

◆   ◆   ◆

As the 2020 election drew near, social media companies—driven by internal pressure from employees as well as external pressure from liberal activists—started targeting Trump directly. It seemed an inevitable development, the logical conclusion of censorship that had been mounting since 2016. Despite clear signs that censorship was coming, Republicans hadn't taken strong enough action to deter the tech giants. They would pay the price for their inaction in November.

It began on May 26, when Trump fired off two tweets about the Democrats' push for widespread use of mail-in balloting:

> There is NO WAY (ZERO!) that Mail-In Ballots will be anything less than substantially fraudulent. Mail boxes will be robbed, ballots will be forged & even illegally printed out & fraudulently signed. The Governor of California is sending Ballots to millions of people, anyone living in the state, no matter who they are or how they got there, will get one....
>
> That will be followed up with professionals telling all of these people, many of whom have never even thought of voting before, how, and for whom, to vote. This will be a Rigged Election. No way![41]

In what would become a standard practice, Twitter quickly appended both tweets with an exclamation point followed by a link where users of the site could "get the facts" about mail-in ballots.[42] That link led to a short statement from Twitter saying that "Trump makes unsubstantiated claim that mail-in ballots will lead to voter fraud," with a short summary of "facts" about mail-in voting.[43]

Twitter's contention was downright false. Trump's claims were backed by hard evidence and expert opinion. As discussed throughout this book, mail-in ballots are known to be more susceptible to fraud. For decades, experts of differing political persuasions had expressed grave concerns about mail-in voting. While Trump may not have cited their studies in a footnote, he was hardly making a reckless claim. It just so happened that Trump's opinion now clashed with the Democratic Party line.

Further, the "facts" about mail-in voting that Twitter presented as an alternative to Trump's tweet were convoluted, misleading, and made a complete hash of the issue.[44] An article in *Wired* magazine, which otherwise applauded Twitter for censoring the president, lamented, "It's remarkable that, after having years to prepare for the portentous moment of calling out a false Trump tweet, Twitter couldn't even bulletproof its own fact-check."[45]

The censors would strike again just days later, on May 29. As riots consumed Minneapolis following the death of George Floyd, Trump sent two tweets:

> I can't stand back & watch this happen to a great American City, Minneapolis. A total lack of leadership. Either the very weak Radical Left Mayor, Jacob Frey, get his act together and bring the City under control, or I will send in the National Guard & get the job done right....
>
> These THUGS are dishonoring the memory of George Floyd, and I won't let it happen. Just spoke to Governor Tim Walz and told him that the Military is with him all the way. Any difficulty and we will assume control but, when the looting starts, the shooting starts. Thank you.

Within minutes, Twitter hid Trump's second tweet and replaced it with a message that read, "This Tweet violated the Twitter Rules about glorifying violence. However, Twitter has determined that it may be in the public's interest for the Tweet to remain accessible."[46] Users could see the tweet, but not retweet it, quote tweet it, or respond to it.

The White House Twitter account soon fired back, "Twitter, in an email to the White House moments ago, admitted that the very tweet they are censoring does not violate any Twitter rules. So why are they still censoring it?"[47] The tweet included a photo of the letter, which said, "We have investigated the reported content and could not identify any violations of the Twitter Rules.... Accordingly, we have not taken any action at this time."[48] The baseless censorship would continue unabated from there on out.

Another few days later, Twitter completely blocked another Trump tweet that read, "There will never be an 'Autonomous Zone' in Washington, D.C., as long as I'm your President. If they try they will be met with serious force!"[49] Twitter's justification for censoring the president was that the tweet violated a site policy about "the presence of a threat of harm against an identifiable group." Since there was no "autonomous zone" in Washington, who was the "identifiable group" Trump was threatening? And since when was promising to uphold the law against criminals and anarchists "threatening?" If state-sanctioned force is not justified against violent anarchists, when does Twitter think it is justified? The president is, after all, the nation's chief law enforcement officer.

The dam had broken. For the rest of the election, Twitter would regularly block or otherwise censor the president's tweets. The censorship exposed egregious double standards. At a hearing before the Israeli Knesset in July, a representative of Twitter was asked why the company was censoring Trump but had done nothing about Iran's Ayatollah Khamenei, who had repeatedly called for the destruction of Israel and Jewish genocide.[50] Just over a week before Trump's censored tweet about looting, Khamenei had tweeted, "The only remedy until the removal of the Zionist regime is firm, armed resistance," and Twitter did nothing.[51]

The response from Twitter to the Knesset was disingenuous, to put it mildly. Khamenei got a free pass because "comments on political issues of the day, or foreign policy saber-rattling on economic or military issues are generally not in violation of our Twitter rules."[52]

Again, the more likely explanation is that Twitter, much like the executives at all the other tech companies, despised Trump and his politics. Twitter's executive in charge of "site integrity," who is largely responsible for devising and implementing the platform's new fact-checking policies, is a man with thin journalistic credentials named Yoel Roth.[53] Roth has used his own Twitter account to express his vitriolic and anti-Trump political opinions. "I'm just saying, we fly over those states that voted for a racist tangerine for a reason," he tweeted.[54] In another tweet he declared there were "ACTUAL NAZIS IN THE WHITE HOUSE."[55]

The latter accusation merited its own fact-check, but either way, Roth's bias against Trump, never mind ordinary conservative users of Twitter, is obvious. No one has any reason to expect Twitter executives are capable of being judicious and fair when determining what viewpoints are permissible in a political debate.

◆   ◆   ◆

Facebook was not to be outdone by Twitter's heavy-handed censorship. Unlike Twitter, which took it upon itself to engage in censorship directly, Facebook was eager to maintain the veneer of neutrality. As a result, it outsourced its "fact-checking" to other media organizations. Facebook compensated these organizations well, thus further extending its influence over the media landscape.

But the power was more important than the money. Legacy media outlets were all too eager to silence conservative news sources that challenged their reporting or called their standards into question. Censorship was now a cornerstone of liberal political orthodoxy.

On September 27, Project Veritas released footage purporting to expose an illegal vote-brokering scheme.[56] The story centered on

Minneapolis's Somali immigrant community in the controversial Democratic representative Ilhan Omar's congressional district. In the videos Project Veritas recorded, a Somali man explains how men go door-to-door with absentee ballot forms, telling voters, "This year, you will vote for Ilhan.... When we sign the voting document and they fill it out is when they give us the money."[57]

While Project Veritas's report wasn't documented proof of voter fraud, it was newsworthy and contained enough details to demand further reporting. Immigrant communities were often sources of voter fraud. In 2000, an investigative report in the *Wall Street Journal* detailed fraud problems with mail-in ballots in Hispanic communities that exploited elderly immigrants who often didn't speak English.[58] Similarly, the fraud that took place in Paterson, New Jersey, earlier that year appeared to exploit the city's immigrant communities.[59]

But not only did news outlets refuse to follow up on the Veritas report, they tried to suppress it. Less than forty-eight hours after the release of the Veritas video, the *New York Times*'s coverage of the report began with this sentence: "A deceptive video released on Sunday by the conservative activist James O'Keefe, which claimed through unidentified sources and with no verifiable evidence that Representative Ilhan Omar's campaign had collected ballots illegally, was probably part of a coordinated disinformation effort, according to researchers at Stanford University."[60] The headline was even more declarative: "Project Veritas Video Was a 'Coordinated Disinformation Campaign,' Researchers Say."[61]

The article offered no proof that Project Veritas's report was a "disinformation campaign."[62] The *Times*'s entire report was premised on speculation. Since Project Veritas's report came out soon after a big *New York Times* report on President Trump's leaked tax returns, the *Times* hubristically assumed the voter fraud report was released for the sole purpose of stealing the limelight from its own reporting. To lend its untethered explanation the air of legitimacy, the *Times* quoted academic experts who asserted that the timing *seemed* suspicious.

The *Times* went on to publish a number of follow-up articles similarly dismissive of the Veritas report, calling it "deceptive," "disinformation," and "false."[63] *USA Today*, one of Facebook's official fact-checking partners, cited the *Times*'s reporting when it published an article headlined, "Fact Check: No Proof of Alleged Voter Fraud Scheme or Connection to Rep. Ilhan Omar."[64] Naturally, Project Veritas's report was soon censored by Facebook.

Project Veritas defends the integrity of its report to this day. It has sued the *New York Times* for defamation.[65] In March 2021, a New York State Supreme Court judge rebuked the *Times* for pioneering a novel defense against libel in the case. The paper argued that it hadn't libeled Project Veritas, since *New York Times* reporters are entitled to assert opinions in news stories without labeling or distinguishing opinion from fact.[66]

"Veritas contends that NYT's own ethical policies—which NYT publishes on its website—prohibit news reporters from injecting their subjective opinions into news stories published by NYT, and thus a reasonable reader would expect a news reporter's statements to be assertions of fact and not opinion," wrote Judge Charles D. Wood.[67]

As of this writing, the outcome of Project Veritas's libel suit is unresolved.

The Veritas report was just one piece of explosive news that the media and Big Tech censored before the election. It is an instructive example in how different groups conspired to throw the game to Joe Biden.

Facebook once touted its ability to shut off 80 percent of the internet traffic to any link it deems misleading.[68] When deciding whom to censor, Facebook relied on media "fact-checkers" who consider themselves the opposition party. Biased journalists were given the power to scrub their rivals from the internet, thanks more to the legacy of their places of employment than their own work. This process of erroneous or slanted liberal media reports informing Facebook "fact checks" played out through Trump's entire presidency and reelection effort.[69] It suppressed dozens of news stories in the public interest and helped get Biden over the finish line.

◆   ◆   ◆

While tech platforms censored and banned conservative media outlets, their founders were eager to insert themselves more directly into the democratic process. The power to shape public opinion was not enough. They wanted the power to determine election outcomes.

And to an alarming degree, Democrats achieved control over elections in 2020. What made 2020 different was that for the first time ever, the groups that supported Democrats were allowed, on a widespread basis, to cross that bright red line that separates government officials who administer an election from political operatives. Unelected liberal activists were allowed to embed in government offices and actually take over election administration duties in crucial battleground states. They were given vast amounts of voter information and even put in charge of designing, distributing, and collecting ballots.

While there are always activist groups on both the right and the left fighting over candidates and election rules, the battles over electioneering in the 2020 election were substantially different. It was as if the Dallas Cowboys were allowed to hire and train their own family members to serve as referees and then got angry the losing team didn't publicly accept a narrow loss with several controversial calls. In 2020, liberal organizations, corporate interests, and a tech billionaire spent hundreds of millions of dollars getting access to the levers of government power in key states with the goal of ousting Donald Trump. This privatization of election administration tainted the entire election. There was no concern about this outrageous arrangement from the media and other watchdogs. Instead, they dishonestly spun it as a triumph of voting rights and clean elections.

Months after the 2020 presidential election, *Time* magazine published its triumphant story of how the election was won by "a well-funded cabal of powerful people, ranging across industries and ideologies, working together behind the scenes to influence perceptions, change rules and laws, steer media coverage and control the flow of information. They were not rigging the election; they were fortifying it."[70]

The article was written by Molly Ball, a journalist who had recently published a biography of Democratic Speaker of the House Nancy Pelosi that the *Wall Street Journal*'s Barton Swaim described as "one of the most cloyingly adulatory paeans to a living politician I've ever read." He added, "If I ever write anything so mindlessly celebratory about any elected official, living or dead, liberal or conservative, I hope the editor of these pages will have the decency to fire me and suggest a career in advertising or political consultancy."[71]

The book was uncomfortably friendly to the powerful Democrat and confirmed that Ball had close ties to Democratic leaders. Of all people, she was in a position to know the story of what happened in 2020.

In her piece, Ball told a cheerful story about a "conspiracy unfolding behind the scenes," the "result of an informal alliance between left-wing activists and business titans."[72] She purported to tell "the inside story of the conspiracy to save the 2020 election."[73]

Of course, the leaders of the Democratic Party weren't trying to "save" the election. They were out to win it by hook or by crook, no matter Ball's gauzy reframing. And the same tech oligarchs whose companies silenced Donald Trump and his allies were bankrolling the operation.

Former Obama White House associate counsel Ian Bassin told Ball, "[I]t's massively important for the country to understand that it didn't happen accidentally. The system didn't work magically. Democracy is not self-executing."[74] It would be more accurate to say that Bassin wasn't ultimately concerned about "democracy" in a larger sense. These activists were much more concerned about enabling the Democratic Party's push to expand mail-in voting and focus its get-out-the-vote operation on mail-in voting. If it could get local and state governments to assist in that partisan effort, Trump would be defeated.

Bassin's group Protect Democracy, which Ball described as nonpartisan, is an unabashedly leftist group. It sued President Trump's 2016 campaign for alleged collusion with Russia, the conspiracy theory that the Democratic National Committee and Clinton campaign had secretly launched and laundered through the media and bureaucracy to affect the previous elections. Bassin's group sued Wisconsin in 2020 to oppose its ballot security laws.[75] Ball wrote of the group of Democratic leaders:

> Their work touched every aspect of the election. They got states to change voting systems and laws and helped secure hundreds of millions in public and private funding. They fended off voter-suppression lawsuits, recruited armies of poll workers and got millions of people to vote by mail for the first time. They successfully pressured social media companies to take a harder line against disinformation and used data-driven strategies to fight viral smears. They executed national public-awareness campaigns that helped Americans understand how the vote count would unfold over days or weeks, preventing Trump's conspiracy theories and false claims of victory from getting more traction. After Election Day, they monitored every pressure point to ensure that Trump could not overturn the result.[76]

In Ball's telling, the effort to control the election began in 2019 when Mike Podhorzer, a senior advisor to the president of the AFL–CIO, a Democratic special interest group, began to worry Trump would win. Podhorzer co-chairs Catalist, a firm that provides data, software, and analytics for left-progressive groups and candidates. That group is closely aligned with Democracy Alliance, a major liberal donor clearinghouse that helps distribute hundreds of millions of dollars every year to a variety of liberal causes.[77]

A coalition of "resistance" groups called the Fight Back Table began to plan scenarios about how to secure victory for Democrats.[78]

They gathered liberal activists across the country into something called the Democracy Defense Coalition to further plan and strategize. Podhorzer put together a network that included "the labor movement; the institutional left, like Planned Parenthood and Greenpeace; resistance groups like Indivisible and MoveOn; progressive data geeks and strategists, representatives of donors and foundations, state-level grassroots organizers, racial-justice activists and others."[79] Tellingly, Ball reported that the BLM riots were a key part of their effort to impact the election, as the leaders of these groups "drew energy from the summer's racial-justice protests, many of whose leaders were a key part of the liberal alliance."

In April 2020, Podhorzer began hosting hours-long Zoom sessions every week to coordinate the effort to secure the 2020 election for Biden. "The meetings became the galactic center for a constellation of operatives across the left who shared overlapping goals but didn't usually work in concert," Ball wrote.[80] "The first task was overhauling America's balky election infrastructure—in the middle of a pandemic."[81]

Podhorzer's effort was the operational complement to Democratic lawyer Marc Elias's structural reforms. He wanted to raise an army of progressive activists to administer the election at the ground level. But even progressive armies need money. Podhorzer needed to hire staff to work mail-in balloting and get-out-the-vote operations, cornerstones of the Democratic Party's plan for 2020. He needed to buy scanners and other equipment to process mail-in ballots.

Podhorzer and other activists lobbied the federal government to pay for the parts of Democrats' mail-in ballot strategy that state and local governments themselves could do, claiming it was necessary because of the coronavirus. Congress allocated hundreds of millions of dollars, but the progressive activists needed much more to accomplish their vision. That's when "[p]rivate philanthropy stepped into the breach," according to *Time*.[82]

Big Democratic donors funded a dizzying array of liberal nonprofit groups to assist the Democratic effort to win in 2020. These groups may have technically been nonpartisan, but they all had strong, nearly exclusive, ties to the Democratic Party.

The Voter Participation Center, for example, helped the effort by running focus groups, sending out ballot applications to millions of people, and running ads encouraging the get-out-the-vote operation. "All the work we have done for 17 years was built for this moment of bringing democracy to people's doorsteps," *Time* quoted Tom Lopach, the center's CEO, as saying. Lopach was a longtime Democratic activist and the former executive director of the Committee for a Democratic Majority.[83] The Voter Participation Center itself has always been run by Democrats, who focused on registering groups that lean Democratic. Even the liberal *Washington Post* admitted in 2020 that the group, while technically nonpartisan, was "aligned with efforts to defeat the president."[84]

"Even though the group was officially nonpartisan, for tax purposes, there was no secret that the goal of all its efforts was to generate new votes for Democrats," wrote Sasha Issenberg in *The Victory Lab: The Secret Science of Winning Campaigns*.[85]

Ball also highlighted All Voting Is Local, a left-leaning get-out-the-vote operation.[86] Hannah Fried, the organization's national campaign director, worked on Obama's re-election campaign and was a deputy general counsel on the 2016 Hillary Clinton campaign. That group focused its 2020 efforts not nationwide, but on the same states Democrats had identified as their primary targets: Arizona, Georgia, Nevada, Pennsylvania, Florida, Michigan, Ohio, and Wisconsin.

Ball also highlighted the Brennan Center for Justice at N.Y.U, another group that is technically nonpartisan but is in practice fiercely liberal. The center was named for former Supreme Court justice William Brennan, known as the father of judicial activism, and has a history of supporting far-left judicial activism. It would help groups file lawsuits when needed.

Time highlighted other groups "fortifying" the election, all affiliated with the left and boasting strong ties to the Democratic Party.[87] The Voting Rights Lab's co-founders are affiliated with Everytown for Gun

Safety, an anti–gun rights organization, and NARAL Pro-Choice America, two groups that are key members of the Democratic coalition. Into Action, which spread state-specific memes about mail-in balloting, is run by former Obama administration official Yosi Sergent. The National Vote at Home Institute partners with progressive and leftist organizations, including the Democracy Fund, Common Cause, Nonprofit VOTE, and Rock the Vote. Stephen Silberstein, a megadonor in Democracy Alliance, is on the board. Dozens of these groups were involved with the effort to "secure" the election for Democrats by pushing mail-in balloting.[88]

And the plan worked. Nearly half of voters voted by mail, and another quarter voted early. It was, Ball wrote, "practically a revolution in how people vote."[89] The money for the effort was funneled by billionaires through dark money groups. One billionaire in particular took a prominent and public role in the effort. And it was his money that enabled these far-left groups to embed within the voting system itself. That billionaire was Facebook founder Mark Zuckerberg.

◆　　◆　　◆

"At Facebook, we took our responsibility to protect the integrity of this election very seriously.... We've built sophisticated systems to protect against election interference," CEO Mark Zuckerberg told ABC News shortly after the election. He highlighted his censorship work, which he described as a fight against "misinformation."[90]

Zuckerberg didn't just help Democrats by censoring their political opponents. He directly funded liberal groups running partisan get-out-the-vote operations. In fact, he helped those groups infiltrate election offices in key swing states by doling out large grants to crucial districts. That funding was the means by which Podhorzer and other activists achieved their "revolution" and changed the course of the 2020 election.[91]

The Chan Zuckerberg Initiative, an organization led by Zuckerberg's wife Priscilla, gave more than $400 million to nonprofit groups that were part of the conspiracy to control the 2020 election. Most of those funds—colloquially called "Zuck Bucks"—were funneled through the Center for Tech and Civic Life (CTCL), a group led by three Democrats with a long history of activism.[92] The couple also heavily funded the Center for Election Innovation and Research, a group run by a man who used to be the senior attorney at the left-wing People for the American Way. That group also funneled Zuck Bucks to governmental entities.[93]

Shortly before the election, David Plouffe, who is best known for running President Barack Obama's successful 2008 presidential campaign, published a book that said the 2020 election "may come down to block-by-block street fights in Detroit, Philadelphia, and Milwaukee."[94] Since 2017, he had been doing policy and advocacy work for the Chan Zuckerberg Initiative. He was advising the group when it decided to give so much money toward privatizing and controlling the nation's election system in 2020.[95] Plouffe, one of the Democratic Party's most successful campaigners, innately understood exactly what needed to happen for a lackluster Biden campaign to pull off a victory. He was part of the organization that gave millions of dollars to state and local governments, paving the way for liberal activists to gain entry into election offices in important state battlegrounds.

CTCL is another voter outreach organization that, though technically nonpartisan, boasts strong ties to the Democratic Party. One of its founders is Tiana Epps-Johnson, a former Obama Foundation fellow who previously worked on the Voting Rights Project for the Lawyers' Committee for Civil Rights, a politically liberal advocacy group funded by progressive powerhouse foundations such as George Soros's Open Society Foundations.

Epps-Johnson founded CTCL with Whitney May and Donny Bridges. All three worked on activism relating to election rules until 2015 for the New Organizing Institute (NOI), which the *Washington Post* described as "the Democratic Party's Hogwarts for digital wizardry."[96] Some on the right had called the influential Democratic training organization "the Left's New Death Star."[97] NOI disbanded shortly after eight senior staff, including the trio that formed CTCL, walked out over frustration with how it was being managed in 2015.

The $350 million from Zuckerberg would turn the relatively new and narrowly focused CTCL into a power player in the 2020 election. In 2018, CTCL's budget had been only $1.4 million. Now flush with cash, CTCL would disburse hundreds of millions of dollars in grants to election officials and local governments across the country.

The private funding was billed publicly as "COVID-19 response grants," ostensibly to help municipalities acquire protective gear for poll workers or otherwise help prevent election officials and volunteers from contracting the virus.[98] In practice, relatively little money was spent on measures to guard the health of election workers. Here, as in other cases, COVID-19 provided the cover to institute the left's political wish list.

CTCL has been reluctant to share information about how its operation was run, but it did list the local governments it funded.[99] Through open records requests, researchers have been able to piece together the massive effort to control the 2020 election.

The money was purportedly given to counties regardless of their political leaning, but National Public Radio notes that not all grants were the same size. Some election officials and localities received small packets of CTCL funding, while others received enough grant money to "fund their dream election."[100] Democratic areas regularly received massively more funding than Republican counties, whether in terms of total dollar amount or per capita.

When the Associated Press covered the effort in September 2020, it noted that conservatives were concerned about the "Democratic origins" of CTCL and that "its donations have predominantly been in areas where Democrats depend on votes."[101] The report claimed that the group intended to give some money to lower-population Republican areas, but only after it had flushed piles of cash into Democratic areas throughout the summer.[102]

"I don't think anybody would disagree that Philly would get substantially more money than some of these [smaller] counties. But proportionally, it appears to look as though some red counties were patted on the head and said, 'Oh, here you go' to say that money went to red and blue counties combined," Representative Seth Grove (R-York County) told Broad and Liberty about the disparate funding in his state.[103]

The effect of the operation was monumental.

According to the Foundation for Government Accountability (FGA), Georgia received more than $31 million in Zuck Bucks for the general election alone, one of the highest amounts in the country.[104] It worked out to nearly 9 percent of all Zuckerberg funding, even though Georgia has just over 3 percent of the population of the country.[105]

The money was not spent on COVID-related issues. For instance, the three counties that received the most Zuck Buck funding spent only 1.3 percent of that funding on personal protective equipment.[106] The rest was spent on salaries, laptops, vehicle rentals, attorneys' fees for public records requests, mail-in balloting, and other measures that allowed elections offices to hire activists to work the election.[107]

Not all 159 counties in Georgia received the funding. Of those that did, Trump-voting counties received an average of $1.91 per registered voter, while Biden-voting counties received, on average, $7.13 per voter.[108]

"Put simply, Zuckerbucks counties in the Biden column were granted nearly four times as many Zuckerbucks per registered voter than were Zuckerbucks counties won by Trump," the FGA reported.[109] They looked at it another way, too. Trump won Georgia by more than five points in 2016. He lost it by three-tenths of a percentage point in 2020. On average, as a share of the two-party vote, most counties moved Democratic by less than one percentage point in that time. Counties that didn't receive Zuck Bucks showed hardly any movement, but counties that were funded by Zuck Bucks moved, on average, 2.3 percentage points more Democratic.[110]

Likewise, in Georgia counties that did not receive Zuck Bucks, "roughly half saw an increase in Democrat votes that offset the increase in Republican votes, while roughly half saw the opposite trend." But in counties that did receive Zuck Bucks, three quarters of them "saw a significant uptick in Democrat votes that offset any upward change in Republican votes," including the highly populated Fulton, Gwinnett, Cobb, and DeKalb counties.[111]

The Zuck Bucks kept flowing even after Election Day, as Georgia faced a run-off election to determine who its two senators would be. At least $14.5 million more in funding came in, with more than 60 percent allocated to the Democratic counties of Fulton and DeKalb alone. "Yet again, Democrat districts were targeted, and Democrat votes were boosted," the FGA reported.[112]

Georgia's election results moved more than five points in the direction of the Democratic presidential candidate from 2016 to 2020, resulting not just in Trump's defeat but the capture by Democrats of two key Senate races. Florida, by contrast, moved two points in Trump's direction in the same years. Even though Georgia's population is roughly half of Florida's population of 21.5 million people,[113] it received many times the funding from left-wing groups.

Of the more than $7 million given to Florida counties, the vast majority went to Democratic strongholds. More money could have swung Florida in a pro-Biden direction, analysis by the FGA suggested. A comparison of adjacent counties with historically similar voting patterns showed that Leon County, which received Zuck Bucks, saw an increase in Democratic voter turnout that more than offset the increase in Republican turnout. The neighboring Gadsden County, which received no Zuck Bucks, saw the opposite trend, an increase in Republican turnout that more than offset the increase in Democratic turnout.

"The same exact patterns were visible in several other pairs of contiguous counties, including Brevard and Volusia counties, Lake and Polk counties, and Wakulla and Liberty counties—indicating a trend of greater Democrat performance compared to 2016 in counties that received Zuckerbucks relative to their neighboring counties," the FGA reported.[114]

Democratic counties in Pennsylvania were also targeted for Zuck Buck infusions. The Capital Research Center determined that Biden won eight of the ten highest-funded CTCL counties in the state, which together received $21,047,163, or more than 95 percent of all grants statewide.[115] A Biden-winning county was over 3.5 times more likely to be funded by CTCL than a Trump-winning county. Trump counties received an average of $0.59 per capita, while Biden counties averaged $2.85 per capita.[116] Philadelphia, the most richly funded Biden county, received $6.32 per capita, compared to a mere $1.12 for Berks, the most richly funded Trump county.[117]

"Seasoned election observers went into November saying that Pennsylvania was a critical swing state for the presidential election and that Philadelphia would be ground zero for the Democratic candidate's hopes. CTCL partisans knew this too, and their investments in Pennsylvania show it," said Scott Walter, the president of the Capital Research Center.[118]

In Wisconsin, CTCL gave $6.3 million to the cities of Racine, Green Bay, Madison, Milwaukee, and Kenosha to ensure voting could be "done in accordance with prevailing public health requirements" to "reduce the risk of exposure to coronavirus."[119]

Wisconsin law says voting is a right, but that voting absentee is a privilege. "[V]oting by absentee ballot must be carefully regulated to prevent the potential for fraud or abuse; to prevent overzealous solicitation of absentee electors who may prefer not to participate in an election."[120] It also says that elections are to be run by clerks or other government officials.

The five cities of Wisconsin that received Zuck Bucks outsourced much of their election operation to private liberal groups. In one case, the private group's control was so extensive that a government official frustrated at being sidelined by Zuckerberg-funded out-of-state activists quit her job before the election.

That was by design. Cities that received grants were not allowed to use the money to fund outside help unless CTCL specifically approved the plan in writing. CTCL kept tight control of how money was spent, and it had an abundance of "partners" to help with anything the cities needed.

Some government officials were willing to do whatever CTCL recommended. "As far as I'm concerned I am taking all of my cues from CTCL and work with those you recommend," Celestine Jeffreys, the chief of staff to Green Bay mayor Eric Genrich, wrote in an email.[121] And CTCL had plenty of recommendations.

The left-wing group CTCL said it had a "network of current and former election administrations and election experts available" to scale up "your vote by mail processes" and "ensure forms, envelopes, and other materials are understood and completed correctly by voters."[122]

Each group was comprised of progressive activists who supported the Democratic Party, albeit from a posture of official nonpartisanship. Both Republicans and Democrats have such support groups and have for decades. Usually, that's just politics. But not in 2020.

CTCL's network groups offered services that would have a direct effect on election results.[123] Power the Polls, a liberal group recruiting poll workers, promised to help with ballot curing. The liberal Mikva Challenge worked to recruit high school–age poll workers. And the left-wing Brennan Center could help with "election integrity," including "postelection audits" and "cybersecurity."[124]

The Center for Civic Design, an election-administration policy organization that frequently partners with left-of-center organizations such as liberal billionaire Pierre Omidyar's Democracy Fund, designed absentee ballots and voting instructions, often working directly with an election commission to develop a new envelope design and create an advertising and targeting campaign.[125] The Elections Group, another group linked to the Democracy Fund, provided technical assistance in handling drop boxes and conducted voter outreach. The communications director for the Center for Secure and Modern Elections, a left-of-center advocacy organization created to promote sweeping changes to the elections process, ran a conference call to help Green Bay develop Spanish-language radio ads and geofencing to target voters in a predefined area.

Digital Response, a nonprofit launched in 2020, offered to "bring voters an updated elections website," "run a website health check," "set up communications channels," "bring poll worker application and management online," "track and respond to polling location wait times," "set up voter support and email response tools," "bring vote-by-mail applications online," "process incoming VBM applications," and help with "ballot curing process tooling and voter notification."[126]

The amount of services Digital Response offered to officials was stunning:

- "If your state does not provide online [vote-by-mail] applications, we can help you set one up—improving the application process for both you and your voters."[127]
- "We can help you set up tools to quickly notify voters with rejected ballots—and then guide them through the ballot cure process."[128]
- "We'll help you monitor wait times at the polls—helping you respond where needed and improving the voting experience."[129]
- "We'll help you set up the tools you need to share information with your voters across social, email, text, and web."[130]

The National Vote at Home Institute was presented as a "technical assistance partner" that could "support outreach around absentee voting," provide and oversee voting machines, consult on methods to cure absentee ballots, and even take the duty of curing absentee ballots off of Green Bay's hands.[131]

A few weeks after the cities received their grant, CTCL emailed Claire Woodall-Vogg, the executive director of the Milwaukee Election Commission, to offer "an experienced elections staffer that could potentially embed with your staff in Milwaukee in a matter of days."[132]

The staffer leading Wisconsin's portion of the National Vote at Home Institute was an out-of-state Democratic activist named Michael

Spitzer-Rubenstein. As soon as he met with Woodall-Vogg, he asked for contacts at the Wisconsin Elections Commission and in the other cities.

Spitzer-Rubenstein would eventually take over much of Green Bay's election planning from the official charged with running the election, Green Bay city clerk Kris Teske. Teske was not happy at being replaced by Spitzer-Rubenstein and his team. A few weeks before the election, she would take Family and Medical Leave Act leave, quitting shortly thereafter.

Emails from Spitzer-Rubenstein show he was managing much of the election process. To one government official he wrote, "By Monday, I'll have our edits on the absentee voting instructions. We're pushing Quickbase to get their system up and running and I'll keep you updated. I'll revise the planning tool to accurately reflect the process. I'll create a flowchart for the vote-by-mail processing that we will be able to share with both inspectors and also observers."[133]

Once early voting started, Woodall-Vogg would provide him with a daily update on the numbers of absentee ballots returned and still outstanding in each ward, prized information for a political operative. "Here's what I'll need," Spitzer-Rubenstein wrote to her in late October, "1) Number of ballot preparation teams, 2) Number of returned ballots per ward, 3) Number of outstanding ballots per ward."[134]

Amazingly, he even asked for direct access to the Milwaukee Election Commission's voter database.

> We're hoping there's an easier way to get the data out of Wis-Vote than you having to manually export it every day or week. To that end, we have two questions: 1. Would you or someone else on your team be able to do a screen-share so we can see the process for an export? 2. Do you know if WisVote has an API or anything similar so that it can connect with other software apps? That would be the holy grail (but I'm not expecting it to be that easy).[135]

Even for Woodall-Vogg, who had been providing daily reports to the Democratic activist working for the nonprofit, that was too much. "While I completely understand and appreciate the assistance that is trying to be provided," she wrote, "I am definitely not comfortable having a non-staff member involved in the function of our voter database, much less recording it."[136]

When the emails were released in 2021, they stunned Wisconsin observers. "What exactly was the National Vote at Home Institute doing with its daily reports? Was it making sure that people were actually voting from home by going door-to-door to collect ballots from voters who had not yet turned theirs in? Was this data sharing a condition of the CTCL grant? And who was really running Milwaukee's election?" asked Dan O'Donnell, whose election analysis appeared at Wisconsin's MacIver Institute, a conservative think tank.[137]

"The rigging of the election happened in front of our face, you know?" said O'Donnell of what happened in Wisconsin.

Wisconsin law stipulates elections are to be conducted by clerks, not by mayors or outside groups. Months before the election, Teske, an election clerk, wrote that she was being sidelined by the mayor's office and the outside funding. "I haven't been in any discussions or emails as to what they are going to do with the money. I only know what has been on the news/in the media.... Again, I feel I am being left out of the discussions and not listened to at the meetings," Teske wrote on July 9.[138]

"I just attended the Ad Hoc meeting on Elections.... I also asked when these people from the grant give us advisors, who is going to be determining if their advice is legal or not.... I don't think it pays to talk to the Mayor because he sides with Celestine [Jeffreys], so I know this is what he wants. I just don't know where the Clerk's Office fits in anymore," Teske wrote in early July.[139]

By August, she was worried about legal exposure. "I don't understand how people who don't have the knowledge of the process can tell us how to manage the election," Teske wrote on August 28, 2020.[140]

She had good reason to worry.

Even though state law clearly states that the city clerk is in charge of the election, Democratic Green Bay mayor Eric Genrich delegated that authority to agents from outside groups and gave them leadership roles in collecting absentee ballots, fixing ballots that would otherwise be voided for failure to follow the law, and even supervising the counting of ballots.

"The grant mentors would like to meet with you to discuss, further, the ballot curing process. Please let them know when you're available," Genrich's chief of staff, Celestine Jeffreys, told Teske. Spitzer-Rubenstein explained that the National Vote at Home Institute had done the same for other cities in Wisconsin.[141] "We have a process map that we've worked out with Milwaukee for their process. We can also adapt the letter we're sending out with rejected absentee ballots along with a call script alerting voters. (We can also get people to make the calls, too, so you don't need to worry about it.)"[142]

Emails show that Spitzer-Rubenstein, a non-governmental official who was funded by the Democratic effort, had keys to the central counting facility and access to all the machines before Election Night. His name was on contracts with the hotel hosting the ballot counting.

"The city of Green Bay literally gave the keys to the election to a Democratic Party operative from New York," wrote M. D. Kittle, an investigative reporter.[143]

Sandy Juno, who was clerk of Brown County, where Green Bay is located, testified about the problems in a legislative hearing after the fact. "He was advising them on things. He was touching the ballots. He had access to see how the votes were counted," Juno said of Spitzer-Rubenstein. Others testified that he was giving orders to poll workers and seemed to be the person running the count operation on Election Night.[144]

"I would really like to think that when we talk about security of elections, we're talking about more than just the security of the internet. You know, it has to be security of the physical location, where you're not giving a third party keys to where you have your election equipment," Juno said.

She noted that there were irregularities in the counting, too, with no consistency in how the various tables were processing ballots. Some even had absentee ballots face-up, so anyone could see how they were marked. Juno said poll workers were observed reviewing the ballot not just to see that they'd been appropriately checked by the clerk, but "reviewing how they were marked." And when poll workers were fixing ballots, they used the same color pens as the ones ballots had been filled out in, contrary to established procedures designed to make sure observers could differentiate between a voter's marks and a poll worker's mark.[145]

After the election, concerned citizens raised the alarm. A complaint was filed with the Wisconsin Elections Commission, but it was dismissed. Meagan Wolfe, the administrator of the Wisconsin Elections Commission, said the commission "doesn't have any sort of statutory authority over private grant funding. And so [the complaint] was dismissed."[146] The plan by Democratic strategists to bring their activist groups into the election offices worked in part because no legislature had ever imagined that a nonprofit could take over so many election offices so quickly and so easily. "If it can happen to Green Bay, Wisconsin, sweet little old Green Bay Wisconsin, these people can coordinate any place," said Janel Brandtjen, a state representative in Wisconsin.

Democrats were willing to take extreme measures to keep the privatized funding that enabled their political activists to embed in the election system. After the Wisconsin legislature passed a bill banning private funding of election operations by a 60–36 margin in the state assembly and by an 18–14 margin in the state senate, Governor Tony Evers vetoed the ban. Without tech oligarchs' buying the administration of the state's elections, Democrats stand to lose.

What happened in Green Bay by means of the large grant from Zuckerberg also happened in countless Democrat-run cities across the country. Cities and counties took money from the left-wing Center for Tech and Civic Life to help with elections. The strings attached to the money required officials to work with "partner organizations" to massively expand mail-in voting and staff their operation with activists.

These partner organizations were all left-wing groups that then ran a Democratic get-out-the-vote operation through the election offices themselves.

It was a genius plan. And because no one ever imagined that a coordinated operation could pull off the privatization of the election system, laws were not built to combat it. In fact, nobody even really figured it out until Ball's article and the emails in Green Bay came to light months after the fact.

"Big Tech got meaner, bigger, stronger, and they were crazed," Trump says, reflecting on their election meddling by means of censorship and algorithms. And as for the rigging by means of interference of liberal activists in administering elections, Trump is even more blunt.

"Zuckerberg should be in jail," he says.

CHAPTER EIGHT

Burying Biden Corruption

Café Milano is a Georgetown restaurant that caters to Washington, D.C.'s rich and powerful. Go there at night, and you're likely to see a line of town cars and blacked-out government SUVs dropping off power brokers jonesing for the truffle pappardelle. The restaurant's own website touts a quote from the *New York Times* calling Café Milano where the "powerful gather to hold court."[1] The *Washington Post* has declared it "Washington's ultimate place to see and be seen." If you don't want to be seen, the dining room is very dimly lit, and there are private rooms available.[2]

Naturally, one of Café Milano's private rooms was the perfect meeting place for Vice President Joe Biden and his son Hunter to meet with the corrupt Ukrainian, Russian, and Kazakh "businessmen" Hunter was working with. The meeting took place on April 16, 2015. Those in attendance included former Moscow mayor Yury Luzhkov (husband to Russian billionaire Yelena Baturina, who'd sent one of Hunter's firms a $3.5 million wire transfer the year before the meeting); Karim Massimov, the former prime minister of Kazakhstan; and Vadym

Pozharskyi, an executive of the Ukrainian energy company Burisma. The firm was paying Hunter a million dollars annually to serve on its board, despite the fact that he had no energy sector expertise. Even if he did, such compensation for serving on a board was unheard of. Hunter Biden's chief qualification was that his father was overseeing Ukraine policy in the White House.[3] Apparently, Burisma considered that worth paying a premium for.

The meeting was documented by emails found on Hunter Biden's laptop, which Hunter reportedly left at a computer repair shop in Delaware for so long that it became the legal property of the shop owner. The laptop contained detailed emails confirming the meeting. "Dear Hunter, thank you for inviting me to DC and giving an opportunity to meet your father and spent [sic] some time together.... It's realty [sic] an honor and pleasure," wrote Pozharskyi the day after the dinner.[4]

That wasn't the only email confirming the meeting. "Deer [sic] Hunter, Thank you for an amazing evening, wonderful company and great conversation. I look forward to seeing you soon and to many opportunities to work closely together," wrote Marc Holtzman, who was chairman of Kazakhstan's largest bank.[5] A photo of the Bidens with Holtzman, Karim Massimov, and Kenes Rakishev, a Kazakh energy oligarch, was posted online in 2019.[6] The photo was taken at Café Milano.

Throughout his 2020 campaign, Joe Biden insisted that he had never met any of his son's business partners or talked to Hunter about his business dealings that had attracted public scrutiny. "I have never spoken to my son about his overseas business dealings," Biden said.[7] There was already a mountain of facts suggesting Joe Biden was directly involved in his son's corrupt deals, and the evidence on Hunter's laptop confirmed that Biden was lying.

When the *New York Post* dropped its first report on Hunter's laptop in October 2020, major news outlets immediately labeled reports sourced to Hunter's laptop "Russian disinformation."[8] They offered no proof to back up claims of disinformation, and ignored corroborating sources and evidence confirming the information from the laptop was accurate. The Biden campaign didn't even deny that the emails and other laptop evidence were authentic.

The media's hysterical and hyper-partisan reaction to the reports emerging about Hunter's laptop was all the excuse progressive social media companies needed to censor the news of the Biden family's corruption. Twitter wouldn't even let users send links to the *New York Post* story in private messages.[9]

A month after the election, the Biden campaign would reveal that Hunter Biden was the target of a long-running Justice Department investigation into his foreign business dealings. But by then his father and possible partner-in-crime was on his way to the White House.

There's reason to believe the Hunter Biden news blackout was a decisive factor in Biden's narrow victory. A post-election poll of 1,750 voters in seven swing states commissioned by the right-leaning Media Research Center found that 45 percent of Biden voters were unaware of any financial scandals involving Hunter Biden.[10] One in six Biden voters said they would not have voted for President Biden had they known the full extent of the financial corruption scandals involving Hunter Biden.[11]

What happened with the Hunter Biden story wasn't about mere media bias or double standards, nor was it about the establishment's giving a pass to the ne'er-do-well son of a politician. At every point, the media and their Big Tech allies deliberately controlled the information surrounding a major political corruption story involving a man who is now president, who knowingly let his family exploit his political power to strike deals with communist China and the violent oligarchs that emerged from the corrupt wasteland of the former Soviet Union. They withheld information on this corruption by any means necessary, eventually resorting to censorship and publishing disinformation in order to help Joe Biden win an election.

◆　　◆　　◆

The Biden campaign always knew that Joe's son Hunter would be a problem.

Joe Biden's youngest son had been a public embarrassment for several years. His life was a mess, to say nothing of the financial and political corruption he was mixed up in. The campaign team clearly felt they had no choice but to get out ahead of a story that was destined to roil the presidential race. And so, just before the Democratic primary began in earnest, in July 2019 the *New Yorker* published a splashy article about Hunter Biden that purported to reckon with his problems head-on.[12]

The article was written by former *Washington Post* reporter Adam Entous, who, according to his *New Yorker* bio, won "a Pulitzer Prize and a special Polk Award for stories that led to the firing of President Trump's first national-security adviser and to the appointment of a special prosecutor to investigate Russia's role in the 2016 Presidential election."[13] Suffice to say, Entous was a sympathetic and partisan reporter, and the resulting ten-thousand-word profile—"Will Hunter Biden Jeopardize His Father's Campaign?"—was skillfully crafted with an eye toward not harming Biden's presidential ambitions.

But there was only so much Entous could do, as Hunter Biden made Billy Carter look like Mother Teresa.[14] His drug-fueled escapades and corruption were so profligate that in its efforts to address all the possible future accusations, Entous's profile felt less like a piece of journalism and more like an emetic.

In May 2013, Hunter joined the Navy Reserve, despite the fact that he never would have been eligible for military service had his father not been vice president at the time. At forty-three years old, Hunter was too old to join up, requiring a special waiver from the Navy. Further, the *Wall Street Journal* reported that Hunter was given a second waiver for a "drug-related incident when he was a young man."[15] A month after Hunter enlisted, on his first official day serving in the Navy, he was given a drug test which found cocaine in his system. He was discharged in February 2014.

Despite Biden's long history of drug abuse, the *New Yorker* article dutifully—and preposterously—recounted Hunter Biden's claim that he only tested positive because he had bummed a cigarette from two men from South Africa at a bar near the White House. That cigarette, Hunter maintained, must have been laced with cocaine.

Hunter soon returned to the tabloids in 2016, when Kathleen Biden, Hunter's wife and mother to three of his children, filed for divorce, claiming that Hunter had a habit of extravagant spending on "drugs, alcohol, prostitutes, strip clubs, and gifts for women with whom he has sexual relations."[16] Hunter publicly denied hiring prostitutes in the wake of these allegations.

Hunter was also having an affair with Hallie Biden, the widow of his brother Beau—the former attorney general of Delaware who died of brain cancer. The affair reportedly began around the time of Beau's death in 2015. When the story broke in 2017, the Bidens tried to put a brave face on the development. Joe Biden issued a statement saying, "We are all lucky that Hunter and Hallie found each other as they were putting their lives together again after such sadness."[17] According to the *New Yorker*, Joe Biden didn't become aware of Hunter's relationship with his deceased brother's wife until the *New York Post* called his office for comment. According to Hunter, the only reason the Bidens issued a statement supportive of Hunter and Hallie's relationship was that Hunter begged them to. "I said, 'Dad, if people find out, but they think you're not approving of this, it makes it seem wrong,'" Hunter said.[18]

In May 2019, Lunden Alexis Roberts, an Arkansas woman who had worked under the stage name "Dallas" at a strip club a few blocks from the White House, sued Hunter Biden for paternity of her child.[19] The child was conceived and born while Hunter was still reportedly in a relationship with Hallie Biden.[20] When the *New Yorker* article was published a month after the paternity suit, Hunter was still publicly denying he had fathered the child. A DNA test later that year confirmed the child was his, and Hunter settled the paternity suit out of court.[21]

Throughout all of this personal drama, Hunter's drug problems remained out of control, as the *New Yorker* reported in the hopes that the Biden campaign could stay one step ahead of GOP opposition researchers. In the fall of 2016, a Hertz rental car office in Arizona "found a crack pipe in [Hunter Biden's] car and, on one of the consoles, a line of white-powder residue. Beau Biden's attorney-general badge was on the dashboard."[22] Also in the car was a "plastic baggie containing a 'white powdery substance,' a Secret Service business card, credit cards, and Hunter's driver's license."[23] Hertz reported this to the police, who filed a narcotics offense report. In the end, Secret Service agents assured the Prescott, Arizona, police department that Hunter Biden was "secure/well."[24] No charges against Hunter were filed by the police.

Many Americans can relate to dealing with someone they care about struggling with serious addiction issues. It would be hard to hold Joe Biden responsible for the personal decisions of a middle-aged wayward son—even if he did get sucked into publicly defending some of his son's poor choices.

Ultimately, the problem for Joe Biden was that Hunter's problems weren't confined to his personal life. Hunter Biden's poor decision-making and track record of dishonesty was an issue of public corruption. No serious person could argue that Hunter hadn't leveraged his father's status as vice president to make a series of lucrative deals with shady foreign entities. And in one instance, Hunter had even taken an overt bribe.

Entous asked Hunter Biden about a "large diamond" his wife referenced in their divorce proceedings. The story behind it turned out to be truly alarming.[25] Hunter Biden had a meeting in Miami with "Chinese energy tycoon Ye Jianming, who was trying to make connections in Washington among prominent Democrats and Republicans." Hunter claimed that he was trying to get Jianming to make a donation to a nonprofit he was on the board of, World Food Program USA.[26] In exchange, he "offered to use his contacts to help identify investment opportunities for Ye's company, CEFC China Energy, in liquefied-natural-gas projects in the United States."[27]

> After the dinner, Ye sent a 2.8-carat diamond to Hunter's hotel room with a card thanking him for their meeting. "I was, like, Oh, my God," Hunter said.[28] (In Kathleen's court motion, the diamond is estimated to be worth eighty thousand dollars. Hunter said he believes the value is closer to ten thousand.) When I asked him if he thought the diamond was intended as a bribe, he said no: "What would they be bribing me for? My dad wasn't in office." Hunter said that he gave the diamond to his associates, and doesn't know what they did with it. "I knew it wasn't a good idea to take it. I just felt like it was weird," he said.[29]

For years now, the media had obsessed over the Trump family's finances—especially any deals their worldwide real estate empire had made overseas—in a desperate attempt to establish that foreign dictators had leverage over the president. Here Hunter Biden, despite his attempts to deny it, admitted that he had taken a bribe worth tens of thousands of dollars from a Chinese businessman with close ties to that country's communist government—and it was buried more than seventy paragraphs into an article few voters would read in a magazine with a target audience of liberal elites.

Despite its best efforts, the *New Yorker* couldn't inoculate Joe Biden from the blowback of Hunter Biden's questionable dealings.

In 2009, just after his father became vice president, Hunter Biden went into business with another privileged scion of Washington—Christopher Heinz, stepson of Massachusetts senator and failed Democratic presidential candidate John Kerry. At the time, Kerry was chairman of the powerful Senate Foreign Relations Committee;[30] in 2013, Kerry would be appointed secretary of state for the second term of the Obama–Biden administration.

Hunter Biden and Heinz, along with a third partner, Heinz's college roommate, Devon Archer, formed an international private equity company under the moniker Rosemont Seneca.[31] Heinz was an heir to the family condiment fortune, and this new venture was backed by his family's investment fund, Rosemont Capital. The Bidens had much to gain from this relationship. The Biden family, while still quite wealthy, wasn't nearly as rich as other D.C. politicians and couldn't bring seed money to such an ambitious venture.

Hunter Biden had no special expertise to aid Rosemont Seneca. In fact, his prior career history suggested that he would be a liability. He had had an undistinguished career at the law firm Boies Schiller Flexner and a handful of politically connected jobs.[32] He worked as a lobbyist for several years until he abruptly quit in 2008, when the Obama campaign made it clear that it did not take kindly to Biden's having a lobbyist in the family.

Hunter Biden had one previous foray as a partner in an investment fund with his uncle, James Biden, but it was a disastrous failure. In 2006, the two men purchased Paradigm Capital Management. Paradigm would later develop a business relationship with another investment firm, Stanford Capital, managing a "jointly branded" $50 million fund for the two firms. That arrangement became an issue when Stanford Capital was exposed as a "$7 billion Ponzi scheme."[33] Allen Stanford is now serving a 110-year prison sentence, but the Bidens didn't face any charges of wrongdoing for their involvement with his firm.

Though not on the hook for the Ponzi scheme, the Bidens were still implicated in messy litigation regarding their tenure with Paradigm. Former business partner Anthony Lotito Jr. sued the pair over allegations of fraud and breach of fiduciary duty for shutting him out of the deal to purchase Paradigm. Lotito also claims that the deal to purchase Paradigm was hatched because Hunter Biden needed to find other lucrative work so that he could quit his job as a lobbyist, per his father's request. The Bidens settled out of court in 2008, with the *Washington Post* observing, "[T]he dispute highlights Hunter Biden's unusual dual roles as lobbyist and investment executive at a time when hedge funds face greater regulatory scrutiny."[34]

When it came to the founding of Rosemont Seneca, Hunter Biden had no money to contribute and had already demonstrated he had neither the skill nor judgment necessary to run an investment firm. What he did have to offer was his last name—and by 2009 his father had improbably made the leap from an unremarkable, if affable, senator to a heartbeat away from being the most powerful leader on the planet. Rosemont Seneca, unlike most financial firms, didn't set up shop in New York or Connecticut. Its offices were in Georgetown, and the firm was soon leveraging its connections to raise billions of dollars.

"Over the next seven years, as both Joe Biden and John Kerry negotiated sensitive and high-stakes deals with foreign governments, Rosemont entities secured a series of exclusive deals often with those same foreign governments," observes Peter Schweizer in his book *Secret Empires: How the American Political Class Hides Corruption and Enriches Family and Friends*.[35] "Some of the deals they secured may remain hidden. These Rosemont entities are, after all, within a private equity firm and as such are not required to report or disclose their financial dealings publicly."[36]

China, in particular, seemed eager to do business with Rosemont Seneca. In the Middle Kingdom it was an established cultural and business practice to curry favor with powerful people by paying off their children. The recipients of such largesse were sometimes known as "princelings," and there is even a Chinese word for the practice of exploiting familial connections: *guanxi*.[37] In recent times, U.S. companies desperate to do business in China's enormous growing economy have even run into legal trouble for practicing *guanxi*. J. P. Morgan, for example, was charged with violating the Foreign Corrupt Practices Act (FCPA) for giving Chinese princelings lucrative sinecures.

"But it is important to note that the FCPA prevents American corporations from hiring or doing special business deals with the children of foreign officials," Schweizer notes.[38] "It does not prevent foreign entities from hiring or doing special deals with the children of American officials."[39]

The materials Rosemont Seneca distributed to prospective clients explicitly promoted Biden as the son of the vice president, and the Chinese seemed to instinctively understand what Rosemont Seneca was all about. Within a year, the American princelings had teamed up with another firm, the Thornton Group, and soon they were taking meetings with the biggest names in Chinese finance. The story behind the Thornton Group was another tale of political privilege. The founder of the Thornton Group was James Bulger, the son of Billy Bulger, the longest-serving president of the Massachusetts State Senate and a longtime political ally of John Kerry. Billy Bulger was the younger brother of notorious Boston gangster Whitey Bulger, who is believed to have killed at least nineteen people and was the inspiration for Jack Nicholson's character in Martin Scorsese's film *The Departed*. Despite being a notorious criminal figure for decades, Whitey Bulger's political and law enforcement connections helped him avoid serious criminal charges until 2013.

Rosemont Seneca's relationship with China reached its apex in 2013. In December of that year, Hunter Biden and his daughter Finnegan accompanied Joe Biden on board Air Force Two to China, where the Biden family was greeted with much public fanfare.[40] During the trip Joe Biden spent over five hours in a private meeting with Chinese president Xi Jinping and took a meeting with the U.S.–China Business Council. There is almost no public record of what Hunter Biden was doing in China during the trip.

The timing of the Biden family trip, however, has raised questions ever since. Ten days after the trip, Rosemont Seneca signed a deal to form a joint venture with the government-owned Bank of China, an institution known for using its massive financial clout to further China's international ambitions. The joint venture was to be called "Bohai Harvest RST," a name derived from a gulf in the Yellow Sea and the initials for Rosemont Seneca Thornton.[41] Despite being a relatively new and comparatively small fund, Rosemont Seneca's involvement in Bohai Harvest

RST made it the first Western firm allowed to operate out of the recently created Shanghai Free-Trade Zone, opening up a slew of lucrative investment opportunities unavailable to other American investors. The deal was reportedly worth $1.5 billion.

"In short," says Schweizer, "the Chinese government was literally funding a business that it co-owned along with the sons of two of America's most powerful decision makers."[42]

While the financial and national security implications of the venture with the Bank of China dwarf what happened next, Hunter's subsequent deal would get the attention of political critics.

Hunter Biden was appointed to the board of the politically connected Ukrainian gas company Burisma in May 2014, shortly after his father was named the Obama administration's "point person" on Ukraine.[43] Hunter regularly attended Burisma's twice-yearly board meetings, which took place outside of Ukraine.[44] Joe Biden has always insisted that this arrangement did not affect his dealings with Ukraine on behalf of the United States. "I did not know he was on the board of that company," Biden told PBS in 2020. When Biden was asked a follow-up question about whether he would have interceded if he had known about Hunter joining Burisma's board, Biden, who had been sharply critical of Trump on the campaign trail for having his children work at the White House, didn't answer the question. He reiterated that it hadn't been established that Hunter had done "anything wrong."[45]

Biden's claim of ignorance isn't remotely believable—members of the Obama administration had directly raised concerns about Hunter Biden's role at Burisma to the White House while Biden was vice president.[46] Further, on April 16, 2014, Hunter's business partner at Rosemont Seneca, Devon Archer, showed up at the White House for a lengthy meeting. On April 21, Joe Biden arrived in Kiev to meet with Ukrainian officials. The next day, April 22, it was announced that Devon Archer was joining Burisma's board. Hunter Biden's announcement came a few weeks later, on May 13.[47] Also in May, Burisma hired lobbyist David Leiter, former chief of staff for the

Obama administration's new secretary of state John Kerry, stepfather to Chris Heinz, Biden and Archer's partner.[48]

From the beginning, the Burisma arrangement reeked of corruption. Ukraine is considered one of the most corrupt countries on the planet, and several prominent observers considered Burisma one of the most corrupt companies in a country defined by corruption. At the time Biden joined its board, the British government's anti-fraud office was busy seizing millions in assets from Burisma founder Mykola Zlochevsky.

According to Reuters, "[R]ecords show 18 months in which two payments of $83,333 per month were paid to [Hunter Biden's company] Rosemont Seneca Bohai for 'consulting services.'"[49] Evidently one of the $83,333 payments was for Hunter Biden's board service, while the other was for his business partner and co–Burisma board member Devon Archer. The payments amounted to approximately $1 million annually each for Hunter Biden and Archer, an unheard-of amount of compensation for serving on a corporate board.[50] A 2017 Harvard study looked at the compensation of board members at private companies with annual revenue of less than $500 million.[51] Board members were typically paid between $55,230 and $82,986 annually. In 2018, Burisma reportedly had revenue of $400 million.[52] Burisma paid Biden more every month than board members at similar-sized companies could expect to receive in a year.[53]

There's more than enough evidence to suggest that Hunter Biden was being paid for something other than consulting services or advice on topics related to corporate governance. Reporting shows that Biden and Archer were instrumental in organizing meetings for Burisma with the State Department while Biden was vice president and Kerry was secretary of state,[54] along with other events where the company had access to elected officials.[55]

Much attention has also been focused on the fact Joe Biden threatened to withhold $1 billion in U.S. aid to Ukraine to oust the country's top corruption prosecutor, Viktor Shokin. Shokin would later claim he was ousted after being told to back off his investigation into Burisma.[56]

Biden partisans countered that Shokin was being pressured because he wasn't doing enough to combat Ukrainian corruption, and noted that other international groups, such as the International Monetary Fund, also shared that view.[57]

Regardless, Hunter Biden's joining Burisma also coincided with some suspicious moves that proved beneficial for the company. In July 2013, four Democratic senators authored a letter requesting that the Obama administration give aid for the Ukrainian energy industry.[58] Controversial oligarch Ihor Kolomoisky, who owned a controlling interest in Burisma, had been barred from entering the United Sates over concerns about his criminal activities. In 2015, while Biden was still on the board of Burisma, the State Department reversed its previous decision and allowed Kolomoisky to travel to the United States again. Also in 2015, Joe Biden and John Kerry began publicly championing $1.8 billion in International Monetary Fund loans to Ukraine backed by U.S. taxpayers.[59] The $1.8 billion in loans was eventually deposited into a bank owned by Kolomoisky, where it promptly vanished—embezzled and laundered through a series of offshore entities.[60]

But despite the mounting evidence of Hunter Biden's corruption, the media showed less interest in covering the story than in covering it up. Their primary concern was ensuring that Republicans were unable to use any of this evidence of corruption to damage Joe Biden's chances of winning the 2020 election. To the extent the media covered any Biden corruption at all, it was through a heavily politicized lens. A typical *New York Times* headline in May 2019 read, "Biden Faces Conflict of Interest Questions That Are Being Promoted by Trump and Allies."[61] And if the media weren't going to probe Biden family corruption, who would investigate the Bidens? The media had spent the entire Trump presidency wildly speculating a foreign government might have leverage over the president. But now that the same issue was being credibly raised regarding Biden, the press had very little to say about it.

Donald Trump ended up forcing the issue of examining these conflicts of interest when he asked Ukrainian president Volodymyr Zelensky during a July 25 phone call to investigate the Bidens for political corruption. Democrats would later premise Donald Trump's first impeachment on this phone call, but the impeachment presented a dilemma for Democrats. If Hunter Biden really was engaged in corruption that compromised or implicated his father, Trump had a legitimate reason to investigate it as a national security concern. Consequently, Representative Adam Schiff, the Democrats' impeachment leader, ended up taking wholly unprecedented steps for Democrats to control the impeachment proceedings. After the first witness in the House impeachment inquiry resulted in a bevy of bad publicity for Democrats, Schiff made sure from then on that all the witnesses in the impeachment inquiry were deposed in a way that forbade committee members from discussing what was said publicly. Any information Republicans unearthed about Hunter Biden's corruption in Ukraine couldn't be aired publicly without congressional Republicans' facing ethics charges. This secrecy and control over the process was unprecedented for a constitutional procedure as important as an impeachment trial. The corporate media, which are supposed to have a vested interest in transparency, saw no problem with this.

The press may not have wanted to talk about Biden family scandals, but the Trump campaign certainly did. And they were receiving more evidence of Hunter's suspect behavior by the day.

On September 23, with the election just over a month away, the U.S. Senate Committee on Homeland Security and Governmental Affairs and the U.S. Senate Committee on Finance released an eighty-seven-page report on Hunter Biden's business activities that painted a damning and detailed picture of corruption.[62]

The report was a laundry list of eye-popping corruption, but perhaps the most damning finding in the report was this: "Hunter Biden received a $3.5 million wire transfer from Elena Baturina, the wife of the former mayor of Moscow."[63] There were even bigger examples of financial corruption swirling around Hunter Biden, but this one was politically potent. After years of asserting Trump was colluding with and financially compromised by Russia, the much-hyped Mueller report had produced no evidence of any alarming links between Russia and Trump or his family. But here was hard evidence that Joe Biden's son was getting paid an exorbitant amount by a Russian politician, and the media didn't care.

Tellingly, when the Senate report came out, the stories in the *Washington Post*, *New York Times*, CNN, NPR, *The Hill*, Daily Beast, *Wall Street Journal*, CBS News, and *Forbes* didn't mention the Russian wire transfer. Instead, the coverage was brazenly biased and protective of Joe Biden. The headline on the *Washington Post*'s news story on Grassley and Johnson's report read, "GOP Senators' Report Calls Hunter Biden's Board Position with Ukraine Firm 'Problematic' but Doesn't Show It Changed U.S. Policy."[64] That's a highly debatable characterization for an allegedly neutral news story, and the report had officials on record saying Hunter Biden's position at Burisma hampered U.S. anti-corruption efforts.

Regardless, the most potent finding in the report was almost completely blacked out of the news coverage, such that less than a week later, when Trump asked Biden about the Russian wire transfer at the first presidential debate, it was the first time most Americans had heard about it. In response to the question, Biden responded by saying the claim was "totally discredited. Totally discredited."[65] Given that it was a direct allegation in a government document and Biden was flatly denying it, this would have been a perfect opportunity for the media to dig in and sort out the truth of the claim.

Trump had forced the issue, and the media, always eager to dissect the most trivial GOP claim and declare it a falsehood, chose to obfuscate rather than clarify the issue. *USA Today*'s fact-checking operation said, "Claims That Hunter Biden Received $3.5M from Russia Are Unproven, Lack Context."[66] PolitiFact was even more circumspect, refusing to rate the claim true or false, using a dubious rationale similar to that used by *USA Today*'s fact-checker and regurgitating the Biden campaign spin on the matter. "Biden's lawyer says he did not co-found the partnership [that received the money] and had no stake in it," noted PolitiFact, adding, "Democrats say they reviewed the Republicans' documentation but did not find a specific link to Hunter Biden."[67]

Serious journalists would see this for the artful dodge that it is. No one disputes that Treasury Department documents showed Elena Baturina wired $3.5 million to Hunter Biden's firm, Rosemont Seneca Thornton, for a vague "consultancy agreement."[68] Hunter Biden's lawyer was suddenly, and quite dubiously, disputing his client's involvement in his own business firm without providing any evidence to back up the denial. Senate Democrats, in turn, had a partisan interest in separating Hunter Biden from the source of the tainted cash, and their denial was obviously parsed.

However, a corrupt and credulous press never seriously attempted to confront Joe Biden about any of this. Biden's ongoing denials were the fig leaf they needed to keep ignoring one of the biggest political corruption scandals in modern history. But ignoring and downplaying the Biden corruption wasn't going to be enough. If the media wanted to help Biden win the presidential election by burying his scandals, they would soon have to take much more drastic action.

◆   ◆   ◆

It was a classic October surprise.

The *New York Post* reported on October 14 that the paper had obtained a slew of incriminating emails and other materials on Hunter Biden. The information came from a computer repair shop in Delaware, not far from Biden's residence.[69] Hunter Biden had reportedly dropped off his water-damaged laptop and simply forgotten to pick it up, despite repeated attempts by the shop to contact him and return his computer. According to the terms of service at the repair shop, any computers abandoned without payment became the property of the shop. The owner of the shop then turned the laptop over to the FBI, but not before he made a copy of the hard drive to give Trump confidant Rudy Giuliani.[70]

In addition to lewd videos and photos depicting Hunter taking drugs and engaged in sex acts, the laptop contained emails that indicated

Hunter was running a pay-for-play scheme. The allegations in the emails were explosive and confirmed much of what had been reported in previous months, while also introducing new information.

In an email to Ye Jianming, the government-connected owner of the Chinese energy company CEFC who featured prominently in the Senate report, Biden demanded Jianming pay him $10 million a year "for introductions alone."[71] The emails also detailed how Biden was trying to broker a larger deal with Jianming's doomed company, CEFC, that he described as "interesting for me and my family."[72] The proposed venture with CEFC was to be called "SinoHawk."[73] An email to Hunter Biden proposed ownership stakes in the new company, with percentages for each investor. Those stakes included 10 percent for "Jim" and "10 held by H for the big guy."[74] Neither "Jim" nor "the big guy" was identified, but speculation immediately arose that "Jim" was James Biden and "the big guy" was none other than Joe Biden.[75]

Even for a press corps that repeatedly demonstrated a cartoonish hostility to Trump, the reaction to the *New York Post*'s scoop was on another level. The immediate reaction was to discredit the story without even attempting to prove the *Post*'s reporting was inaccurate, despite the fact the Biden campaign didn't dispute the authenticity of the emails.

The day after the first *Post* laptop story ran, Natasha Bertrand, a *Politico* reporter who had been criticized even by the *Washington Post*'s media columnist for her credulous reporting on the Steele dossier, wrote a piece headlined "Hunter Biden Story Is Russian Disinfo, Dozens of Former Intel Officials Say."[76] Bertrand cited a public letter signed by fifty former members of the military and American intelligence agencies warning that the *Post*'s story "has all the classic earmarks of a Russian information operation."[77] Though Russian disinformation was the headline, the same letter also admitted that the intelligence officials, many of whom had track records of partisan activism, had no proof of anything. "We want to emphasize that we do not know if the e-mails, provided to the *New York Post* by President Trump's personal attorney Rudy Giuliani, are genuine or not and that we do not have evidence of Russian involvement," said the letter.[78] Signatories to the letter included former Obama director of national intelligence James Clapper and former CIA director John Brennan, both of whom had been caught lying to Congress and were instrumental in foisting the Steele dossier and Russia collusion hoax on the media.

That same day, the *New York Times* also reported, "Trump Said to Be Warned That Giuliani Was Conveying Russian Disinformation," and, further, that Trump had "shrugged off" the warning about his aide who was involved in bringing the laptop story to light.[79] These reports were naturally buttressed by more outspoken members of the "intelligence community."[80]

The default media explanation for the laptop became—yet again—a Vladimir Putin–backed conspiracy, where the laptop was invented as part of a Russian disinformation campaign to meddle in American elections. By contrast, the notion that erratic Hunter Biden, who once left his drugs and crack pipe in a rental car, had forgotten to pick up his laptop at a computer repair shop a short distance from his house was deemed too far-fetched.

The managing editor of taxpayer-funded NPR declared it a "waste of time" to report on the Hunter Biden allegations.[81] *Vice* tried to tell readers "why almost none of this actually matters and you should go outside and stare into the sun" rather than read the *New York Post*'s story on Biden.[82] *The Atlantic*'s Anne Applebaum assured us, "Those who live outside the Fox News bubble and intend to remain there do not, of course, need to learn any of this stuff [about Hunter Biden]."[83] David Frum, Applebaum's colleague at *The Atlantic*, went even further. "The people on far right and far left who publicized the obviously bogus [*New York Post*] story were not dupes. They were accomplices. The story could not have been more obviously fake if it had been wearing dollar-store spectacles and attached plastic mustache," he wrote.[84]

But the media's conspiracy theories and frantic condemnations were downstream from the most unprecedented and frightening reaction to the *Post*'s scoop. The biggest social media companies censored the story as soon as it appeared.

The morning the story appeared online, Andy Stone, Facebook's policy communications manager, tweeted: "While I will intentionally not link to the *New York Post*, I want be clear that this story is eligible to be fact checked by Facebook's third-party fact checking partners. In the meantime, we are reducing its distribution on our platform."[85] Stone, whose résumé includes stints working for Democratic senator Barbara Boxer and the Democratic Congressional Campaign Committee, also preposterously claimed, "This is part of our standard process to reduce the spread of misinformation. We temporarily reduce distribution pending fact-checker review."[86] The last four years had been marked by dozens of untrue accusations leveled at President Trump in major publications that were much less credible than the *Post*'s reporting on Biden's laptop. The social media giant hadn't lifted a finger to stop any of those stories.

Twitter's approach was even more draconian—the site simply made it impossible to post a link to the *New York Post* story. The website locked the accounts of users trying to share the story, including White House press secretary Kayleigh McEnany. Twitter's justification for its Orwellian measures was that the *Post*'s story violated the site's policy against disseminating hacked materials, but there was no evidence that the materials from Hunter Biden's laptop had been hacked, and by all accounts the owner of the computer repair shop had legally gained possession of it. Stories that did involve ill-gotten information, such as the *New York Times*'s coverage of Trump's illegally leaked tax returns, were not censored.[87] Twitter shut the *New York Post*—the oldest continuously published newspaper in America, founded by none other than Alexander Hamilton—out of its own Twitter account unless it agreed to delete its initial tweet promoting the story.[88] The *New York Post* got access to its Twitter account restored over two weeks later, and only after Twitter CEO Jack Dorsey had been summoned to testify before Congress to explain the censorship.

The censorship, combined with the wholly unproven "Russian disinformation" narrative, largely neutralized the revelations. Biden appeared at an ABC News town hall on October 15, the day after the first *Post* laptop story ran. George Stephanopoulos, the former Clinton White House official who now presents himself as an impartial news anchor, didn't ask Biden a single question related to either of the two *Post* stories about his son's corruption and the allegations he had helped directly facilitate it.[89]

Prominent journalists, who are supposed to have a vested interest in creating a culture of free speech and rooting out public corruption, lined up to defend the censorship. "Honestly, they [Facebook and Twitter] are not even doing one-tenth of what they should be doing," CNN media analyst Brian Stelter told the BBC. Stelter added that he thought Trump and Republican voters had brought this censorship on themselves.[90] "There's a lot more indecency and BS...being spread by the right. It's sad, hopefully it will stop, but right now it's true and that's what the platforms are reacting to," he said.[91]

With the election less than two weeks away, the Trump campaign had one last blow to drop on Biden—but there was a fight behind the scenes at a major newspaper to keep the information from coming out. Tony Bobulinski, one of Hunter Biden's partners in the deal with Ye Jianming, was willing to go on record with the *Wall Street Journal* and make an astonishing claim—the "big guy" being cut in on Hunter's China deal was indeed Joe Biden. Not only did Bobulinski claim to have personally met with Joe Biden to discuss the deal, he provided texts, emails, voicemails, and other evidence supporting his claims. Bobulinski was a former naval officer, and there was no obvious reason to doubt his credibility.

It was a blockbuster story—and one that the *Wall Street Journal* refused to print.[92] After ten days of sitting on the Bobulinski story, the Trump campaign finally got exasperated and, two hours before the second presidential debate, staged a press conference in which Bobulinski himself outlined his claims and provided evidence that Joe Biden was profiting off his son's corruption.[93] At the presidential debate later that night, Biden wasn't forced to answer any specific allegations made by Bobulinski. When Trump brought up Hunter's laptop, Biden hid behind the letter signed by intelligence community officials. "There are 50 former national intelligence folks who said that what [Trump's] accusing me of is a Russian plan," he said.[94]

With the *Journal* stalling, the Bobulinski documents were handed out to conservative publications and any other media willing to write about them. By then, it was an open secret that the *Wall Street Journal* newsroom had been sitting on the Bobulinski claims for weeks. A few hours after Bobulinski's press conference started making waves, the *Wall Street Journal* newsroom made the curious decision to finally publish its story on the matter, well after its exclusive had been squandered. And the framing of the news story was peculiar, to say the least.

The subhead to the story read, "Former vice president says he had no involvement; corporate records reviewed by The Wall Street Journal show no role for Joe Biden."[95] On the issue of Biden's denial, a credible witness had provided personal on-the-record testimony and documents contradicting Joe Biden—that was the heart of the story. Biden's denial wasn't especially credible or newsworthy. And the issue of "corporate records" seemed almost willfully misleading—Bobulinski was specifically alleging that Hunter Biden would secretly hold Joe Biden's stake in the deal so as to shield it from the public. The entire point was Joe Biden's name wouldn't be found on any paperwork.

The one reported detail the *Wall Street Journal*'s story had that was missing from other accounts of the Bobulinski allegations was a cagey denial from James Gilliar, another businessman involved in the deal. "I am unaware of any involvement at any time of the former vice president," he told *Wall Street Journal* reporters. "The activity in question never delivered any project revenue."[96] But Gilliar authored the infamous email referencing a 10 percent stake in the deal being "held by H for the big guy." Gilliar did not respond to a request for comment from the *Wall Street Journal* about the email.

After the *Wall Street Journal*'s news story finally emerged, a strange media narrative coalesced around discrediting the Bobulinski allegations. Oddly enough, one of the first notable stories on the Bobulinski claims was written by *Wall Street Journal* opinion columnist Kim Strassel and appeared a few hours ahead of the *Wall Street Journal*'s belated news article. Strassel noted that the allegations looked very bad for Biden, but her story was typically detailed and careful.

Other reporters seized on the news story's pro-Biden framing to try and attack Strassel. "No Evidence for Trump Claim That Joe Biden Earned Money in China, According to the Wall Street Journal, Contradicting Its Editorial Section," was the headline at Business Insider.[97] Jennifer Epstein, the reporter covering the Biden campaign for Bloomberg, tweeted, "This article will run in tomorrow's print WSJ, as will an opinion piece making claims that the article debunks."[98] *Vanity Fair* even wrote an entire article about the "Wall Street Journal Cold War," claiming "Journal reporters blew up corruption allegations against the Biden family amplified on the Opinion page, exposing a rift between the paper's newsroom and conservative editorial operation."[99]

The problem, however, was that not a single fact reported in the *Wall Street Journal*'s news story contradicted Strassel's carefully reported column. *Vanity Fair* was right about there being a simmering conflict at the *Wall Street Journal*, but that didn't discredit Strassel: it offered a possible explanation for why the paper's newsroom botched the Bobulinski story so badly. The previous summer, three hundred *Journal* employees had signed a letter criticizing the *Wall Street Journal*'s conservative opinion pages for their allegedly sloppy reporting. They also demanded that the paper's news reporters be allowed to publicly criticize the opinion side of the paper without professional consequences. Many of the *Wall Street Journal*'s reporters' complaints about the opinion section were political—the letter objected to an op-ed on "The Myth of Systemic Racism," as if such a broad topic can't be debated.[100] The two authors of the Bobulinski news story at the *Journal*, Andrew Duehren and James Areddy, were signers of this letter, which left little doubt as to where their personal political sympathies lay.

When Biden eked out an incredibly narrow victory at the beginning of November, it wasn't long before reporters started patting themselves on the back for suppressing the Hunter Biden story. *Politico* ran a post-election feature on "How 'Obamagate' and Hunter's 'Laptop from Hell' Fizzled," arguing that the stories failed to gain traction because they were "riddled with falsehoods, exaggerations and assumptions."[101] Later in November, *Politico* editor Sam Stein, then working at The Daily Beast, argued that the media's suppression of stories about Hunter kept Joe Biden from losing such a close election.

"According to Biden campaign metrics, online chatter about the Hunter Biden story during the election's last week was greater than it was around Hillary's emails during last month of '16," observed Stein. "The difference: it never spilled over into mainstream outlets."[102]

In December 2020, the Biden campaign admitted Hunter was under federal investigation for his financial dealings, including with China.[103] Not only did the documents and emails published by the *New York Post* appear to be authentic, a Daily Beast report noted that there was evidence that could have been used to verify the *Post*'s story hiding in plain sight.[104]

One of the FBI documents from the laptop published by the *Post* "included a case number that had the code associated with an ongoing federal money laundering investigation in Delaware, according to several law enforcement officials who reviewed the document. Another document—one with a grand jury subpoena number—appeared to show the initials of two assistant U.S. attorneys linked to the Wilmington, Delaware, office."[105] If other media outlets had bothered to examine the documents in the *Post* story instead of rushing to press with tendentious reports discrediting the story, voters could have learned the truth.

Shortly after the election, Twitter CEO Jack Dorsey told the Senate Judiciary Committee that his platform had been wrong to censor the *Post*. "We recognize it as a mistake that we made, both in terms of the *i*ntention of the policy and also the enforcement action of not allowing people to share it publicly or privately," said Dorsey.[106]

But it was only a mistake if you believe America's media companies care about stopping disinformation. If you believe that the goal of censoring the *Post* story was to help Joe Biden win an election, Twitter and the rest of the media knew exactly what they were doing. The same journalists who spent the entire Trump presidency screaming about the erosion of political norms suddenly had no problem rejecting the most sacred ideals of their profession and embracing an unprecedented campaign to censor and discredit legitimate reporting on political corruption weeks before an election.

Theirs was another attempt to rig the election in their candidate's favor, and it succeeded. Two days before the election, on November 1, the *New York Times* took a victory lap celebrating the media's efforts to suppress the growing number of Biden corruption stories. "Welcome to November. For Trump, the October Surprise Never Came," was the headline in the *Times*. "Trump's hope that an economic recovery, a Covid vaccine or a Biden scandal could shake up the race faded with the last light of October."[107]

CHAPTER NINE

Fourteen Seconds Too Late

In retrospect, the most notable thing about Election Day was how quiet it was.

In the weeks and months ahead of November 3, the Trump political operation had charted out six different combinations of state victories that could put Trump over the required number of Electoral College votes. Those six different combinations covered seventeen different states.

Because of all the things that can go wrong when voting or counting votes, the Trump team put together extensive legal teams for each of the seventeen states. Three national law firms were procured, dividing up the seventeen states between them.[1] Then state-level law firms were brought onto the effort, along with additional lawyers and political operatives in key cities. State directors of the operation had been on board since around April, but new lawyers and operatives were added in the fall. Biden had bragged that summer about having hired six hundred lawyers for his litigation strategy.[2] Both sides claimed they needed lawyers to stop the other side from "stealing" the election.[3]

A big Trump legal team was set up in North Carolina. The Tar Heel state had been a tremendous problem for the campaign heading into

Election Day.[4] In September, the two Republicans on the state's board of elections had resigned in protest. (There are five members on the board, with a majority of seats given to the political party of the governor.) The North Carolina Alliance for Retired Americans, an advocacy group represented by Democrats' top election lawyer Marc Elias, had sued the state over its rules for mail-in balloting.[5] Rather than defend the laws passed by the state's elected representatives in court, the state's Democratic attorney general settled the lawsuit, letting Elias's demands rewrite the state's election laws.[6]

The new rules, which were litigated all the way to the United States Supreme Court, made it so that mail-in ballots in the state would be accepted up to nine days after Election Day, a full six days more than the old limit.[7] The new rules also eliminated several security provisions around the state's ballot "curing" procedures—the process of fixing any problems with a mail-in ballot after it's been mailed in.[8] Elias had great success with this "sue-and-settle" approach to changing laws, particularly in states with Democratic secretaries of state, attorney generals, or governors.[9]

Despite the concerns created by these abrupt changes in the law, North Carolina turned out to have few problems on Election Day—in part because Trump won the state by a margin just large enough that ballot disputes didn't become an issue, and both campaigns focused their fight elsewhere.

The biggest team of attorneys and operatives was set up in Florida, because, well, it was Florida. In 2000, an intense recount and legal battle had kept the country unclear on who the winner of the Electoral College was until the United States Supreme Court handed down a ruling on December 12 of that year. Because it was such a mess, Florida had reformed its election system, but county-level officials and systems could still be a problem. The Trump team was not going to let Florida be a problem. And it wasn't, with a decisive victory early on Election Night.

◆   ◆   ◆

Pennsylvania was another big legal effort. It's a huge state with two major cities, one with a history of problems for Republicans. "Bad things happen in Philadelphia,"[10] President Trump had said during the first presidential debate in September. Media and other activists insisted it wasn't true. But Philadelphia, which is overwhelmingly Democratic, has a long and storied history of election fraud. A federal judge had to overturn the results of a 1993 state senate election after it was determined that Democrats had forged hundreds of absentee ballots.[11]

In 2008, the left-wing Association of Community Organizations for Reform Now (ACORN) was shown to have registered voters by filling names out of the phone book and falsifying signatures.[12] Nearly one hundred fraudulent voter registrations submitted by ACORN in Delaware County prompted the district attorney to issue an identity theft alert.[13]

On Election Day in 2008, the New Black Panthers, a black nationalist group, stood outside a polling place brandishing a weapon. It was a clear-cut case of voter intimidation, and charges were filed against the New Black Panthers by the Justice Department. The charges were later dropped by the Obama administration.[14]

In 2012, Republican poll watchers were either barred from or kicked out of some seventy-five polling locations.[15] Later in the day, a judge issued an emergency order demanding they be allowed in. In twenty wards, voter turnout was greater than 97 percent, a figure of great concern to those who knew that the voter rolls were bloated with dead people and others who hadn't been removed as they should have been.[16] By comparison, voter turnout nationwide in 2012 averaged 58.6 percent of the eligible voting population.

In 2017, polling place workers were charged with intimidating voters, casting bogus ballots, and falsely certifying results during a special election for a state house seat in North Philadelphia.[17]

In 2020, South Philadelphia judge of elections Domenick DeMuro pleaded guilty to taking bribes to stuff the ballot box in multiple elections.[18] Another Democrat, former U.S. representative Michael Myers—also implicated in the Abscam FBI sting investigation in the 1970s—was also charged in the voter fraud scheme.[19]

The *Philadelphia Inquirer* wrote that after Myers was released from prison for the Abscam situation, he consulted with candidates "looking to navigate the intricacies of ward politics in South Philadelphia," but that it wasn't quite clear exactly what they were paying him for.[20]

It's exceedingly difficult to convict anyone of voter fraud, and difficult to indict for it, because it's very difficult to find conclusively. But vigilance on Election Day, when people report odd occurrences and questionable actions, is a first step.

Unlike the other sixty-six counties in Pennsylvania, Philadelphia has a special dedicated election court where Democratic and Republican attorneys can bring issues to a judge quickly.[21] That's where Linda A. Kerns, a civil litigator who practices in the state and federal courts of Pennsylvania and New Jersey, would station herself. When the Trump campaign needed an attorney to cover southeastern Pennsylvania, there was no question they'd reach out to Kerns.

"She's a straight shooter, extremely good lawyer, and knows the system better than anyone," said James Fitzpatrick, the state director for Election Day operations.[22]

Kerns got up to speed on Philadelphia's notoriously corrupt election practices by helping the Philadelphia Republican City Committee each Election Day. A tenacious and meticulous attorney, she got Freddie Ramirez, the Democratic candidate for the 197th Legislative District, ousted from the ballot in 2017 by proving he was lying about where he lived.[23] Ramirez, a clinical social worker, had claimed he lived around the corner from a treatment center he owned in Feltonville, a working-class neighborhood of North Philadelphia. He testified that he occasionally spent the night in the Roxborough neighborhood, where his teenage daughter lived, and over in Bristol, where his girlfriend lived, but that he spent four or five nights a week at the Feltonville address.[24]

Kerns had been tipped off that he was lying, but to prove it she had to interview neighbors, pore through evidence, and write up filings in just a few hours' time. Election law moves at a breakneck pace because of the natural deadlines for printing up ballots and holding elections.

Neighbors of the Feltonville house testified that Ramirez didn't live there, and other evidence showed Ramirez spent time in Bristol, a borough twenty miles north of Philadelphia in Bucks County.[25]

Kerns pored through utility records going back to January 2015 that showed electricity used at the Roxborough home he claimed to spend only some time at was up to seventeen times more than that used at his supposed Feltonville residence. And the Water Revenue Bureau information showed that if he was living at the Feltonville home, he certainly wasn't using the toilet there. The number of flushes per day was impossibly low for a residence.[26]

Candidate residency is almost never challenged, even less likely to be tried, and almost never won. However, Commonwealth Court judge Anne Covey threw Ramirez off the ballot in a decisive fifty-page opinion. The *Philadelphia Public Record* said that the unquestioned winner of the story was "the diligent effectiveness of Kerns and her team in the arcane thickets of election law."[27]

"I am horrified at what these Democrats did here," said Kerns. "I hope this is a lesson to them. I may only be one person but I'm not going away."[28]

◆　　◆　　◆

Over the years, Kerns had become wise to some of the problems that would arise in Philadelphia. When a poll watcher hired by Republicans in 2016 reported that one of the machines at a polling location already had votes on it when it was started for the day, Kerns got the machine impounded.[29] That same year, liberal special interest groups were bringing in bundles of "emergency absentee ballots" that they had collected at nursing homes and hospitals.[30] Pennsylvania didn't have mail-in balloting at the time, just absentee balloting. But the state did have something called emergency absentee balloting. If a voter fell ill within a few days of the election, he or she could submit an emergency absentee ballot, as long as a judge signed off on it.[31]

Bundlers of the ballots would collect them in large groups, often from vulnerable and easily pressured populations in nursing homes and hospitals, and ask a judge to issue a blanket order accepting them. The law said that anyone could have a hearing on each emergency absentee ballot, so Kerns would do that, slowing down the process of such ballot harvesting, which was and is technically illegal in the state.[32]

The Pennsylvania legislature dramatically changed its election laws in 2019, one year before the presidential election.[33] The legislature got rid of straight-ticket voting, in which voters could vote for just one party, and added mail-in balloting. It was a huge win for Democrats, and at not much cost.

The Republican Party was not in any way prepared for what hit it. The Republicans in the legislature were thrilled to get rid of straight-party voting that they thought helped Democrats, and they didn't put much thought into growing integrity problems associated with mail-in voting. GOP chairman Val DiGiorgio resigned in disgrace months prior to the passing of the legislation in a sexting scandal. Election integrity was clearly not his focus at the time.[34]

The changes, combined with the COVID-19 pandemic, meant a massive increase in mail-in balloting. The rushed change to mail-in balloting caused headaches for everyone. When tens of thousands of ballots were rejected in the primary for failing to comply with a provision to ensure the votes were secretly cast, everyone realized that the November counting would be rough. "November is going to be a train wreck involving a clown car getting rear-ended into a burning dumpster full of old tires, to be precise," Logan Churchwell, a spokesman for the conservative Public

Interest Legal Foundation, which is dedicated to litigating election integrity issues, said.[35]

◆   ◆   ◆

Usually, Philadelphia would count its hundreds of thousands of votes by bringing cartridges—small devices somewhat bigger than a thumb drive—that held ballot data from the thousands of voting machines spread across the city to the two main election offices. They'd also tally the limited absentee and provisional ballots. In 2020, there were hundreds of thousands of mail-in ballots that weren't supposed to be counted until Election Day. That meant observation of the mail-in vote counting was key for Republicans.

For weeks prior to Election Day, Republicans had begged election officials to see the layout of the convention center where mail-in ballots would be counted. They needed to secure poll watchers and had no idea if they needed ten poll watchers or hundreds. Election officials refused to give Republicans a tour. The night before Election Day, the Republicans wondered if they should have a food delivery ordered for inside the convention center just to get a report of how tables were arranged by interviewing the person who delivered the food.

The attorneys and operatives who arrived at the convention center early in the morning on November 3 immediately phoned Kerns over at the election court. It was worse than anybody had feared. GOP poll watchers couldn't see a thing. Parade gates had been set up, and the counting was happening so far away behind those gates that the poll watchers couldn't tell what was going on at all. Votes were being counted on tables set up in row after row. Visibility was limited even at the tables in the nearest row. Seeing what was happening seven rows away was flat-out impossible. The poll watchers said that it was like standing in one end zone trying to observe something in the opposite end zone.

Kerns had already been fighting against a similar poll-watching issue months prior. The City of Philadelphia had received more than ten million dollars in Zuck Bucks, some of which was spent on satellite offices where, in their words, voters could "request a mail-in ballot in-person, receive it, fill it out, and return it to cast their vote."[36] The language alarmed the Trump campaign, because early voting isn't legal in Pennsylvania. Nevertheless, Philadelphia would open seventeen such locations where people could vote in September and October, prior to the election. Nearly $35 million in Zuckerberg funds flowed into government offices in Democratic strongholds of Pennsylvania to assist Democrats with their mail-in voting push.[37]

Pennsylvania election code permits municipalities to set up election offices as needed to conduct business. Philadelphia has two, one in city hall for executive offices and one on Spring Garden Street near the Delaware River, where they process votes. Philadelphia officials interpreted the law to mean they could open additional offices, where people could pick up a ballot, fill it out, and return it, all in one transaction.

Publicly, Philadelphia kept advertising what was happening in these new satellite locations as "voting," but when Republicans inquired about witnessing what was happening, they were told it wasn't voting.[38] Members of the Trump campaign tried to enter one of the voting locations, but they were told they couldn't. The Trump campaign sent cameras over to the site to record that they were being blocked from observing. An attorney for the city said that since the city wasn't recording the votes, it wasn't voting. But votes aren't recorded at polling locations on Election Day, either, yet poll watchers are encouraged and allowed to be there.

If it wasn't a polling place, it was a public building, the Trump campaign surmised. They tried to enter on the grounds it was a public building but were told that they couldn't come into the building because of COVID-19 concerns. The Trump campaign was willing to put observers in full hazmat suits and follow any protocol, so long as they could observe the early voting, yet they were not allowed in. The Trump campaign sued over what was happening and lost.[39]

Judge Gary Glazer of the Philadelphia County Court of Common Pleas ruled that satellite offices didn't qualify as polling places and that state law "contains no provision that expressly grants the Campaign and its representatives a right to serve as watchers at satellite offices of the Board of Elections."[40]

The Trump campaign appealed the decision to the Commonwealth Court and lost there as well. Judge Patricia McCullough wrote a blistering dissent to the rulings, which, she said, "effectively deprive both presidential candidates, and by extension, every party and candidate, of their statutory right to have poll watchers present at places where electors cast and submit votes in person and in numbers unparalleled in our times."[41]

Zuck Bucks were also used to set up drop boxes for ballots. The drop boxes were unmanned and had minimal security. Ballot harvesting is not allowed in Pennsylvania because of concerns that the practice violates the sanctity of the secret ballot. There are very narrow exceptions for voters with disabilities, in which case a "designated agent" form can be filled out for someone else to turn in the ballot. The drop boxes made it all but impossible to enforce that law.[42]

The Trump campaign realized that ballot harvesting was happening. In just a short period of time at one ballot box at Philadelphia City Hall, three people were observed illegally dropping multiple ballots into the box. According to the Pennsylvania Supreme Court, an absentee ballot cast in violation of the requirements was supposed to be voided. The campaign immediately sounded the alarm, saying they believed "these to be just the tip of the iceberg."[43] They asked for election officials to man the drop boxes, and other relief. But instead of election officials' doing anything about the problem, the Trump campaign got in trouble.

The media were enraged that the Trump campaign was taking voter integrity seriously. "The Trump campaign has been videotaping Philadelphia voters while they deposit their ballots in drop boxes, leading Pennsylvania's attorney general to warn this week that the campaign's actions fall outside of permitted poll watching practices and could amount to illegal voter intimidation," the *New York Times* wrote.[44] Oddly enough, the article was itself illustrated with a photo of "a voter depositing a ballot on Saturday at a drop box in Philadelphia," the same type of photo that had drawn the rebuke for the Trump campaign.[45] In fact, when the Trump campaign had observed the ballot trafficking, they had been stationed behind a local TV news crew that was recording people dropping off ballots at the ballot box.

The *Philadelphia Inquirer* ran a similar story, uncritically pushing Democratic attorney general Josh Shapiro's claim that observing ballot box election fraud was "voter intimidation."[46] Its story was illustrated with a picture of a prominent city resident dropping off his ballots. "Philadelphia Mayor Jim Kenney delivers his mail ballot outside City Hall on Monday," read the caption.[47]

The only problem? The Democratic mayor was pictured with two ballots, in clear violation of the law. When the Trump campaign sounded the alarm again, the mayor's office admitted that the picture was as it seemed, but claimed that he had been saved in the nick of time from actually violating the law.

"The Mayor was also carrying a mail-in ballot belonging to a person with whom he is personally close," Kenney's spokesman, Mike Dunn, told the *Delaware Valley Journal*.[48] "The elections official standing with him in the photograph informed him that he was not allowed to deposit that person's ballot. The Mayor then deposited only his own ballot into the drop box."[49]

The Trump campaign said that since the mayor himself "almost broke the law, " they were right to ask for a Board of Elections representative to staff drop boxes to stop illegal voting.[50] Nevertheless, while illegal voting was occurring, Philadelphia officials didn't care, and the state and national media coverage was so hostile to the Trump campaign's documentation of it that the campaign moved on to other issues.

Voting in Pennsylvania was a mess in ways that were obvious well before November 3, so it came as little surprise that GOP poll watchers were being rebuffed on Election Day. Back at the convention center,

Kerns immediately petitioned the judge that her poll watchers be allowed within six feet of the counting of ballots. The judge denied it, albeit with a request that election commissioners investigate moving the barriers if they could.[51]

Kerns appealed to the Commonwealth Court, one of the state's two intermediate appellate courts.[52] In other Pennsylvania courts, when a lawyer files a complaint, he or she is assigned a judge. The Commonwealth Court functions a bit like a lottery, with attorneys not knowing which judge will be assigned. Kerns filed her appeal that morning, and the court scheduled a conference call for that night. It was just Kerns on her side of the case, because the other Trump campaign lawyers were busy and it was such a seemingly simple request for access to the vote counting. But there were about thirty attorneys on the other side—including Marc Elias's team—because powerful Democratic interests had intervened in the case. Democrats clearly did not want Republican observers to have access to the counting of mail-in ballots at the Philadelphia convention center. Despite the disparity in the numbers and prominence of the legal counsel on each side, when the judge appeared, Kerns immediately thought she'd win.

That was because the judge was a woman with the memorable name of Christine Fizzano Cannon. When Fizzano Cannon was up for election across the state in 2017, Philadelphia's disastrous handling of her race nearly derailed her electoral chances. Half of the voting machines in Philadelphia had her name one way—as Christine Fizzano—and half had her as another—Christine Fizzano Cannon.[53] Her campaign was livid.

"It is hard to fathom how, out of 67 counties, this would only happen in the City of Philadelphia where Fizzano Cannon's principal opposition is a sitting Philadelphia Judge," campaign spokesman Pete Peterson said in a statement.[54] If any Pennsylvania judge were to understand Philadelphia shenanigans and their significance, it would be Fizzano Cannon.

The Trump campaign offered to turn in its filings on the case the next morning by 8:00 a.m., since time was of the essence and ballots were being counted the whole time even though Republican observers were being kept at bay.[55] The Democrats were urging a delay, saying they needed to explain the history of the election code and do a deep dive into why the access was limited. Further, they hoped the judge would order the Trump campaign to file its briefs first and then give the Democrats a chance to respond.[56]

The judge was having none of the delay tactics. She said the briefs for both sides were due the next morning, after which she quickly issued her ruling saying that the Trump campaign was allowed within six feet of the ballot counting.[57]

Kerns waded through the protesters and police outside the convention center to deliver the ruling. The lawyers for the city tried to stop the ruling from going into effect immediately, saying they'd need to analyze it. Kerns insisted that they had to let the Trump observers watch the ballot counting from six feet away. Instead, the city shut down ballot counting and immediately appealed the case to the Supreme Court of Pennsylvania.[58] That action meant that Fizzano Cannon's ruling was stayed, and that the trial court order—which had said that the city didn't have to allow Republican observers within six feet of the counting—was in effect.[59] The Democrats in Philadelphia did not have to allow the Trump campaign any observation of the vote counting.

As the Trump campaign began litigating election issues in various battleground states, the media and other partisans would obsessively reiterate that there was no widespread fraud being alleged. But fraud is difficult to find in elections, even under the circumstances most advantageous to finding it conclusively. And it's more difficult to find if groups aren't allowed to observe the election process.

Without ballot observers, it's impossible to say whether an election— let alone an election in a city such as Philadelphia with a storied reputation for corruption—is being conducted fairly. There's a process with mail-in ballots that must be followed to help ensure fraud isn't occurring—either with the ballots themselves or among poll counters. Election workers are supposed to review each envelope that contains a ballot and determine that it has been filed legally.

If anything, spuriously obstructing a campaign's legal right to have observers present puts into question an election's fairness, if not its legitimacy. The Trump campaign had a legal right to observers within a reasonable distance from the counting. Why did election officials in overwhelmingly Democratic Philadelphia go out of their way to deprive the campaign of that right?

In theory, mail-in balloting procedures should mimic the anti-fraud provisions of in-person balloting as much as possible. With in-person balloting, a voter identifies himself or herself publicly, so that the rest of the community is assured he or she is a legal voter. Then the person votes in secret, to assure that undue pressure is not applied to the voter. In Pennsylvania, the mail-in voter is supposed to sign and date a legal declaration on the outside of the envelope—just as he or she would sign and date an entry in a voter log if doing in-person voting—and then put the ballot inside of a secrecy envelope that goes inside the regular envelope. Failure to do any of these things is supposed to cause a rejection, just as it would in in-person voting.

To mimic the security provisions, a form is printed on the envelope for the mail-in ballot asking each voter if he or she signed the following declaration in his or her own handwriting and if he or she put the ballot inside a secrecy envelope. The declaration reads:

> I hereby declare that I am qualified to vote from the below stated address at this election; that I have not already voted in this election; and I further declare that I marked my ballot in secret. I am qualified to vote the enclosed ballot. I understand I am no longer eligible to vote at my polling place after I return my voted ballot. However, if my ballot is not received by the county, I understand I may only vote by provisional ballot at my polling place, unless I surrender my

balloting materials, to be voided, to the judge of elections at my polling place.[60]

The Pennsylvania voter is supposed to sign the declaration, mark the date he or she signed it, print his or her name, and write his or her address. Failure to do these things renders the vote invalid, according to the election code.[61]

Since the ballot itself is separated from the outside envelope during the counting process, it's very important for poll watchers to observe whether the election workers are handling that process ethically. Were they really setting aside all the ballots that should be rejected for failure to conform to the anti-fraud provisions of the law? Nobody had any idea.

The Pennsylvania election code holds that once election workers count all the ballots, they must set aside any ballots that may be rejected for failure to comply with election rules. The rejected ballots are then supposed to go to a review board, where three commissioners sit on a bench and the supervisor comes with the rejected ballots. Out of the 365,000 ballots submitted by mail in Philadelphia, only a small number had been rejected. About 1,200 ballots were set aside because the envelope was signed but the declaration wasn't filled out. About 1,250 were set aside because they were signed, but not dated. And about 550 were set aside because the name was not printed.

The commissioners are then to vote on whether to accept the ballots or not, by the category of disqualification. The law does give a campaign the right to appeal the counting of entire categories of ballot acceptance or rejection to a judge. So all the ballots that were missing a signature could be accepted or rejected en masse, and that ruling could be appealed en masse.

In Philadelphia, the ballots were accepted. The Trump campaign appealed and lost.

Republican state senate candidate Nicole Ziccarelli also appealed the counting of an entire category of ballots that had been improperly cast.[62] She ran against incumbent senator Jim Brewster for the Forty-Fifth

Senatorial District, which straddles more than one county. In the portion of the district in the mostly Democratic Allegheny County, mail-in ballots that arrived without an indication of the date upon which they were signed were counted.[63] In the portion of the district in the mostly Republican Westmoreland County, the elections officials did not count the ballots, since the state election code clearly stated that mail-in ballots needed to be dated. Before the improper Allegheny County votes were counted, Ziccarelli was winning the seat. On election night, Ziccarelli was up ten thousand votes. She would end up losing by fewer than one hundred votes.[64]

The law and the official election guidance from the state were clearly supportive of Ziccarelli's claim. Pennsylvania law repeatedly declared that voters "shall"—not "may," but "shall"—date their declarations.[65]

On September 28, 2020, Secretary of State Kathy Boockvar sent out "Guidance Concerning Civilian Absentee and Mail-in Ballot Procedures," which clearly and repeatedly said, "A ballot return envelope with a declaration that is not filled out, dated, and signed is not sufficient and must be set aside, declared void and may not be counted."[66]

Pennsylvania attorney general Josh Shapiro even told the United States Supreme Court that the dating requirement was so key, serious, and enforceable that the state should be allowed to accept late-arriving ballots. "Further, the mail-in ballot envelope contains a Voter's Declaration that must be signed and dated by the qualified elector.... Lying on this declaration constitutes voter fraud. Voter fraud in Pennsylvania is a third-degree felony, carrying a maximum 7-year prison term," he wrote in his brief before the court, filed on October 5, 2020.[67]

The Commonwealth Court ruled in Ziccarelli's favor, noting in its ruling that the law clearly required the votes to be thrown out, and that not enforcing it would be "absolving [voters] of their responsibility to execute their ballots in accordance with law."[68] That court's ruling was overturned by the liberal Pennsylvania Supreme Court, which admitted that the ballots were violations of the election code, but said that they should be counted in any case. Failure to follow the law's clear anti-fraud provisions, such as signing a ballot, was "at worst, entirely immaterial" and did not invalidate the ballot, three of the liberal justices on the court ruled.[69]

The Pennsylvania Supreme Court decision allowed the improper votes to be counted, but only three of the four justices who so ruled thought the matter was "immaterial" or unimportant.[70] The controlling opinion and deciding vote came from Justice David Wecht, who said that his vote was only for the particular circumstances of Ziccarelli's election challenge and that it should not apply going forward.[71] He said the law that ballots be dated was given in "unambiguously mandatory terms" and so "in future elections, I would treat the date and sign requirement as mandatory in both particulars, with the omission of either item sufficient without more to invalidate the ballot in question."[72]

The next Pennsylvania election was in May 2021. Despite his controlling opinion that ballot declarations had to be dated "in future elections," a Philadelphia review board voted to accept 1,300 ballots—about 2 percent of the 64,000 mail-in ballots received—even though the voters had not dated their declarations.[73] Republicans in the Pennsylvania legislature threatened impeachment, and Philadelphia ultimately reversed course and rejected the undated ballots.[74]

The 2020 larger court battle raised what would become another major issue. If voters in one area of Pennsylvania had to follow the law in order to have their votes counted, but voters in another area were not required to follow the law, that disenfranchises the voters in the law-abiding region relative to the voters in the non-law-abiding region. Every county was making different decisions as to what was permitted and what was not. Not all voters were being treated equally under the Pennsylvania law.

"Based on the Pennsylvania Supreme Court's judgment, mail-in ballots will be counted or not counted based solely on the happenstance of which county election board reviews the ballot," Ziccarelli wrote when she unsuccessfully challenged the Pennsylvania Supreme Court ruling in a federal court.[75]

Ziccarelli said the process was appalling and frustrating. "We didn't want anything special. We just wanted the courts to follow the law. It's a shame when courts become activists instead of places where you go to seek justice," she said after the federal court rejected her claim.

She may have failed, but her case drew the attention of U.S. Supreme Court associate justice Clarence Thomas, who cited it in his blistering dissent of a Supreme Court dismissal of a case that would have decided whether courts have the right to rewrite election laws passed by legislatures.[76] He said that the country was fortunate that some of the disputes about court-ordered changes hadn't resulted in election disputes, but that there was no guarantee it wouldn't going forward. Further, he noted that Ziccarelli would have won under the legislative rule of how to conduct elections, but that another candidate was seated because different rules were followed.[77]

"That is not a prescription for confidence. Changing the rules in the middle of the game is bad enough. Such rule changes by officials who may lack authority to do so is even worse. When those changes alter election results, they can severely damage the electoral system on which our self-governance so heavily depends," Thomas wrote.[78] "If state officials have the authority they have claimed, we need to make it clear. If not, we need to put an end to this practice now before the consequences become catastrophic."[79]

Back in November, Republican candidates and attorneys began to realize that disparate interpretation of Pennsylvania election law and lower standards for mail-in balloting relative to in-person voting were benefiting Democratic candidates in significant ways.

"Voters in Pennsylvania were held to different standards simply based on how they chose to cast their ballot, and we believe this two-tiered election system resulted in potentially fraudulent votes being counted without proper verification or oversight," Matt Morgan, the Trump general counsel, said at the time.[80]

Pennsylvania was supposed to be one of the only states where ballots could not be opened until Election Day. The Republican-led legislature and the Democratic governor Tom Wolf discussed allowing counties to open ballots early but never actually changed the law to permit it.[81]

Well before Election Day, Republicans began seeing that Philadelphia Democrats were advertising on Facebook and Twitter that they had jobs for "curing" or fixing ballots well ahead of the election. Pennsylvania law says that any mail-in ballots received prior to Election Day are to be kept in sealed or locked containers until Election Day. Voters were reporting on social media that they were getting calls about not having filled out their declarations correctly or having forgotten the required secrecy envelope. On October 27, 2020, Philadelphia city commissioners even put a notice on the city's website that voters who received notification that their ballots were canceled likely fell into one of three categories: They had notified the city they had changed their mind and wanted to vote in person, the ballot was undeliverable, or it had no signature.[82] That last category was stunning.

Some election officials in Philadelphia, and perhaps other parts of the state, were clearly beginning to inspect the mail-in ballots and were allowing voters to fix their problems. That would be one thing if it were happening with all the millions of mail-in ballots, but just as Allegheny County had counted ballots that hadn't been dated while Westmoreland County held off, there was a partisan divide on this issue as well. Republican-dominant counties tended to interpret the law strictly to mean that they couldn't begin that process until 7:00 a.m. on Election Day. Mail-in voters in areas that included more Republicans weren't being given an opportunity to "cure" or fix ballots, while voters in Democrat-heavy areas had interpreted the law more loosely, which privileged the Democratic-leaning voters in those areas.

Several lawsuits were filed alleging that not following this practice uniformly across the state had a disparate impact on Republicans and Democrats, but no judge found it compelling.[83] "I do not understand how the integrity of the election was affected," U.S. District Court judge Timothy Savage said about a lawsuit from one Republican congressional candidate.[84]

◆ ◆ ◆

Election Day had come and gone without producing a definitive presidential winner. But within a day or two, the Trump campaign had narrowed down the list of seventeen states they were fighting in to just six: Pennsylvania, Michigan, Wisconsin, Georgia, Arizona, and Nevada.

It was never entirely clear why Nevada was one of those states. Yes, the state had a history of voter integrity problems and had recklessly sent out universal mail-in ballots, but the margin was not considered winnable by the campaign. Two of Trump's most effective surrogates, former ambassador to Germany Ric Grenell and American Conservative Union chairman Matt Schlapp, had been sent to Nevada and had uncovered problems, but the campaign wished they had been sent to Arizona instead, a much tighter race that was taking forever to count.

It turned out there was cause for concern about what was happening with get-out-the-vote efforts in Nevada. The Nevada Native Vote Project, an organization that works with Native Americans, posted an ad on its Facebook page for a "virtual Raffle for tribal members, residents and employees" in the Reno–Sparks area. Those who sent in a photo of themselves wearing an "I voted" sticker or a picture of a completed ballot were then eligible to win one of several gift cards ranging in value from $25 to $500. This was not just one event—the Nevada Native Vote Project appears to have sponsored similar raffles all over the state.[85] According to the *Washington Examiner*, one of the people involved in promoting one of these Native American raffles "is shown wearing a Biden-Harris anti-virus mask and in front of the Biden-Harris campaign bus."[86]

Incredibly, this was defended by a lawyer for the Nevada Native Vote Project on the grounds that raffles are a "cultural staple" in Native American communities.[87] However, the U.S. code is very clear that "an expenditure to any person, either to vote or withhold his vote" is against the law,[88] so it appears that the Nevada Native Vote Project was engaged in coordinating widespread illegal activity. These vote-buying schemes were potentially impactful—there are about sixty thousand Native American voters in Nevada, a state Trump lost by thirty-three thousand votes.

Even without the problems in Nevada, campaign leadership worried it would look bad to take any of the six states "off the board." Momentum was a key concern, especially after Fox News's decision to call Arizona early. Any sign of weakness or retreat could bury the campaign's efforts to litigate under an avalanche of negative headlines.

Arizona was a state that the political operation very much believed Trump would win. They thought it would be close, but that Trump would eke out a victory in the end. They watched intently as each batch of ballots came in over the course of many long days.

Arizona was slow, but the state ran elections cleanly, the campaign believed. They got a break when they came across what they called the "green button" issue.[89] Some machines, they found, had showed voters an error message that contained a green button. If the person feeding the ballot pushed that green button, the machine would count a legitimate vote as an over-vote, the term for when someone votes for too many candidates for a position. If someone had voted for both Trump and Biden, that would be an over-vote.[90] The machine incorrectly made it appear that some people had cast over-votes.

The glitch, and erroneous guidance given by election officials to voters about how to deal with the glitch, only affected Election Day voters in Maricopa County. That meant that Democratic-leaning early voters got greater care and treatment than Republican-leaning day-of voters.

The problem was determined to have affected as many as ten thousand in-person ballots, which would have very important repercussions for a race that came down to about that many votes.[91] The state's recount statute is exceedingly narrow, only allowing a recount if a candidate is within two hundred votes of his or her opponent. Even the notoriously close Bush–Gore race in 2000 wouldn't have qualified for a recount under the statute. The only recourse a losing campaign has to fight, then, is through legal battles.

Kory Langhofer, a well-known election attorney with Statecraft, a Phoenix law firm, pursued a lawsuit regarding the green button problem.[92] As more was discovered about the glitch, it became clear that while it was true that it had affected ten thousand ballots, it only would have affected a couple hundred votes in the presidential race, with the problems of the green button being spread throughout the ballot and affecting other races.

Katie Hobbs, the Democratic secretary of state, pressured Langhofer to drop his case as soon as he filed it, suggesting that if he didn't withdraw his lawsuit, she would move for sanctions against him and his law firm. She also threatened sanctions against other attorneys in Arizona who filed legitimate lawsuits.

Hobbs is an extremely partisan Democrat who has repeatedly disparaged Republicans in public. She tweeted that Trump "has made it abundantly clear he's more interested in pandering to his neo-nazi base than being @POTUS for all Americans."[93] She had condescendingly maligned Republican voters by saying, "There are Trump t-shirts. And people not embarrassed to wear them. In airports."[94] She accused Trump of having "racist, sexist, homophobic" policies, and said that if he won the presidential election, "we won't have a country to move out of."[95] She also said, "There is so much deplorable at Trump rallies it's hard to keep track."[96]

Some of the most significant effects on the 2020 election were the elections in years prior when Democrats won key control over secretary of state offices. That project really began in 2006, when far-left political operatives created the Secretary of State Project to wrest control from Republicans.[97] Though the group folded within a few election cycles, winning secretary of state elections remained a top priority for the party. Arizona's Hobbs managed to flip the office from the Republicans in 2018, as did Jocelyn Benson in Michigan.[98] Pennsylvania's Boockvar was a Democrat, appointed by a Democratic governor. And Democrats controlled the election board in North Carolina.

When *Politico* wrote up the Secretary of State Project in an article headlined "Secretaries of State Give Dem Firewall," it explained that

Democrats wanted control not just so they could turn away from the Republican emphasis on preventing fraud, but because it was "more important" to be in a "more advantageous position when it comes to the interpretation and administration of election law" on Election Day.[99]

That was certainly true in Arizona, where the secretary of state applied pressure against legal challenges. On November 13, Langhofer told the court the case was moot relative to the election contest, and the judge accepted his declaration and dismissed the case.[100]

Bill Stepien and Justin Clark gave President Trump the bad news. The case being moot likely meant Arizona was lost, because it was the only realistic case for the state. Disappointed in his campaign's legal team's efforts, President Trump tweeted the next day that Rudy Giuliani was now in charge of fighting the campaign's post-election battles.[101]

"I look forward to Mayor Giuliani spearheading the legal effort to defend OUR RIGHT to FREE and FAIR ELECTIONS! Rudy Giuliani, Joseph diGenova, Victoria Toensing, Sidney Powell, and Jenna Ellis, a truly great team, added to our other wonderful lawyers and representatives!" Trump said in a tweet.[102]

The failure in Arizona had triggered the decision, and putting Giuliani in charge would prove disastrous to the legal efforts in Pennsylvania and beyond.

◆   ◆   ◆

The Pennsylvania Trump team had previously decided to sue in federal court on the issue of how ballots were being treated differently in different areas of the state, filing in the Middle District of Pennsylvania. Since ballots across the state were counted according to dramatically different legal protocols, the case alleged, the state had violated the equal protection clause of the Fourteenth Amendment mandating uniform legal treatment for Americans.[103] It was the same argument that had merit in *Bush v. Gore*, the federal case that determined who would be the forty-third president of the United States.

Kerns, with the help of powerhouse law firm Porter Wright, filed the case. The judge set a tight and aggressive schedule. Briefs were due later that week, and the hearing was scheduled for the following Tuesday.

The Lincoln Project, a Democratic political action committee that bills itself as a group of former Republicans, had learned of the lawsuit and began a campaign of personal destruction against the lawyers working the case. They published the names of Ron Hicks and Carolyn McGee, two attorneys with Porter Wright, the Pittsburgh law firm working to protect Pennsylvania voters.[104]

"Here are two attorneys attempting to help Trump overturn the will of the Pennsylvanian people," a tweet from the group said, identifying them by name and photo. "Make them famous."[105] Within minutes, the law firm was being deluged with vulgar and vicious attacks as well as death threats.

Any attorney working on the case was being verbally assaulted. Kerns was repeatedly called a "cunt," a "fucking bitch," a "traitor," "stupid," "treacherous," a "fucking Nazi," and a "whore." Some expressed hope that she would lose her possessions, her law license, and her life. "We know where you live, where your office is, and where your court dates will be. Thousands of us will wait for you outside, licking our chops. You and your partners on this case are scumbag pieces of shit, and I'd love for nothing more than to see you begging for your life," wrote one emailer. "The people will rise, the mobs will ascend on you and your colleagues, and you will die a painful, scary death. This country knows how to deal with treason." In addition to threats such as this, two explicit death threats brought the attention of the FBI.

It was one thing to have to field threats and attacks from random supporters of Democrats—that was almost to be expected in highly politicized litigation such as this. But one of the harassing phone calls came from an attorney in the Washington, D.C., office of Kirkland & Ellis, the outside counsel to Boockvar. The code of professional conduct for legal practitioners in the Middle District of Pennsylvania includes a commitment to "treat with civility and respect the lawyers, clients, opposing parties, the court and all the officials with whom I work."[106] When Kirkland & Ellis was notified of the voice mail attack, the firm at first suggested it might not have been from one of its attorneys. Later, the firm admitted it had come from one of its attorneys, even if he was not working on that particular election lawsuit, and acknowledged that it was "discourteous and not appropriate."[107] Kerns asked the judge to sanction the firm for the shocking behavior of one of its lawyers. "It is sad that we currently reside in a world where abuse and harassment are the costs of taking on a representation unpopular with some. It is sanctionable when that abuse and harassment comes from an elite law firm representing the Secretary of State," she told the judge.[108]

On Thursday, Porter Wright withdrew from the case.[109] The threats from Democratic mobs were endangering the firm and its clients. Kerns was now the only public face representing the Trump campaign in the lawsuit. The briefs were due the next day.

In Porter Wright's absence, the Trump campaign brought on respected Texas attorneys John Scott and Douglas Bryan Hughes. Helping with the briefs were a slew of former Supreme Court clerks, avoiding leftist mobs by working behind the scenes to get the case through its hearings. It was the best shot the Trump campaign had, and the facts of the case were in their favor.

The Texas attorneys entered into the case. To practice law in a state, attorneys have to be admitted to the bar. If they haven't been admitted but desire to participate in a particular case, they can be allowed to participate *pro hac vice*, Latin for "for this occasion." The attorney who requests the authorization has to request permission from the court, and usually gets the main local attorney on the case to sponsor his or her participation. Kerns had no problem agreeing to sponsor the Texas attorneys, and they granted her request to admit them.

Prior to this case's being heard, Rudy Giuliani had held a press conference at the Four Seasons Total Landscaping company, where instead of talking about all of the legitimate issues affecting the Pennsylvania election—and there were so many—he put forth dramatic claims about voter fraud. The first person he brought up as a witness to irregularities was a man named Daryl Brooks, who said he was a paid GOP poll watcher. "They did not allow us to see anything. Was it corrupt or not? But give us an opportunity as poll watchers to view all the documents—all of the ballots," said Brooks.[110] But in addition to being a convicted sex offender with strong Democratic Party ties, Brooks was well known as a perennial candidate in New Jersey.[111] He was not an ideal witness, to put it mildly.

The veteran Republican lawyers were at best confused by Giuliani's approach and at worst completely opposed to it. Giuliani called Kerns and told her he was taking over her Pennsylvania litigation. She didn't agree with the direction he wanted to take the federal case, and so she was not willing to sponsor his participation, as she had done for the Texas lawyers. It wouldn't matter: Giuliani found another attorney to help him enter into the case, and he took it over that way.

Kerns filed a petition to withdraw, as did the two Texas attorneys. While the Texas attorneys were allowed out of the case, Kerns was not permitted out. Because of the departure of the Porter Wright attorneys, the judge was adamant that at least one attorney should stick with the case all the way. "I believed it best to have some semblance of consistency in counsel ahead of the oral argument," Judge Matthew Brann wrote, denying her request.[112]

The threats against Trump attorneys were out of control at this point. Out of fear for her safety, Kerns was brought through the back door of the courthouse by U.S. Marshals.

The hearing went on for hours, with Giuliani talking about fraud that he could not substantiate with evidence. The judge asked Kerns to speak, and she noted that no one was talking about equal protection, the original complaint the campaign had filed.[113] Courts look extremely unkindly on attorneys who fail to stick with the arguments in the original complaints. Kerns asked again to be let out of a case that was running off the rails. Giuliani asked her to stay. She called the judge the next day and asked to be let out and was finally allowed off the case.[114] The judge quickly approved the defendant's motion to dismiss in a blistering opinion saying Giuliani had presented the court with "strained legal arguments without merit and speculative accusations."[115] The Obama-appointed judge had been open to the case and its legal arguments at the beginning, but showed little tolerance for what it had become.

Giuliani regularly downplayed very real issues with the 2020 election in Pennsylvania by emphasizing less relevant—and less actionable— claims. For instance, the Public Interest Legal Foundation had sued Pennsylvania over the twenty-one thousand dead people that were on its voter rolls.[116] The group's data, which it filed under seal with the U.S. District Court for the Middle District of Pennsylvania, showed thousands of dead people on the voter rolls, some of them for many years. It said that hundreds of them had shown up as voters in 2016 or 2018.

"AT LEAST 21K Dead People on Pennsylvania Voter Rolls '9,212 registrants have been dead for at least five years, at least 1,990 registrants have been dead for at least ten years, and at least 197 registrants have been dead for at least twenty years,'" Giuliani tweeted on November 6.[117]

Media coverage of the tweet and the issue of dead people being on voter rolls was predictably awful. "No, 21,000 Dead People in Pennsylvania Did Not Vote," was the *New York Times* headline on November 6, although no one had actually made that claim.[118] The claim was that dead people's names remained on Pennsylvania voter rolls years after they had died, which increased opportunities for fraud. The *Times* dismissed the legitimacy of the case, saying the judge overseeing it was "doubtful" of it.[119] News organizations purported to check the fact of whether Pennsylvania had dead people on its rolls. Snopes rated it "false," while FactCheck.org said it had "thin" evidence.[120]

The Public Interest Legal Foundation had asked a judge before the election for an injunction to stop any of the dead people listed on voter rolls from voting, but it wasn't granted. However, less than five months after the November election, Pennsylvania settled with the Public Interest Legal Foundation and agreed to remove the dead voters on its list before the 2021 municipal elections.[121]

Still, the focus on the relatively marginal issue of dead people on the voter rolls was far less pertinent than the issue that Kerns and the previous legal team had raised. Kerns's suit identified an issue that had affected all 6.1 million Pennsylvania voters. Her suit raised a fundamental legal question, drawing attention to the problems caused when law-abiding voters are treated differently than non-law-abiding voters depending on where they live in a state. That issue potentially affected the actual outcome of the 2020 race in a way that the dead voter roll issue wouldn't and couldn't.

For perspective, the initial Republican legal strategy was to keep the margin of Biden's lead relative to total ballots cast down to .5 percent, the threshold that would trigger an automatic recount. As votes kept being located and counted, Biden would eventually be certified the victor by more than eighty thousand votes, yielding Biden 1.2 percent more of the vote than Trump—more than twice what he needed to prevent a recount.

By wasting time on less relevant claims, an important lawsuit failed. It had catastrophic effects for the remaining legal battles. Pennsylvania could have been the first domino to fall for the Trump campaign in a sequence of tightly contested courtroom victories. Instead, it was the beginning of the end for the campaign's effort to hold Democrats accountable for foul play. It also had a ripple effect throughout the legal community. The media were soon dismissing all legal challenges as baseless attempts to prove widespread fraud, ignoring more substantive claims. The avalanche of bad publicity scared off credible lawyers from participating in further election challenges on behalf of the Trump campaign, and it made judges inclined to view any such challenges, no matter how merited, with suspicion.

◆　　◆　　◆

Wisconsin was also fairly quiet on Election Day, a relief for a state that had endured months of tumultuous riots. The *Washington Post*'s last poll before the election claimed that Biden was on track to win the state by seventeen points.[122] When all was said and done, Biden would be certified as the winner with only seven-tenths of one percentage point.[123]

Democrats had targeted Wisconsin early and had set out to make it difficult for Trump to win. The state kept 234,000 invalid voter registrations on its voter rolls, even when ordered to remove them by a court.[124] The clerks of the two biggest Democratic counties got tens of thousands of people to claim they were "indefinitely confined," enabling them to vote by mail without showing any identification.[125]

But one of the most important things Wisconsin Democrats did was disenfranchise the Green Party presidential ticket and otherwise work to keep third-party candidates off the ballot. Amazingly, despite filing nearly twice the number of signatures necessary to appear on the ballot, the Green Party nominee Howie Hawkins was kept off the ballot.[126] Kanye West was denied access to the ballot on an absurd technicality.[127]

In 2016, Trump had won Wisconsin by just 22,000 votes.[128] The Green Party candidate that year, Jill Stein, had taken 30,000 votes.[129] Many Democrats blamed her for the Clinton loss, since she had won more votes than Clinton's margin of defeat in Michigan, Wisconsin, and Pennsylvania. But that didn't take into account that Trump had even greater problems posed by third-party candidates. For instance, in Wisconsin, Libertarian Party candidate Gary Johnson, a former Republican governor of New Mexico, took more than 100,000 votes.[130]

"We have a much bigger problem than the Green Party. We have the Libertarian Party. The Libertarian Party got almost 4 percent of the vote. The Green Party got less than 1 percent," Trump says of 2016. Johnson received 3.6 percent of the vote that year, while Stein received 1.07 percent.[131]

In any case, in 2020 the Wisconsin Elections Commission went out of its way to disqualify the Green Party candidate from the Wisconsin ballot in a party-line vote at its August meeting. A Democratic donor and activist named Allen Arntsen had lodged a complaint, without providing evidence, that the Green Party's vice presidential candidate may have listed an incorrect address on the party's nominating petition. The Wisconsin Elections Commission did not allow the Green Party to make the case that the candidate had merely moved during the process of collecting signatures to get placed on the Wisconsin ballot.[132]

Instead, the commission voted on whether to accept 1,834 signatures that appeared on petitions listing vice presidential candidate Angela Walker's old address. The three Democrats on the commission voted against them, while the three Republicans voted to validate them. The commission interpreted that vote to mean that the signatures were not validated and therefore kept the Green Party off the ballot for failing to meet the signature threshold.[133]

But Wisconsin law says that the burden of proof for invalidating signatures rests with the challenger, a burden that was never met. It was improper for the Wisconsin Elections Commission to place the burden of proving validity on the candidate; the commission was legally required to presume the signatures were valid.

The Wisconsin Supreme Court heard the Green Party's case that it had wrongly been kept off the ballot. The court's three liberal justices were joined in their decision to uphold the commission's ruling by Brian Hagedorn, a recently elected justice and aide to former Republican governor Scott Walker. He had been viewed as conservative prior to his rulings in election litigation.[134]

The majority didn't rule on whether the election commission had violated the law, that was clear as day. Instead, they came up with a new standard that would get them the result they wanted. According to the court, it was simply too close to the election to reprint ballots. The Green Party would be kept off the ballot because the court thought upholding the party's rights would be inconvenient.[135]

The conservative dissenters were appalled. The Green Party candidates had "satisfied all requirements necessary to secure their spot on the ballot as candidates of the Green Party, but the Wisconsin Elections

Commission, with the outrageous acquiescence of the majority, denies them their rightful place."[136]

The conservative minority were upset that the court "reward[ed] rather than rebuff[ed]" the "unlawful maneuvers" of the Wisconsin Elections Commission. They cited how Alabama state officials in 1968 left black candidates off general election ballots "in response to some comparably concocted but meritless challenge."[137] When that happened, the United States Supreme Court required Alabama to hold a new election.[138]

A similar effort to keep the Green Party candidate off the ballot in Pennsylvania occurred in the run-up to the 2020 election.[139]

The Green Party gathered signatures of Pennsylvania voters from March through August of 2020 for five candidates for federal and state offices. On August 3, 8,500 signatures were submitted to the Office of the Secretary of the Commonwealth in Harrisburg. Only 5,000 were required. Because the Green Party convention wasn't held until July, the petition used stand-in candidates to fill in for the eventual nominees who would be picked later in the year. When the petitions were submitted, they included a "notarized candidate affidavit" for nominees Howie Hawkins and Angela Walker.[140] After submitting the petitions, the party filed two substitute nomination certificates to formally replace the stand-in candidates with the actual candidates.

It was at that time that Democrats asked the Commonwealth Court "to have the Green Party slate removed from the general election ballot based upon the presidential and vice presidential candidates' alleged failure to comply with the requirements of the Election Code pertaining to candidate affidavits and substitutions."[141] They claimed that Walker had faxed a copy of her affidavit without a cover letter and hadn't followed up to ensure it was received. The Commonwealth Court said that such a "bureaucratic snafu" was not a "fatal defect" and rejected the Democrats' request to ban the Green Party from the ballot.[142]

But the Democrats would not be denied. Democratic activists appealed to the Pennsylvania Supreme Court, which had a strong Democratic majority. Unlike the lower court, the Pennsylvania Supreme Court said the aforementioned "bureaucratic snafu" was, in fact, "fatal" to the Green Party's slate.[143]

The final margin in Pennsylvania in 2020 was just over eighty thousand votes. Keeping the leftist party that received fifty thousand votes three years prior off the ballot was a huge victory for Biden. CNN called it "a sweeping victory for Democrats."[144]

Wisconsin also kept rapper-turned-presidential-candidate Kanye West off the ballot, claiming he was fourteen seconds late in filing.[145] The decision was Kafkaesque.

Wisconsin law said that nomination papers for independent candidates for president and vice president may not be filed later than 5:00 p.m. on the first Tuesday in August preceding a presidential election. That was August 4, 2020. The West campaign spoke with the Wisconsin Elections Commission staff to ensure they followed proper procedure to make the deadline. They were told that the commission's office building in Madison would be locked and that the second layer of double doors to the main floor of the building would also be locked. Three West campaign staffers arrived before 5:00 p.m. and searched in vain for a phone number outside the building to call to gain access to the building. Finally, after some digging, they found the number and called to notify staff that they were outside prior to 5:00 p.m. A staff member unlocked the inner layer of double doors on the main floor of the building and gave them access. The commission election specialist accepted the papers as "not later than 5 p.m.," but later declared the acceptance to be late because, supposedly, they actually came fourteen seconds—yes, fourteen seconds—later than 5:00 p.m. The West campaign alleged that the multiple layers of locked doors had impeded their access and ability to deliver nominating papers.[146]

A circuit court ruled that the Wisconsin Elections Commission had acted appropriately in ruling the paperwork fourteen seconds late because the law clearly said that it had to be in by five o'clock. A challenge to that ruling in the U.S. District Court of the Eastern District of Wisconsin also failed.[147]

Keeping third-party candidates off the ballot was part of a larger Democratic project to minimize the public exposure of third-party candidates. Third-party candidates who might hurt Biden's chances were kept off the air, marginalized, and even disparaged. Liberal *New York Times* columnist Gail Collins wrote on September 16, 2020, "Throwing your support to a third-party candidate with no hope whatsoever of getting elected is, however, a good way to dodge responsibility."[148] Corporate media also kept the third-party candidates out of polling questions, unlike in 2016 when they did everything in their power to amplify even the most absurd third-party races, such as the Never Trump movement's push to get behind Evan McMullin, a Capitol Hill staffer who had a brief stint with the CIA.[149] In 2020, the tables had turned. Third parties posed a significant challenge not to Trump but to Biden, and so coverage was dropped.

The Democratic strategy of suppressing competing parties and candidates worked, particularly when compared to the situation with parties that compete for Republican votes. In Wisconsin, the Libertarian candidate far exceeded the margin of Biden's victory, and in Pennsylvania, it came just under it.

◆   ◆   ◆

Republican election observers in Wisconsin faced the same problems that Republican election observers faced in Pennsylvania and other states. Though technically allowed in the facilities, they were kept as far away as possible from the areas where absentee ballots were deemed valid or not.

Republican politicians have long asserted that statewide Republican candidates need tens of thousands of extra votes to take care of the fraud problems coming out of Milwaukee. Putting aside media claims to the contrary, Milwaukee, much like Philadelphia, also has a long and storied history of voter fraud.

In the 2000 election, the Al Gore campaign faced a problem when one of its key donors, a Manhattan socialite named Connie Milstein, was embroiled in what came to be known as the "smokes-for-votes" scandal.[150] Milstein, who had given Democrats more than $400,000 that year, was caught by the local news handing out cigarettes to homeless men she and other Gore volunteers had brought to Milwaukee City Hall to fill out absentee ballots.[151]

Wisconsin law prohibits bribing people for votes or giving anything valued at more than $1 for a vote. The Milwaukee district attorney was investigating the bribery of a few dozen homeless men. Milstein admitted to a TV interviewer that she'd "been pretty busy, going to the local shelters."[152] While the Democratic district attorney decided against pressing charges, Milstein agreed to pay a $5,000 civil forfeiture for the bribery.[153]

Incidentally, when Tucker Carlson mentioned the scandal in 2014, PolitiFact rated him only "half true" for saying Democrats gave "Newports to the homeless to get them to the polls."[154] "There is no evidence that the cigarettes were Newports," PolitiFact said.[155]

The problem of illegal voting was so widespread that Milwaukee police created a special investigative unit to crack down on it. In February 2008, the unit released a sixty-seven-page report on what Mike Sandvick, the head of the unit, called an "illegal organized attempt to influence the outcome of [the 2004] election in the state of Wisconsin."[156] The *Wall Street Journal* reported on the findings, highlighting that around five thousand more votes were recorded in Milwaukee than the number of voters recorded as having cast ballots. Absentee ballots were cast by people who didn't live in Wisconsin; felons not only voted but were poll workers; and some people voted more than once.[157]

Because Wisconsin law provided that same-day registrants who didn't have photo ID only had to have another person vouch for them, campaign workers for Democratic nominee John Kerry allegedly had "other staff members who were registered voters vouch for them by corroborating their residency."[158] Sandvick referred sixteen members of the

Kerry campaign for prosecution, but the Democratic district attorney declined to take action.[159]

Kevin Clancy, a special registration deputy for Milwaukee who also worked for ACORN, was charged with falsely procuring voter registrations after he submitted multiple registrations for the same people. He was convicted and sentenced to ten months in jail.[160] A total of four ACORN workers were convicted in an illegal voter registration scheme. Frank Walton, a special registration deputy who also worked for the Community Voters Project, was sentenced to fifty-two days in jail after he was found to have falsely registered dozens of forms. He and two other Community Voters Project staff were convicted on vote fraud charges.[161]

Even though, or perhaps because, Sandvick's unit was so effective, it was shut down by Democratic mayor Tom Barrett in 2008, and police officers were barred from being at polling locations.[162] "We know what to look for," Sandvick, who then resigned, told the *Wall Street Journal*, "and that scares some people."[163]

In 2012, Milwaukee refused to check newly registered voters against a list of convicted felons.[164] In 2016, nearly one thousand suspected cases of vote fraud were referred to local district attorneys, but very few were investigated, much less prosecuted.[165]

The distrust of Milwaukee has a lengthy history, compounded by the 2018 election, when Republican incumbent Governor Scott Walker was headed to a comfortable win over Democrat Tony Evers until Milwaukee reported late-counted ballots well after everyone else had completed tallying.[166]

The same thing happened in 2020. After the rest of the state reported its vote totals and Trump had a sizable lead, Milwaukee came in with a vote total that tipped the race to a twenty-thousand-vote victory for Biden.[167]

"For a second straight election, the City of Milwaukee seemed to have waited until officials knew exactly how many votes needed to be counted to ensure a statewide Democrat win," wrote Dan O'Donnell for the MacIver Institute.[168] "As one frustrated voter put it on Twitter, 'The only thing we did on Election Day was tell them how many votes they needed on Election Night.'"[169]

It was in this environment that Republicans were concerned about rates of absentee and mail-in ballot rejection in 2020.

In a February 2021 commentary piece for the MacIver Institute, Dan O'Donnell noted that the ballot rejection rate in the April 2016 Wisconsin presidential primary was 2.5 percent, with a 1.4 percent rejection rate the following November. The April 2020 rejection rate was well within the normal range at 1.8 percent, but then it suddenly dipped to a minuscule 0.2 percent. He called it a "stunning anomaly."[170]

In came *USA Today* to assert that the issue was in O'Donnell's imagination, not the rejection rates. November elections regularly had lower rejection rates than other elections, and 2016 was an anomaly because of compliance with a new law on witness verification.[171] Of the nearly one million absentee ballots cast in Wisconsin during the April 2020 general election, more than 23,000 ballots were rejected.[172] Of the two million absentee ballots cast in the November general, only 4,270 were rejected.[173] *USA Today* claimed that lower November rejections were due to the fact that mail-in absentee voting was a larger percentage of the absentee vote in April than in November. In Wisconsin, early voting is counted as absentee voting, too.[174]

Studies have shown that first-time mail voters are up to three times more likely to have their votes rejected. But analysis of the 2020 election by Nathaniel Rakich at FiveThirtyEight showed that the dramatic increase in first-time mail voters in 2020 was met, somehow, with a decreasing rejection rate.[175] In twenty of the twenty-three states he studied, the rejection rate went down from 2016. He described it as a "success story," which assumes without investigation or evidence that all the ballots that should have been rejected were rejected.[176] He cited as reasons for the lowered rejection Democrats' and the media's lengthy public relations campaign encouraging voters to submit their votes well ahead of the election, ballot boxes, Center for Tech and Civic Life funding and help with states' design of the ballots, and laws expanding how late ballots could arrive and still be counted.[177]

Not everyone shared the left's innate trust in the integrity of absentee balloting procedures. The Trump campaign sued in Wisconsin over four major voting integrity issues tied to absentee ballots. The margin of votes separating Biden and Trump in Wisconsin was just under twenty-one thousand votes.[178]

As mentioned earlier, in Wisconsin law, voting absentee is merely "a privilege exercised wholly outside the traditional safeguards of the polling place."[179] The legislature said that the "privilege of voting by absentee ballot must be carefully regulated to prevent the potential for fraud or abuse" and to prevent people from being bullied to vote or being unduly influenced to vote for a particular candidate.[180] The law specifically says that ballots cast in contravention of specified procedures "may not be counted" and "may not be included in the certified result of any election."[181]

In the lawsuit, the Trump campaign tried to have the Wisconsin State Supreme Court strike all ballots cast by voters who claimed after March 25 to be indefinitely confined. The clerks of Milwaukee and Dane counties had erroneously told people they could and should claim to be indefinitely confined, only updating that guidance on March 25 when told to do so by the courts. The move had enabled tens of thousands of people to vote without showing any identification whatsoever. Because there was no way to separate legitimately confined voters from non-legitimately confined voters in these counties, the court said the request had no merit.[182]

The Trump campaign also argued that a form used for in-person absentee voting was not a written application and that such ballots were invalid, that municipal officials improperly added witness information on absentee ballots and that they were therefore invalid, and that ballots harvested at two Democracy in the Park events held by the City of Madison were illegal.[183]

The two Madison events had shocked Republicans as an egregious flouting of Wisconsin election laws. They found out about it through

Biden for President campaign radio ads, an indication of unlawful coordination to promote illegal in-person absentee voting in each and every one of the city's 206 parks.

According to Wisconsin law, under certain conditions a municipality can put forth an alternate site for absentee voting. It has to be as near as possible to the clerk's office, can't advantage one political party over another, and has to be designated weeks prior to when ballots are made available. Republicans originally tried to stop the event, which they worried was illegal, and also tried to separate the 17,271 absentee ballots improperly cast at the events.[184] Those efforts failed, but a challenge to the Democracy in the Park events would form a major part of their lawsuit.

The court's three liberal members and Hagedorn said that it was too late to bring these concerns, and they declined to hear the case.[185]

The conservative justices were outraged. In a blistering dissent written by Justice Rebecca Bradley and signed by two other conservatives, she said they found "troubling allegations of noncompliance with Wisconsin's election laws" for which "the majority's failure to act leaves an indelible stain on our most recent election."[186] The majority's refusal to act would "profoundly and perhaps irreparably impact all local, statewide, and national elections going forward, with grave consequence to the State of Wisconsin and significant harm to the rule of law," Bradley wrote.[187]

The case wasn't about whether Trump or Biden would win, they said, but about whether Wisconsin was required to follow its own laws for how to handle absentee voting.

"While some will either celebrate or decry the court's inaction based upon the impact on their preferred candidate, the importance of this case transcends the results of this particular election," Bradley wrote.[188] "The majority takes a pass on resolving the important questions presented by the petitioners in this case, thereby undermining the public's confidence in the integrity of Wisconsin's electoral processes not only during this election, but in every future election."[189]

The three conservatives who dissented argued each of the remaining challenges on the merits.[190] They found that the in-person absentee voting sufficiently satisfied the application requirement. But on the issue of municipal clerks filling in witness verification on absentee ballots, they said that was clearly contrary to the law. They also said that the more than two hundred early voting locations operated in Madison clearly violated the law.

Of particular concern for Bradley was that "the majority's failure to discharge its duty perpetuates violations of the law by those entrusted to administer it."[191]

Justice Annette Kingsland Ziegler also weighed in, saying the court was presented with a straightforward question. Were the ballots cast according to the law as stated and, if not, what, if any, remedy exists? "The people of Wisconsin deserve an answer—if not for this election, then at least to protect the integrity of elections in the future."[192]

Nevertheless, Democrats' efforts in Wisconsin and Pennsylvania had survived in the courts and paid off tremendously. But that was nothing compared to Georgia, where it was Republican officials themselves who helped Democrats achieve their stunning victory in that state.

CHAPTER TEN

The Trouble with Fulton County

On Election Night, Georgia Republican field organizer Michelle Branton was told to go to State Farm Arena in Atlanta, where Fulton County was counting hundreds of thousands of mail-in absentee ballots. She was joined by fellow field organizer Mitchell Harrison.[1]

Georgia election operations are difficult to monitor on a good day. The Peach State boasts 159 counties, more than any other state in the union but Texas. Fulton County is the largest of the bunch, with more than one million residents. It's one of the most reliably Democratic counties in the entire country.

By the time Michelle Branton and Mitchell Harrison arrived, State Farm Arena—where the NBA's Atlanta Hawks play—had already made news that day. A water main had broken, or so the media reported, causing a delay in ballot counting.[2] But the reported cause and scope of the waterworks would get smaller and smaller as Election Night went on. The reason given for the leak soon went from a broken water main to a burst pipe. Still later, an investigator would claim that the problem was an overflowing urinal, hardly enough of a problem to warrant extreme delays.[3]

Republicans thought that the ever-changing story, though suspicious, may have just pointed to Fulton County's incompetence and trouble with effective communication. With time, the bizarre news story would look less like poor communication and more like deliberate obfuscation. Fulton County's behavior was raising eyebrows.

When they got to the arena, Branton and Harrison, together with a camera crew from a Fox affiliate news station, were sent to a large, angular room where they were told to stay behind a rope at one end of the space. They couldn't see a thing. The distance "effectively prevented our actual observation of the process," Branton said in an affidavit.[4]

A machine that copied electronically received ballots—usually called UOCAVA ballots for the Uniformed and Overseas Citizens Absentee Voting Act that authorizes them—could only be viewed from the side, and doors to the area where the machine sat obstructed even that view. The machines used to scan the hundreds of thousands of mail-in absentee ballots simply weren't visible to the observers at all.

Regina Waller, the public affairs manager for elections in Fulton County, explained the setup to Branton and Harrison. That was the only way they even knew that scanners were on site. Top Fulton County Democrats were there, including Robb Pitts, the powerful chairman of the Fulton County Commission, the top position in the county. Branton remembers finding it odd that Pitts was spending so much time around the ballot counting.

Election workers had been processing ballots since that morning. After Branton and Harrison arrived, employees began wrapping up their work. The last employee finished her stack of envelopes around 10:30 p.m.

Across the room, a woman—she seemed to Branton and Harrison to be the supervisor—told everyone to stop counting and to come back at 8:30 a.m., at which point counting would resume. All but about four people left.

A Republican Party officer had instructed the poll watchers to make sure they got the number of ballots that had been counted and the number of ballots remaining to be counted before they left. They asked

Waller, who they later said seemed "uncomfortable," for the information three times, but she declined to give it. She called someone for advice on how to respond to the information request, finally telling the duo that the information could be found "on the website."[5]

Branton and Harrison left, along with the Fox TV news crew. They headed back to the Fulton County Board of Elections warehouse across town. Waller arrived shortly thereafter. But then they began to read on social media that counting hadn't, in fact, stopped. It was still going on. Harrison rushed back to State Farm Arena with Trevin McKoy, another Republican poll watcher. When they got to the building shortly before 1:00 a.m., they were told that counting had kept going after they left, but was now stopped. They demanded to get access to the ballot counting area, where they witnessed no one counting ballots and were told that the counting had "just finished."[6]

Late on Election Night and into the early morning hours, reports of pausing or stopping for the night in other swing states filled the news and social media. Cities in Pennsylvania, Michigan, and Wisconsin all had reports of counters taking a break or stopping. But the evidence suggests that they didn't actually stop. The vote-counting was continuing in every state. And that led to another alarming situation that night: Biden was getting huge spikes in his number of votes, allowing him to take the lead or almost take the lead in multiple swing states.

To make matters worse, in some states nobody could even guess how many ballots were outstanding. Alarm bells about the lack of transparency were ringing for Republicans across the country. As hours turned into days in Georgia, Biden took the lead as more and more votes were found and counted. Republican complaints about the State Farm Arena situation began to go viral.

As soon as the Trump campaign realized that their poll watchers had been improperly cleared from State Farm Arena on Election Night, they sued in the Superior Court of Chatham County, Georgia, to demand the enforcement of election laws.[7] It was the beginning of an onslaught of litigation in Georgia that would last months.

Meanwhile, the media and Democrats argued that nothing untoward had happened in Georgia or anywhere else. David Shafer, the chairman of the Georgia Republican Party, tweeted in frustration, "Let me repeat. Fulton County elections officials told the media and our observers that they were shutting down the tabulation center at State Farm Arena at 10:30 p.m. on election night only to continue counting ballots in secret until 1:00 a.m.[8] No one disputes that Fulton County elections officials falsely announced that the counting of ballots would stop at 10:30 p.m. No one disputes that Fulton County elected officials unlawfully resumed the counting of ballots after our observers left the center.[9] The [*Atlanta Journal-Constitution*] is gaslighting you when they report that there is no evidence of irregularity in the election."

And, of course, the tweets were labeled by Twitter with a note saying, "This claim about election fraud is disputed!"[10]

While Fulton County officials would claim they had never told anyone they were shutting down, the GOP poll watchers had an abundance of evidence on their side.

"We saw absentee ballot counting at State Farm Arena wrap up at 10:30. Workers will be back in the morning," Matt Johnson, a reporter for WSBTV, tweeted around 11:20 p.m.[11]

The *Atlanta Journal-Constitution* itself reported that night, "They planned to stop scanning absentee ballots at 10:30 p.m. and pick it up back in the morning. No official could explain before press time why Fulton was stopping its count of absentee ballots at that time, only saying that was the procedure."[12]

"Fulton Co spokeswoman tells me absentee ballot counters at State Farm Arena were sent home at 10:30, will be back at 8:30 a.m. to work on finishing processing absentee ballots," reported Joe Henke of 11Alive News.[13]

Several other outlets, both local and national, made statements confirming the discrepancy between the time Fulton County officials said they were stopping the count and when they actually did.[14] No matter how much the Trump team complained, though, the media insisted that there wasn't a problem.

Unlike the other states that were causing the Trump campaign trouble, Georgia had a Republican governor and a Republican secretary of state. But that only made the problems the Trump campaign faced more daunting, as Georgia Republicans had been complicit in many of the electoral changes that had occurred in the preceding year.

Many of those changes happened in Democratic Fulton County, the real hub of electoral dysfunction in the state. The county's long history of mismanaging elections had drawn headlines months earlier in Georgia's primary election on June 9. Hours-long lines formed early and lasted throughout the day. Many people failed to receive the absentee ballots they requested. A state investigation found that Fulton County's elections office broke the law when it failed to process and deliver hundreds of absentee ballot requests for the June primary.[15]

The June 9 primary became a national spectacle and was a humiliation for Georgia secretary of state Brad Raffensperger. The problems were so vast that the state elections board decided to sue the county, eventually settling the suit in a consent decree between the state and Fulton County. The negative headlines led the Republican Raffensperger and his office to do whatever they could to win over the press and their liberal allies. He was a large part of the problem for the Trump campaign and would prove to be one of their greatest obstacles.

For months, the Trump campaign had felt that the Republican establishment had not fought Marc Elias or his demands as much as it should have. It was one of the reasons why the Trump campaign took over such election lawsuits during the early summer.

◆　◆　◆

The Trump campaign's frustrations with how the Georgia election had been conducted, and worries about how a similarly conducted election would hurt the party in the required runoff for two all-important Senate seats, drove a huge wedge between the secretary of state's office and the campaign.

The disputes that arose between the campaign and the state created some interesting conflicts of interest. Taylor English attorneys were representing Georgia election officials in a long-running voting suit while representing the Trump campaign in the 2020 election.[16] And Russo, the top elections lawyer, was extremely close with Secretary of State Brad Raffensperger. He was one of the lawyers who had signed off on the mail-in ballot settlement from March 2020 that acquiesced to Marc Elias's demands on curing ballots and making it more difficult to challenge mismatched signatures.

The White House sent two additional teams of attorneys down to the state. Chief of Staff Mark Meadows dispatched Cleta Mitchell, a former elected Democrat who had become a top Republican election lawyer and conservative activist.[17] And Trump aide Johnny McEntee sent Office of Personnel Management's Paul Dans as well. Mitchell couldn't believe that the Trump campaign was relying so much on Russo considering his closeness to Raffensperger, the man who had overseen the handling of the election they were challenging in courts.

There were also lawyers such as Sidney Powell and Lin Wood, who were pushing unsubstantiated claims of voter system fraud and foreign meddling. Both right-wing activists and the media obsessively focused on their claims at the expense of paying attention to legitimate problems raised by the others. Some of the activists keyed into Powell and Wood's claims were getting increasingly worked up and threatening Georgia election officials.[18]

Rudy Giuliani also hovered around the periphery. Following the embarrassing drama with the Four Seasons Total Landscaping press conference in Pennsylvania, as well as failures in key court cases, Giuliani led a movement to hold hearings in state legislatures about election fraud and other improprieties.[19] In Michigan and Georgia, people testified about problems they'd experienced and witnessed at their polling or ballot-counting locations.[20]

Giuliani appeared more interested in creating a public relations spectacle than mounting a credible legal challenge. As his questionable strategy faltered, many of the big law firms that had signed onto the Trump campaign's legal effort didn't quit so much as quietly back away. Mitchell and the rest of her team kept working, putting together a powerful lawsuit that former federal prosecutor Andrew McCarthy of *National Review* called Trump's "best legal challenge mustered so far."

The Georgia Supreme Court had previously ruled that challengers to an election don't need to show definitive fraud with particular votes, just that there were enough irregular ballots or violations of election procedures to place doubt in the result. Judges never want to overturn the results of an election, but under Georgia law, if it is showed that there were enough problems to cast doubt, then a new election is to be held. One was already scheduled for early January for Senate runoff races.

The lawsuit alleged up to 143,986 illegal votes, as well as violations of election law in how ballots were cast and in how signature match was conducted. McCarthy said the case, unlike other Trump-related cases he'd read, was "a linear, cogently presented description of numerous election-law violations, apparently based on hard data."[21]

In early December, Mitchell's team found security footage from Georgia's State Farm Arena that showed dozens of ballot counters, media, and Republican observers leaving en masse at the same time from the ballot-counting area for Fulton County, just as the Republican poll watchers had said. The video showed that after they left, a small remnant of about four workers began pulling trunks containing thousands of ballots from underneath a table with a long tablecloth and running ballots through machines.

The video was presented as part of a larger hearing before a Georgia Senate Judiciary Committee subcommittee. The hearing included "jaw-dropping allegations of alleged election fraud," reported a local CBS affiliate. It appeared to show "ballots being counted without oversight." The local CBS affiliate said it was "the biggest bombshell presented to lawmakers" and allegedly showed "people taking out at least four boxes of ballots from underneath a table, and then counting them after hours with no election supervisors present."[22]

The video exploded across the internet and conservative media and was shared widely around the same time that Georgia was completing a recount—different than an earlier audit—of the presidential election. Like the audit, it would gain some votes for Trump, putting the margin at 11,779 votes.

Democrats knew that the video looked absolutely awful, particularly since Biden had received a huge spike in numbers from Fulton County at the same time as the footage was timestamped.[23] In came liberal media to tell people not to believe their lying eyes—there was no problematic behavior in the suspicious footage.

After mentioning how some prominent conservative pundits had described the video as troubling, the *Washington Post*'s Erik Wemple said, "Of course, there's another explanation, one offered on Friday by Fulton County Director of Registration and Elections Richard L. Barron: 'According to my staff, that's just normal.'"[24]

The *Washington Post* also quoted Barron as saying, "No one from my staff made an announcement for anyone to leave."[25]

With that, the *Washington Post* was satisfied. Never mind that in addition to the video, there were multiple affidavits from poll watchers and dozens of media reports on Election Night saying that they were told the counting was done for the night. There was no curiosity about why everyone had left at the same time if no one had made an announcement for anyone to leave. Barron's claim was at best lawyerly and narrow: they didn't technically ask anyone to leave. Such a sophistical answer wouldn't hold up against the most modest level of scrutiny. Luckily for Barron, the media wasn't interested in providing any.

For many in the media, an election supervisor's disputing a claim made by a Republican meant the case was closed. But though election officials are supposed to be nonpartisan, they frequently aren't. And Barron was no exception. In fact, the Fulton County elections board hired Barron in 2013 in part because of his problems with Republicans at his prior job.

When Barron had served as election administrator for Williamson County, Texas, an election held on his watch had to be redone when more than one hundred wrong ballots were handed out in a race that came down to three votes. In that election, he had three law enforcement officers boot a Republican poll watcher. Both actions led to a no-confidence vote he narrowly survived.

In the run-up to his appointment as Fulton County election administrator, the *Atlanta-Journal Constitution* speculated that "Barron's run-in with Republicans may boost his chances with a panel where Democrats have a 5–2 majority."[26] Apparently, the Fulton County Board of Commissioners considered the fact Barron had run afoul of Republicans a credential rather than a liability.

Barron was not the only one who asserted that the video of Fulton County poll workers did not merit serious consideration. Another group purporting to debunk the video was an outfit called Lead Stories, which relies on funding from Silicon Valley tech giants Google and Facebook, in addition to ByteDance, a Chinese-operated company headquartered in Beijing that operates the social media platform TikTok.[27] Lead Stories relied on the same line as the *Washington Post*, saying, "There was never an announcement made to the media and other observers about the counting being over for the night and them needing to leave, according to [Frances Watson, chief investigator for the Georgia secretary of state], who was provided information by the media liaison, who was present."

While Lead Stories didn't name the media liaison, the media liaison who was present that night, according to the affidavits, was Regina Waller, the Fulton County public affairs manager for elections. And it was Regina Waller who "told ABC News that the election department sent the State Farm Arena absentee ballot counters home at 10:30 p.m."[28] In their affidavits, the GOP poll watchers noted that "Regina Waller was sending an email, as she relayed to us, when we left."[29]

Months later, an email timestamped at 10:22 p.m. on Election Night from Regina Waller to Barron and other county officials would be discovered that supported the GOP poll watchers' claim. In it, she said, "The workers in the Absentee Ballot Processing area will get started again at 8 am tomorrow."[30] Obviously, workers can only get started again if they have stopped.

What's more, Fulton County election commissioner Mark Wingate said that Barron called him after 10:00 p.m. on Election Night to say that there was an issue at State Farm Arena when Ralph Jones Sr., one of the county's top registration officials, needed to leave for the night to deal with a personal emergency. They were going to have to shut down operations for the night. "I said, Rick, are you kidding? This is election night. This is a highly contested presidential election. Are you going to then be able to face what's going to come at you in terms of you as the director, allowing the operation to shut down at 10:30 PM election night?" Wingate recalled. According to Wingate, Barron said he was heading to the State Farm Arena to try to keep things open.

When the video came out, Wingate couldn't help but notice that Ralph Jones Sr., who reportedly had claimed that he needed to leave the premises, appeared to have stuck around while ballots were counted. It made no sense. Why was Jones Sr. there?

Ralph Jones Sr. is no stranger to scandal. He was embroiled in an election controversy of his own in 2018 when a consulting firm registered to him was paid thousands of dollars by Atlanta mayoral candidate Keisha Lance Bottoms. Bottoms would go on to win by a razor-thin margin of 832 votes.[31]

The *Atlanta Journal-Constitution* described it as an "alarming lack of separation between a top election employee and active political campaign," since Jones Sr. oversaw the division that "maintains master voter lists, purges criminal and deceased voters from the polls, verifies petitions and mails absentee ballots."[32]

Ralph Jones Sr. is known for his hospitality toward the candidates whose elections he oversees, hosting an annual party where many of them are invited guests. "The optics are unfathomable," Wingate said. And to make matters worse, his son Ralph Jones Jr. was the company's "incorporator" and served as social media communications director for Bottoms's campaign.

"It's almost like saying, having a big arrow going, 'Hey, look at me, I'm doing something corrupt. Check it out,'" said Caren Morrison, a former federal prosecutor who is a law professor at Georgia State University. However, at the time, Barron said that Jones Sr. had not violated his oath.

The father–son act would continue in 2020. Ralph Jones Jr. moved on from working for Bottoms to act as the communications director for none other than Raphael Warnock, a Democratic candidate in the 2020 Senate election and runoff, a race Warnock would eventually win.[33]

A *Newsweek* story attempting to quash the concern over the video said Raffensperger's office claimed a designated election observer was "at that spot all night, the entire time."[34] But it wasn't true. Lead Stories itself emphasized that while partisan observers may not have been present, an "unnamed state election board monitor" was present from 11:52 p.m. until about 12:45 a.m., and the "deputy chief investigator for the secretary of state's office was present beginning at 12:15 a.m."[35] The Trump campaign's claim that there were no media, no partisan monitors, and no independent overseers present during the counting of ballots for more than an hour was true, not debunked.

The unnamed state election board monitor was a man named Carter Jones, who was employed by a contractor called Seven Hills Strategies. Months later, it would emerge that Seven Hills Strategies had submitted a twenty-nine-page memo in November to the Georgia secretary of state's office. The memo detailed extensive problems with how Fulton County's elections were conducted, providing an almost hourly accounting of problems with the election administration and ballot counting from November 2 through November 7. According to the memo, thousands of ballots were coming in to be counted in insecure rolling bins. "This seems like a massive chain of custody problem. It is my understanding that the ballots are supposed to be moved in numbered, sealed boxes to protect them," Jones wrote. Jones also flagged numerous other concerns involving double counting of votes, insecure ballot storage, and privacy violations.[36]

The memo raised deep concerns over the integrity of Fulton County's process. But instead of voicing these concerns, Secretary of State Brad Raffensperger decided to bury them. He appeared on *60 Minutes* in January and announced, "We had safe, secure, honest elections."[37]

In July 2021, Raffensperger would sing a different tune about Fulton County after lawsuits kept the county's 2020 election integrity problems in the news. "Fulton County's continued failures have gone on long enough with no accountability. Rick Barron and Ralph Jones, Fulton's registration chief, must be fired and removed from Fulton's elections leadership immediately. Fulton's voters and the people of Georgia deserve better," Raffensperger tweeted.[38]

◆   ◆   ◆

While the media may "call" a race, it is elected or appointed officials who certify it. Certification is when an election official says that each valid vote is included in the official canvass. "For an election official, the canvass means aggregating or confirming every valid ballot cast and counted—absentee, early voting, Election Day, provisional, challenged, and uniformed and overseas citizen," explains the U.S. Election Assistance Commission.[39]

The problems in Fulton County were so extensive that neither of the Republican commissioners voted to certify the election.[40] For one thing, the first certification was on November 13, but the county was still finding, processing, and tabulating absentee ballots as late as

November 12. Later, during the runoff, the county would discover thumb drives accidentally left in voting machines, further worrying the Republican commissioners about chain-of-custody issues and inventory management.

The Republican commissioners also drew attention to the fact that there was no chain-of-custody information provided for the thirty-eight ballot drop boxes spread throughout the county. The commissioners asked for, but were never provided, a document showing who had picked up the ballots or dropped them off, and when, much less whether, all ballots placed into the boxes were accounted for during their transport.[41]

The Republican commissioners also doubted whether Fulton County had even attempted to meaningfully match signatures. And it wasn't for lack of technology. In July that same year, the Fulton County elections division had acquired a new platform to handle absentee-by-mail ballots from a company called BlueCrest. The stations they purchased had the ability to scan the oath envelope, open the envelope, remove the ballot, and flatten the ballot itself in order to start the scanning process. The system also had optional capabilities for matching signatures to official signatures on file. While Barron had indicated to commissioners that the match capability was being brought into use, the Republicans later found out that the managers never had any intention of using that system. Consequently, there was no effective signature match going on at all.

Even statewide, almost no ballots or applications to receive ballots were rejected for having an improper signature match, leading some critics of mail-in balloting to wonder if any meaningful signature match took place in the state.[42]

Following the November election but before the Senate runoff, Wes Cantrell, a Georgia state representative, posted to Twitter an image of his real signature next to one that looked nothing like it. Cantrell had used the latter to request his mail-in ballot. Nevertheless, the state sent him a ballot. When he turned in the ballot, he signed the ballot envelope with yet another signature. He included a jagged middle initial and distinct letters in his last name; there was not a single letter that matched his original signature. His ballot was accepted without incident. "Signature Verification for Mail-In Ballots is a joke!" Cantrell said.[43]

Other Republicans in the state conducted similar experiments and got the same result.[44] They were able to vote and request ballots despite using signatures that looked nothing like their own. With signature match being one of the only security measures present for mail-in ballots during the election, the lack of rigor in checking them was disconcerting to many.

Finally, the Republican Fulton County election commissioners also had a problem with how Fulton County maintains its registered voter database. Active voter registrations in the county total more than 95 percent of the adult population of the county, an improbably high percentage. Nationwide, the Census Bureau said that in the 2016 presidential election, 70 percent of the voting-eligible population was registered to vote.[45]

The Republican commissioners felt they were asked to simply trust that everything had been done properly, despite their legitimate concerns. They posed important questions to officials only to get stonewalled and told off.

"If you don't get what you're asking for, you've got one or two ways to go," Wingate said about his many concerns. "Either you accept it, or you don't. And obviously with what's going on, there's many, many, many people that don't accept it. I was one of them."

◆   ◆   ◆

Though Fulton County was the hub of the dysfunction in Georgia, problems extended across the state.

Voter rolls were a major issue everywhere. In their lawsuit, the Trump campaign claimed that tens of thousands of voters had moved without registering to vote in their new residence. To get the figures about changes of address, the campaign looked at the National Change of

Address data set, a secure data set of information on people who have filed a change of address with the United States Postal Service.

Someone's filing a change-of-address form with the post office doesn't conclusively mean the person is no longer eligible to vote at his or her former address. Some of those address changes could be students at college or military members serving elsewhere. They would still be eligible to vote at the address they changed their mail from being delivered to. But many of them reflected permanent moves to new cities and states. In fact, with around 10 percent of the population moving each year, and inadequate maintenance of voter rolls, experts say there are literally millions of bogus registrations on voter rolls all over the country.[46] Such a situation doesn't necessitate fraud, but it does make the situation ripe for fraud or the illegal casting of votes.

There were around 122,000 Georgia voters in 2020 who told the Postal Service they were moving to a new county in Georgia with a "move effective date" of more than thirty days before the election and who failed to re-register in their new county in time to be eligible to vote in the general election.

The secretary of state specifically instructs, citing Georgia law, that doing this means "you have lost your eligibility to vote in the county of your old residence." Voters are required to register in the new county. "Remember, if you don't register to vote by the deadline, you cannot vote in that particular election," the secretary of state instructed.[47]

The vast majority of the 122,000 voters who moved obeyed the law and did not try to vote in their old county. But thousands of voters appeared to break the law by casting a vote in a county in which they didn't live. And most did so by voting absentee ballot, albeit many by early in-person absentee voting rather than mail-in voting.

Nearly all of these voters appeared to have voted in the wrong state house district, and more than 85 percent appeared to have voted in the wrong state senate district. Nearly two-thirds appeared to have voted in the wrong congressional district. And all of them appeared to be illegal votes in all races, since they would be ineligible to vote by law. Those who made similar moves but did not register to vote at their new address, and therefore didn't vote, had obeyed the law.

The issue is important because it shows "the folks who obeyed the law didn't get to vote, and the folks who broke it did get to vote," says Mark Davis, the Republican data expert in Georgia who raised alarms about the problem.

Davis was a fighter for election integrity in a state that could be lax about enforcing its basic laws. He drew attention to several problems. Some had been simmering for decades, but one—the problem of double voting—was new, a product of rule changes and mass mail-in voting.

◆   ◆   ◆

Mark Davis got into data analysis in college after his father, Guy Davis, was the Republican nominee for governor in Georgia in 1986. At that time, the Republican National Committee was the only organization in Georgia that had voter data, and it was on reel-to-reel magnetic tape. It annoyed him so much he began building voter databases himself on a mainframe, and he's been doing it ever since. His voter files are much sought after by Republican candidates throughout the state.

In the process of developing voter databases, Davis became aware of many of the problems with the voting system in Georgia, and he's been trying to get them fixed for decades.

"For years and years and years, I've kind of been that nerd over there that will bore you to tears talking about election integrity," he jokes. He's been an expert witness in five different election cases, usually dealing with problems caused by failure to place voters in their proper municipal district or related to change-of-address issues.

In the summer of 2020, Davis was involved in a dispute for a Long County probate judge who lost his election by nine votes. While working on that case, Davis learned of a man boasting to friends and neighbors that he had voted twice, once by mail and once in person, to test the system. The polling station failed the test and counted both votes.[48]

After speaking with the man, Davis realized that the problem of double voting may be more widespread with the increase in mail-in voting. Long County had opened up and counted absentee ballots before Election Day. That meant that if someone came to vote in person on Election Day and asked to have his absentee ballot canceled, it may have been too late to catch or remove it from the voting pile, as it could have already been separated from its identifying envelope and counted. Davis wondered if the smaller number of double voters he found in that one small county wasn't just the tip of the iceberg statewide.

"If there's an exploit out there, who knows whether or not people have been taking advantage of it deliberately," Davis said.

While election workers were supposed to check if someone had submitted his or her ballot already, that clearly hadn't happened in the case of many voters, such as that of the man in Long County. More than one thousand voters in the June primary voted more than once. Of those who did, 60 percent requested Democratic ballots.[49] No one was prosecuted for the crime, but when Raffensperger suggested to the public that he was going to take it seriously because double voting was an intentional act, the *Atlanta Journal-Constitution* defended double voters on the grounds of the ambiguity of handling ballot cancellation.

Raffensperger said, "Those that make the choice to game the system are breaking the law. And as secretary of state, I will not tolerate it."

"How the secretary of state can be so sure of this, we don't know," responded the *Atlanta Journal-Constitution*. "A confusing and often inexact electoral bureaucracy is a likely defense."[50]

Clearly, the opportunity to vote multiple times was a major flaw in the system. The lack of prosecutions concerned Republicans.

"I am not sure the secretary of state has the backbone for this," Fulton County poll manager Suzi Voyles told RealClearInvestigations. The highest concentration of double voters was in Fulton County. "We have turned in thousands of unlawful voters and not one of them has been prosecuted."[51]

Davis decided to look into the double voting situation statewide for the presidential election in November. He asked the secretary of state for an enumerated list of voters eligible to vote on November 5. They told him they would not give it to him, and that he should request it straight from the counties. Cobb County had the data easily available, but the four other large counties he wanted to begin with would not give him the data.

Later, when the secretary of state's office asked Davis to do an investigation of double voting, he reminded them that they wouldn't give him the data he had requested under open-records laws. They told him they could give it to him if he signed a non-disclosure agreement. He declined. Their investigation by another person found more than four hundred double voters in the November election, although it did not look into the issue of people who canceled their absentee ballot after they voted, of particular issue for the one hundred-plus Georgia counties that began counting early.

To do his analysis on change-of-address issues, Davis asked the secretary of state's office for a certified copy of the qualified list of voters, the list of names of all eligible voters that is due five days before an election. The office sent a file that was a complete mess, missing names and demographic information. The format has been the same since the National Motor Voter Law required the records to be kept in 1993. Davis messaged Gabriel Sterling, his childhood acquaintance and the chief operating officer at the secretary of state's office. Sterling told Davis that all of their data people had quit and the new guy had only been there for a week and a half. He couldn't get it replaced.

When Davis asked for the same information for the runoff, he received a file that looked perfect, except it was missing the one field he needed for his project, the last change date. The file looked to him as if it had been deliberately edited to remove a field. When he asked about it, the file was replaced immediately with a good file. He wondered why he could get that runoff data file replaced immediately but not the one that was such a mess from the general election in November.

Davis brought these issues to the Trump campaign and was working with the campaign to identify change-of-address concerns. His push for clear information would cause a major dustup between the campaign and the state—one that was twisted by the media into a national scandal.

The Trump campaign attorneys, including Cleta Mitchell and Kurt Hilbert, attempted to get the official information from the secretary of state a half-dozen times, according to leaked audio of a January 2, 2021, call they and President Trump had with Raffensperger, secretary of state counsel Ryan Germany, and White House chief of staff Mark Meadows. Raffensperger kept claiming that the Trump legal team's data showing ineligible voters was wrong, but he declined to share the state's data to back it up.[52]

The Trump campaign's lawsuit needed to show that more votes were in question than Biden's margin of victory. Between the in-state voters that had moved without registering and the out-of-state voters that had moved, the campaign identified fifty thousand votes. Working with Solomon Brothers as outside counsel, they determined that even if they assumed that fully half of them were military or college—a percentage they felt was outlandishly generous—that left them with twenty-five thousand votes, more than twice the number needed to seek relief of a new election.

As legitimate as the lawsuit was, it couldn't get heard—stifled by bureaucratic gamesmanship. At the same time, attorneys associated with Marc Elias and Perkins Coie began filing *pro hac vice* requests, where attorneys ask to appear in court for a particular trial even though they're not admitted to the bar in that state. The attorneys began filing all sorts of special motions to dismiss, even before they were given permission to practice law in Georgia.

Fulton County judge Constance Russell, assigned by lottery to the case, turned out to be ineligible because the law says the judge hearing the case can't be an active sitting judge from the county where the suit is filed. But before she left the case, she entered an interim order that the case was going to go on a normal procedural course, "which means it will not be resolved any time soon," as the *Journal-Constitution* put it.[53]

The Trump team had filed their lawsuit with an emergency temporary restraining order request to prevent certification of the election. When Raffensperger certified the election, the Trump team withdrew their motion and filed a new emergency motion to decertify.[54]

With no hearing in sight, the Trump team—desperate to get to a court date before the Electoral College convened—appealed to the Georgia Supreme Court, asking it to grant immediate review of that interim order slow-walking the case, as well as an order assigning a judge. That court said it couldn't do anything about the interim order because it lacked final jurisdiction. It did get a liberal senior judge from Cobb County, Adele Grubbs, to handle the case. She set January 8 as the date for a hearing, which was of no help to the Trump team as it was after January 6, when Congress would process the Electoral College vote.[55]

This was the context for the campaign's call with the secretary of state to get the information out in a timely fashion. The call, which included Trump's making exaggerated claims about the size of the errors alleged in the lawsuit, included Trump's claim that they had found tens of thousands of votes that were illegal, requiring the election to be redone.[56]

Again, if more than 11,779 ineligible votes were found, that meant that the election should be redone, according to the Trump campaign's understanding of state law. Trump said in the call, "All I want to do is this. I just want to find 11,780 votes, which is one more than we have because we won the state."[57]

The media portrayed this request as Trump asking Raffensperger to steal the election for him and fraudulently create new votes to put him over the top.[58] The false interpretation of the sound bite even made it into the article of impeachment the second time Democrats impeached the president.[59]

Anyone familiar with the lawsuit knew Trump was saying his team had already "found" nearly 150,000 problematic votes, not just votes from people who had allegedly moved but also people who had allegedly registered improperly or were otherwise ineligible to cast votes, and simply needed the secretary of state's office to agree. He was saying they didn't need to agree that all 150,000 were bad, just that fewer than 10 percent of them were problematic.

In any case, the secretary of state's office refused, and refused to share the information the campaign claimed would prove their contention.

It was one thing to not take the claims of illegal votes seriously. But leaking the audio to a press corps that was out for blood, days before a runoff election that Democrats would win, was a different matter entirely. It spoke to a level of unprofessionalism, if not downright corruption, that was unimaginable in an official acting in good faith.

"I think they were circling the wagons. They did not want Raffensperger to be held responsible for these errors," Davis said.

Fox News's Martha MacCallum asked Raffensperger directly if he had authorized the leak of the second call, and he repeatedly refused to answer the question. Raffensperger admitted to MacCallum that it coincided with his anger at Republican senator David Perdue, whom he blamed for animosity directed at his wife after Perdue called for him to resign.[60]

On January 9, the *Washington Post* published a bombshell report about what President Trump had reportedly said in another phone call to a Georgia elections investigator. The headline was "'Find the Fraud': Trump Pressured a Georgia Elections Investigator in a Separate Call Legal Experts Say Could Amount to Obstruction."

The original story was influential. "The president's attempts to intervene in an ongoing investigation could amount to obstruction of justice or other criminal violations, legal experts said, though they cautioned a case could be difficult to prove," reported the *Post* story.

A few weeks later, House Democrats would cite the article and its fabricated quotes on page ten of their impeachment brief, as well as highlight the article and its fake quotes in oral arguments during the televised impeachment trial.[61]

On March 11, months after the damage was done, the *Post* quietly changed the headline and added a stunning correction:

> Correction: Two months after publication of this story, the Georgia secretary of state released an audio recording of President Donald Trump's December phone call with the state's top elections investigator. The recording revealed that The Post misquoted Trump's comments on the call, based on information provided by a source. Trump did not tell the investigator to "find the fraud" or say she would be "a national hero" if she did so. Instead, Trump urged the investigator to scrutinize ballots in Fulton County, Ga., asserting she would find "dishonesty" there. He also told her that she had "the most important job in the country right now." A story about the recording can be found here. The headline and text of this story have been corrected to remove quotes misattributed to Trump.[62]

Even accurately reported, the story may have been newsworthy or unflattering to Trump. But there's a huge difference in criminal intent between a frustrated and addled Trump asking an investigator to look into problems he genuinely believes are real versus pressuring the investigator to invent fraud. For what it's worth, once the investigator on the phone call was identified, she told local news "she did not perceive any pressure from the president's call."[63]

A correction two months after the fact, when the story has already played a significant role in shaping perceptions of political events, seems wholly inadequate. The headline on the *Post*'s follow-up story was given an anodyne headline: "Recording Reveals Details of Trump Call to Georgia's Chief Elections Investigator."[64]

Originally, the fabricated quotes were sourced to "an individual familiar with the call who spoke on the condition of anonymity because of the sensitivity of the conversation." What had been revealed about how the story was reported made both the *Post*'s reporting and the secretary of state's office look worse, not better:

> The Washington Post reported on the substance of Trump's Dec. 23 call in January, describing him saying that Watson should "find the fraud" and that she would be a "national hero," based on an account from Jordan Fuchs, the deputy secretary of state, whom Watson briefed on his comments. In fact, he did not use those precise words. Rather, Trump urged the investigator to scrutinize Fulton County, where she would find "dishonesty," he said. He also said, "whatever you can do, Frances, it would be—it's a great thing. It's an important thing for the country. So important. You've no idea. So important. And I very much appreciate it."[65]

Revealing the source of the quotes shows the *Post* had cause for more scrutiny, not less. According to the chairman of the Georgia Republican Party, "The Secretary of State's office secretly recorded the conversation, mischaracterized its contents to The Washington Post and then attempted to delete the recording. It was recently discovered in a laptop 'trash' folder as part of an open records search."[66]

In sum: the *Washington Post* anonymously printed fabricated quotes it knew were from a secondhand source in the office of a politician publicly hostile to Trump, couldn't confirm the quotes with additional sourcing, still attributed them to the sitting president of the United States, and used those quotes as a basis to speculate the president had committed a crime.

But it gets much worse. Several other major media outlets—including NBC, ABC, *USA Today*, PBS, and CNN—"confirmed" the fabricated quotes from the *Post*'s anonymous source by citing their own anonymous sources.[67]

◆　　◆　　◆

Jordan Fuchs, the deputy secretary of state who was accused in both of those leaks, did not have a background in election management or experience running a large organization when she was made deputy secretary of state. Fuchs received an outsized role in orchestrating the election—a role that she may not have been prepared for. She also had a history of partisan statements that raised questions about whether she was able to conduct a fair election.

Even the mildest of criticisms of the secretary of state's performance met brutal pushback from Fuchs, which caused a serious deterioration in the office's relationship with the legislature and many Republicans, even before she leaked phone calls.[68] Fuchs's Twitter account featured anti-Trump sentiments and claims that concerns about election integrity were a "big lie."[69] It didn't exactly build confidence that she knew what she was doing, was able to separate her emotions from her work, or was capable of understanding legitimate complaints about how she manages elections.

Leaking phone calls on the eve of an all-important senate runoff was bad enough, but many Republican activists had been frustrated with the secretary of state's office all year. Fuchs's apparent goal after Georgia's primary election fiasco was to drive up early and mail-in absentee voting in the struggling Democratic counties as much as possible.[70] Since Democrats had made mail-in balloting their primary campaign goal, that meant the office was subsidizing the Democrats' get-out-the-vote operations.

Some of the money was taxpayer-funded, such as the more than $10 million Georgia received in Help America Vote Act funding to help with mail-in balloting.[71] The secretary of state's office also received more than $5.5 million from the Mark Zuckerberg–linked Center for Election Innovation and Research. The group said Georgia used the funds to "encourage voters to apply for a ballot online" and to "counteract disinformation, issuing public service announcements warning voters of disinformation and encouraging them to report fraud to the Secretary of State hotline."[72] And that doesn't count the $45 million sent to the counties themselves to privately fund the handling of mail-in voting with a tech oligarch's money.

To assist with the effort, the secretary of state's office unilaterally mailed nearly seven million absentee ballot applications to Georgia residents, further undermining what little security mail-in ballots had.[73] The method of indiscriminately mailing out ballot applications to more than seven million registered voters led to greater instability of the signature match system, even in the unlikely case that poll workers were checking for matches.

Moreover, signature match couldn't verify that the person to whom the ballot was sent was a legitimate voter or wasn't lying about whom the ballot was for. If the same person signed both the ballot application and the ballot itself, the signature matched, but that didn't prove the identity of the voter was accurate. And sending out millions of ballot applications provided ample opportunity for malefactors to procure bogus ballots, knowing that a signature wouldn't prove they were fraudulently obtained to begin with.

"It's like putting cyanide in your cake and trying to eat around it," said Mark Rountree, the president of Landmark Communications, a top Georgia political consulting firm. Rountree ran Raffensperger's secretary of state campaign and had previously employed both Jordan Fuchs and Gabriel Sterling. "You can't. It is embedded into the cake."

Ballots were sent to nearly 150 addresses where more than 50 voters were registered. Some were homeless shelters, such as one with more than 2,000 registered voters that had used that address over the years. Republicans and Democrats agree that homeless people have the right to vote, but the location in which they vote is important, both for legal reasons and for districting issues. "I'm told this is encouraged," Davis said of homeless registrations at county buildings or shelters. "I see a lot of potential for fraud here."

Other addresses with more than fifty registrations included commercial mail-receiving agencies, parking lots, college dining halls, and single-family dwellings. More than fifty registrations at an extended-stay hotel was one thing, but more than fifty registrations at a Courtyard Marriott looked less justified.

The operation helped the secretary of state at least look better initially in the November election, and it helped Democrats win. "They basically spent huge amounts of federal money to increase Democratic turnout," said Davis.

Raffensperger and his staff seemed to welcome the change in coverage from the June 9 primary. They were no longer under the barrel of the media's gun. But Raffensperger paid a high price for that early good coverage and would soon find himself under fire again. Republicans were upset.

"It is not that they should have put the thumb on the scale for Trump," said Rountree. "But they definitely shouldn't have put the thumb on the scale for Biden."

Few of the concerns raised by Republicans could get meaningful attention from the office. When Raffensperger did try to quell Republican discontent, he often seemed to be more interested in protecting his reputation than addressing their concerns. After Republicans complained about signature match problems statewide, Raffensperger did an audit of fifteen thousand signatures in Cobb County. But Cobb County was generally considered a well-run portion of the state, and the audit found virtually no problems. Asked why it wasn't auditing Fulton County, the site of so many problems, the office claimed it hadn't received any complaints about the problem there.

Raffensperger and the secretary of state's office would be forced to address problems that had been ignored after Joe Biden was sworn in as president and the spotlight went away, tacitly validating many of the issues the Trump campaign had tried to bring to his attention earlier.

On May 7, Davis announced that he had evidence of 10,559 voters who had updated their voter registration after the election to the address they had told the Postal Service they had moved to at least thirty days before the election, but who had voted at the old address. He said an average of fifty-seven such confirmations were coming in per day.

He posted his information publicly and asked people to pressure the secretary of state to take action.[74] The secretary of state's office opened an investigation into the residency issue problem that day.

In addition to the official investigation into residency issues, the secretary of state opened an investigation in December 2020 into outside groups deliberately trying to get people with eligibility problems to vote.[75] Raffensperger announced an investigation into several progressive groups, including one founded by Stacey Abrams and previously run by Warnock called the New Georgia Project. Complainants alleged the groups were soliciting registrations in the name of dead people, those ineligible to vote, and those who had moved away years prior.[76] Social media reports indicated that the effort to get people to vote in Georgia was nationwide, with voters out of state claiming they had received requests for them to register in Georgia.

But it was too little too late. In the months since the 2020 election, data has been put forth showing strong reason to question the legality of more votes than the margin Biden won by. Had a court been willing to hear the argument, and had Trump's attorneys been able to show the data in the weeks following the election, a good argument could have been made for holding a new election.

And that doesn't even count the tens of millions of Zuck Bucks that flowed into the coffers of Democratic counties in Georgia, much less the millions the secretary of state's office used to help Democrats with their get-out-the-vote balloting scheme.

"Trump actually won the state. And I'm not crazy when I say that," said Rountree.

Consent of the Losers

"**D**emocracy depends on the consent of the losers," wrote *The Atlantic*'s Yoni Appelbaum in 2019 during the impeachment of President Trump.[1] Appelbaum wasn't writing about the refusal of his fellow Democratic partisans to accept their 2016 presidential loss, or their forming a "resistance," or their unceasing efforts to remove Trump from office. Rather, he was talking about Republicans' needing to understand and accept, without putting up much of a fight, the unavoidable electoral losses that were headed their way.

While it is true that democracy depends on the consent of the losers, Democrats had made a habit of questioning the legitimacy of elections they had lost since at least George H. W. Bush's election. As bad as their earlier objections were, they paled in comparison to Democrats' refusal to accept the outcome in 2016.

The widespread attempts to discredit the 2016 election went far beyond the usual protests Democrats made in the wake of electoral losses. Riots, investigations, impeachments, and a non-stop resistance spurred on by the Democratic Party harmed the country in grievous ways that eclipsed the objections dozens of congressional Democrats made to certifying the 2016 Electoral College vote.[2]

After decades of Democrats' taking exception to election results, the fact that large numbers of voters and members of Congress objected to the outcome of the 2020 election wasn't new, or even surprising. What was different this time was that it was Republicans who didn't trust the election's integrity. Previously, the republic had held together in part because Republicans accepted losses and put up with Democrats' recurring refusal to accept election results. This time, after copious foul play in the months leading up to the election, some Republicans had had enough.

With nearly 160 million Americans voting in 2020, Democrat Joe Biden won the Electoral College vote 306 to 232. But the margin was much narrower than the Electoral College count would suggest. The election was exceedingly close to producing a very different outcome.[3] Biden won Arizona, Georgia, and Wisconsin by fewer than 43,000 votes combined. Had just 22,000 of those votes across three states flipped from Biden to Trump, Trump would have won those states and the Electoral College would have been tied at 269 votes for each candidate. Such ties are decided by one vote for each House delegation, of which Republicans controlled a majority.[4]

It was massively hypocritical to suggest that whoever lost a presidential race in such close circumstances wasn't entitled to an aggressive challenge. When Donald Trump defeated Hillary Clinton in similarly close fashion in 2016—she lost by just eighty thousand votes in Michigan, Pennsylvania, and Wisconsin—Clinton joined recount efforts and tried to derail the Electoral College vote.[5] She and her allies used lies about colluding with Russia to undermine President Trump and launch a special counsel probe with the purpose of ousting him by means of impeachment. And she spent the next four years publicly claiming the election had been stolen from her.[6]

The 2020 election was unlike any in the nation's history. Thirty-nine states modified their election laws or procedures, or both, ahead of the general election.[7] The Constitution provides that state legislatures oversee elections, but in 2020 many courts and election administrators changed the rules without the approval of their state legislature. The changes—or, in many cases, lack of changes—led to more than 500 lawsuits and subsequent appeals filed by Democrats and Republicans.[8] Nearly 250 of the lawsuits dealt with a rushed expansion of mail-in balloting procedures that Democrats were pushing as part of their campaign strategy for winning the White House and other races.[9]

Democrats won several important rulings in key states ahead of the election. Some cases were settled prior to the election, others were settled after. Some were dismissed or unheard before the election because there wasn't sufficient time to review before the election or because no harm could be shown as the election hadn't happened yet. Others were dismissed after the election because it was too late to do anything about them or they were rendered moot by the outcome of the election.

While these were short-term and even long-term wins for the Democratic Party, the failure of the courts to clearly define whether the Democratic Party's revolution in voting was constitutional, much less legal, was setting up to be something of a crisis.

Republicans asked the United States Supreme Court to review a Pennsylvania Supreme Court ruling prior to the election, and to do so in an expedited fashion. The Supreme Court said it didn't have time, but Associate Justice Samuel Alito, joined by Associate Justices Clarence Thomas and Neil Gorsuch, worried about "post-election problems."[10]

The case seemed clear-cut. Pennsylvania's legislature had set a clear deadline for counting votes and had declined an opportunity to revise it after the global pandemic hit. That's when the Pennsylvania Supreme Court took matters into its own hands and issued a decision that "squarely alters" the law, according to Supreme Court justice Samuel Alito.[11]

Alito wrote that it would be "highly desirable" to have the court decide the issue of constitutionality.[12] "The provisions of the Federal Constitution conferring on state legislatures, not state courts, the authority to make rules governing federal elections would be meaning-less if a state court could override the rules adopted by the legislature," Alito wrote, noting that just because the court wasn't deciding it before the election didn't mean it couldn't or shouldn't decide it after.[13]

But in February, the Supreme Court decided the case was moot, though it didn't explain precisely why. Justice Clarence Thomas wrote a blistering dissent:

> One wonders what this Court waits for. We failed to settle this dispute before the election, and thus provide clear rules. Now we again fail to provide clear rules for future elections. The decision to leave election law hidden beneath a shroud of doubt is baffling. By doing nothing, we invite further confusion and erosion of voter confidence. Our fellow citizens deserve better and expect more of us. I respectfully dissent.[14]

It really was inexplicable. Ruling on the case would not change any election results, particularly since the number of ballots in question—about ten thousand—was less than Biden's margin of victory in Pennsylvania. Both sides of the dispute agreed that the case needed to be settled, and a federal court had ruled on the same issue in a different state in a different way from the Pennsylvania Supreme Court, a classic example of the type of case the Supreme Court exists to decide.

Statewide elections are complex operations. Legislatures make difficult decisions about how to best structure and conduct an election, and thousands of state and local officials and volunteers must implement those decisions on the ground both before the election and as the votes are counted. A lot can go wrong, especially when the rules have not been set in stone.

Legal clarity prior to elections is paramount, as Associate Justice Brett Kavanaugh wrote regarding an earlier Supreme Court decision involving the Wisconsin election. "When an election is close at hand, the rules of the road should be clear and settled," he wrote.[15] Clarity from the courts "not only prevents voter confusion but also prevents election administrator confusion—and thereby protects the State's interest in running an orderly, efficient election and in giving citizens (including the losing candidates and their supporters) confidence in the fairness of the election."[16]

For obvious reasons, declared winners of elections have more confidence in the fairness of elections. The key is that elections must be run in such a way that losers, too, have confidence.

Thomas agreed with this earlier reasoning by Kavanaugh, but he went a step further. The absence of evidence of fraud, Thomas noted, was not sufficient to settle debates about fraud, something that the media refused to understand. Strong systems must be in place to deter and detect fraud—and, just as important, to inspire confidence among candidates and citizens. "An election free from strong evidence of systemic fraud is not alone sufficient for election confidence. Also important is the assurance that fraud will not go undetected," wrote Justice Thomas.[17]

The raft of changes the Democrats rushed in undermined many of the measures in place to detect fraud. By unilaterally issuing these changes, the Democrats undermined the faith of millions of Republicans in the election. They chose not to conduct an election that their opponents could have confidence in, and acted surprised when the declared loser challenged the results. Luckily for them, those challenges failed to trigger a full-blown constitutional crisis. But they very much could have, and might yet if Democrats insist on conducting future elections in such a partisan way in the future.

◆   ◆   ◆

Shortly after the election, dozens of state-based challenges to the election confusion instituted by the rush to mail-in balloting failed. The Trump campaign's six paths to victory through different combinations of seventeen different states narrowed and narrowed. With no legal play in Arizona, and procedural dismissals of cases in Pennsylvania, Wisconsin, and Georgia, Trump's new legal team sought a theory of the case that would be big enough to involve several states. A win in a single state was not going to be sufficient.

Time and again, courts up to and including the United States Supreme Court avoided settling disputes.[18] It was an abdication of duty, regardless of how they might have ruled.

The Trump campaign's best chance was *Texas v. Pennsylvania*, a lawsuit filed directly at the Supreme Court by Texas attorney general Ken Paxton and joined by seventeen other state attorney generals. The court declined to hear the case, arguing that Texas lacked "standing," a legal term meaning that Texas could not demonstrate that its interest had been harmed by the defendant.

The case was a long shot, but there was a difference between the Supreme Court's explaining why it was wrong on the merits and simply refusing to even consider the arguments. That refusal, along with so many others at the federal and state level, went a long way to amping up the frustration of the losing side, culminating in a riot at the Capitol on January 6.

At the same time the legal team was working its way through the courts, however unsuccessfully, the conversation among Trump advisors and supporters turned to fraud.

Prominent Trump affiliates began hyping dramatic claims about problems with Dominion Voting Systems, one of the companies that supplied voting machines used in many states. Rudy Giuliani and others suggested the election had experienced fraud sufficient to overturn the results nationwide.[19] The media soon characterized all of the legal fights as nothing more than discussions of "widespread fraud," when that wasn't at all relevant to the claims made in several lawsuits. Further, they said if "widespread fraud" was not found, it meant that there was nothing to worry about with the election.[20]

Many of these claims gained currency and were damaging to the political discourse—there's no doubt about that. Nonetheless, the mainstream right is disgusted by the disparate treatment given to the conspiracies and violence hatched by Democrats. It was prominent Democrats and the media who had sounded the alarm about voting system security right up until November 3, 2020.

On October 26, 2020, for example, *PBS NewsHour* aired a seven-minute segment on concerns outside experts had with Georgia's new $107 million Dominion voting system.[21] Reporter Miles O'Brien described the system as a "complex assortment of laptops, iPads, magnetic cards, touch screens, printers, and scanners."[22]

"They have set up a complicated system, which is centralized and doesn't seem to have any safeguards," said security consultant Harri Hursti in the segment.[23]

PBS noted that the rollout of the system for the June primary resulted in significant problems. "The poll pads took as long as 30 hours to download the voter database, displayed the wrong races, and would randomly shut down. And the power-hungry ballot-marking devices blew circuit-breakers in numerous locations. Poll workers, many of whom had no hands-on training because of the pandemic, were often befuddled by the new technology," O'Brien said.[24]

J. Alex Halderman, a University of Michigan professor of computer science, said he'd analyzed the voting system, which issues a "QR" code for each ballot—a machine-readable optical label that contains information about the item to which it is attached—and found that "there's nothing that stops an attacker from just duplicating one, and the duplicate would count the same as the original bar code."[25] Halderman had also tested whether voters could catch deliberately placed errors on their ballot, and only 7 percent did.

None of this was presented as crackpot theorizing, but instead these were treated as legitimate concerns.

Democratic senators had likewise spent years expressing deep concern over the difficulty of catching fraud with voting systems. At a 2018 Senate hearing, then senator Kamala Harris of California said, "I actually held a demonstration for my colleagues here at the Capitol, where we brought in folks who, before our eyes, hacked election machines."[26]

Fellow senator Amy Klobuchar of Minnesota said, "We're very concerned because there's only three companies. You could easily hack into them. It makes it seem like all these states are doing different things. But in fact, three companies are controlling them."[27]

And Senator Ron Wyden of Oregon said, "Forty-three percent of American voters use voting machines that researchers have found have serious security flaws, including back doors. These companies are accountable to no one. They won't answer basic questions about their cybersecurity practices and the biggest companies won't answer any questions at all. Five states have no paper trail, and that means there is no way to prove the numbers the voting machines put out are legitimate. So much for cybersecurity 101."[28]

Even Democratic voting rights guru Marc Elias was pushing theories about voting machines as part of his three-month challenge of Republican Claudia Tenney's victory in a New York congressional race, delaying her seating in Congress.[29] While the judge didn't find value in the claim, he didn't rule it outside the bounds of appropriate discourse.

There was little reason to believe the liberal media had any concern about wild claims of voter fraud when those claims were made by Democrats. But after the 2020 election, media personalities and other partisans used the most outlandish claims made by Republicans to dismiss all of the many legitimate concerns about election integrity as a "big lie."[30]

CNN's Jake Tapper was particularly fond of calling it a "big lie." Adolf Hitler, of all people, coined the term to describe the propaganda technique of a lie so audacious that no one could believe it was made up. Hitler claimed Jews used the technique by blaming Germany's World War I loss on a nationalist political leader.

Jake Tapper kept using Hitler's language to attack Republicans' widespread concern about election integrity.

Amazingly, it was Tapper himself, along with his colleagues, who obsessively pushed the lie that Trump had illegitimately won the 2016 election by colluding with Russia. Tapper was one of four reporters who wrote CNN's story that ended up popularizing the wildly inaccurate Steele dossier, which was used by the FBI to spy on the Trump campaign and launch years of conspiratorial fake news.[31]

The lies behind the Russia collusion story were definitely convincing to Democrats. Asked if they believed the Trump campaign had colluded with the Russian government to influence the 2016 presidential election, 86 percent of Democrats said yes, even more than a year after the election. In the summer of 2018, a full three-quarters of Democrats still said they believed the conspiracy theory. Even nineteen months after Trump took office, three out of every four Democrats believed the lie that the Trump campaign had colluded with the Russian government to influence the election and that the Russian government had *kompromat*—blackmail material—on Trump.[32]

◆   ◆   ◆

Despite the media and other activists' saying that the 2020 election must be accepted without question, strong majorities of Republicans have reason to complain—and they aren't backing down. From their perspective, they were the victims of an election that was rigged from the day Trump won the presidential election in November 2016.

When Trump surprised the world by defeating Clinton, the left immediately began to protest and riot nationwide. Thousands took to the streets of Chicago. In Oakland, rioters set trash cans, cars, and a building on fire. They smashed store windows, hurt police, and blocked a freeway.[33] Other protests formed in Atlanta, Boston, Cleveland, Dallas, Detroit, Houston, Los Angeles, Miami, New York, Omaha, Philadelphia, Portland, Richmond, San Diego, and San Francisco.[34]

Nationwide, the left caused chaos. Protests and riots spread to the White House, where Trump was meeting with President Obama, as well as Austin, Grand Rapids, Greensboro, Louisville, Madison, Milwaukee, Minneapolis, Pittsburgh, and Tampa.

The left's riots and protests continued on November 11, 2016, hitting the cities of Anchorage, Bakersfield, Denver, Des Moines, Eugene, Fort Worth, Iowa City, Nashville, New Haven, and Orlando.[35]

On the first weekend after Trump's election, the left organized massive marches to protest his victory.[36] More than ten thousand Angelenos shut down Wilshire Boulevard.[37] In New York, a crowd of twenty-five thousand marched on Trump Tower.[38]

Liberals refused to show up to their jobs, and school students across the country staged walkouts because they claimed they were so upset.[39] When Vice President–Elect Mike Pence attended a showing of *Hamilton* on Broadway, the cast, who reportedly "could barely go on stage" after the election because of the difficulty they had coping with Trump's victory, read a statement to the prominent member of the audience.[40]

On Inauguration Day, more riots erupted in Washington, D.C. Hundreds were arrested as black-clad rioters set cars on fire, threw bricks, and injured police. One in three Democratic House members joined the protest by refusing to attend the inauguration, claiming Trump's election was not legitimate.[41]

Democrats attempted to thwart the Electoral College vote for Trump by having James Clapper, Obama's director of national intelligence who had previously had to apologize for lying to Congress, brief the Electoral College on Trump's fitness for office and allege foreign interference in the election.[42]

In a secret January 5, 2017, meeting in the Oval Office, Obama gave guidance to key officials who would be tasked with protecting his administration's utilization of a secretly funded Clinton campaign operation to spy on Trump campaign affiliates.[43] That campaign operation alleged Trump was involved in a treasonous plot to collude with Russia, and Obama and his officials wanted to keep it from being discovered, much less stopped, by the incoming administration.

Shortly thereafter, high-level operatives began intensely leaking selective information to a compliant press that supported a supposed Russia–Trump conspiracy theory. The incoming national security advisor was ambushed by the FBI and forced to resign, and the incoming attorney general was forced to recuse himself from oversight of investigations of President Trump.[44] At each major point in the operation, explosive media leaks were a key strategy in the operation to take down Trump.[45]

Throughout the administration, leftists pushed the idea that Trump should be ousted by means of a unique reading of the Twenty-Fifth Amendment to the Constitution.[46] Further, they alleged that Trump administration officials and even his supporters should be attacked in public.

"Let's make sure we show up wherever we have to show up. And if you see anybody from that Cabinet in a restaurant, in a department store, at a gasoline station, you get out and you create a crowd. And you push back on them. And you tell them they're not welcome anymore, anywhere," Representative Maxine Waters told a crowd of cheering Democrats in 2018.[47] Throughout the Trump presidency, liberal activists did just that, attacking Trump officials in restaurants and at their homes.

◆　　◆　　◆

It is impossible to understand Republican opposition to the handling of the 2020 election without dealing honestly with what was done to Trump, his administration, and his supporters by his rabid and obsessed enemies every day of the preceding four years.

In his book on the 2020 presidential election *Neither Free Nor Fair*, Joel Pollak notes that an election can only be considered free and fair if it is free and fair throughout the process. "[V]oting is not the only event in an election, just as the verdict is not the only event in a trial, though it is the decisive one. An election is the culmination of a process, which includes campaigns by the candidates, appealing to voters both directly and through the media, motivating them to participate and asking for their support," he writes.[48]

A corrupt media corrupts the integrity of elections, and the constant flow of negative stories from journalists out to get Trump undermined public faith in their ability to report basic facts. They could hardly cover daily stories of little importance without denigrating the president. How could they be expected to stand as neutral arbiters of a contested election?

The media lied about Trump's successes, made up damaging stories, and worked with anonymous sources to publish fake stories for four years. White House press correspondents reacted histrionically to everything the president said or did. Corporate media hid or downplayed the Trump administration's accomplishments, such as historic peace agreements in the Middle East, no new wars, hostage rescues, the repositioning of the country to take on China, bolstering U.S. energy production so that the county was less reliant on foreign adversaries, and the strengthening of NATO by directing countries to fund more of their own defense. The pre-COVID wage and job growth was creating what Trump called a "blue-collar boom," which was a boon to all ethnic groups, but it was downplayed in favor of liberals' alleging Trump was racist.[49]

Just as the 2020 general election campaign got going, media-induced hysteria over the coronavirus sent not just the country but the world into a tailspin. Any attempt to hold the communist government of China accountable for unleashing the virus was met with cries from the media and other powerful Democrats that such assignation of responsibility was racist. If Trump said something, the media immediately treated it as untrue because he'd said it. Their hostile posture had real consequences.

That's not to say that Trump didn't say or do unwise things, about the coronavirus and many other things. But whenever great challenges have faced American presidents, the question is whether they achieve the big things, not the little things. When Roosevelt began commanding U.S. forces in World War II, or when the Manhattan Project began, or when Abraham Lincoln defended the Union, they made mistakes, some of them major. But these presidents were still credited for the big things they got right.

But the media obsessed over mistakes made by Trump, failing to credit him for tearing down the bureaucratic barriers preventing a quick development of a vaccine and devoting considerable resources to Operation Warp Speed. As a result of Trump's actions, the United States developed a lifesaving vaccine in record time, and it was being administered to millions before he left office.

The onslaught of fake news stories was relentless. Corporate media polls pushed falsehoods about the nature of U.S. elections, routinely overestimating the level of support Biden had, and, more important, underestimating the level of support Trump had.[50] They were more push polls than real polls, intended to demoralize Republicans and lift the spirits of Democrats. When the media narrative, day in and day out for months, was not that the race was close but that Biden would win by large margins, it was a massive in-kind contribution to Democrats.

One of the standards for a free and fair election is that it be free from political violence. The 2020 election happened at the same time that the left embraced wanton political violence to achieve its ends. But ever since 2016, prominent Democratic officials had encouraged their followers to assault Trump supporters. The media even went after high school kids who supported the president, lying about a boy from Covington, Kentucky, who had attended a pro-life rally.

Part of the left's effort to control the 2020 election included, according to the infamous *Time* magazine article, coordination with the organizers of the Black Lives Matter riots. The article said that the coordinated effort included plans for more riots if Trump had won. The trauma of the summer of violence included dozens of deaths, billions of dollars in damage, and the destruction of major sections of cities across America.

Any attempt to quell the violence was treated as reprehensible, in part because the media kept lying by claiming the deadly riots were "mostly peaceful." When the White House, federal courts, and city police stations were attacked or even taken over, the media asserted that the rioters were well-intentioned crusaders for racial justice and deemed any strong response unacceptable. At the same time, they used the widespread violence wrought by the left against other Americans to discredit Trump's argument that he was a peace-and-prosperity president.

Republicans also know that powerful tech companies began rigging the election from the moment Trump won. They put in place algorithms to decrease the spread of conservative arguments, privileged so-called "fact checks" from liberal groups as a means to do so, and instituted widespread censorship campaigns against individuals and stories to help their fellow Democrats.[51]

Tech companies inserted themselves into the 2020 election, deciding to work against one party and one candidate. Twitter began meddling in the election by censoring and limiting the reach of tweets from Donald Trump, whether about election rigging, the summer of violence, the origin and treatment of COVID-19, or any other issue it felt compelled to weigh in on.[52] Meanwhile, the political speech of fellow Democrats, no matter how disputed, was left untouched. It was yet another massive in-kind contribution to Democrats.

And all that was before the media conspired with tech companies to suppress the distribution of facts about the Biden family's corruption, including a blackout on corporate media coverage of Hunter Biden's scandal-ridden laptop featuring lurid details about the Biden family business of selling access to their powerful patriarch. Tech oligarchs intervened to censor the distribution of the story from other media outlets, part of a pattern of controlling discourse to favor political allies.

The media, polling, and Big Tech rigging alone would have been enough to cause Republicans to doubt any election loss, but what Democrats did to the manner in which people vote was further destabilizing to the country.

Democrats took advantage of the coronavirus global pandemic to foist upon the country election rules explicitly designed to favor their party. Since before the country was founded, Americans have been fighting about how to hold elections in a free and fair manner.

Long-standing historical concerns about the integrity of elections led to the development of a single Election Day, a secret ballot, and governmental running of elections—all developments that went a long way toward building up trust in America's electoral process. In recent years, Democrats have lobbied to move away from each of those things, saying that efforts to stop them from doing so were "voter suppression."[53] In the months leading up to 2020, Democrats were able to convince legislatures, courts, and election officials to open elections up to ballot trafficking, voting without showing identification, voting without following state laws or guidelines, and counting ballots without oversight from independent observers. Meager checks on fraud, such as signature matching, were watered down to the point of meaninglessness.

Most dramatically, Democrats were able to embed their army of nonprofit groups inside America's election system through generous grants from Mark Zuckerberg and other high-powered Democratic donors. The money went to election officials with strings attached, including that the election officials would work only with that network of left-wing groups that had spent decades advancing Democratic Party ideals in voting practices.

The left spent hundreds of millions of dollars on its scheme to embed operatives in governmental election systems that aren't supposed to take sides. Republican voters had no idea what had been done until it was too late.

While some judges did admirable work in the fight for election integrity, some courts helped Democrats keep third-party candidates off ballots or make last-minute changes to election procedures. After the election was said and done, the courts did very little to help make sense of the conflicting mess of election guidance. States across the union reported disparate handling of the new laws based on how carefully cities and counties held to the letter of the law.

And then Democrats tried to make permanent all of the radical changes they had made by passing legislation to ban voter ID, legalize vote trafficking, weaken absentee voter verifications, and make it more difficult to keep updated lists of voters.

While the corrupt and partisan media strongly supported passing a law to do those things, the provisions are remarkably unpopular with most Americans. Sixty-four percent of voters surveyed said they wanted to strengthen safeguards to prevent fraud, not eliminate them.[54]

"Voters want it to be easy to vote, but also hard to cheat," said Jason Snead, executive director of the Honest Elections Project.

More than three-quarters of Americans surveyed support voter ID requirements, which are standard in Europe. Only 11 percent think ballot harvesting should be legal. The vast majority think it should be illegal for political operatives and paid organizers to have unsupervised control of absentee voters' ballots or direct access to absentee voters as they vote.

In the wake of what the left itself describes as a revolution in voting, followed by widespread distrust in the integrity of the election, after repeated instances of electoral losers lacking trust in the outcome, perhaps the worst response to the crisis of confidence in the electoral system would be to open it up to more opportunities to commit fraud. So, yes, millions of American citizens have reason to be concerned about the integrity of the 2020 election. They have reason to doubt that the corrupt media have any interest in providing them with a true account of what happened. They have reason to believe that the process was politicized in dramatic fashion to get the result Democrats wanted.

The 2020 election is just the tip of the iceberg. The left's vehement anti-Trumpism—and willingness to lie, contort reality, and ruin Trump's supporters to advance its agenda—has undermined half the country's faith in America's most vaunted institutions. Restoring that trust will take a gargantuan effort. And regrettably, it does not look like anyone in the political and cultural establishment is willing to do the work required to do so.

◆   ◆   ◆

It is certainly true that "democracy depends on the consent of the losers." But the establishment's norm-obliterating failure to accept Trump's legitimate victory in 2016 came at a republic-threatening cost.

What many ordinary Americans saw from 2016 to 2020 was a willingness on the part of the establishment to do whatever it took to defeat its political opponents. The Democrats invented and perpetrated the Russia collusion hoax against Trump, ringing up his affiliates on process crimes as a message to never work against the establishment again. They impeached him and regularly tried to oust him through underhanded means. They invented encyclopedic volumes of fake news. They rioted for years. They pushed fake polls. They refused to give voice to the tens of millions of Americans who were fed up with the establishment's decades of failure on immigration, foreign policy, and economic policy.

The most believable thing in the world is that these powerful media and political entities wouldn't just rig tech algorithms, media coverage, public opinion surveys, debate commissions, and powerful governmental investigations, but the electoral process itself.

The establishment needed in 2020 what it sought in 2016, not just Trump's defeat but to disgrace him and obliterate the coalition he had built. While Trump's opponents were able to heave over the finish line a mediocre politician who poses no threat to the establishment, they failed at killing the movement. And while Trump wasn't able to win in the rigged system, he did very well relative to the wipeout that the establishment had promised and done so much to achieve.

Against all odds, Trump broke through against the establishment in 2016. His presidency was an embarrassment to his opponents, as he succeeded in showing their impotence and failures. He worked to stop their endless wars, instead negotiating trade deals and Middle East peace treaties. He pushed for economic policies that benefited the working class and the national security of the United States, not Wall Street and China. And he revealed how far the establishment was willing to go to preserve power.

Even after what the ruling groups put Trump and his supporters through for four years, the movement gained twelve million new voters. The voters he gained were the ones that the Republican Party had been desperate to make inroads with for years. The Republican Party became a seventy-five-million-voter-strong, multiracial, working-class party. That coalition is real and potent and, for the first time, aware of the extreme lengths the establishment is willing to go to stop it.

The establishment fought back and won the 2020 battle, but it was unable to completely crush the growing rebellion. The left's path to future victory requires it to cow its opposition into silence, to throw its political opponents in jail, and to censor any discussion that threatens its one-party state. The left's vision is fundamentally anti-American, and its increasingly brazen activities aimed at crushing dissent will only alienate it from the American people.

A growing number of Americans are outraged by the way the left seizes and deploys power. They are sick of the lies, manipulation, and distortion that a corrupt ruling class spins on a regular basis. Those courageous citizens, not the decaying establishment, will determine the fate of the nation. Their efforts will ensure that we pass on our beloved republic to future generations.

In the fights to come, those men and women will have the best weapon—truth—on their side. The only question is whether their leaders will have the courage to use it.

Note to Readers

This book is based on interviews of dozens of people, including former president Donald J. Trump, cabinet officials, high-ranking former White House and campaign officials, dozens of elected officials, and dozens of activists and authorities in states throughout the country.

These people graciously gave of their time and knowledge, many sitting for multiple interviews. The vast majority of the interviews were conducted "on background," which means that the information could be used, but the source asked not to be identified.

This account draws heavily from contemporaneous news reports, books, and resources such as Ballotpedia and InfluenceWatch. The Capital Research Center and MacIver Institute's work was influential. Sasha Issenberg's *The Victory Lab*, Allum Bokhari's *#Deleted*, and Joel Pollak's *Neither Free nor Fair* heavily shaped my thinking.

This book also relies on the personal knowledge of the author, acquired through her reporting work during the Trump administration, the 2020 campaign, and its aftermath. This includes reporting trips to Iowa and New Hampshire. It also includes traveling with former vice president Mike Pence as he campaigned in Florida in 2020, when he told the author that he learned through his barnstorming throughout the country that the enthusiasm for the Republican ticket was even greater in 2020 than it had been in 2016. Nearly twelve million additional votes later, it is clear he was correct.

This book arose out of a desire to do what the media failed to do: investigate how the election was handled in a year when states, counties, and cities rapidly changed their election procedures with minimal oversight.

Acknowledgments

This book would not have been possible without the help and support of many people. I apologize in advance for any I have unintentionally omitted.

My editor Paul Choix tackled this project with wisdom beyond his years and a focused vision on what the finished book needed to accomplish. His edits always improved this complicated story and he made them on an unbelievably tight deadline. I thank Tom Spence and Regnery for taking on this whirlwind of a project, and for supporting authors in the face of rampant censorship and blacklisting. Alyssa Cordova's years-long campaign to get me to write another book paid off.

One dear friend in particular, who wishes to remain nameless, envisioned this book and its importance and pushed me to stand against the immense pressure of D.C. to write it. I'm so grateful for his counsel, wisdom, courage, and mentoring.

My colleagues at The Federalist enthusiastically and graciously supported my work. Thank you in particular to Ben Domenech, Sean Davis, and Joy Pullmann. Much of the reporting of this book previously appeared or began at The Federalist. Thank you to senior contributor Margot Cleveland for her tenacious and detailed reporting on this topic as well. Thank you to my readers at The Federalist and viewers at Fox News. Their feedback and support gave me the courage to speak out in a city where conformity is demanded.

Thanks are also owed to Tom Kuntz, Peder Zane, and the rest of the crew at RealClearInvestigations. They've facilitated my husband Mark's work on electoral integrity issues and are otherwise doing important hard-hitting reporting the corporate media refuse to do.

My colleagues at Hillsdale College, particularly Matthew Spalding and Matt Mehan, provided ready counsel, supportive words, and excellent advice. Hillsdale College's Kirby Center provided me with non-stop support. Kristyna Skurk, my main research assistant for two books, now, provided in-depth research on everything from massive historical topics down to minor factual issues in the footnotes. Her cheerfulness, wit, and friendship were an added bonus.

Research coordinator Emily Weston Kannon led a team of valiant research assistants, including research assistant Allison Schuster, graduate research assisant Nathaniel Esbenshade, and interns Robert J. Norris and Alden G. Di Dio. My Federalist intern Maggie Hroncich merged their work into the manuscript.

Earlier in the project, Hillsdale's undergraduate program coordinator Jennifer Lessnau led interns Elise Robinson, Chase Bufkin, Lily McHale, Mary Greco, Lucy Cuneo, Cydney McKeel, and Alex Nester on research projects.

Thank you to my many sources for tremendous generosity with their time and stories, for their patience in explaining to me everything from the intricacies of campaign operations to the distinctions in each state's campaign laws, and for their participation in the country's political process. I am particularly grateful to the time and insight President Trump afforded me over three interviews at his Mar-a-Lago home. I thank Vice President Mike Pence and his team for their time and generosity, both in office and out. Attorney General Bill Barr provided much needed perspective on the challenges of dealing with riots throughout American cities and growing problems within the Department of Justice.

For a project such as this, many interviews with Trump officials were required. Jason Miller was of tremendous assistance in securing those interviews and answering my many questions.

I would also like to thank Christian Adams, Michael Ahrens, Ric Andersen, Steve Armbruster, Nate Bailey, Allum Bokhari, Jase Bolger, Nathan Brand, Janel Brandtjen, Buzz Brockaway, Representative Mo Brooks, David Burrell, Robert Cahaly, Spencer Carr, Justin Clark, Ann Corkery, Marjorie Dannenfelser, Mark Davis, Jackie Pick Deason, Kristen Eastlick, Jordan Gehrke, Hogan Gidley, Victor Davis Hanson, Heather

Higgins, Kurt Hilbert, Linda A. Kerns, Andrew Kloster, Kerri Kupec, Jack Langer, Kory Langhofer, Hayden Ludwig, Nicholas Luna, Stephanie Maloney, Jenny Beth Martin, Margo Martin, Ronna McDaniel, Mark Meadows, Molly Michael, Cleta Mitchell, Matt Morgan, Nick Nordseth, Dan O'Donnell, James O'Keefe, Carter Page, Brad Parscale, Joel Pollak, Justin Riemer, Maureen Riordan, Mark Rountree, Tony Sayegh, Adam Schaeffer, Carrie Severino, Roger Severino, Todd Shepherd, Marc Short, Brad Smith, Jason Snead, Hans von Spakovsky, Representative Claudia Tenney, Paul Teller, Eliza Thurston, Nick Trainer, James Troupis, Donald Trump Jr., Scott Walter, Drew Wierda, Mark Wingate, Megan Wold, and Nicole Ziccarelli.

Thank you to Immanuel Lutheran Church, my congregation, and my pastors Christopher Esget and Noah Rogness for their spiritual care. Many friends supported me and my family during this book writing, none as much as Matthew Braun and Julia Habrecht.

Thank you also to my parents, Larry and Carolyn Ziegler, and my siblings, Kirsten Pratt and Erich Ziegler. Thank you also to my in-laws Bill and Kathy Hemingway, for their unflinching support.

Mark Hemingway, my amazing husband, is the uncredited co-author of this book. Not only did he lead the way in reporting on election integrity problems in the United States in recent years, and much of his work is repurposed here, but he served as a constant co-writer, editor, and encourager. I'm grateful to God for the gift of Mark as my husband of fifteen years. The children and I are fully reliant on him as the head of our household and we can never express our gratitude sufficiently.

Notes

Prologue: You're Not Wrong

1. Jim Geraghty, "Hillary Clinton in 2002: George W. Bush Was 'Selected, Not Elected,'" *National Review,* October 20, 2016, https://www.nationalreview.com /corner/hillary-clinton-2002-george-w-bush-was-selected-not-elected/.
2. For example, see Mark Crispin Miller, *Fooled Again: How the Right Stole the 2004 Election and Why They'll Steal the Next One Too (Unless We Stop Them)* (New York: Basic Books, 2005).
3. Mike Figueredo, "10 Years after HBO's Hacking Democracy, Electoral Vulnerabilities Still Exist," Huffpost, December 13, 2016, https://www.huffpost .com/entry/ten-years-after-hbos-hacking-democracy-electoral_b_584f8d14e4b0 016e5043070b.
4. William Cummings, "'You Can Have the Election Stolen from You,' Hillary Clinton Warns 2020 Democrats," *USA Today,* May 6, 2019, https://www.usato day.com/story/news/politics/onpolitics/2019/05/06/hillary-clinton-warns-2020 -democratic-candidates-stolen-election/1116477001/.
5. Trilby Beresford, "Hillary Clinton Calls for Impeachment, Says Trump 'Poses a Direct Threat' to America," *Hollywood Reporter,* September 26, 2019, https:// www.hollywoodreporter.com/news/politics-news/hillary-clinton-identifies-trump -as-a-threat-america-calls-impeachment-1243742/.
6. Ibid.
7. Bill Chappell, "Jimmy Carter Says He Sees Trump as an Illegitimate President," NPR, June 28, 2019, https://www.npr.org/2019/06/28/737008785/jimmy-carter -says-he-sees-trump-as-an-illegitimate-president.
8. "I Don't See Trump as a 'Legitimate President'—the Russians Helped Him Win: Veteran Congressman Claims 'Conspiracy' to Beat Clinton," *Daily Mail,* January 13, 2017, https://www.dailymail.co.uk/news/article-4118562/I-don-t-Trump-legi timate-president-Russians-helped-win-Veteran-Democrat-congressman-claims-co nspiracy-beat-Clinton.html.
9. Kevin Merida, "So Close, So Far: A Texas Democrat's Day without Sunshine," *Washington Post,* January 21, 2001, https://www.washingtonpost.com/wp-dyn /articles/A24413-2001Jan20.html.
10. Simone Pathé, "Here Are the Democrats Skipping Trump's Inauguration," *Roll Call,* January 17, 2017, https://www.rollcall.com/2017/01/17/here-are-the-democ rats-skipping-trumps-inauguration/.
11. "The Entire GOP Are Traitors. It's That Simple," Daily Kos, July 16, 2018, https:// www.dailykos.com/stories/2018/7/16/1780958/-The-entire-GOP-are-traitors-It -s-that-simple.

12. Special Counsel's Office, Department of Justice, *Report on the Investigation into Russian Interference in the 2016 Presidential Election* (Mueller Report), vol. 2 (Washington, D.C.: U.S. Government Publishing Office, 2019), 2.

13. "The 2018 Pulitzer Prize Winner in National Reporting," Pulitzer Prizes, n.d., https://www.pulitzer.org/winners/staffs-new-york-times-and-washington-post.

14. Josh Zeitz, "Worried about a Rigged Election? Here's One Way to Handle It," *Politico*, October 17, 2016, https://www.politico.com/magazine/story/2016/10/donald-trump-2016-rigged-nixon-kennedy-1960-214395/.

15. Molly Ball, "The Secret History of the Shadow Campaign That Saved the 2020 Election," *Time*, February 4, 2021, https://time.com/5936036/secret-2020-election-campaign/.

16. Ibid.

Chapter One: Over Before It Began

1. Daniela Flamini, "Trump's Opa-Locka Rally Draws Thousands, Raising COVID Concerns," NBC News, November 2, 2020, https://www.nbcmiami.com/news/politics/decision-2020/trump-to-host-evening-rally-in-opa-locka/2314852/.

2. Susan Milligan, "Where's Joe Biden?," U.S. News & World Report, August 7, 2020, https://www.usnews.com/news/elections/articles/2020-08-07/wheres-joe-biden-not-on-the-campaign-trail.

3. Ibid.

4. Kelly Fisher, "Last Poll before Election Shows Trump Up in Ohio, Biden Stops in Cleveland," iHeart Radio, November 2, 2020, https://www.iheart.com/content/2020-11-02-last-poll-before-election-shows-trump-up-in-ohio-biden-stops-in-cleveland/.

5. "February 4, 2020: State of the Union Address," Miller Center of Public Affairs, University of Virginia, https://millercenter.org/the-presidency/presidential-speeches/february-4-2020-state-union-address.

6. "Trump Wins Electoral College amid Nationwide Protests," BBC News, December 20, 2016, https://www.bbc.com/news/world-us-canada-38374749.

7. Ross Douthat, "The 25th Amendment Solution for Removing Trump," *New York Times*, May 16, 2017, https://www.nytimes.com/2017/05/16/opinion/25th-amendment-trump.html.

8. Luke O'Neil, "'I Am a Gaffe Machine': A History of Joe Biden's Biggest Blunders," *The Guardian*, April 25, 2019, https://www.theguardian.com/us-news/2019/apr/25/joe-biden-2020-public-gaffes-mistakes-history.

9. Kevin Roberts, "'Mostly Peaceful' Lets Black Lives Matter off the Hook for Real Violence," Texas Public Policy Foundation, September 24, 2020, https://www.texaspolicy.com/mostly-peaceful-lets-black-lives-matter-off-the-hook-for-real-violence/; Roudabeh Kishi and Sam Jones, *Demonstrations & Political Violence in America: New Data for Summer 2020* (ACLED, September 3, 2020), https://acleddata.com/acleddatanew/wp-content/uploads/2020/09/ACLED_USData Review_Sum2020_SeptWebPDF_HiRes.pdf, 3.

10. Jennifer A. Kingson, "Exclusive: $1 Billion-Plus Riot Damage Is Most Expensive in Insurance History," Axios, September 16, 2020, https://www.axios.com/riots-cost-property-damage-276c9bcc-a455-4067-b06a-66f9db4cea9c.html.

11. Joe Concha, "CNN Ridiculed for 'Fiery but Mostly Peaceful' Caption with Video of Burning Building in Kenosha," *The Hill*, August 27, 2020, https://thehill.com/homenews/media/513902-cnn-ridiculed-for-fiery-but-mostly-peaceful-caption-with-video-of-burning.

12. Dave Boyer, "Biden Calls Trump Supporters 'Chumps' at Pennsylvania Rally," *Washington Times*, October 24, 2020, https://www.washingtontimes.com/news/2020/oct/24/biden-calls-trump-supporters-chumps-pennsylvania-r/.

13. Sophia Ankel, "Joe Biden Snaps at 'Ugly' Trump Supporters Who Disrupted His Minnesota Rally by Beeping Car Horns," Business Insider, October 31, 2020, https://www.msn.com/en-us/news/politics/joe-biden-snaps-at-ugly-trump-supporters-who-disrupted-his-minnesota-rally-by-beeping-car-horns/ar-BB1aztnc.

14. Jessica Chasmar, "Trump Supporters Chant 'Four More Years' during Biden Speech in Ohio," *Washington Times*, October 13, 2020, https://www.washingtontimes.com/news/2020/oct/13/trump-supporters-chant-four-more-years-during-biden/.

15. MJ Lee (@mj_lee), "Practically a Trump drive-in rally here now outside the Biden drive-in event. Biden has just finished speaking," Twitter, October 24, 2020, 12:15 p.m., https://twitter.com/mj_lee/status/1320036248002711554.

16. Act of January 23, 1845, 28 Cong. Ch 1; 5 Stat. 721 (codified as 3 U.S.C. § 1).

17. Ben Leubsdorf, *Election Day: Frequently Asked Questions*, Congressional Research Service report prepared for Members and Committees of Congress, January 6, 2021, 2.

18. Olivia B. Waxman, "This Is How Early Voting Became a Thing," *Time*, November 6, 2020, https://time.com/4539862/early-voting-history-first-states/.

19. Pam Fessler, "Voting Season Begins: North Carolina Mails Out First Ballots," NPR, September 4, 2020, https://www.npr.org/2020/09/04/909597279/voting-season-begins-north-carolina-mails-out-first-ballots.

20. "Analysis of Absentee/Mail-In Voting, 2016–2018," Ballotpedia, n.d., https://ballotpedia.org/Analysis_of_absentee/mail-in_voting,_2016-2018.

21. Brittany Renee Mayes and Kate Rabinowitz, "The U.S. Hit 73% of 2016 Voting before Election Day: At Least 101.9 Million Voted Early Nationwide," *Washington Post*, November 3, 2020, https://www.washingtonpost.com/graphics/2020/elections/early-voting-numbers-so-far/.

22. CNN, "Barr Interview Gets Tense When Pressed on Mail-In Voting," YouTube, September 2, 2020, https://www.youtube.com/watch?v=dC6PxLJ3dDU.

23. Eldon Cobb Evans, "History of the Australian Ballot System in the United States" (Ph.D. dissertation, University of Michigan, 1917), 3–6.

24. Ibid., 1.

25. Ibid., 7.

26. Ibid., 3.

27. Ibid., 12.

28. Craig C. Donsanto and Nancy L. Simmons, *Federal Prosecution of Election Offenses* (Washington, D.C.: U.S. Department of Justice, Criminal Division, Public Integrity Section, August 2007), 244.

29. Evans, "History of the Australian Ballot System in the United States," 19.

30. "South Carolina: At Last," *Time*, May 1, 1950, http://content.time.com/time/subscriber/article/0,33009,812302,00.html.

31. Jan Teorell, Daniel Ziblatt, and Fabrice Lehoucq, "An Introduction to Special Issue: The Causes and Consequences of Secret Ballot Reform," *Comparative Political Studies* 50, no. 5 (April 26, 2016): 531–54, https://journals.sagepub.com/doi/10.1177/0010414016641977.

32. Evans, "History of the Australian Ballot System in the United States," 35.

33. Paula Wasley, "Back When Everyone Knew How You Voted," *Humanities* 37, no. 4 (Fall 2016).

34. "VOPP: Table 13: States That Are Required to Provide Secrecy Sleeves for Absentee/Mail Ballots," National Conference of State Legislatures, May 5, 2020, https://www.ncsl.org/research/elections-and-campaigns/vopp-table-13-states-that-are-required-to-provide-secrecy-sleeves-for-absentee-mail-ballots.aspx.

35. Pierre-Paul Bermingham, "France Split over 'American' Mail-in Ballots for 2021 Regional Elections," *Politico*, November 16, 2020, https://www.politico.eu/article/france-is-split-over-american-mail-in-ballots-2021-regional-election/.

36. *Building Confidence in U.S. Elections: Report of the Commission on Federal Election Reform* (Center for Democracy and Election Management, September 2005), 46.

37. Ibid.

38. *Voting: What Is, What Could Be* (California Institute of Technology / Massachusetts Institute of Technology Voting Technology Project, July 2001), 10.

39. Ibid., 36.

40. Ibid., 39.

41. Adam Liptak, "Error and Fraud at Issue as Absentee Voting Rises," *New York Times*, October 6, 2012, https://www.nytimes.com/2012/10/07/us/politics/as-more-vote-by-mail-faulty-ballots-could-impact-elections.html.

42. David A. Fahrenthold, "Selling Votes Is Common Type of Election Fraud," *Washington Post*, October 1, 2012, https://www.washingtonpost.com/politics/decision2012/selling-votes-is-common-type-of-election-fraud/2012/10/01/f8f5045a-071d-11e2-81ba-ffe35a7b6542_story.html.

43. Maggie Haberman, "Clinton Hires Campaign Lawyer Ahead of Likely Run," *New York Times*, March 4, 2015, https://www.nytimes.com/politics/first-draft/2015/03/04/clinton-hires-campaign-lawyer-ahead-of-likely-run/.

44. Michael Kranish, "Clinton Lawyer Kept Russian Dossier Project Closely Held," *Washington Post*, October 27, 2017, https://www.washingtonpost.com/politics/clinton-lawyer-kept-russian-dossier-project-closely-held/2017/10/27/e7935276-ba68-11e7-be94-fabb0f1e9ffb_story.html.

45. Mollie Hemingway, "Media Silent as Christopher Steele 'Hero' 'Spymaster' Narrative Crumbles," The Federalist, August 3, 2020, https://thefederalist.com/20 20/08/03/media-silent-as-christopher-steele-hero-spymaster-narrative-crumbles/.

46. For example, see David Corn, "A Veteran Spy Has Given the FBI Information Alleging a Russian Operation to Cultivate Donald Trump," *Mother Jones*, October 31, 2016.

47. Jonathon Allen and Amie Parnes, *Shattered: Inside Hillary Clinton's Doomed Campaign* (New York: Crown, 2017), 394–95, Kindle edition.

48. Adam Entous, Devlin Barrett, and Rosalind S. Helderman, "Clinton Campaign, DNC Paid for Research That Led to Russian Dossier," *Washington Post*, October 24, 2017, https://www.washingtonpost.com/world/national-security/clinton-cam paign-dnc-paid-for-research-that-led-to-russia-dossier/2017/10/24/226fabf0-b8e4 -11e7-a908-a3470754bbb9_story.html?utm_term=.c938bb9a67a3.

49. Tristan Justice, "Intel Community Blog Founder Admits Nunes Was Right about Spygate from the Beginning," The Federalist, December 19, 2019, https://thefedera list.com/2019/12/19/intel-community-blog-founder-admits-nunes-was-right-abo ut-spygate-from-the-beginning/.

50. Kenneth P. Vogel (@kenvogel), "When I tried to report this story, Clinton campaign lawyer @marcelias pushed back vigorously, saying 'You (or your sources) are wrong,'" Twitter, October 24, 2017, 6:38 p.m., https://twitter.com/kenvogel/sta tus/922955410327425027.

51. Maggie Haberman (@maggieNYT), "Folks involved with funding this lied about it, and with sanctimony, for a year," Twitter, October 24, 2017, 7:07 p.m., https:// twitter.com/maggieNYT/status/922962880206647297.

52. Manu Raju and Jeremy Herb, "Exclusive: In Hill Interviews, Top Dems Denied Knowledge of Payments to Firm behind Trump Dossier," CNN, October 26, 2017, https://www.cnn.com/2017/10/26/politics/john-podesta-debbie-wasserman-schu ltz-trump-dossier/index.html.

53. Arno Rosenfeld, "Marc Elias, Democratic Power-Lawyer, Is Hero of the Election in Many Circles," The Forward, December 29, 2020, https://forward.com/news /461074/marc-elias-democratic-lawyer-voting-rights-campaign-finance-trump/; Jeremy B. White, "California Republicans Spark National Feud Over 'Harvesting' Ballot Boxes," *Politico*, October 15, 2020; Dylan Jackson and Dan Roe, "Big Firms Bring in Millions as Hundreds of Election Lawsuits Rage across the Country," Law.com, October 15, 2020, https://www.law.com/americanlawyer/2020/10/15 /big-firms-bring-in-millions-as-hundreds-of-election-lawsuits-rage-across-the-co untry/?slreturn=20210612190547; David Wasserman, "The Hidden Mess That Could Cost Democrats Up to Two Points in November," Cook Political Report, July 31, 2020, https://cookpolitical.com/analysis/national/national-politics/hidden -mess-could-cost-democrats-two-points-november.

54. Kenneth P. Vogel and Patricia Mazzei, "In Florida Recount Fight, Democratic Lawyer Draws Plaudits and Fire," *New York Times*, November 14, 2018, https:// www.nytimes.com/2018/11/14/us/politics/florida-governor-recount.html.

55. Kenneth P. Vogel, "The Man behind the Political Cash Grab," *Politico*, December 14, 2014, https://www.politico.com/story/2014/12/democratic-lawyer-crafted-campaign-finance-deal-113549.

56. Robert Barnes, "The Crusade of a Democratic Superlawyer with Multimillion-Dollar Backing," *Washington Post*, August 7, 2016, https://www.washingtonpost.com/politics/courts_law/the-crusade-of-a-democratic-super-lawyer-with-multimillion-dollar-backing/2016/08/07/2c1b408c-5a54-11e6-9767-f6c947fd0cb8_story.html.

57. Charles P. Pierce, "Iowa Taxpayers Will Have to Pay for the Legal Defense of an Assault on Their Own Voting Rights," *Esquire*, March 9, 2021, https://www.esquire.com/news-politics/politics/a35786687/iowa-voter-suppression-bill-lawsuit/.

58. Reid Wilson, "Meet the Lawyer Democrats Call When It's Recount Time," *The Hill*, November 14, 2018, https://thehill.com/homenews/campaign/416847-meet-the-lawyer-democrats-call-when-its-recount-time.

59. Associated Press, "Coleman, Franken Race Still Undecided," *Cape Cod Times*, November 5, 2008, https://www.capecodtimes.com/article/20081105/NEWS11/81105014.

60. Pat Doyle, "Judges Rule Franken Winner; Coleman to Appeal," *Star Tribune*, April 15, 2009, http://www.startribune.com/politics/national/senate/42932907.html.

61. Sasha Issenberg, *The Victory Lab: The Secret Science of Winning Campaigns* (New York: Crown, 2013), 10.

62. Ibid., 11.

63. John Fund, "Felons for Franken," *Wall Street Journal*, July 14, 2010, https://www.wsj.com/articles/SB10001424052748704518904575365063352229680.

64. Ibid.

65. Steven Lemongello and Gray Roher, "Florida Governor's Race Faces Recount as Senate Race Gets Even Tighter," *Orlando Sentinel*, November 8, 2018, https://www.orlandosentinel.com/politics/os-ne-florida-governor-recount-close-20181108-story.html.

66. Matt Dixon and Marc Caputo, "Florida Readies for Massive Recount," *Politico*, November 8, 2018, https://www.politico.com/story/2018/11/08/florida-senate-elections-scott-nelson-2018-recount-975805.

67. Steve Contorno, "Florida Recount Timeline: How Did We Get Here?," *Tampa Bay Times*, November 13, 2018, https://www.tampabay.com/florida-politics/buzz/2018/11/13/florida-recount-timeline-how-did-we-get-here/.

68. Donald J. Trump (@realDonaldTrump), "As soon as Democrats sent their best Election stealing lawyer, Marc Elias, to Broward County they miraculously started finding Democrat votes. Don't worry, Florida—I am sending much better lawyers to expose the FRAUD!" Twitter, November 9, 2019, https://twitter.com/realDonaldTrump/status/1060938144336367616?ref_src=twsrc%5Etfw. Trump's account has since been suspended.

69. Marco Rubio (@marcorubio), "Not very comforting to #Florida voters that #Broward County supervisor, in whose hands may rest outcome of Senate &

cabinet race has in the past: 1. Illegally destroyed ballots 2. Secretly opened mail ballots 3. Sent voters too many ballot pages 4. Left const question off ballot," Twitter, November 9, 2018, 9:29 a.m, https://twitter.com/marcorubio/status/1060902128955392000.

70. Warren Richey, "Why Did Broward Destroy 2016 Ballots? Sanders Ally Seeks US Probe," *Christian Science Monitor*, December 15, 2017, https://www.csmonitor.com/USA/Politics/2017/1215/Why-did-Broward-destroy-2016-ballots-Sanders-ally-seeks-US-probe.

71. Marco Rubio (@marcorubio), "A U.S. Senate seat & a statewide cabinet officer are now potentially in the hands of an elections supervisor with a history of incompetence & of blatant violations of state & federal laws," Twitter, November 8, 2018, 1:16 p.m, https://twitter.com/marcorubio/status/1060596885617025024.

72. Jeb Bush (@JebBush), "There is no question that Broward County Supervisor of Elections Brenda Snipes failed to comply with Florida law on multiple counts, undermining Floridians' confidence in our electoral process. Supervisor Snipes should be removed from her office following the recounts," Twitter, November 12, 2018, 1:53 p.m., https://twitter.com/JebBush/status/1062055907629109249.

73. Anthony Man, "Trump Bashes Broward County and Brenda Snipes Over Election Issues," *South Florida Sun Sentinel*, November 9, 2018, https://www.sun-sentinel.com/news/politics/fl-ne-florida-voting-ballots-senate-friday-20181109-story.html.

74. Jed Shank et al., *Audit of Supervisor of Elections*, Report No. 20-12 (Broward County, Florida: Office of the County Auditor, April 22, 2020), https://www.broward.org/Auditor/Reports/Reports/050520_Exh1_AuditofSOE_RptNo20-12.pdf.

75. Ibid., 23.

76. Ibid., 2.

77. Caroline Spiezio, "5th Circuit Keeps Sanctions against Marc Elias in Voting Case," Reuters, June 30, 2021, https://www.reuters.com/legal/government/5th-circuit-keeps-sanctions-against-marc-elias-voting-case-2021-06-30/.

78. Marc Elias, "We Are Not Counting Every Vote," Medium, January 13, 2020, https://medium.com/@marceelias/we-are-not-counting-every-vote-e3b91b4a96f1.

79. Marc Elias, "How to Fix Our Voting Rules before November," *The Atlantic*, April 5, 2020, https://www.theatlantic.com/ideas/archive/2020/04/how-fix-voting-right-now/609454/.

80. Ibid.

81. Ibid.

82. Ibid.

83. Quinn Scanlan, "Here's How States Have Changed the Rules around Voting amid the Coronavirus Pandemic," ABC News, September 22, 2020, https://abcnews.go.com/Politics/states-changed-rules-voting-amid-coronavirus-pandemic/story?id=72309089.

84. Ibid.

85. Ronna McDaniel, "RNC Chairwoman: Democrats Don't Want to Play by the Same Voting Rules," *Washington Post*, August 27, 2020, https://www.washingt

onpost.com/opinions/2020/08/27/ronna-mcdaniel-rnc-chairwoman-poll-watch
ers-voting/.

86. Ibid.

87. "2012 Obama Campaign Legacy Report," available on the Time website at https://
time.com/wp-content/uploads/2015/02/legacy-report.pdf.

88. Ben Schreckinger, "Inside Donald Trump's Election Night War Room," *GQ*,
November 7, 2017, https://www.gq.com/story/inside-donald-trumps-election-nig
ht-war-room.

89. Julia Manchester, "GOP Chairwoman Suggests RNC Plans to Get 'Litigious' Over
Push for National Popular Vote," *The Hill*, February 28, 2020, https://thehill.com
/homenews/campaign/485146-gop-chairwoman-suggests-rnc-plans-to-get-litig
ious-over-push-for-national.

90. Virginia Gordan, "Lawsuit Challenges Michigan's Signature Matching
Requirement for Absentee Ballots," NPR, October 31, 2019, https://www.michi
ganradio.org/post/lawsuit-challenges-michigans-signature-matching-requirement
-absentee-ballots.

91. Statement from Marc Elias, "Another Victory for Voting Rights," press release,
April 21, 2020, available on Democracy Docket website at https://www.democra
cydocket.com/wp-content/uploads/sites/45/2020/04/PR_20200421_MI-SOS-Re
vises-Signature-Match-Process-As-a-Result-of-Federal-Lawsuit-1.pdf.

92. Gus Burns, "Court Invalidates Michigan Rule on How to Verify Absentee Ballot
Application Signatures," MLive, March 16, 2021, https://www.mlive.com/public
-interest/2021/03/court-invalidates-michigan-rule-on-how-to-verify-absentee-bal
lot-application-signatures.html.

93. "Republican National Committee v. Gill, No. 03971 EQCV193154 (Iowa Dist.
Ct., Woodbury Cnty.)," Stanford-MIT Healthy Elections Project, https://healthy
elections-case-tracker.stanford.edu/detail?id=226.

94. Alex Isenstadt and Natasha Korecki, "Trump Campaign Ready to Unleash
Thousands of Poll Watchers on Election Day," *Politico*, October 8, 2020, https://
www.politico.com/news/2020/10/08/trump-election-poll-watching-427008.

95. "2016 Florida Results," *New York Times*, updated August 1, 2017, https://www
.nytimes.com/elections/2016/results/florida.

96. "Florida Election Results 2018," *Washington Post*, updated April 6, 2019, https://
www.washingtonpost.com/election-results/florida/.

97. "Florida Presidential Results," *Politico*, updated January 6, 2021, https://www.po
litico.com/2020-election/results/florida/.

98. "Wisconsin: McCain vs. Obama," RealClearPolitics, n.d., https://www.realclear
politics.com/epolls/2008/president/wi/wisconsin_mccain_vs_obama-549.html.

99. "Wisconsin: Romney vs. Obama," RealClearPolitics, n.d., https://www.realclear
politics.com/epolls/2012/president/wi/wisconsin_romney_vs_obama-1871.html.

100. "Wisconsin: Trump vs. Clinton," RealClearPolitics, n.d., https://www.realclearpo
litics.com/epolls/2016/president/wi/wisconsin_trump_vs_clinton-5659.html#!.

101. Alexander Burns and Jonathan Martin, "Election at Hand, Biden Leads Trump
in Four Key States, Poll Shows," *New York Times*, November 1, 2020, https://

www.nytimes.com/2020/11/01/us/politics/biden-trump-poll-florida-pennsylvania
-wisconsin.html.

102. Chris Jackson et al., "In Wisconsin, Biden Leads Trump in Final Days before
Election," Ipsos, November 1, 2020, https://www.ipsos.com/en-us/news-polls/presi
dential_election_2020_WI.

103. Jacob Pramuk, "Biden Narrowly Leads Trump in Six Swing States before Election
Day, Poll Shows," CNBC, November 2, 2020, https://www.cnbc.com/2020/11
/02/2020-election-polls-biden-leads-trump-in-six-swing-states.html; Jennifer
Agiesta, "CNN Polls: Biden Leads in Michigan and Wisconsin as Campaign Ends,
with Tighter Races in Arizona and North Carolina," CNN, November 1, 2020,
http://cdn.cnn.com/cnn/2020/images/10/31/rel2_wi.pdf.

104. Jonathan Martin, "Biden Has Narrow Lead in Iowa and Senate Race Is Tight, Poll
Shows," *New York Times*, October 21, 2020, https://www.nytimes.com/2020/10
/21/us/politics/poll-iowa-biden-trump.html.

105. Kayleigh McEnany (@kayleighmcenany), "It's time to call FLORIDA! FACT:
President @realDonaldTrump will WIN Florida QUESTION: How long will it
take for the media to acknowledge it?" Twitter, November 3, 2020, 9:33 p.m.
https://twitter.com/kayleighmcenany/status/1323815506244182016.

106. Marco Rubio (@marcorubio), "Trump is up in #Florida by 3.5 points & 381000
votes with 91% reporting & 50000 votes left to count. It's over. So why won't they
call the race? To deny Trump an early swing state win until Arizona and Nevada
close," Twitter, November 3, 2020, 9:50 p.m., https://twitter.com/marcorubio/sta
tus/1323819918534578181.

107. Ron DeSantis (@RonDesantisFL), "President @realDonaldTrump is up in Florida
by almost 400,000 votes with more than 90% of precincts reporting. Why haven't
networks called the race? It's a done deal and the refusal to recognize the obvious
speaks volumes about the (lack of) objectivity of these outlets," Twitter, November
3, 2020, 9:57 p.m., https://twitter.com/RonDeSantisFL/status/13238215666989
38368.

108. In the interest of disclosure, the author is a contributor at Fox News. The following
quotations are from Fox News's "Democracy 2020," November 3, 2020.

109. Doug Ducey (@dougducey), "It's far too early to call the election in Arizona.
Election Day votes are not fully reported, and we haven't even started to count
early ballots dropped off at the polls. In AZ, we protected Election Day. Let's count
the votes—all the votes—before making declarations," Twitter, November 3, 2020,
11:57 p.m., https://twitter.com/dougducey/status/1323851735408930822.

110. Jason Miller (@JasonMillerinDC), "WAY too soon to be calling Arizona...way
too soon. We believe over 2/3 of those outstanding Election Day voters are going
to be for Trump. Can't believe Fox was so anxious to pull the trigger here after
taking so long to call Florida. Wow," Twitter, November 3, 2020, 11:27 p.m.,
https://twitter.com/JasonMillerinDC/status/1323844198580264964.

111. Mike Murphy, "Other News Organizations Finally Call Arizona for Biden,"
Market Watch, November 13, 2020, https://www.marketwatch.com/story/other
-news-organizations-finally-call-arizona-for-biden-11605243924.

112. Molly Ball, "The Secret History of the Shadow Campaign That Saved the 2020 Election," *Time,* February 4, 2021, https://time.com/5936036/secret-2020-election-campaign/.

113. Ibid.

Chapter Two: Taking On the Establishment

1.   Steven A. Holmes, "The 1992 Campaign: The Challenger; Buchanan Quest: Turning Protest Votes into Delegates," *New York Times,* March 5, 1992.

2.   Wilson Andrews, Kitty Bennett, and Alicia Parlapiano, "2016 Delegate Count and Primary Results," *New York Times,* last updated July 5, 2016, https://www.nytimes.com/interactive/2016/us/elections/primary-calendar-and-results.html.

3.   "Donald J. Trump for President, Inc.," DemocracyinAction.us, July 15, 2020, https://www.democracyinaction.us/2020/trump/trumporg.html.

4.   Ibid.

5.   Frank Phillips, "In Rebuke to Charlie Baker; State GOP Picks Conservative to Lead Party," *Boston Globe,* January 19, 2019, https://www.bostonglobe.com/metro/2019/01/19/rebuke-charlie-baker-state-gop-picks-conservative-lead-party/9yUUsBEC6SEgSAY9zACm5J/story.html.

6.   Stephanie Murray, "Massachusetts Republicans Move to Protect Trump in 2020 Primary," *Politico,* May 6, 2019, https://www.politico.com/story/2019/05/06/massachusetts-republicans-trump-2020-primary-1302875.

7.   "RNC Delegate Guidelines from Kentucky, 2016," Ballotpedia, n.d., https://ballotpedia.org/RNC_delegate_guidelines_from_Kentucky,_2016.

8.   Colby Itkowitz, "'No Path Right Now for Me': Kasich Won't Run for President against Trump," *Washington Post,* May 31, 2019, https://www.washingtonpost.com/politics/no-path-right-now-for-me-kasich-wont-run-for-president-against-trump/2019/05/31/8291cd66-83c6-11e9-933d-7501070ee669_story.html.

9.   John Bowden, "Bill Weld Secures One Iowa Delegate in Longshot Primary Challenge to Trump," *The Hill,* February 2, 2020, https://thehill.com/homenews/campaign/482454-bill-weld-secures-one-iowa-delegate-in-longshot-primary-challenge-to-trump.

10. David Shortell and Evan Perez, "Two of Four FISA Warrants against Carter Page Declared Invalid," CNN, January 23, 2020, https://www.cnn.com/2020/01/23/politics/fisa-carter-page-warrants/index.html.

11. Johnathan Easley, "GOP Report: Clapper Told CNN Host about Trump Dossier in 2017," *The Hill,* April 27, 2018, https://thehill.com/policy/national-security/385278-gop-report-clapper-told-cnn-host-about-trump-dossier-in-2017.

12. Kara Scannell, "Flynn Charge Suggests Arcane Law Is 'Leverage' for Special Counsel Investigation," CNN, December 1, 2017, https://www.cnn.com/2017/12/01/politics/michael-flynn-logan-act/index.html.

13. Kelsey Snell, "Congressional Republicans Divided on Whether to Support Flynn," *Washington Post,* February 13, 2017, https://www.washingtonpost.com/news/po

werpost/wp/2017/02/13/graham-flynn-has-a-problem-that-he-needs-to-fix-with
-this-president/.

14. Ibid.

15. Jeff Greenfield, "Why Sessions Recused Himself," *Politico*, March 2, 2017, https://
www.politico.com/magazine/story/2017/03/sessions-recuses-himself-trump-russia
-214857/.

16. Erin Dooley, "Lawmakers Praise Special Counsel Appointed to Oversee Russia
Investigation," ABC News, May 17, 2017, https://abcnews.go.com/Politics/lawma
kcrs-praise-special-counsel-appointed-oversee-russia-investigation/story?id=4747
4713.

17. Jason Chaffetz (@jasoninthehouse), "Mueller is a great selection. Impeccable
credentials. Should be widely accepted," Twitter, May 17, 2017, 6:04 p.m., https://
twitter.com/jasoninthehouse/status/864964765608624130.

18. Jeremy Herb, "Ethics Committee Clears Intelligence Chairman Devin Nunes,"
CNN, December 7, 2017, https://www.cnn.com/2017/12/07/politics/ethics-com
mittee-devin-nunes/index.html.

19. Shortell and Perez, "Two of Four FISA Warrants."

20. "February 4, 2020: State of the Union Address," Miller Center of Public Affairs,
University of Virginia, https://millercenter.org/the-presidency/presidential-speec
hes/february-4-2020-state-union-address.

21. Ibid.

22. Ibid.

23. Ibid.

24. Ibid.

25. Congresswoman Ayanna Pressley (@RepPressley), "The State of the Union is
hurting because of the occupant of the White House, who consistently demonstrates
contempt for the American people," Twitter, February 4, 2020, 3:31 p.m., https://
twitter.com/RepPressley/status/1224792604094627843.

26. "February 4, 2020: State of the Union Address."

27. Ibid.

28. Ibid.

29. Ibid.

30. "Full Text of Clinton's Speech on China Trade Bill," *New York Times*, March 9,
2000, https://archive.nytimes.com/www.nytimes.com/library/world/asia/03090
0clinton-china-text.html.

31. Bob Davis, "How China's Trade Concessions Made It Stronger," *Wall Street
Journal,* August 12, 2016, https://www.wsj.com/articles/BL-REB-36410.

32. Matthew Impelli, "Donald Trump's Views on Abortion and Roe v. Wade in His
Own Words," *Newsweek*, September 29, 2020, https://www.newsweek.com/do
nald-trumps-views-abortion-roe-vs-wade-his-own-words-1534954.

33. "Road to the White House 2016, Presidential Candidates Debate," C-SPAN, aired
October 19, 2016, https://www.c-span.org/video/?414228-1/presidential-nominees-
debate-university-nevada-las-vegas.

34. Ibid.

35. "The Border Wall System Is Deployed, Effective, and Disrupting Criminals and Smugglers," Department of Homeland Security, October 29, 2020, https://www .dhs.gov/news/2020/10/29/border-wall-system-deployed-effective-and-disrupting -criminals-and-smugglers.

36. Carol Morello and Adam Taylor, "Trump Says U.S. Won't Rush to Defend NATO Countries If They Don't Spend More on Military," *Washington Post*, July 21, 2016, https://www.washingtonpost.com/world/national-security/trump-says-us-wont -rush-to-defend-nato-countries-if-they-dont-spend-more-on-military/2016/07/21 /76c48430-4f51-11e6-a7d8-13d06b37f256_story.html.

37. "Transcript: Donald Trump on NATO, Turkey's Coup Attempt and the World," *New York Times*, July 21, 2016, https://www.nytimes.com/2016/07/22/us/polit ics/donald-trump-foreign-policy-interview.html.

38. "February 4, 2020: State of the Union Address."

39. Zeke Miller, Deb Riechmann, and Robert Burns, "Trump Says US Forces Cornered IS Leader in Dead-End Tunnel," Associated Press, October 27, 2019, https://apne ws.com/article/donald-trump-syria-ap-top-news-international-news-abu-bakr-al -baghdadi-2c2c48e64f934d329c72a7af3dc284b1.

40. "February 4, 2020: State of the Union Address."

41. Ibid.

42. Ibid.

43. Ibid.

44. Ibid.

45. Ibid.

Chapter Three: Designed in a Lab

1.   "Presidential Approval Ratings—Donald Trump," Gallup, n.d., https://news.gal lup.com/poll/203198/presidential-approval-ratings-donald-trump.aspx.

2.   Willis L. Krumholz, "Paul Krugman Said Markets Would 'Never' Recover from Trump. The Dow Is Up 10,000 Points Since 2016," The Federalist, December 26, 2019, https://thefederalist.com/2019/12/26/paul-krugman-said-markets-would-ne ver-recover-from-trump-the-dow-is-up-10000-points-since-2016/.

3.   Kimberly Amadeo, "Dow Jones Highest Closing Records," The Balance, June 25, 2021, https://www.thebalance.com/dow-jones-closing-history-top-highs-and-lo ws-since-1929-3306174.

4.   Brendan Cole, "Donald Trump Is First President Since Jimmy Carter Not to Enter U.S. Troops into New Conflict," *Newsweek*, November 25, 2020, https://www .newsweek.com/donald-trump-first-president-since-jimmy-carter-not-enter-us-tr oops-new-conflict-1549037.

5.   "Abraham Accords Peace Agreement," treaty signed by the United Arab Emirates and the State of Israel, September 15, 2020, https://www.state.gov/wp-content/up loads/2020/09/UAE_Israel-treaty-signed-FINAL-15-Sept-2020-508.pdf.

6. Alana Semuels, "As COVID-19 Crashes the Economy, Workers and Business Owners Wonder If Anything Can Save Them from Financial Ruin," *Time*, March 18, 2020, https://time.com/5805526/coronavirus-economy-layoffs/.

7. Jim Carlton, "How Coronavirus Changed Election 2020 Voting and Polling Stations," *Wall Street Journal*, November 3, 2020, https://www.wsj.com/articles /how-coronavirus-changed-election-2020-voting-and-polling-stations-1160444 4111.

8. Rahm Emanuel, "Opinion: Let's Make Sure This Crisis Doesn't Go to Waste," *Washington Post*, March 25, 2020, https://www.washingtonpost.com/opinions /2020/03/25/lets-make-sure-this-crisis-doesnt-go-waste/.

9. "COVID-Related Election Litigation Tracker," Stanford–MIT Healthy Elections Project, n.d., https://healthyelections-case-tracker.stanford.edu/.

10. Ibid.

11. Ethan Kaplan and Haishan Yuan, "Early Voting Laws, Voter Turnout, and Partisan Vote Composition: Evidence from Ohio," *American Economic Journal: Applied Economics* 12, no. 1 (January 2020): 32–60, https://www.aeaweb.org/ar ticles?id=10.1257/app.20180192.

12. Tyrone Beason, "Bernie Sanders and Joe Biden Spring to the Finish in Michigan Primary amid Coronavirus Crisis," *Los Angeles Times*, March 9, 2020, https:// www.latimes.com/politics/story/2020-03-09/sanders-biden-michigan-sprint-to -the-finish.

13. Scott Neuman, "Tom Hanks, Wife Rita Wilson Test Positive for Coronavirus," National Public Radio, March 12, 2020, https://www.npr.org/2020/03/12/8148 07838/tom-hanks-wife-rita-wilson-test-positive-for-coronavirus; Jabari Young, "NBA Suspends Season Indefinitely after Utah Jazz Player Tests Positive for Coronavirus," CNBC, March 12, 2020, https://www.cnbc.com/2020/03/12/coro navirus-nba-suspends-season-after-player-tests-positive.html; Taylore Telford and Thomas Heath, "U.S. Stocks Nosedive, Trading Paused as Emergency Fed Action Fails to Mollify Investors," *Washington Post*, March 16, 2020, https://www.was hingtonpost.com/business/2020/03/16/stocks-markets-live-updates-coronavirus/.

14. "A Timeline of COVID-19 Developments in 2020," American Journal of Managed Care, updated January 1, 2021, https://www.ajmc.com/view/a-timeline-of-covid19 -developments-in-2020.

15. Nick Corasaniti and Stephanie Saul, "Ohio's Governor Postpones Primary as Health Emergency Is Declared over Virus," *New York Times*, March 16, 2020, https://www.nytimes.com/2020/03/16/us/politics/virus-primary-2020-ohio.html.

16. Adam Edelman and Alex Seitz-Wald, "Wisconsin Primary in-Person Voting Suspended by Governor amid Coronavirus Concerns," MSNBC News, April 6, 2020, https://www.nbcnews.com/politics/2020-election/wisconsin-gov-evers-sus pends-person-voting-tuesday-primary-amid-coronavirus-n1177746.

17. Dan O'Donnell, "Why Wasn't Wisconsin's Election Postponed? Two Words: Tony Evers," News Talk 1130, April 5, 2020, https://newstalk1130.iheart.com/featured /common-sense-central/content/2020-04-05-why-wasnt-wisconsins-election-pos tponed-two-words-tony-evers/.

18. "Wisconsin's Faux Outrage Election," MacIver Institute, April 8, 2020, https://www.maciverinstitute.com/2020/04/wisconsins-faux-outrage-election/.

19. O'Donnell, "Why Wasn't Wisconsin's Election Postponed?"

20. "Groups Call on Court to Postpone Wisconsin's Spring Election," Fox 11 News, March 27, 2020, https://fox11online.com/news/election/groups-call-on-court-to-postpone-wisconsins-spring-election.

21. "In the Supreme Court of the United States," *Washington Post*, https://context-cdn.washingtonpost.com/notes/prod/default/documents/10cc3393-cb94-4aa5-baf3-7ea5c133d945/note/41de9a23-9f01-4fb1-8503-97208d9ed8dd.

22. Natasha Korecki, "Wisconsin Democrats Apoplectic over Governor's Handling of Tuesday Primary," *Politico*, April 2, 2020, https://www.politico.com/news/2020/04/02/tony-evers-wisconsin-democrats-primary-election-161423.

23. Nick Corasaniti, "'I'm Scared': Wisconsin Election Puts Poll Workers at Risk of Virus," *New York Times*, April 2, 2020, https://www.nytimes.com/2020/04/02/us/politics/wisconsin-election-coronavirus.html.

24. Alex Seitz-Wald and Shaquille Brewster, "GOP Lawmakers Reject Wisconsin Governor's Call for Delay in Election Results," NBC News, April 3, 2020, https://www.nbcnews.com/politics/2020-election/wisconsin-governor-calls-special-legislative-session-consider-delaying-election-deadline-n1176186.

25. Amy Gardner et al., "Wisconsin Supreme Court Blocks Order by Governor to Stop Tuesday's Elections in State's Latest Whipsaw," *Washington Post*, April 7, 2020, https://www.washingtonpost.com/politics/wisconsin-governor-suspends-in-person-voting-in-tuesdays-elections-amid-escalating-coronavirus-fears/2020/04/06/9d658e2a-781c-11ea-b6ff-597f170df8f8_story.html.

26. Laurel White, "Postmark Irregularities Could Disqualify Ballots Sent on or before Election Day in Wisconsin," Wisconsin Public Radio, April 10, 2020, https://www.wpr.org/postmark-irregularities-could-disqualify-ballots-sent-or-election-day-wisconsin.

27. Lisa Lerer, "Wisconsin Votes Tomorrow. In Person," *New York Times*, April 6, 2020, https://www.nytimes.com/2020/04/06/us/politics/on-politics-wisconsin-coronavirus.html.

28. John McCormack, "CDC Study Shows No COVID-19 Spike from Wisconsin's April Election," *National Review*, July 31, 2020, https://www.nationalreview.com/2020/07/cdc-study-wisconsin-elections-caused-no-coronavirus-spike/.

29. David Wahlberg, "No COVID-19 Surge in Milwaukee from Wisconsin's April 7 Election, CDC Says," *Wisconsin State Journal*, August 3, 2020, https://madison.com/wsj/news/local/health-med-fit/no-covid-19-surge-in-milwaukee-from-wisconsins-april-7-election-cdc-says/article_1ab8aab7-4099-5189-a5af-2ec25d75d062.html.

30. Patrick Marley, "Thousands of Absentee Ballots in Wisconsin Weren't Counted because of Mailing Problems and Tech Glitches," *Milwaukee Journal Sentinel*, May 19, 2020, https://www.jsonline.com/story/news/politics/2020/05/19/glitches-mailing-problems-mar-absentee-voting-wisconsin/5219371002/.

31. Ibid.

32. Ibid.
33. *April 7, 2020, Absentee Voting Report* (Wisconsin Elections Commission: May 15, 2020), https://elections.wi.gov/sites/elections.wi.gov/files/2020-05/April%202 020%20Absentee%20Voting%20Report.pdf.
34. Marisa Iati, "A Judge Ordered Up to 234,000 People to Be Tossed from the Registered Voter List in a Swing State," *Washington Post*, December 14, 2019, https://www.washingtonpost.com/politics/2019/12/14/judge-ordered-up-people -be-tossed-registered-voter-list-swing-state/.
35. Mitch Smith, "Wisconsin Elections Officials Held in Contempt for Refusing to Purge Voters," *New York Times*, January 13, 2020, https://www.nytimes.com/20 20/01/13/us/wisconsin-voter-purge.html.
36. Scott Bauer, "Wisconsin Supreme Court Says Don't Purge Voters from Rolls," Associated Press, April 9, 2021, https://apnews.com/article/wisconsin-state-elec tions-elections-courts-voter-registration-3b22c017bf78784cec38b2733b13f3e3.
37. Dan O'Donnell, "How the Wisconsin Elections Commission Destroyed Fair Elections in Wisconsin," MacIver Institute, November 5, 2020, https://www.ma civerinstitute.com/2020/11/how-the-wisconsin-elections-commission-destroyed -fair-elections-in-wisconsin/.
38. *Meeting of the Wisconsin Elections Commission* (Wisconsin Elections Commission: May 20, 2020), https://elections.wi.gov/sites/elections.wi.gov/files/20 20-05/WEC%205-20-2020%20PowerPoint%20Presentation.pdf.
39. "A Quarter-Million Wisconsin Voters Claim to Be 'Indefinitely Confined' and Not Bound by Voter ID," MacIver Institute, October 29, 2020, https://www.maciverin stitute.com/2020/10/a-quarter-million-wisconsin-voters-claim-to-be-indefinitely -confined/.
40. Dan O'Donnell, "How the Wisconsin Elections Commission Destroyed Fair Elections in Wisconsin," MacIver Institute, November 5, 2020, https://www.ma civerinstitute.com/2020/11/how-the-wisconsin-elections-commission-destroyed -fair-elections-in-wisconsin/.
41. Scott Bauer, "Trump-Backed Tom Tiffany Retains Northern Wisconsin Congressional Seat for GOP," *Wisconsin State Journal*, May 13, 2020, https://ma dison.com/wsj/news/local/govt-and-politics/trump-backed-tom-tiffany-retains-no rthern-wisconsin-congressional-seat-for-gop/article_ae2521a5-d239-5efd-a7f1-5e e290a052ee.html.
42. "Wisconsin's 7th Congressional District Election, 2016," Ballotpedia, n.d., https:// ballotpedia.org/Wisconsin%27s_7th_Congressional_District_election.
43. Donald Judd, "Donald Trump Holds 'Tele-Rally' in Campaign First amid Coronavirus Pandemic," CNN, July 18, 2020, https://www.cnn.com/2020/07/18 /politics/donald-trump-telerally-campaign-event/index.html.
44. Bauer, "Trump-Backed Tom Tiffany Retains."
45. Jerry Zremski, "NY-27 Race Portends a Presidential Election Night Like No Other," *Buffalo News*, July 20, 2020, https://buffalonews.com/news/ny-27-race -portends-a-presidential-election-night-like-no-other/article_2c4ef58c-c790-11ea -8f9f-e7a7cd647816.html.

46. Ibid.
47. Amber Philips, "New Poll Confirms Republicans' Wariness of Voting by Mail," *Washington Post*, September 10, 2020, https://www.washingtonpost.com/politics/2020/09/10/new-poll-confirms-republicans-wariness-voting-by-mail/.
48. Phillip Bump, "Only 1 in 5 Republicans Say They're Likely to Vote by Mail," *Washington Post*, August 11, 2020, https://www.washingtonpost.com/politics/2020/08/11/only-1-in-5-republicans-say-theyre-likely-vote-by-mail/.
49. Reid J. Epstein, "Democrats' Vote-by-Mail Effort Won in Wisconsin: Will It Work Elsewhere?," *New York Times*, last updated September 14, 2020, https://www.nytimes.com/2020/05/10/us/politics/Wisconsin-election-vote-by-mail-.html.
50. Ibid.
51. Ibid.
52. Ibid.
53. "Lessons Learned from Wisconsin's April Election," Fair Fight Action, April 29, 2020, https://archive.is/o/eXEqE/https://fairfight.com/wp-content/uploads/2020/04/WisLessons.pdf.
54. Epstein, "Democrats' Vote-by-Mail Effort Won in Wisconsin."
55. Emma Hurt, "Refusal to Concede an Election Isn't a New Concept in Georgia," National Public Radio, November 18, 2020, https://www.npr.org/2020/11/18/936096359/refusal-to-concede-an-election-isnt-a-new-concept-in-georgia.
56. Maya King, "How Stacey Abrams and Her Band of Believers Turned Georgia Blue," *Politico*, November 8, 2020, https://www.politico.com/news/2020/11/08/stacey-abrams-believers-georgia-blue-434985.
57. *Democratic Party of Georgia v. Raffensperger*, No. 1:19-cv-5028 (N.D. Ga. 2019), https://www.dscc.org/wp-content/uploads/2019/11/Georgia-Absentee-Voting-Lawsuit.pdf.
58. Joel B. Pollak, "Fact Check: Trump Is Right, AP Wrong, about Georgia Signature Matching," Breitbart, November 16, 2020, https://www.breitbart.com/2020-election/2020/11/16/fact-check-trump-is-right-ap-wrong-about-georgia-signature-matching/.
59. Mark Niesse, "Lawsuit Settled, Giving Georgia Voters Time to Fix Rejected Ballots," *Atlanta Journal-Constitution*, March 7, 2020, https://www.ajc.com/news/state--regional-govt--politics/lawsuit-settled-giving-georgia-voters-time-fix-rejected-ballots/oJcZ4eCXf8J197AEdGfsSM/.
60. Ibid.
61. 11Alive, "Georgia House Election Security Stream Today Live," YouTube, December 23, 2020, https://www.youtube.com/watch?v=8yDF1mnfQL4.
62. Mollie Hemingway, "Media's Entire Georgia Narrative Is Fraudulent, Not Just the Fabricated Trump Quotes," The Federalist, March 17, 2021, https://thefederalist.com/2021/03/17/medias-entire-georgia-narrative-is-fraudulent-not-just-the-fabricated-trump-quotes/.
63. "Compromise Settlement Agreement and Release," Perkins Coie LLC, March 6, 2020, https://demdoc2.perkinscoieblogs.com/wp-content/uploads/sites/45/2020/07/GA-Settlement-1.pdf.

64. "Election Results, 2020: Analysis of Rejected Ballots," Ballotpedia, n.d., https://ballotpedia.org/Election_results,_2020:_Analysis_of_rejected_ballots.
65. Caroline Linton, "Georgia Postpones Presidential Primary Originally Scheduled for March 24," CBS News, March 14, 2020, https://www.cbsnews.com/news/georgia-postpones-presidential-primary-scheduled-for-march-24-2020-03-14/.
66. Ben Nadler, "Georgia Postpones Primaries Again because of Coronavirus," Associated Press, April 9, 2020, https://apnews.com/article/public-health-primary-elections-us-news-ap-top-news-elections-d0a07a2989f7399c6b14e2276b482526.
67. Richard Fausset and Reid J. Epstein, "Georgia's Election Mess: Many Problems, Plenty of Blame, Few Solutions for November," *New York Times*, June 10, 2020, https://www.nytimes.com/2020/06/10/us/politics/georgia-primary-election-voting.html.
68. Ibid.
69. Ibid.
70. Ibid.
71. Ibid.
72. Eric Geller, "Georgia Likely to Plow Ahead with Buying Insecure Voting Machines," *Politico*, March 28, 2019, https://www.politico.com/story/2019/03/28/georgia-voting-machines-safe-1241033.
73. Ibid.
74. Ibid.
75. Mark Niesse, "Threats to Georgia Elections Loom Despite New Paper Ballot Voting," *Atlanta Journal-Constitution*, August 7, 2019, https://www.ajc.com/news/state--regional-govt--politics/threats-georgia-elections-loom-despite-new-paper-ballot-voting/c5blwnfcwaGh8yTRQSn2uJ/.
76. Ibid.
77. Richard Fausset et al., "'I Refuse Not to Be Heard': Georgia in Uproar over Voting Meltdown," *New York Times*, updated June 11, 2020, https://www.nytimes.com/2020/06/09/us/politics/atlanta-voting-georgia-primary.html.
78. Ibid.
79. Neena Satija et al., "As Georgia Rolls Out New Voting Machines for 2020, Worries about Election Security Persist," *Washington Post*, December 23, 2019, https://www.washingtonpost.com/politics/as-georgia-rolls-out-new-voting-machines-for-2020-worries-about-election-security-persist/2019/12/23/c5036d74-2017-11ea-bed5-880264cc91a9_story.html.
80. Ibid.
81. Ben Brasch, "Fulton, State Sign Deal to End Investigation of June 9 Voting Debacle," *Atlanta Journal-Constitution*, October 30, 2020, https://www.ajc.com/news/atlanta-news/fulton-state-sign-deal-to-end-investigation-of-june-9-voting-debacle/WH256PK6HZHIXLYS6GZFAHJSII/.
82. Ibid.
83. Ronn Blitzer, "DOJ to Send Election Monitors to 44 Jurisdictions in 18 States," Fox News, November 2, 2020, https://www.foxnews.com/politics/doj-election-monitors-44-jurisdictions-18-states.

84. "CEIR 2020 Voter Education Grant Program," Center for Election Innovation & Research, n.d., https://electioninnovation.org/research/ceir-2020-voter-education-grant-program/.

85. Hayden Ludwig and Sarah Lee, "Ludwig, Lee: Left-Wing Groups Flooded Georgia with 'Dark Money' and Mail-in Ballots in 2020," *North State Journal*, July 7, 2021, https://nsjonline.com/article/2021/07/ludwig-lee-left-wing-groups-flooded-georgia-with-dark-money-and-mail-in-ballots-in-2020/.

86. "CEIR 2020 Voter Education Grant Program."

87. Matt Taibbi, "Yesterday's Gone: Iowa Was Waterloo for Democrats," *Rolling Stone*, February 8, 2020, https://www.rollingstone.com/politics/politics-features/iowa-caucus-democrats-disaster-trump-sanders-949655/.

88. "Judicial Watch: Eight Iowa Counties Have Total Registration Rates Larger Than Eligible Voter Population—at Least 18,658 Extra Names on Iowa Voting Rolls," press release, Judicial Watch, February 3, 2020, https://www.judicialwatch.org/press-releases/judicial-watch-eight-iowa-counties-have-total-registration-rates-larger-than-eligible-voter-population-at-least-18658-extra-names-on-iowa-voting-rolls-2/.

89. "Media Release: Official Data Rebuts False Claims Regarding Iowa Voter Registration," Office of the Iowa Secretary of State, February 2, 2020, https://sos.iowa.gov/news/2020_02_02.html.

90. Philip Bump, "Judicial Watch's Voter Fraud Fear-Mongering Finds a New Opponent: A Pro-Voter-ID Iowa Official," *Washington Post*, February 3, 2020, https://www.washingtonpost.com/politics/2020/02/03/judicial-watchs-voter-fraud-fear-mongering-finds-new-opponent-pro-voter-id-iowa-official/.

91. Joe Malinconico, "Paterson Voter Fraud Charges Expand in New Indictments from NJ Attorney General," North Jersey, March 5, 2021, https://www.northjersey.com/story/news/paterson-press/2021/03/05/2020-election-voter-fraud-new-charges-paterson-nj-attorney-general/4577142001/.

92. Mark Hemingway, "Widespread Fraud in New Jersey Mail-In Election," RealClearPolitics, June 26, 2020, https://www.realclearpolitics.com/2020/06/26/widespread_fraud_in_new_jersey_mail-in_election_515452.html.

93. Anna Sturla, "Judge Invalidates Paterson, NJ, City Council Election after Allegations of Mail-In Voter Fraud," CNN, updated August 20, 2020, https://www.cnn.com/2020/08/20/politics/paterson-new-jersey-city-council-voter-fraud/index.html.

94. Hemingway, "Widespread Fraud in New Jersey."

95. Ibid.

96. Jonathan Dienst and Joe Valiquette, "Corruption Allegations Keep Growing in Paterson Vote-by-Mail Election," NBC News, May 13, 2020, https://www.nbcnewyork.com/news/local/corruption-allegations-keep-growing-in-paterson-vote-by-mail-election/2416111/.

97. Ibid.

98. Joe Malinconico, "Post Office Says Mail-in Ballots Were Left on Floor in Paterson Buildings," New Jersey, August 14, 2020, https://www.northjersey.com/story/ne

ws/passaic/paterson/2020/08/14/paterson-nj-election-ballots-were-left-floor-post
-office-says/5582951002/.

99. Hemingway, "Widespread Fraud in New Jersey."
100. Ibid.
101. Ibid.
102. Ibid.
103. Ibid.
104. Ibid.
105. Ibid.
106. Jeffery Cawood, "COVID-19 Pandemic: Examining the Early 'Warnings' Trump Allegedly 'Ignored,'" The Daily Wire, March 6, 2020, https://www.dailywire.com/news/covid-19-pandemic-examining-the-early-warnings-trump-allegedly-igno red.
107. "Public Screening to Begin at Three U.S. Airports for 2019 Novel Coronavirus," Centers for Disease Control, January 17, 2020, https://www.cdc.gov/media/relea ses/2020/p0117-coronavirus-screening.html#:~:text=Starting%20January%2017 %2C%202020%2C%20travelers,Los%20Angeles%20(LAX)%20airports.
108. Elizabeth Cohen, "Vaccine for New Chinese Coronavirus in the Works," CNN, January 20, 2020, https://www.cnn.com/2020/01/20/health/coronavirus-nih-vac cine-development/index.html.
109. "CDC Emergency Operations Center Activations," CDC, n.d., https://emergency .cdc.gov/recentincidents/.
110. Rebecca Ballhaus, "Trump Announces Coronavirus Taskforce," *Wall Street Journal*, January 29, 2020, https://www.wsj.com/articles/trump-announces-coro navirus-task-force-11580359187.
111. Michael Corkery and Annie Karni, "Trump Administration Restricts Entry into U.S. from China," *New York Times*, January 31, 2020, https://www.nytimes.com/2020/01/31/business/china-travel-coronavirus.html.
112. Rosie Spinks, "Who Says It's Not Safe to Travel to China?," *New York Times*, February 5, 2020, https://www.nytimes.com/2020/02/05/opinion/china-travel-co ronavirus.html.
113. Ibid.
114. Ibid.
115. Megan Thielking and Lev Facher, "Health Experts Warn China Travel Ban Will Hinder Coronavirus Response," STAT, January 31 2020, https://www.statnews .com/2020/01/31/as-far-right-calls-for-china-travel-ban-health-experts-warn-co ronavirus-response-would-suffer/.
116. Nicole Wetsman, "Trump Bans Foreign Nationals Who Have Traveled to China from Entering the US," The Verge, January 31, 2020, https://www.theverge.com/2020/1/31/21117403/trump-coronavirus-ban-travel-non-us-citizens-china.
117. Dan Diamond (@ddiamond), "Yes—in late January, Trump's initial coronavirus moves were widely hailed as strong and appropriate response…," Twitter, March 8, 2020, 9:22 a.m., https://twitter.com/ddiamond/status/1236643371734765568.

118. Gerry Shih et al., "As Deadly Coronavirus Spreads, U.S. to Expand Screening of Passengers from China at 20 Airports," *Washington Post*, January 27, 2020, https://www.washingtonpost.com/health/as-deadly-coronavirus-spreads-us-to-expand-screening-of-passengers-from-china-at-20-airports/2020/01/27/deb0fb78-412e-11ea-aa6a-083d01b3ed18_story.html.

119. Paul Gosar (@RepGosar), "Vox has deleted this tweet…," Twitter, March 24, 2020, 9:31 p.m., https://twitter.com/RepGosar/status/1242625203844325376.

120. Lenny Bernstein, "Get a Grippe, America. The Flu Is a Much Bigger Threat Than Coronavirus, for Now," *Washington Post*, February 1, 2020, https://www.washingtonpost.com/health/time-for-a-reality-check-america-the-flu-is-a-much-bigger-threat-than-coronavirus-for-now/2020/01/31/46a15166-4444-11ea-b5fc-eefa848cde99_story.html.

121. J. Edward Moreno, "Government Health Agency Official: Coronavirus 'Isn't Something the American Public Need to Worry About,'" *The Hill*, January 26, 2020, https://thehill.com/homenews/sunday-talk-shows/479939-government-health-agency-official-corona-virus-isnt-something-the.

122. KPIX CBS SF Bay Area, "Speaker Pelosi Visits SF's Chinatown to Show Support amid Coronavirus Fears," YouTube, February 24, 2020, https://www.youtube.com/watch?time_continue=134&v=eFCzoXhNM6c&feature=emb_title.

123. David Siders, "Dems Sweat Trump's Economy: 'We Don't Really Have a Robust National Message Right Now,'" *Politico*, April 28, 2019, https://www.politico.com/story/2019/04/28/democrats-economy-2020-trump-1291371.

124. Ben White, "Warning to Democrats: Economy Points to a Trump Win," *Politico*, October 15, 2019, https://www.politico.com/news/2019/10/15/warning-to-democrats-economy-points-to-a-trump-win-047021.

125. Ryan Lizza and Daniel Lippman, "The General Election Scenario That Democrats Are Dreading," *Politico*, May 26, 2020, https://www.politico.com/news/2020/05/26/2020-election-democrats-281470.

126. Mark Landler and Stephen Castle, "Behind the Virus Report That Jarred the U.S. and the U.K. to Action," *New York Times*, April 2, 2020, https://www.nytimes.com/2020/03/17/world/europe/coronavirus-imperial-college-johnson.html.

127. Alan Reynolds, "How One Model Simulated 2.2 Million U.S. Deaths from COVID-19," Cato Institute, April 21, 2020, https://www.cato.org/blog/how-one-model-simulated-22-million-us-deaths-covid-19.

128. Andrew O'Reilly, "Pelosi Says Trump Has Downplayed Severity of Coronavirus: 'As the President Fiddles, People Are Dying,'" Fox News, March 29, 2020, https://www.foxnews.com/politics/pelosi-says-trump-has-downplayed-severity-of-coronavirus-as-the-president-fiddles-people-are-dying.

129. Emily Tillett and Margaret Brennan, "Former Trump Deputy National Security Adviser Matt Pottinger Details 'Grave Misstep' in Pandemic Response," CBS News, February 20, 2021, https://www.cbsnews.com/news/former-deputy-nsa-matt-pottinger/.

130. Jacqueline Howard, "Masks May Actually Increase Your Coronavirus Risk If Worn Improperly, Surgeon Warns," CNN, March 2, 2020, https://www.cnn.com/2020/03/02/health/surgeon-general-coronavirus-masks-risk-trnd/index.html.

131. Reis Thebault et al., "How to Prepare for Coronavirus in the U.S.," *Washington Post*, March 11, 2020, https://www.washingtonpost.com/health/2020/02/26/how-to-prepare-for-coronavirus/?utm_medium=social&utm_source=twitter&utm_campaign=wp_main.

132. Scottie Andrew, "There's Been a Run of Surgical Masks in the US because of the Coronavirus Scare. You Don't Need Them, Physicians Say," CNN, January 28, 2020, https://t.co/Q5xiN6GqMd?amp=1.

133. Scottie Andrew and Jessie Yeung, "Masks Can't Stop the Coronavirus in the US, but Hysteria Has Led to Bulk-Buying and Price-Gouging," CNN, February 29, 2020, https://edition.cnn.com/asia/live-news/coronavirus-outbreak-02-29-20-intl-hnk/h_60c0416ca901c2006c1c7c91010b70a4.

134. Rosemary Guerguerian, "Main Focus for Preventing Coronavirus Spread Should Be Hand Hygiene, Not Face Masks," NBC News, February 28, 2020, https://www.nbcnews.com/health/health-news/main-focus-preventing-coronavirus-spread-should-be-hand-hygiene-not-n1144346?cid=sm_npd_ms_tw_ma.

135. Ken Dilanian et al., "Mismanagement, Missed Opportunities: How the White House Bungled the Coronavirus Response," NBC News, March 14, 2020, https://www.nbcnews.com/politics/white-house/mismanagement-missed-opportunities-how-white-house-bungled-coronavirus-response-n1158746.

136. Jason Breslow, "Fauci: Mixed Messaging on Masks Set U.S. Public Health Response Back," NPR, July 1, 2020, https://www.npr.org/sections/health-shots/2020/07/01/886299190/it-does-not-have-to-be-100-000-cases-a-day-fauci-urges-u-s-to-follow-guidelines.

137. Alana Wise, "Nancy Pelosi Calls Trump 'Cowardly' for Not Wearing Mask, Supports Federal Mandate," NPR, June 26, 2020, https://www.npr.org/2020/06/26/884039346/house-speaker-nancy-pelosi-talks-about-the-coronavirus-police-reform-and-health-.

138. Sydney Ember, "Biden Calls Trump a 'Fool' for Not Wearing Mask in Coronavirus Crisis," *New York Times*, August 13, 2020, https://www.nytimes.com/2020/05/26/us/politics/joe-biden-facemasks-trump-coronavirus.html.

139. Quint Forgey, "McEnany's Husband Attends White House Press Briefing without Mask," *Politico*, December 2, 2020, https://www.politico.com/news/2020/12/02/sean-gilmartin-mcenany-mask-white-house-442244.

140. Andrew Beaujon, "Kayleigh McEnany Conducted Thursday's Briefing without a Mask. Are White House Reporters Concerned?" *The Washingtonian*, October 2, 2020, https://www.washingtonian.com/2020/10/02/kayleigh-mcenany-conducted-thursdays-briefing-without-a-mask-are-white-house-reporters-concerned/.

141. Stephen Collinson, "Trump Peddles Unsubstantiated Hope in Dark Times," CNN, March 20, 2020, https://www.cnn.com/2020/03/20/politics/donald-trump-coronavirus-false-hope/index.html.

142. Elizabeth Cohen et al., "Trump Says This Drug Has 'Tremendous Promise,' but Fauci's Not Spending Money on It," CNN, April 10, 2002, https://www.cnn.com/2020/03/28/health/coronavirus-hydroxychloroquine-trial/index.html.

143. "Opinion: Trump Is Spreading False Hope for a Virus Cure—and That's Not the Only Damage," *Washington Post*, March 25, 2020, https://www.washingtonpost.com/opinions/global-opinions/trump-is-spreading-false-hope-for-a-virus-cure—and-thats-not-the-only-damage/2020/03/25/587b26d8-6ec3-11ea-b148-e4ce3fbd85b5_story.html.

144. Michael A. Cohen, "Trump Is Spreading Misinformation about the Coronavirus—Time to Take Away His Microphone," *Boston Globe*, March 20, 2020, https://www.bostonglobe.com/2020/03/20/opinion/take-away-trumps-microphone/.

145. Sonam Sheth and Jake Lahut, "'I Cannot Stress This Enough, This Will Kill You': Fox News Host Neil Cavuto Was Shocked by Trump's Announcement That He's Taking Hydroxychloroquine to Prevent Coronavirus," Business Insider, May 18, 2020, https://www.businessinsider.com/fox-news-neil-cavuto-shocked-trump-hyroxychloroquine-announcement-video-2020-5.

146. Erika Edwards and Vaughn Hillyard, "Man Dies after Taking Chloroquine in an Attempt to Prevent Coronavirus," NBC News, March 23, 2020, https://www.nbcnews.com/health/health-news/man-dies-after-ingesting-chloroquine-attempt-prevent-coronavirus-n1167166.

147. Alana Goodman, "Police Investigating Death of Arizona Man from Chloroquine Phosphate," Washington Free Beacon, April 28, 2020, https://freebeacon.com/coronavirus/police-investigating-death-of-arizona-man-from-chloroquine-phosphate/.

148. Ibid.

149. Mandeep R. Mehra et al., "Hydroxychloroquine or Chloroquine with or without a Macrolide for Treatment of COVID-19: A Multinational Registry Analysis," *The Lancet* (May 22, 2020), https://www.thelancet.com/journals/lancet/article/PIIS0140-6736(20)31180-6/fulltext.

150. Curtis Houck, "CNN Gave over 90 Minutes in One Day to Now-Retracted Hydroxychloroquine Study," NewsBusters, June 4, 2020, https://www.newsbusters.org/blogs/nb/curtis-houck/2020/06/04/cnn-gave-over-90-minutes-one-day-now-retracted-hydroxychloroquine.

151. Mollie Hemingway, "Trump Was Right, Cuomo Was Wrong about Ventilator Needs," The Federalist, April 8, 2020, https://thefederalist.com/2020/04/08/trump-was-right-cuomo-was-wrong-about-ventilator-needs/.

152. John Roberts (@johnrobertsFox), "New York Governor @andrewcuomo announces that beginning tomorrow, the State will begin treating some patients with a combination of Hydroxychloroquine and Azithromycin," Twitter, March 23, 2020, 11:27 a.m., https://twitter.com/johnrobertsFox/status/1242110848262422528.

153. Noah Higgins-Dunn, "People Are Stealing Masks and Other Medical Equipment from Hospitals, New York Gov. Cuomo Says," CNBC, March 31, 2020, https://

www.cnbc.com/2020/03/06/people-are-stealing-face-masks-from-local-hospitals-gov-cuomo-says.html.

154. Sean Collins, "Trump Could Help Solve the Mask Problem. Instead He's Making Baseless Attacks on New York Nurses," Vox, March 30, 2020, https://www.vox.com/policy-and-politics/2020/3/30/21199538/coronavirus-mask-trump-new-york-hospital-stealing.

155. CBS News (@CBSNews), "Gov. Cuomo says President Trump was right to question the WHO on pandemic warning sign…," Twitter, April 10, 2020, 12:04 p.m., https://twitter.com/CBSNews/status/1248642998281396225.

156. Dominick Mastrangelo, "Rob Reiner: 'Donald Trump Is Actively Trying to Kill Our Children,'" *Washington Examiner*, July 16, 2020, https://www.washingtonexaminer.com/news/rob-reiner-donald-trump-is-actively-trying-to-kill-our-children.

157. Eliza Shapiro, "N.Y. Schools Can Reopen, Cuomo Says, in Contrast with Much of U.S.," *New York Times*, September 1, 2020, https://www.nytimes.com/2020/08/07/nyregion/cuomo-schools-reopening.html.

158. TheEllenShow, "Trevor Noah Is a 'Cuomosexual,'" YouTube, April 20, 2020, https://www.youtube.com/watch?v=O93vQQamzAw.

159. Marina Villeneuve, "Cuomo Set to Earn $5M from Book on COVID-19 Crisis," ABC News, May 17, 2021, https://abcnews.go.com/Entertainment/wireStory/cuomo-set-earn-5m-book-covid-19-crisis-77741418.

160. Joseph Wulfsohn, "CNN Blasted for Now Declaring 'Wuhan Virus' as 'Racist' after Weeks of Network's 'China's Coronavirus' Coverage," Fox News, March 12, 2020, https://www.foxnews.com/media/cnn-china-wuhan-coronavirus.

161. U.S. Department of State, "March 18, 2020, Members of the Coronavirus Task Force Hold a Press Briefing," YouTube, March 18, 2020, https://www.youtube.com/watch?v=W7AI0FwWrUE.

162. Justin Baragona, "Trump Addresses 'Kung-Flu' Remark, Says Asian Americans Agree '100 Percent' with Him Using 'Chinese Virus,'" The Daily Beast, March 18, 2020, https://www.thedailybeast.com/trump-addresses-kung-flu-remark-says-asian-americans-agree-100-with-him-using-chinese-virus.

163. Kamala Harris (@VP), "Calling it the 'Chinese coronavirus' isn't just racist, it's dangerous and incites discrimination against Asian Americans and Asian immigrants…," Twitter, March 10, 2020, 12:52 p.m., https://twitter.com/VP/status/1237421056358518785.

164. Gail Collins, "Let's Call It Trumpvirus," *New York Times*, February 26, 2020, https://www.nytimes.com/2020/02/26/opinion/coronavirus-trump.html.

165. Bill D'Agostino, "Study: Trump-Bashing Takes Up Majority of CNN's Coronavirus Coverage," NewsBusters, February 28, 2020, https://www.newsbusters.org/blogs/nb/bill-dagostino/2020/02/28/study-trump-bashing-takes-majority-cnns-coronavirus-coverage.

166. Peter Hessler, "How China Controlled the Coronavirus," *New Yorker*, August 10, 2020, https://www.newyorker.com/magazine/2020/08/17/how-china-controlled-the-coronavirus.

167. Alexander Nazaryan, "'They Know How to Keep People Alive': Why China's Coronavirus Response Is Better Than You Think," Yahoo, March 13, 2020, https://www.yahoo.com/lifestyle/they-know-how-to-keep-people-alive-why-ch inas-coronavirus-response-is-better-than-you-think-211702070.html.

168. Steven Lee Myers and Alissa J. Rubin, "Its Coronavirus Cases Dwindling, China Turns Focus Outward," *New York Times*, March 18, 2020, https://www.nytimes .com/2020/03/18/world/asia/coronavirus-china-aid.html.

169. Keith Bradsher and Liz Alderman, "The World Needs Masks. China Makes Them, but Has Been Hoarding Them," *New York Times*, April 2, 2020, https:// www.nytimes.com/2020/03/13/business/masks-china-coronavirus.html.

170. Helen Davidson, "First COVID-19 Case Happened in November, China Government Records Show—Report," *The Guardian*, March 13, 2020, https:// www.theguardian.com/world/2020/mar/13/first-covid-19-case-happened-in-no vember-china-government-records-show-report.

171. "China Investigates Respiratory Illness Outbreak Sickening 27," Associated Press, December 31, 2019, https://apnews.com/article/wuhan-health-international-news -china-severe-acute-respiratory-syndrome-00c78d1974410d96fe031f67edbd86ec.

172. Drew Holden (@DrewHolden360), "It wouldn't be right not to also spotlight how terrible @WHO has handled all of this. I've got whole threads dedicated to the subject, but here's just a few w/ time stamps," Twitter, April 28, 2020, 6:10 p.m., https://twitter.com/DrewHolden360/status/1255258226137972741.

173. Julia Hollingsworth, "A Lot Has Changed since China's SARS Outbreak 17 Years Ago. But Some Things Haven't," CNN, January 24, 2020, https://www.cnn.com /2020/01/24/asia/china-sars-coronavirus-intl-hnk/index.html.

174. Kim Hjelmgaard et al., "This Is What China Did to Beat Coronavirus. Experts Say America Couldn't Handle It," *USA Today*, April 1, 2020, https://www.usato day.com/story/news/world/2020/04/01/coronavirus-covid-19-china-radical-mea sures-lockdowns-mass-quarantines/2938374001/.

175. Hilary Brueck et al., "China Took at Least 12 Strict Measures to Control the Coronavirus. They Could Work for the US, but Would Likely Be Impossible to Implement," Business Insider, March 24, 2020, https://www.businessinsider.com /chinas-coronavirus-quarantines-other-countries-arent-ready-2020-3.

176. James Griffiths, "China Wants to Take a Victory Lap over Its Handling of the Coronavirus Outbreak," CNN, March 10, 2020, https://www.cnn.com/2020/03 /10/asia/china-coronavirus-propaganda-intl-hnk/index.html.

177. Jeremy Page et al., "How It All Started: China's Early Coronavirus Missteps," *Wall Street Journal*, March 6, 2020, https://www.wsj.com/articles/how-it-all-started-ch inas-early-coronavirus-missteps-11583508932.

178. Jeremy Youde, "Does the World Health Organization Have the Freedom to Do What It Needs to Do about COVID-19?," *Washington Post*, March 4, 2020, https://www.washingtonpost.com/politics/2020/03/04/does-world-health-organi zation-have-freedom-do-what-it-needs-do-about-covid-19/.

179. Paulina Firozi, "Tom Cotton Keeps Repeating a Coronavirus Fringe Theory That Scientists Have Disputed," *Washington Post*, February 17, 2020, https://www.washingtonpost.com/politics/2020/02/16/tom-cotton-coronavirus-conspiracy/.

180. Richard H. Ebright (@R_H_Ebright), "That was scenario discussed in your Fox interview...," Twitter, February 16, 2020, 11:05 p.m., https://twitter.com/R_H_Ebright/status/1229255646350127104. https://twitter.com/SenTomCotton/status/1229202136094953473.

181. David E. Sanger, "Pompeo Ties Coronavirus to China Lab, Despite Spy Agencies' Uncertainty," *New York Times*, June 14, 2021, https://www.nytimes.com/2020/05/03/us/politics/coronavirus-pompeo-wuhan-china-lab.html.

182. Bernie Sanders (@SenSanders), "There are legitimate questions we must ask about the Chinese government's inability to contain the virus...," Twitter, May 4, 2020, 8:43 a.m., https://twitter.com/SenSanders/status/1257289630099165185.

183. NBC News (@NBCNews), "Fact check: A coronavirus vaccine could come this year, President Trump says. Experts say he needs a 'miracle' to be right," Twitter, May 15, 2020, 12:12 p.m., https://twitter.com/NBCNews/status/1261328497991131137.

184. Yamiche Alcindor (@Yamiche), "President Trump just now at the WH on a coronavirus vaccine: 'We're looking to get it by the end of the year...,'" Twitter, May 15, 2020, 12:52 p.m., https://twitter.com/yamiche/status/1261338735355899906?lang=en.

185. "The Upside of Crisis," Kite and Key Media, March 2021, https://www.kiteandkeymedia.com/videos/covid-19-crisis-management-federal-government-coronavirus-pandemic-emergency-vaccine/?utm_source=social&utm_medium=twitter.

186. NPR (@NPR), "Fact Check: President Trump said of a vaccine: 'It's ready. It's going to be announced within weeks.' This lacks evidence...," Twitter, October 22, 2020, 10:09 p.m., https://twitter.com/NPR/status/1319461002287742977.

187. ABC News (@ABC), "Pres. Trump's Claim: 'Now, we're weeks away from a vaccine.' Fact Check: Most prominent public health experts...," Twitter, September 29, 2020, 11:23 p.m., https://twitter.com/abc/status/1311144648048611329.

188. Adam Cancryn and Sarah Owermohle, "Pfizer Trying to Defuse Critics amid Push for Vaccine before Election Day," *Politico*, October 9, 2020, https://www.politico.com/news/2020/10/09/coronavirus-vaccine-pfizer-election-day-428371.

189. Matthew Herper, "COVID-19 Vaccine from Pfizer and BioNTech Is Strongly Effective, Early Data from Large Trial Indicate," STAT, November 9, 2020, https://www.statnews.com/2020/11/09/covid-19-vaccine-from-pfizer-and-biontech-is-strongly-effective-early-data-from-large-trial-indicate/comment-page-7/#comment-3047884.

190. Philip Melanchthon Wegmann (@PhilpWegmann), "The @PressSec says of Fauci's emails, 'it's obviously not advantageous for me to re-litigate the substance of emails from 17 months ago,'" Twitter, June 3, 2021, 1:17 p.m., https://twitter.com/PhilipWegmann/status/1400502035078856707.

Chapter Four: Summary of Violence

1. "How Groups Voted in 2016," Roper Center, Cornell, https://ropercenter.cornell
   .edu/how-groups-voted-2016.
2. Ronald Kessler, *Inside the White House* (New York: Simon & Schuster, 1996), 33.
3. Doris Kearns Goodwin, *Lyndon Johnson and the American Dream* (New York:
   Harper & Rowe, 1976), 169.
4. Daniel Patrick Moynihan, "Chapter II. The Negro American Family," in *The
   Negro Family: The Case for National Action* (U.S. Department of Labor, March
   1965), https://www.dol.gov/general/aboutdol/history/webid-moynihan/moynchap
   ter2.
5. Donald Trump (@realDonaldTrump), "We ALL must be united & condemn all
   that hate stands for. There is no place for this kind of violence in America. Let's
   come together as one," Twitter, August 12, 2017, 1:19 p.m. Account has since been
   suspended; tweet found at https://www.thetrumparchive.com.
6. "Full Transcript and Video: Trump's News Conference in New York," *New York
   Times*, August 15, 2017, https://www.nytimes.com/2017/08/15/us/politics/trump
   -press-conference-transcript.html.
7. Dareh Gregorian, "'Justice Will Be Served!': Trump Weighs in on George Floyd
   Case," NBC News, May 27, 2020, https://www.nbcnews.com/politics/donald-tr
   ump/justice-will-be-served-trump-weighs-george-floyd-case-n1216026.
8. Jemima McEvoy, "'It's Just Devastating': Some Minneapolis Businesses Still
   Fighting to Survive a Year after George Floyd Unrest," *Forbes*, May 25, 2021,
   https://www.forbes.com/sites/jemimamcevoy/2021/05/25/its-just-devastating-so
   me-minneapolis-businesses-still-fighting-to-survive-a-year-after-george-floyd-un
   rest/?sh=7a66db8c3f77.
9. Tony Daniel, "Minneapolis Rioters Burned One of America's Most Beloved
   Independent Bookstores to the Ground," The Federalist, June 1, 2020, https://the
   federalist.com/2020/06/01/minneapolis-rioters-burned-one-of-americas-most-be
   loved-independent-bookstores-to-the-ground/.
10. Tristan Justice, "Factory Burned Down in Minneapolis Riots Will Leave City,"
    The Federalist, June 9, 2020, https://thefederalist.com/2020/06/09/factory-burned
    -down-in-minneapolis-riots-will-leave-city/.
11. Sam Jones, "US Crisis Monitor Releases Full Data for 2020," Armed Conflict
    Location & Event Data Project, February 5, 2021, https://acleddata.com/2021/02
    /05/us-crisis-monitor-releases-full-data-for-2020/.
12. Jamie Knodel, "Twitter Places Warning on Trump Post, Saying Tweet Glorifies
    Violence," NBC News, May 29, 2020, https://www.nbcnews.com/politics/dona
    ld-trump/twitter-says-trump-violated-rules-against-glorifying-violence-places-pub
    lic-n1217591.
13. Barbara Sprunt, "The History behind 'When the Looting Starts, the Shooting
    Starts,'" NPR, May 29, 2020, https://www.npr.org/2020/05/29/864818368/the
    -history-behind-when-the-looting-starts-the-shooting-starts.

14. Kathryn Watson, "Trump Calls George Floyd's Death a 'Terrible Thing,'" CBS News, May 29, 2020, https://www.cbsnews.com/news/trump-calls-george-floyds -death-a-terrible-thing-2020-05-29/.

15. Scott Neuman, "Medical Examiner's Autopsy Reveals George Floyd Had Positive Test for Coronavirus," NPR, June 4, 2020, https://www.npr.org/sections/live-up dates-protests-for-racial-justice/2020/06/04/869278494/medical-examiners-auto psy-reveals-george-floyd-had-positive-test-for-coronavirus.

16. Akshita Jain, "George Floyd's Killing Not a Hate Crime because It Was Systemic Not 'Explicit' Racism, Says Official," *The Independent*, April 26, 2021, https:// www.independent.co.uk/news/world/americas/george-floyd-killing-hate-crime-b1 837419.html.

17. "964 People Have Been Shot and Killed by Police in the Past Year," *Washington Post*, July 2, 2021, https://www.washingtonpost.com/graphics/investigations/poli ce-shootings-database/.

18. Michael Barone, "The Ebbing of 'the Misperception That Bigotry Is Everywhere,'" Jewish World Review, April 23, 2021, http://jewishworldreview.com/michael/ba rone042321.php3.

19. Donald Trump (@realDonaldTrump), "The Lamestream Media is doing everything within their power…," Twitter, May 31, 2021, 12:36 p.m. Account has since been suspended, tweet found at https://www.thetrumparchive.com; Donald Trump, Facebook, May 31, 2020, https://www.facebook.com/DonaldTrump/posts/the-la mestream-media-is-doing-everything-within-their-power-to-foment-hatred-and /10164783908180725/.

20. Matt Taibbi, "On 'White Fragility,'" TK News by Matt Taibbi (Substack), June 28, 2020, https://taibbi.substack.com/p/on-white-fragility.

21. David Azerrad, "The Promises and Perils of Identity Politics," Heritage Foundation, January 23, 2019, https://www.heritage.org/progressivism/report/the-promises -and-perils-identity-politics.

22. Ibid.

23. Nikole Hannah-Jones, "The Idea of America," *New York Times*, August 14, 2019, https://www.nytimes.com/interactive/2019/08/14/magazine/black-history-amer ican-democracy.html.

24. Rich Lowry, "Historians Roast the 1619 Project," *National Review*, January 3, 2020, https://www.nationalreview.com/2020/01/1619-project-top-historians-cri ticize-new-york-times-slavery-feature/.

25. Darcel Rockett, "5 Minutes with Nikole Hannah-Jones, the Architect behind the New York Times' '1619 Project,'" *Chicago Tribune*, October 10, 2019, https:// www.chicagotribune.com/lifestyles/ct-life-nikole-hannah-jones-1619-project-201 91009-20191010-m3rym2hxyncj7ihcn67q2gekdq-story.html.

26. Charles Kesler, "Call Them the 1619 Riots," *New York Post*, June 19, 2020, https:// nypost.com/2020/06/19/call-them-the-1619-riots/.

27. Allison Schuster, "Nikole Hannah-Jones Endorses Riots and Toppling Statues as a Product of the 1619 Project," The Federalist, June 20, 2020, https://thefederalist

.com/2020/06/20/nikole-hannah-jones-endorses-riots-and-toppling-statues-as-a-p
roduct-of-the-1619-project/.

28. Tristan Justice, "Pulitzer Prize–Winning New York Times Writer: 'Destroying
Property Isn't Violence,'" The Federalist, June 3, 2020, https://thefederalist.com
/2020/06/03/pulitzer-prize-winning-new-york-times-writer-destroying-property
-isnt-violence/.

29. Robby Soave, "Public Schools Are Teaching the 1619 Project in Class, despite
Concerns from Historians," *Reason*, January 28, 2020, https://reason.com/2020
/01/28/1619-project-new-york-times-public-schools/.

30. Larry Buchanan, Quoctrung Bui, and Jugal K. Patel, "Black Lives Matter May Be
the Largest Movement in U.S. History," *New York Times*, July 3, 2020, https://
www.nytimes.com/interactive/2020/07/03/us/george-floyd-protests-crowd-size
.html.

31. Joseph Wulfsohn, "MSNBC's Ali Velshi Says Situation Not 'Generally Speaking
Unruly' while Standing outside Burning Building," Fox News, May 29, 2020,
https://www.foxnews.com/media/msnbc-anchor-says-minneapolis-carnage-is-mo
stly-a-protest-as-building-burns-behind-him.

32. Joseph Wulfsohn, "CNN Panned for On-Air Graphic Reading 'Fiery but Mostly
Peaceful Protest' in Front of Kenosha Fire," Fox News, August 27, 2020, https://
www.foxnews.com/media/cnn-panned-for-on-air-graphic-reading-fiery-but-mos
tly-peaceful-protest-in-front-of-kenosha-fire.

33. Lois Beckett, "At Least 25 Americans Were Killed during Protests and Political
Unrest in 2020," *The Guardian*, October 31, 2020, https://www.theguardian.com
/world/2020/oct/31/americans-killed-protests-political-unrest-acled.

34. Caitlin McFall, "Hundreds Mourn David Dorn, Retired St. Louis Police Captain
Killed in Looting," Fox News, June 9, 2020, https://www.foxnews.com/us/hund
reds-honor-david-dorn-retired-st-louis-police-captain-killed.

35. "Race Relations," Gallup, n.d., https://news.gallup.com/poll/1687/race-relations
.aspx.

36. Scott Walter, "The Founders of Black Lives Matter," *First Things*, March 29, 2021,
https://www.firstthings.com/web-exclusives/2021/03/the-founders-of-black-lives
-matter.

37. Ibid.

38. Mike Gonzales, "To Destroy America," *City Journal,* September 1, 2020, https://
www.city-journal.org/marxist-revolutionaries-black-lives-matter.

39. "What We Believe" Black Lives Matter, archive.com, n.d., https://archive.vn
/X4efm.

40. "The Movement for Black Lives," Movement for Black Lives website, n.d., https://
m4bl.org/.

41. "Group Topples George Washington Statue in NE Portland," Koin 6 News, June
18, 2020, https://www.koin.com/news/protests/portland-protests-black-lives-mat
ter-blm-george-floyd-police-reform-racial-justice-demonstration-rally-march-day
-21/; Joel Finkelstein et al., "9/14/20–Network-Enabled Anarchy: How Militant
Anarcho-Socialist Networks Use Social Media to Instigate Widespread Violence

against Political Opponents and Law Enforcement," Network Contagion Research Institute, September 14, 2020, https://networkcontagion.us/reports/network -enabled-anarchy/.

42. Rachel Scully and James Bikales, "A List of the Statues across the US Toppled, Vandalized or Officially Removed amid Protests," *The Hill*, June 12, 2020, https:// thehill.com/homenews/state-watch/502492-list-statues-toppled-vandalized-remo ved-protests; Jonah Gottschalk, "List of 183 Monuments Ruined Since Protests Began, and Counting," The Federalist, July 22, 2020, https://thefederalist.com/20 20/07/22/list-of-183-monuments-ruined-since-protests-began-and-counting/.

43. Letter from Corey Johnson et al. to Mayor Bill de Blasio, June 18, 2020, https://co uncil.nyc.gov/press/wp-content/uploads/sites/56/2020/06/Letter-to-Mayor-de-Bl asio.pdf.

44. Paulina Enck, "Calls to Take Down Emancipation Memorial Ignore Its Great Historical Weight," The Federalist, June 19, 2020, https://thefederalist.com/2020 /06/19/calls-to-take-down-emancipation-memorial-ignore-its-great-historical-we ight/; Christopher Bedford, "Black Community Elders Shutdown and Shame Anti-Statue Protest," The Federalist, June 27, 2020, https://thefederalist.com/2020/06 /27/black-community-elders-shutdown-shame-anti-statue-protest/.

45. Stefan Sykes, "Statue in Boston of Abraham Lincoln with Freed Slave Kneeling at His Feet Is Removed," NBC, December 30, 2020, https://www.nbcnews.com/ne ws/us-news/statue-boston-abraham-lincoln-freed-slave-kneeling-his-feet-removed -n1252554.

46. Callie Ahlgrim, "Here's Everything You Need to Know about Blackout Tuesday and #TheShowMustBePaused Initiatives," Insider, June 2, 2020, https://www.in sider.com/what-is-blackout-tuesday-the-show-must-be-paused-purpose-backlash -2020-6.

47. Jordan Davidson, "These 'Fortune 500' Companies Donated to the Marxist, Anti-Capitalism Black Lives Matter Foundation," The Federalist, July 13, 2020, https:// thefederalist.com/2020/07/13/these-fortune-500-companies-donated-to-the-mar xist-anti-capitalism-black-lives-matter-foundation/.

48. Jonah Gottschalk, "Twitter Mob Attacks Wendy's after Falling for Fake News," The Federalist, June 2, 2020, https://thefederalist.com/2020/06/02/twitter-mob -attacks-wendys-after-falling-for-fake-news/.

49. Chris Cwik, "Drew Brees Addresses NFL Players Kneeling in 2020: 'I Will Never Agree with Anybody Disrespecting the Flag,'" Yahoo, June 3, 2020, https://spor ts.yahoo.com/drew-brees-addresses-nfl-players-kneeling-in-2020-i-will-never-ag ree-with-anybody-disrespecting-the-flag-164423496.html.

50. Drew Brees (@drewbrees), "I would like to apologize to my friends, teammates, the City of New Orleans, the black community, NFL community and anyone I hurt with my comments yesterday…," Instagram, June 4, 2020, https://www.ins tagram.com/p/CBA1P3gHpT_/?utm_source=ig_embed&ig_rid=1668a48f-51e9 -4b48-8a80-f5e8ba533e8b.

51. Associated Press, "Drew Brees' Wife Apologizes for Husband's Comments on Flag: 'We Are the Problem,'" *USA Today*, June 8, 2020, https://www.usatoday.com/st

ory/sports/nfl/2020/06/08/drew-brees-wife-apologizes-for-husbands-comments
-on-flag/111919690/.

52. Tristan Justice, "Washington Redskins Deliberate Name Change to Appease Woke
Mobs," The Federalist, July 3, 2020, https://thefederalist.com/2020/07/03/was
hington-redskins-deliberate-name-change-to-appease-woke-mobs/.

53. Sean Neumann, "WNBA Players Want Atlanta Co-Owner Sen. Kelly Loeffler Out
after She Opposed Black Lives Matter," Yahoo, July 8, 2020, https://www.yahoo
.com/now/wnba-players-want-atlanta-co-164857843.html.

54. Evita Duffy, "WNBA Players Call for Sen. Kelly Loeffler to Step Down as Team
Owner Over 'Black Lives Matter' Remarks," The Federalist, July 10, 2020, https://
thefederalist.com/2020/07/10/wnba-players-call-for-sen-kelly-loeffler-to-step-do
wn-as-team-owner-over-black-lives-matter-remarks/.

55. Kamala Harris (@KamalaHarris), "If you're able to, chip in now…," Twitter, June
1, 2020, 4:34 p.m., https://twitter.com/KamalaHarris/status/126755501812896
5643.

56. Libby Torres, "Drake, Chrissy Teigen, and Steve Carell Are Just Some of the Stars
Who've Donated to Bail-Relief Funds across the US," Insider, June 8, 2020, https://
www.insider.com/minnesota-protests-celebrity-donations-george-floyd-reactions
-2020-5.

57. Tyler Olson, "Minn. Group That Saw $$ Surge, Some from Biden Staffers, Bailed
Out Alleged Violent Criminals: Report," Fox News, August 10, 2020, https://www
.foxnews.com/politics/minnesota-group-that-saw-surge-including-from-biden-st
affers-bailed-out-alleged-violent-criminals-report.

58. Tom Lyden, "Minnesota Nonprofit with $35M Bails Out Those Accused of Violent
Crimes," Fox 9, August 9, 2020, https://www.fox9.com/news/minnesota-nonpro
fit-with-35m-bails-out-those-accused-of-violent-crimes.

59. Peter Hermann, Sarah Pulliam Bailey, and Michelle Boorstein, "Fire Set at Historic
St. John's Church during Protest of George Floyd's Death," *Washington Post,* June
1, 2020, https://www.washingtonpost.com/religion/fire-set-at-historic-st-johns-ch
urch-during-protests-of-george-floyds-death/2020/06/01/4b5c4004-a3b6-11ea
-b619-3f9133bbb482_story.html.

60. Vandana Rambaran, "At Least 60 Secret Service Members Injured during George
Floyd Protests in DC," Fox News, May 31, 2020, https://www.foxnews.com/us
/more-than-60-secret-service-officers-injured-during-violent-george-floyd-protests
-in-washington-d-c.

61. Paul LeBlanc, "Famed DC Monuments Defaced after Night of Unrest," CNN,
May 31, 2020, https://www.cnn.com/2020/05/31/politics/dc-monuments-lincoln
-memorial-defaced/index.html.

62. "Mahatma Gandhi's Statue at Indian Embassy in Washington Desecrated," *The
Week*, June 4, 2020, https://www.theweek.in/news/world/2020/06/04/mahatma
-gandhis-statue-at-indian-embassy-in-washington-desecrated.html.

63. "Trump Says He's 'President of Law and Order,' Declares Aggressive Action on
Violent Protests," CBS News, June 2, 2020, https://www.cbsnews.com/news/tru
mp-protest-president-law-and-order/.

64. Tom Jachman and Carol D. Leonnig, "Report: Park Police Didn't Clear Lafayette Square Protesters for Trump Visit," *Washington Post*, June 9, 2021, https://www.washingtonpost.com/nation/2021/06/09/park-police-lafayette-square/.

65. Carl Hulse and Emily Cochrane, "In Rare Break, Some Republicans Reject Trump's Harsh Response to Unrest," *New York Times*, June 2, 2020, https://www.nytimes.com/2020/06/02/us/trump-republicans-protesters.html.

66. Kevin Roberts, "'Mostly Peaceful' Lets Black Lives Matter off the Hook for Real Violence," Texas Public Policy Foundation, September 24, 2020, https://www.texaspolicy.com/mostly-peaceful-lets-black-lives-matter-off-the-hook-for-real-violence/; Roudabeh Kishi and Sam Jones, *Demonstrations & Political Violence in America: New Data for Summer 2020* (ACLED, September 3, 2020), https://acleddata.com/2020/09/03/demonstrations-political-violence-in-america-new-data-for-summer-2020/.

67. Sanya Mansoor, "93% of Black Lives Matter Protests Have Been Peaceful, New Report Finds," *Time*, September 5, 2020, https://time.com/5886348/report-peaceful-protests/.

68. Joseph Wulfsohn, "MSNBC Mocked for Having Seattle Mayor Refute Kristi Noem's Claim on Violence in Cities Led by Democrats," Fox News, August 26, 2020, https://www.foxnews.com/media/msnbc-mocked-seattle-mayor-kristi-noems-violence-cities.

69. Ian Hanchett, "Seattle Mayor Durkan: 'We Could Have the Summer of Love'—We Have Four Blocks That Are 'More Like a Block Party,'" Breitbart, June 11, 2020, https://www.breitbart.com/clips/2020/06/11/seattle-mayor-durkan-we-could-have-the-summer-of-love-we-have-four-blocks-that-are-more-like-a-block-party/.

70. Mike Baker, "Free Food, Free Speech and Free of Police: Inside Seattle's 'Autonomous Zone,'" *New York Times,* June 11, 2020, https://www.nytimes.com/2020/06/11/us/seattle-autonomous-zone.html.

71. Aaron Colen, "Seattle Police Chief Says Rapes and Robberies Are Occurring in CHAZ Area and Officers Can't Respond to Them," Blaze Media, June 12, 2020, https://www.theblaze.com/news/seattle-police-chief-violence-chaz.

72. Mark Hemingway, "Roots of Antifa: This 'Idea' Has Violent Consequences," RealClearInvestigations, October 30, 2020, https://www.realclearinvestigations.com/articles/2020/10/30/roots_of_antifa_this_idea_has_violent_consequences_125818.html.

73. Conrad Wilson and Jonathan Levinson, "Protests Grow on 52nd Night as Portland Responds to Federal Officers," NPR, July 19, 2020, https://www.npr.org/2020/07/19/892771802/protests-grow-on-52nd-night-as-portland-responds-to-federal-officers.

74. Mark Hemingway, "'Peaceful Riots'? Journalism Bows to the Woke Mob," RealClearPolitics, July 31, 2020, https://www.realclearpolitics.com/articles/2020/07/31/peaceful_riots_journalism_bows_to_the_woke_mob__143855.html?s=09.

75. Mike Balsamo (@MikeBalsamo1), "I watched as injured officers were hauled inside. In one case, the commercial firework came over so fast…," Twitter, July 27, 2020, 12:32 a.m., https://twitter.com/MikeBalsamo1/status/1287606653110517760.

76. Ed Pilkington, "Federal 'Occupying Force' to Pull Out of Portland, Oregon Governor Announces," *The Guardian*, July 29, 2020, https://www.theguardian .com/us-news/2020/jul/29/trump-officials-portland-oregon-governor-protests; Paul LeBlanc, "Portland Mayor Excoriates Trump: 'It's You Who Have Created the Hate,'" CNN, August 30, 2020, https://www.cnn.com/2020/08/30/politics /portland-mayor-donald-trump-protests/index.html.

77. Chris Liedle, "Organizers Cancel Portland Parade Over Threats to Republican Party, Rose Festival on Track," KATU2, April 26, 2017, https://katu.com/news/lo cal/organizers-cancel-portland-parade-over-threats-to-republican-party-rose-festi val-on-track.

78. Donald Trump (@realDonaldTrump), "Does anyone notice how little the Radical Left takeover of Seattle…," Twitter, June 14, 2020, 4:34 p.m. Account has since been suspended, tweet found at https://www.thetrumparchive.com; Donald J. Trump, Facebook, June 14, 2020, https://www.facebook.com/DonaldTrump/po sts/does-anyone-notice-how-little-the-radical-left-takeover-of-seattle-is-being-disc /10164883929640725/.

79. Donald Trump (@realDonaldTrump), "Interesting how ANTIFA and other Far Left militant groups can take over a city without barely a wimpier…," Twitter, June 14, 2020, 4:47 p.m. Account has since been suspended, tweet found at https:// www.thetrumparchive.com.

80. "Remarks by President Trump at South Dakota's 2020 Mount Rushmore Fireworks Celebration | Keystone, South Dakota," Trump White House Archives, July 4, 2020, https://trumpwhitehouse.archives.gov/briefings-statements/remarks -president-trump-south-dakotas-2020-mount-rushmore-fireworks-celebration-ke ystone-south-dakota/.

81. Ibid.

82. Ibid.

83. Ibid.

84. Mollie Hemingway, "Brazen Lying Is Media's Latest Escalation in Campaign against Trump," The Federalist, July 10, 2020, https://thefederalist.com/2020/07 /10/brazen-lying-is-medias-latest-escalation-in-campaign-against-trump/; Robert Costa and Philip Rucker, "Trump's Push to Amplify Racism Unnerves Republicans Who Have Long Enabled Him," *Washington Post*, July 4, 2020, https://www.was hingtonpost.com/politics/trump-racism-white-nationalism-republicans/2020/07 /04/2b0aebe6-bbaf-11ea-80b9-40ece9a701dc_story.html.

85. Robert Costa (@costareports), "President Trump's unyielding push to preserve Confederate symbols and the legacy of white domination was crystallized…," Twitter, July 4, 2020, 12:38 p.m., https://twitter.com/costareports/status/127945 4586659581952.

86. Byron York, "Byron York's Daily Memo: Distorting Trump's Words," *Washington Examiner*, July 6, 2020, https://www.washingtonexaminer.com/opinion/byron -yorks-daily-memo-distorting-trumps-words.

87. Chris Cillizza, "The 28 Most Outrageous Lines from Donald Trump's Mount Rushmore Speech," CNN, July 4, 2020, https://www.cnn.com/2020/07/04/polit ics/donald-trump-mount-rushmore-south-dakota-speech-lines/index.html.

88. Timothy D. Dwyer, "Op-Ed: Could the Racist Past of Mt. Rushmore's Creator Bring Down the Monument?" *Los Angeles Times*, July 3, 2020, https://www.la times.com/opinion/story/2020-07-03/mount-rushmore-sculptor-racist.

89. Justine Coleman, "Duckworth Says Trump's Mt. Rushmore Speech Showed 'His Priorities Are All Wrong,'" *The Hill*, July 5, 2020, https://thehill.com/homenews /sunday-talk-shows/505913-duckworth-on-trumps-mt-rushmore-speech-on-pro tecting-confederate.

90. Joseph Wulfsohn, "NY Times Op-Ed Clears Up 'Defund the Police' Confusion: 'Yes, We Mean Literally Abolish the Police,'" Fox News, June 13, 2020, https:// www.foxnews.com/media/ny-times-op-ed-clears-up-defund-the-police-confusion -yes-we-mean-literally-abolish-the-police.

91. Don Lemon, *CNN Tonight with Don Lemon*, CNN, July 7, 2020, http:// transcripts.cnn.com/TRANSCRIPTS/2007/07/cnnt.01.html.

92. Mark Hemingway, "Protest Violence and the See-No-Evil Media," RealClearPolitics, August 28, 2020, https://www.realclearpolitics.com/articles/20 20/08/28/protest_violence_and_the_see-no-evil_media_144086.html.

93. Joseph Wulfsohn, "CNN's Chris Cuomo Blasted for Suggesting Protesters Don't Have to be 'Peaceful,'" Fox News, June 3, 2020, https://www.foxnews.com/media /cnns-chris-cuomo-blasted-for-suggesting-protesters-dont-have-to-be-peaceful.

94. Justine Coleman, "Biden Condemns Rioting in New Ad," *The Hill*, September 2, 2020, https://thehill.com/homenews/campaign/514738-biden-condemns-rioting -in-new-ad.

95. Ibid.

96. Kevin Robillard, "Joe Biden Turns Speech Condemning Riots into New Television Ad," HuffPost, September 1, 2020, https://www.huffpost.com/entry/biden-riot-sp eech-tv-ad_n_5f4ed898c5b69eb5c035c657.

97. C-SPAN, "First 2020 Presidential Debate between Donald Trump and Joe Biden," YouTube, September 29, 2020, https://www.youtube.com/watch?v=wW1lY5j FNcQ.

98. Eric Tucker and Ben Fox, "FBI Director Chris Wray Says Antifa Is an Ideology, Not an Organization—Testimony That Puts Him at Odds with President Trump," *Chicago Tribune*, September 17, 2020, https://www.chicagotribune.com/nation -world/ct-nw-fbi-director-chris-wray-antifa-20200917-troogvorejfdlg5wzss62l4c la-story.html.

99. Mark Hemingway, "Roots of Antifa: This 'Idea' Has Violent Consequences," RealClearInvestigations, October 30, 2020, https://www.realclearinvestigations .com/articles/2020/10/30/roots_of_antifa_this_idea_has_violent_consequences _125818.html.

100. "The Siege of the Third Precinct in Minneapolis," CrimethInc., n.d., June 10, 2020, https://crimethinc.com/2020/06/10/the-siege-of-the-third-precinct-in-minneapol is-an-account-and-analysis.

101. Joe Biden (@JoeBiden), "Remember: every example of violence Donald Trump decries has happened on his watch. Under his leadership. During his presidency," Twitter, August 27, 2020, 11:20 p.m., https://twitter.com/JoeBiden/status/12991 84932384768001.

102. Frances Fox Piven and Richard Cloward, "The Weight of the Poor: A Strategy to End Poverty," *The Nation*, reprinted March 8, 2010, https://www.thenation.com /article/archive/weight-poor-strategy-end-poverty/.

103. Glenn Beck, "Cloward, Piven and the Fundamental Transformation of America," Fox News, January 5, 2010, https://www.foxnews.com/story/cloward-piven-and -the-fundamental-transformation-of-america.

104. Ezra Klein, "Steve Lerner's Plan," *Washington Post*, March 23, 2011, https://www .washingtonpost.com/blogs/wonkblog/post/steve-lerners-plan/2011/03/10/ABny qcIB_blog.html.

105. Biden (@JoeBiden), "Remember: every example of violence."

Chapter Five: The Revenge of Fake News

1. Glenn Thrush, "Full Transcript: President Trump's Republican National Convention Speech," *New York Times*, August 28, 2020, https://www.nytimes .com/2020/08/28/us/politics/trump-rnc-speech-transcript.html.

2. Sophia Ankel, "The RNC Ended with a Firework Display over the Washington Monument Spelling Out 'TRUMP,'" Business Insider, August 28, 2020, https:// www.businessinsider.com/last-night-rnc-ends-with-trump-fireworks-over-was hington-monument-2020-8.

3. Emily Anne Epstein, "Scenes from the Republican National Convention," *The Atlantic*, July 21, 2016, https://www.theatlantic.com/photo/2016/07/scenes-from -the-republican-national-convention/492428/.

4. Kevin Breuninger, "Here Are the Highlights from Night 2 of the Republican National Convention," CNBC, August 25, 2020, https://www.cnbc.com/2020/08 /25/rnc-highlights-night-2.html.

5. Jim Morrill, "GOP Picks Charlotte for 2020 Convention. Now, the Fundraising and Organizing Begin," *Charlotte Observer*, July 20, 2018, https://www.charlot teobserver.com/news/politics-government/rnc-2020/article215204290.html.

6. "North Carolina," 270 to Win, n.d., https://www.270towin.com/states/North _Carolina.

7. Clyde Hughes, "Democrats Shift August Convention to Smaller, More Virtual Event," United Press International, June 25, 2020, https://www.upi.com/Top_Ne ws/US/2020/06/25/Democrats-shift-August-convention-to-smaller-more-virtual -event/3211593081897/.

8. Alec Tyson, "Republicans Remain Far Less Likely Than Democrats to View COVID-19 as a Major Threat to Public Health," Pew Research Center, July 22, 2020, https://www.pewresearch.org/fact-tank/2020/07/22/republicans-remain-far -less-likely-than-democrats-to-view-covid-19-as-a-major-threat-to-public-health/.

9. Steve Harrison and Lisa Worf, "Top North Carolina Health Official: GOP Should 'Plan for the Worst' for Convention," National Public Radio, May 21, 2020, https://www.npr.org/2020/05/21/860464958/top-north-carolina-health-official-gop-should-plan-for-the-worst-for-convention.

10. Dan Merica, Ryan Nobles, and Jeremy Diamond, "Trump Says GOP Forced to Find New State to Host Convention as North Carolina Stands by Coronavirus Measures," CNN, June 3, 2020, https://www.cnn.com/2020/06/02/politics/republican-national-convention-location/index.html.

11. Jim Morrill, "The RNC Is Gone, Leaving Charlotte to Sort Out Millions in Contract Liabilities," *Charlotte Observer*, June 15, 2020, https://www.charlotteobserver.com/article243540772.html.

12. Ibid.

13. "Lenny Curry," Ballotpedia, n.d., https://ballotpedia.org/Lenny_Curry.

14. Dartunorro Clark, "Republicans Pick Jacksonville, Florida, as Convention Site for Trump to Accept Nomination," NBC News, June 11, 2020, https://www.nbcnews.com/politics/2020-election/rnc-picks-jacksonville-florida-convention-site-trump-accept-gop-nomination-n1230326.

15. Dan Merica and Jeff Zeleny, "Trump to Accept Nomination in Jacksonville after Moving Most of Convention Out of Charlotte," CNN, June 11, 2020, https://www.cnn.com/2020/06/11/politics/republican-convention-jacksonville/index.html.

16. Maanvi Singh, "Donald Trump to Hold Rally in Oklahoma, First since Coronavirus Pandemic Began," *The Guardian*, June 11, 2020, https://www.theguardian.com/us-news/2020/jun/10/donald-trump-rally-tulsa-oklahoma-juneteenth-coronavirus.

17. Tommy Beer, "Trump Says Nearly 1 Million People Have Requested Tickets to Tulsa Rally," *Forbes*, June 15, 2020, https://www.forbes.com/sites/tommybeer/2020/06/15/trump-says-nearly-1-million-people-have-requested-tickets-to-tulsa-rally/?sh=279943e65289.

18. Maggie Haberman and Annie Karni, "The President's Shock at the Rows of Empty Seats in Tulsa," *New York Times*, June 21, 2020, https://www.nytimes.com/2020/06/21/us/politics/trump-tulsa-rally.html.

19. Brian Flood, "Trump Rally Gives Fox News Largest Saturday Night Audience in Its History," Fox News, June 22, 2020, https://www.foxnews.com/media/trump-rally-gives-fox-news-largest-saturday-night-audience-in-history.

20. Holly Ellyatt, "How I Helped Get Trump Elected: The President's Digital Guru," CNBC, November 8, 2017, https://www.cnbc.com/2017/11/08/how-i-helped-get-trump-elected-the-presidents-digital-guru-brad-parscale.html.

21. Ibid.

22. Maggie Haberman, "Trump Replaces Brad Parscale as Campaign Manager, Elevating Bill Stepien," *New York Times*, July 15, 2020, https://www.nytimes.com/2020/07/15/us/politics/trump-campaign-brad-parscale.html.

23. Lacrai Mitchell, "Jacksonville Sheriff Has 'Significant Concerns' about Safely Hosting Republican National Convention," CBS News, July 21, 2020, https://

www.cbsnews.com/news/jacksonville-sheriff-significant-concerns-city-can-safely-host-republican-national-convention/.

24. Caroline Kelly and Fredreka Schouten, "Republican National Convention Will Test Jacksonville Attendees Daily for Coronavirus," CNN, July 6, 2020, https://www.cnn.com/2020/07/06/politics/republican-national-convention-jacksonville-test-attendees-coronavirus/index.html.

25. Maggie Haberman, Patricia Mazzei, and Annie Karni, "Trump Abruptly Cancels Republican Convention in Florida: 'It's Not the Right Time,'" *New York Times*, July 23, 2020, https://www.nytimes.com/2020/07/23/us/politics/jacksonville-rnc.html.

26. Ryan Lizza (@RyanLizza), "Barack Obama just delivered the finest convention speech in modern history…," Twitter, August 19, 2020, 10:47 p.m., https://twitter.com/RyanLizza/status/1296277661472489475.

27. Jim Rutenberg, "Trump Is Testing the Norms of Objectivity in Journalism," *New York Times*, August 7, 2016, https://www.nytimes.com/2016/08/08/business/balance-fairness-and-a-proudly-provocative-presidential-candidate.html.

28. Eli Watkins et al., "Clinton Campaign, DNC Helped Fund Dossier Research," CNN, October 25, 2017, https://www.cnn.com/2017/10/24/politics/fusion-gps-clinton-campaign/index.html.

29. Andrew Prokop, "The 'Pee Tape' Claim, Explained," Vox, April 23, 2018, https://www.vox.com/2018/4/15/17233994/comey-interview-trump-pee-tape-russia.

30. Evan Perez et al., "Intel Chiefs Presented Trump with Claims of Russian Efforts to Compromise Him," CNN, January 12, 2017, https://edition.cnn.com/2017/01/10/politics/donald-trump-intelligence-report-russia/index.html.

31. "The 2018 Pulitzer Prize Winner in National Reporting," The Pulitzer Prizes, n.d., https://www.pulitzer.org/winners/staffs-new-york-times-and-washington-post.

32. Harry Enten, "Latest House Results Confirm 2018 Wasn't a Blue Wave. It Was a Blue Tsunami," CNN, December 6, 2018, https://www.cnn.com/2018/12/06/politics/latest-house-vote-blue-wave/index.html.

33. Barry Meier, "Secret Sharers: The Hidden Ties between Private Spies and Journalists," *New York Times*, May 15, 2021, https://www.nytimes.com/2021/05/15/business/media/spooked-private-spies-news-media.html; Barry Meier, *Spooked: The Trump Dossier, Black Cube, and the Rise of Private Spies* (London: Harper, 2021).

34. Charles Savage, Eric Schmitt, and Michael Schwirtz, "Russia Secretly Offered Afghan Militants Bounties to Kill U.S. Troops, Intelligence Says," *New York Times*, June 26, 2020, https://www.nytimes.com/2020/06/26/us/politics/russia-afghanistan-bounties.html.

35. Ibid.

36. Ibid.

37. Ibid.

38. Ibid.

39. Charlie Savage, "Highlights of the Special Counsel's Case against George Papadopoulos," *New York Times*, October 30, 2017, https://www.nytimes.com

/2017/10/30/us/politics/special-counsel-george-papadopoulos.html; David E. Sanger and Eric Schmitt, "Spy Agency Consensus Grows That Russia Hacked D.N.C.," *New York Times*, July 26, 2016, https://www.nytimes.com/2016/07/27/us/politics/spy-agency-consensus-grows-that-russia-hacked-dnc.html.

40. Jordan Davidson, "Surprise! The 'Russian Bounty' Story Hyped Up by Corrupt Media to Hurt Trump Turned Out to Be Fake News," The Federalist, April 15, 2021, https://thefederalist.com/2021/04/15/surprise-the-russian-bounty-story-hyped-up-by-corrupt-media-to-hurt-trump-turned-out-to-be-fake-news/.

41. Tristan Justice, "Liz Cheney Was a Primary Culprit of Spreading Fake News on Russian Bounties to Undermine Trump," The Federalist, April 16, 2021, https://thefederalist.com/2021/04/16/liz-cheney-was-a-primary-culprit-of-spreading-fake-news-on-russian-bounties-to-undermine-trump/.

42. Josh Lederman (@JoshNBCNews), "This raises the obvious and very serious question: The US had intelligence that Russia was paying militants to kill US & allied troops…," Twitter, June 27, 2020, 4:54 p.m., https://twitter.com/JoshNBCNews/status/1276982370973945863.

43. Office of the Director of National Intelligence, "Statement by DNI Ratcliffe on Recent Press Reporting," News Release No. 25-20, June 27, 2020, https://www.dni.gov/index.php/newsroom/press-releases/item/2128-statement-by-dni-ratcliffe-on-recent-press-reporting.

44. Alyssa Farah (@Alyssafarah), "POTUS wasn't briefed on the reports related to Afghanistan because there is no consensus within the intelligence community on the allegations at this point…," Twitter, June 29, 2020, 1:34 p.m., https://twitter.com/Alyssafarah/status/1277656758178254850.

45. Ken Dilanian and Mike Memoli, "Remember Those Russian Bounties for Dead U.S. Troops? Biden Admin Says the CIA Intel Is Not Conclusive," NBC News, April 15, 2021, https://www.nbcnews.com/politics/national-security/remember-those-russian-bounties-dead-u-s-troops-biden-admin-n1264215.

46. Mollie Hemingway, "Media Are Playing Games Yet Again with Anonymous Russia Leaks," The Federalist, June 30, 2020, https://thefederalist.com/2020/06/30/media-are-playing-games-yet-again-with-anonymous-russia-leaks/.

47. "WMD Commission—Overview," Executive Office of the President, Commission on the Intelligence Capabilities of the United States Regarding Weapons of Mass Destruction, March 31, 2005, https://fas.org/irp/offdocs/wmd_overview.pdf, 14.

48. "The Record on Curveball," National Security Archive, November 5, 2007, https://nsarchive2.gwu.edu/NSAEBB/NSAEBB234/index.htm.

49. "Full Text of Colin Powell's Speech," *The Guardian*, February 5, 2003, https://www.theguardian.com/world/2003/feb/05/iraq.usa.

50. Ibid.

51. Martin Chulov and Helen Pidd, "Curveball: How US Was Duped by Iraqi Fantasist Looking to Topple Saddam," *The Guardian*, February 15, 2011, https://www.theguardian.com/world/2011/feb/15/curveball-iraqi-fantasist-cia-saddam.

52. For example, see *Report of the Select Committee on Intelligence, United States Senate, on Russian Active Measures Campaigns and Interference*, Volume 2,

Report 116-XX, https://www.intelligence.senate.gov/sites/default/files/documents/Report_Volume2.pdf.

53. Jason Slotkin and Mark Katkov, "Trump Says He Was Not Briefed on Russian Bounties because Intelligence 'Not Credible,'" National Public Radio, June 28, 2020, https://www.npr.org/2020/06/28/884407572/trump-denies-briefing-on-russian-bounties-reportedly-placed-on-u-s-troops.

54. Hemingway, "Media Are Playing Games Yet Again."

55. Ibid.

56. Ibid.

57. "'With (Trump) All Roads Lead to Putin': Pelosi," ABC News, June 28, 2020, https://abcnews.go.com/ThisWeek/video/trump-roads-lead-putin-pelosi-71498985.

58. Ibid.

59. "Joe Biden Veterans Roundtable Event & Speech Transcript September 15," Rev.com, September 15, 2020, https://www.rev.com/blog/transcripts/joe-biden-veterans-roundtable-event-speech-transcript-september-15.

60. Andrew Bates (@AndrewBatesNC), "At a time when Trump is giving Russia a pass for putting bounties on the heads of American service members…," Twitter, September 14, 2020, 8:31 p.m., https://twitter.com/AndrewBatesNC/status/1305665426534301696.

61. Sean Davis and Mollie Hemingway, "Schiff Learned of Russian 'Bounty' Intelligence in February, Withheld Information from Congress, and Took No Action," The Federalist, July 2, 2020, https://thefederalist.com/2020/07/02/schiff-learned-of-russian-bounty-intelligence-in-february-withheld-information-from-congress-and-took-no-action/.

62. Maegan Vazquez, "Trump Takes Aim at Schiff ahead of Push to Release Democrats' Memo," CNN, February 5, 2018, https://www.cnn.com/2018/02/05/politics/trump-little-adam-schiff-tweet/index.html.

63. Maggie Miller and Rebecca Kheel, "Biden Administration Says with 'Low to Moderate Confidence' Russia behind Afghanistan Troop Bounties," *The Hill*, April 15, 2021, https://thehill.com/policy/defense/548427-biden-administration-attributes-afghanistan-troop-bounties-to-russia.

64. "Afghan Conflict: US and Taliban Sign Deal to End 18-Year War," BBC News, February 29, 2020, https://www.bbc.com/news/world-asia-51689443.

65. Jeffrey Goldberg, "Trump: Americans Who Died in War Are 'Losers' and 'Suckers,'" *The Atlantic*, September 3, 2020, https://www.theatlantic.com/politics/archive/2020/09/trump-americans-who-died-at-war-are-losers-and-suckers/615997/.

66. Jill Colvin, "Trump Visit to US Cemetery in France Canceled Due to Rain," Associated Press, November 11, 2018, https://apnews.com/article/donald-trump-ap-top-news-weather-world-war-i-north-america-52462add34fd45ecb16319b564045d61.

67. Goldberg, "Trump: Americans Who Died in War."

68. Ibid.

69. Carol E. Lee, "Trump Pays Tribute to the Veterans and Alliances of Two World Wars," NBC News, November 11, 2018, https://www.nbcnews.com/politics/do nald-trump/trump-pays-tribute-veterans-alliances-two-world-wars-n934966.

70. Colvin, "Trump Visit to US Cemetery in France Canceled."

71. Sarah Huckabee Sanders (@SarahHuckabee), "The Atlantic story on @ realDonalTrump is total BS. I was actually there and one of the people part of the discussion…," Twitter, September 3, 2020, 10:03 p.m., https://twitter.com/Sarah Huckabee/status/1301702348071460864.

72. Joseph Wulfsohn, "Does John Bolton's Memoir Undercut the Atlantic on Trump's Canceled Visit to US Cemetery in France?" Fox News, September 4, 2020, https:// www.foxnews.com/politics/john-bolton-memoir-atlantic-trump-france.

73. Rebeccah Heinrichs, "Former Secret Service Director Debunks the Atlantic's Flimsy Trump Hit Piece," The Federalist, September 10, 2020, https://thefederali st.com/2020/09/10/former-secret-service-director-debunks-the-atlantics-flimsy-tr ump-hit-piece/.

74. Bernard Goldberg, "The Atlantic's Trump Report: We Should Know the Sources of a Story This Important," *The Hill,* September 6, 2020, https://thehill.com/opin ion/technology/515289-the-atlantics-trump-report-we-should-know-the-sources -of-a-story-this-important.

75. Matt Taibbi, "16 Years Later, How the Press That Sold the Iraq War Got Away with It," *Rolling Stone,* March 22, 2010, https://www.rollingstone.com/politics /politics-features/iraq-war-media-fail-matt-taibbi-812230/.

76. Julia Reinstein, "Merkel and Macron Embraced at a WW1 Memorial but Trump Couldn't Visit a Different Cemetery Due to Bad Weather," BuzzFeed, November 10, 2018, https://www.buzzfeednews.com/article/juliareinstein/ww1-memorial-an niversary-trump-weather-macron-merkel.

77. Kim Willsher, "Trump Misses Cemetery Visit as Macron and Merkel Vow Unity," *The Guardian,* November 10, 2018, https://www.theguardian.com/world/2018 /nov/10/macron-merkel-trump-armistice-compiegne.

78. Kyriakh Kampouridoy, "Journalist behind Bombshell Trump Report Speaks Out," YouTube, September 7, 2020, https://www.youtube.com/watch?v=IpYDgFoeoFI.

79. "Remarks by President Trump after Air Force One Arrival, Joint Base Andrews, MD, September 3, 2020," Trump White House Archives, September 4, 2020, https://trumpwhitehouse.archives.gov/briefings-statements/remarks-president-tru mp-air-force-one-arrival-joint-base-andrews-md-september-3-2020/.

80. Joe Biden (@JoeBiden), "Mr. President, if you don't respect our troops, you can't lead them," Twitter, September 4, 2020, 12:04 p.m., https://twitter.com/JoeBiden /status/1301913914922299393.

81. Ibid.

82. Jenna Ellis to Jennifer O'Malley Dillon, letter, September 9, 2020, Just the News, https://justthenews.com/sites/default/files/2020-09/Biden%20Letter%20090920 20%20DJTFP_1.pdf.

83. Paul Farhi and Sarah Ellison, "The New York Times Called 'Anonymous' Op-ed Author Miles Taylor a Trump 'Senior Official.' Was That Accurate?" *Washington*

Post, October 28, 2020, https://www.washingtonpost.com/lifestyle/media/anony mous-miles-taylor-new-york-times-senior-official/2020/10/28/73634c0a-1959-11 eb-82db-60b15c874105_story.html.

84. Miles Taylor, "I Am Part of the Resistance inside the Trump Administration," *New York Times*, September 5, 2018, https://www.nytimes.com/2018/09/05/opinion /trump-white-house-anonymous-resistance.html.

85. "How the Anonymous Op-ed Came to Be," *New York Times*, September 8, 2018, https://www.nytimes.com/2018/09/08/reader-center/anonymous-op-ed-trump .html.

86. Chris Cillizza, "13 People Who Might Be the Author of the New York Times Op-Ed," CNN, September 6, 2018, https://www.cnn.com/2018/09/05/politics/do nald-trump-mystery-op-ed/index.html.

87. Ibid.

88. Chris Cillizza, "Here's One Big Clue to the Identity of the Anonymous Op-Ed Writer," CNN, September 6, 2018, https://www.cnn.com/2018/09/06/politics/new -york-times-op-ed-donald-trump/index.html.

89. Ibid.

90. Ibid.

91. Farhi and Ellison, "The New York Times Called."

92. Matt Whitlock (@mattdizwhitlock), "Wow. Miles Taylor wasn't even listed on DHS's senior leadership page when NYT published his op-ed because he was just a policy advisor, not even chief of staff…," Twitter, October 28, 2020, 4:22 p.m., https://mobile.twitter.com/mattdizwhitlock/status/1321548012343250945.

93. Ibid.

94. Manuel Roig-Franzia, "Miles Taylor Spoke Out against Trump as 'Anonymous.' Now He's Gone Public and Is Hiding Out," *Washington Post*, December 1, 2020, https://www.washingtonpost.com/lifestyle/style/miles-taylor-anonymous-trump -profile/2020/11/30/ece1d5c0-28df-11eb-92b7-6ef17b3fe3b4_story.html.

95. Mariam Ahmed, "CNN Hires Taylor as Contributor," Talking Biz News, September 9, 2020, https://talkingbiznews.com/we-talk-biz-news/cnn-hires-taylor -as-contributor/.

96. Hamed Aleaziz and Ryan Mac, "Anonymous Trump Critic and Former DHS Staffer Miles Taylor Has Left Google," BuzzFeed, November 5, 2020, https://www .buzzfeednews.com/article/hamedaleaziz/anonymous-trump-critic-miles-taylor-le aves-google.

97. "Acting DHS Secretary Chad F. Wolf Responds to CNN Contributor Miles Taylor News," Department of Homeland Security, October 28, 2020, https://www.dhs .gov/news/2020/10/28/acting-dhs-secretary-chad-f-wolf-responds-cnn-contribut or-miles-taylor-news.

98. Ryan Mac and Jason Leopold, "A Google Staffer Helped Sell Trump's Family Separation Policy, Despite the Company Denials," BuzzFeed, October 28, 2019, https://www.buzzfeednews.com/article/ryanmac/miles-taylor-family-separation -dhs-despite-google-denial.

99. Jeffrey Martin, "Miles Taylor Says He Owes Anderson Cooper a Beer for Lying about Being 'Anonymous,'" *Newsweek*, October 28, 2020, https://www.newswe ek.com/miles-taylor-says-he-owes-anderson-cooper-beer-lying-about-being-anon ymous-1543089.

100. Thomas Kaplan (@thomaskaplan), "Biden on the USPS at a virtual fund-raiser, via pooler @hollyotterbein…," Twitter, August 14, 2020, 7:35 p.m., https://twitter .com/thomaskaplan/status/1294417266948411392.

101. "USPS Removes Mailboxes in Portland and Eugene, Cites 'Declining Mail Volume,'" *Oregonian*, August 13, 2020, https://www.oregonlive.com/news/2020 /08/usps-removes-mailboxes-in-portland-and-eugene-cites-declining-mail-volume .html.

102. Kylee Zempel, "Joe Biden and Taylor Swift Embrace Bizarre U.S. Postal Service Conspiracy," The Federalist, August 16, 2020, https://thefederalist.com/2020/08 /16/joe-biden-and-taylor-swift-embrace-bizarre-u-s-postal-service-conspiracy/.

103. E. Mazareanu, "United States Postal Service's Total Mail Volume from 2004 to 2020," Statista, March 17, 2021, https://www.statista.com/statistics/320234/ma il-volume-of-the-usps/.

104. Ronn Blitzer, "USPS Flashback: Obama Administration Removed Thousands of Mailboxes," Fox News, August 17, 2020, https://www.foxnews.com/politics/pos tal-service-flashback-obama-admin-removed-thousands-of-mailboxes.

105. "The United States Postal Service Delivers the Facts," United States Postal Service, July 2020, https://about.usps.com/news/delivers-facts/usps-delivers-the-facts.pdf.

106. Barack Obama (@BarackObama), "Everyone depends on the USPS. Seniors for their Social Security, veterans for their prescriptions, small businesses trying to keep their doors open…," Twitter, August 14, 2020, 10:48 a.m., https://twitter .com/BarackObama/status/1294284824325300225.

107. Nancy Pelosi (@SpeakerPelosi), "Alarmingly, Postmaster General DeJoy has acted as an accomplice in the President's effort to cheat the election and manipulate the Postal Service to deny eligible voters access…," Twitter, August 16, 2020, 11:02 a.m., https://twitter.com/SpeakerPelosi/status/1295013098932371456.

108. Taylor Swift (@taylorswift13), "Trump's calculated dismantling of USPS proves one thing clearly: He is WELL AWARE that we do not want him as our president…," Twitter, August 15, 2020, 1:20 p.m., https://twitter.com/taylorswift13/status/12 94685437362155522.

109. Rick Wilson (@TheRickWilson), "The biggest investigative story of this election— on par with Watergate—will be the reporter who run downs the White House and Trump campaign connection to the USPS shutdown…," Twitter, August 15, 2020, 11:17 a.m., https://twitter.com/TheRickWilson/status/1294654395041427457.

110. Jane Mayer (@JaneMayerNYer), "Anyone thinking Trump's assault on the postal service is a rogue move needs to understand that Mike Duncan…," Twitter, August 15, 2020, 11:51 a.m., https://twitter.com/JaneMayerNYer/status/129466305153 5425543.

111. "Following Pressure from Tester, USPS Pauses Mail Collection Box Removal in Montana," U.S. Senator for Montana Jon Tester, August 14, 2020, https://www.tester.senate.gov/?p=press_release&id=7651.
112. Tristan Justice, "Twitter Censors Trump Tweets, but Allows Viral Post Office Conspiracy Theories to Flourish," The Federalist, August 20, 2020, https://thefederalist.com/2020/08/20/twitter-censors-trump-tweets-but-allows-viral-post-office-conspiracy-theories-to-flourish/.

Chapter Six: Stifling Debates

1. Andrew Buncombe, "Trump Finds Out about Ruth Bader Ginsburg Death after Finishing Two-Hour Rally: 'She Just Died? Wow,'" *The Independent*, September 19, 2020, https://www.independent.co.uk/news/world/americas/ruth-bader-ginsburg-dead-trump-reaction-supreme-court-latest-b491380.html.
2. Ibid.
3. Ibid.
4. Mollie Hemingway and Carrie Severino, *Justice on Trial: The Kavanaugh Confirmation and the Future of the Supreme Court* (Washington, D.C.: Regnery Publishing, 2019).
5. Ibid.
6. Ibid.
7. Ibid.
8. Alexander Burns and Adam Nagourney, "Court Vacancy Injects New Uncertainty into Rancorous Election Battle," *New York Times*, September 19, 2020, https://www.nytimes.com/2020/09/19/us/politics/trump-ginsburg-biden.html.
9. Tucker Higgins, "Susan Collins Struggles to Change the Subject from Brett Kavanaugh in Maine Senate Race," CNBC, October 9, 2020, https://www.cnbc.com/2020/10/09/maine-senate-race-susan-collins-brett-kavanaugh-vote.html.
10. Hemingway and Severino, *Justice on Trial*, 21.
11. "Supreme Court Nominee Announcement," C-SPAN, September 26, 2020, https://www.c-span.org/video/?476190-1/president-trump-nominates-amy-coney-barrett-supreme-court.
12. Dartunorro Clark, "Fauci Calls Amy Coney Barrett Ceremony in Rose Garden 'Superspreader Event,'" NBC News, October 9, 2020, https://www.nbcnews.com/politics/white-house/fauci-calls-amy-coney-barrett-ceremony-rose-garden-superspreader-event-n1242781.
13. Elle Thomas, "Sen. Mike Lee Tests Positive for COVID-19," FOX 13, October 2, 2020, https://www.fox13now.com/news/coronavirus/local-coronavirus-news/sen-mike-lee-tests-positive-for-covid-19.
14. Jonah Goldberg, "Ruth Bader Ginsburg and a Question of Eugenics," *Chicago Tribune*, July 16, 2009, https://www.chicagotribune.com/news/ct-xpm-2009-07-16-0907150564-story.html.
15. Tom Hamburger, "Two Students and a Teacher at School Attended by Barrett Children Test Positive for Coronavirus," *Washington Post*, October 9, 2020,

https://www.washingtonpost.com/politics/barrett-children-school-covid/2020/10/09/ac130298-0a40-11eb-9be6-cf25fb429f1a_story.html.

16. Catherine Porter and Serge F. Kovaleski, "An Earthquake, an Orphanage, and New Beginnings for Haitian Children in America," *New York Times*, October 19, 2020, https://www.nytimes.com/2020/10/19/world/haiti-adoptions.html.

17. Ariel Zilber and Geoff Earle, "Boston University Professor Is Urged to Resign for Calling Amy Coney Barrett a 'White Colonizer' Who Is Using Her Two Adopted Haitian Children as 'Props,'" *Daily Mail*, September 27, 2020, https://www.daily mail.co.uk/news/article-8779469/Amy-Coney-Barrett-white-colonizer-adopting -two-black-children-Haiti-professor-says.html.

18. Dominick Mastrangelo, "Barrett Reveals She's Not Using Notes during Confirmation Hearing," *The Hill*, October 13, 2020, https://thehill.com/homene ws/520820-barrett-reveals-shes-not-using-notes-during-confirmation-hearing.

19. "'The Dogma Lives Loudly within You': Revisiting Barrett's Confirmation Hearing," *New York Times*, September 26, 2020, https://www.nytimes.com/20 20/09/26/us/politics/the-dogma-lives-loudly-within-you-revisiting-barretts-confir mation-hearing.html.

20. "Commission on Presidential Debates," Ballotpedia, https://ballotpedia.org/Com mission_on_Presidential_Debates.

21. Ken Thomas, "Debate over Debates Draws Attention to Nonpartisan Commission," *Wall Street Journal*, October 8, 2020, https://www.wsj.com/articl es/debate-over-debates-draws-attention-to-nonpartisan-commission-1160218 7300.

22. Wall Street Journal, "Crowley Interrupts Romney, Social Frenzy Erupts," YouTube, October 17, 2012, https://www.youtube.com/watch?v=Q21rcSrhOM0.

23. Kelly Riddell, "Benghazi Report Points Out Obama, Clinton Lies," *Washington Times*, June 28, 2016, https://www.washingtontimes.com/news/2016/jun/28/ben ghazi-report-points-out-obama-clinton-lies/.

24. Donald Trump (@realDonaldTrump), "The problem is that the so-called Commission on Presidential Debates is stacked with Trump Haters…," Twitter, December 16, 2019, 9:25 a.m. Account has since been suspended, tweets found at https://www.thetrumparchive.com/.

25. Grace Panetta, "Voting in the 2020 Presidential Election Officially Starts Today as North Carolina Sends Out Over 600,000 Mail Ballots," Insider, September 4, 2020, https://www.businessinsider.com/2020-election-voting-begins-september -4-north-carolina-mails-ballots-2020-9.

26. Donald Trump (@realDonaldTrump), "How can voters be sending in Ballots starting, in some cases, one month before…," Twitter, August 6, 2020, 7:44 a.m. Account has since been suspended, tweet found at https://www.thetrumparchive .com.

27. Adam Edelman, "Commission Denies Trump's Request to Move Up Presidential Debates," NBC News, August 6, 2020, https://www.nbcnews.com/politics/2020-elec tion/trump-repeat-campaign-s-calls-move-first-2020-debate-biden-n1236013.

28. Jake Lahut, "Biden Tells Trump to 'Shut up, Man' after 20 Minutes of Constant Bickering in the First Presidential Debate," Insider, September 29, 2020, https://www.businessinsider.com/biden-tells-trump-would-you-shut-up-man-debate-video-2020-9.

29. Kylee Zempel, "Chris Wallace Just Gave the Most Embarrassing Moderator Performance in History," The Federalist, September 30, 2020, https://thefederalist.com/2020/09/30/chris-wallace-just-gave-the-most-embarrassing-moderator-performance-in-history/.

30. "Campaign 2020: Trump-Biden First Debate," C-SPAN, September 29, 2020, https://www.c-span.org/video/?475793-1/trump-biden-debate.

31. Ibid.

32. Emily Jacobs, "Hunter Biden Received $3.5M Wire Transfer from Russian Billionaire: Senate Report," *New York Post*, September 23, 2020, https://nypost.com/2020/09/23/hunter-biden-received-3-5m-from-russian-billionaire-report/.

33. "Campaign 2020: Trump-Biden First Debate."

34. "Combating Race and Sex Stereotyping," Executive Order 13950, 85 Fed. Reg. 60683 (September 22, 2020), https://www.federalregister.gov/documents/2020/09/28/2020-21534/combating-race-and-sex-stereotyping.

35. Martin Luther King Jr., "I Have a Dream," American Rhetoric, delivered August 28, 1963, https://www.americanrhetoric.com/speeches/mlkihaveadream.htm.

36. Robin Opsahl, "Joe Biden Says He Is Not Misrepresenting Trump's 'Fine People on Both Sides' Comment on White Supremacist Protest," *Des Moines Register*, August 8, 2019, https://www.desmoinesregister.com/story/news/elections/presidential/caucus/2019/08/08/joe-biden-donald-trump-white-supremacy-racism-iowa-state-fair-el-paso-texas-shooting-nationalism/1959163001/; Eric Bradner and Maeve Reston, "Joe Biden Takes Trump Head-on over Charlottesville in Announcement Video," CNN, April 25, 2019, https://www.cnn.com/2019/04/25/politics/joe-biden-charlottesville-trump-2020-launch/index.html.

37. Madeline Osburn, "Two-Thirds of Spanish Speaking Telemundo Voters Said Trump Won the First Debate," The Federalist, September 30, 2020, https://thefederalist.com/2020/09/30/two-thirds-of-spanish-speaking-telemundo-voters-said-trump-won-the-first-debate/.

38. Kevin Breuninger, "Joe Biden Struggling with Latino Voters in Key Sate Florida, Polls Show," CNBC, September 9, 2020, https://www.cnbc.com/2020/09/09/joe-biden-struggling-with-latino-voters-in-key-state-florida-polls-show.html.

39. Frank Bruni, "For the Sake of Democracy, Cancel the Trump-Biden Debates," *New York Times*, October 1, 2020, https://www.nytimes.com/2020/10/01/opinion/trump-biden-debates.html.

40. Jeanine Santucci and David Jackson, "White House Adviser Hope Hicks Tests Positive for COVID-19, Trump and First Lady Also Positive," *USA Today*, October 1, 2020, https://www.usatoday.com/story/news/politics/2020/10/01/hope-hicks-tests-positive-covid-after-traveling-trump/5889312002/.

41. Donald Trump (@realDonaldTrump), "Tonight, @FLOTUS and I tested positive for COVID-19. We will begin our quarantine and recovery process immediately.

We will get through this TOGETHER!" Twitter, October 2, 2020, 12:54 a.m. Account has since been suspended, tweet found at https://www.thetrumparchive .com

42. Ben McDonald (@Bmac0507), "Lincoln Project on their game tonight," Twitter, October 2, 2020, 2:05 a.m., https://twitter.com/Bmac0507/status/131191017231 1330816.

43. "Reaction Poll: Trump Contracts COVID," Morning Consult, October 7, 2020, https://morningconsult.com/form/reaction-poll-trump-covid/.

44. Twitter Comms (@TwitterComms), "Tweets that wish or hope for death, serious bodily harm, or fatal disease against *anyone* are not allowed and will need to be removed...," Twitter, October 2, 2020, 7:09 p.m., https://twitter.com/TwitterCo mms/status/1312167835783708672.

45. Mollie Hemingway (@MZHemingway), "I have no words. Washington Post attacks me for, of all things, saying I was 'genuinely disappointed' at the glee some expressed at news of Trump's positive test. Suggests I 'imagined' it," Twitter, October 2, 2020, 8:16 p.m., https://twitter.com/MZHemingway/status/1312184 733925732352; Paul Farhi and Elahe Izadi, "After Trump's Positive Test, Conservative Media Goes after Liberal Critics—Real and Imagined," *Washington Post*, October 2, 2020, https://www.washingtonpost.com/lifestyle/media/after-tr umps-positive-test-conservative-media-goes-after-liberal-critics—real-and-imagi ned/2020/10/02/969a9870-04b6-11eb-b7ed-141dd88560ea_story.html.

46. Kevin Liptak, "Trump Taken to Walter Reed Medical Center and Will Be Hospitalized 'for the Next Few Days,'" CNN, October 3, 2020, https://www.cnn .com/2020/10/02/politics/president-donald-trump-walter-reed-coronavirus/index .html.

47. Jennifer Rubin (@JRubinBlogger), "Totally unacceptable we have not heard from a doctor. Has the 25th amendment been invoked???," Twitter, October 2, 2020, 5:13 p.m., https://twitter.com/JRubinBlogger/status/1312138782259376128.

48. Aaron Zitner, "Biden Scores 14-Point Lead over Trump in Poll after Debate," *Wall Street Journal*, October 4, 2020, https://www.wsj.com/articles/biden-scores-14-po int-lead-over-trump-in-poll-after-debate-11601816400.

49. Josh Kraushaar, "The October of Doom for Republicans," *National Journal*, October 3, 2020, https://twitter.com/hotlinejosh/status/1312442043302436864 ?lang=en.

50. John McCormick, "Trump Fans Show Support outside Walter Reed Medical Center," Fox 5 News, October 4, 2020, https://foxbaltimore.com/news/local/tru mp-fans-show-support-outside-walter-reed-medical-center.

51. Rachel Maddow (@maddow), "'The president has been a phenomenal patient'? this is absolutely ridiculous," Twitter, October 5, 2020, 3:23 p.m., https:// twitter.com/maddow/status/1313198147875803138.

52. Ben Zeisloft, "Harvard Lecturer Pushes Wild Conspiracy Theory about Russian Spies at Walter Reed Hospital," Campus Reform, October 5, 2020, https://www .campusreform.org/?ID=15864.

53. Virginia Kruta, "'Get Well and Get It Together': Jake Tapper Accuses Trump of 'Inflicting' Failures on Americans," Daily Caller, October 4, 2020, https://dailyc aller.com/2020/10/04/get-well-get-it-together-jake-tapper-trump-failures-corona virus/.

54. Barbara Sprunt, "Despite Risks to Others, Trump Leaves Hospital Suite to Greet Supporters," NPR, October 4, 2020, https://www.npr.org/sections/latest-updates -trump-covid-19-results/2020/10/04/920181116/in-brief-drive-by-trump-waves -to-supporters-outside-of-walter-reed.

55. Nicole Lyn Pesce, "Trump Tweets, 'Don't Be Afraid of Covid,' Sparking Heated Twitter Exchange," MarketWatch, October 6, 2020, https://www.marketwatch .com/story/trump-tweets-dont-be-afraid-of-covid-americans-tell-him-why-theyre -still-scared-2020-10-05.

56. Jennifer Rubin (@JRubinBlogger), "You are a menace to everyone around you," Twitter, October 5, 2020, 2:38 p.m., https://twitter.com/JRubinBlogger/status/13 13186875193069570.

57. Wolf Blitzer, "President Trump Set to Return to White House; Awaiting Trump's Departure from Hospital," *The Situation Room*, CNN, October 5, 2020, http:// transcripts.cnn.com/TRANSCRIPTS/2010/05/sitroom.02.html.

58. Joseph Wulfsohn, "CNN Blasts Trump's Departure from Walter Reed: 'This Is the Virus Coming Back to the White House,'" Fox News, October 5, 2020, https:// www.foxnews.com/media/cnn-trump-walter-reed-white-house-coronavirus.

59. "President Trump White House Arrival," C-SPAN, October 5, 2020, https://www .c-span.org/video/?476647-1/president-trump-returns-home-white-house.

60. Joseph Wulfsohn, "Washington Post's Jennifer Rubin Calls to 'Defund' Walter Reed after Trump Announces White House Return," Fox News, October 5, 2020, https://www.foxnews.com/media/jennifer-rubin-defund-walter-reed.

61. Michael Beschloss (@BeschlossDC), "In America, our presidents have generally avoided strongman balcony scenes—that's for other countries with authoritarian systems," Twitter, October 5, 2020, 7:13 p.m., https://twitter.com/BeschlossDC /status/1313256099265609729.

62. Mollie Hemingway, "Trump's Greatest Accomplishments Are What He Hasn't Done," The Federalist, October 21, 2020, https://thefederalist.com/2020/10/21/tr umps-greatest-accomplishments-are-what-he-hasnt-done/.

63. "Campaign 2020: Vice Presidential Candidates Debate," C-SPAN, aired October 7, 2020, https://www.c-span.org/video/?475794-1/vice-presidential-candidates-de bate.

64. Maureen Groppe, "The Prosecutor vs. the 'King of Sound Bites': Why the Harris-Pence Debate Is No Ordinary VP Faceoff," *USA Today*, October 6, 2020, https:// www.usatoday.com/story/news/politics/elections/2020/10/06/mike-pence-kama la-harris-debate-prosecutor-king-sound-bites/5878293002/.

65. Dan McLaughlin, "Kamala Harris's Dishonesty on Abe Lincoln," *National Review*, October 7, 2020, https://www.nationalreview.com/corner/kamala-harris -dishonesty-on-abe-lincoln/.

66. Ibid.

67. "Harris-Pence Debate Fact Check: What They Said about COVID, Jobs, Taxes," *USA Today*, October 8, 2020, https://www.usatoday.com/story/news/politics/elec tions/2020/10/08/kamala-harris-mike-pence-debate-fact-check-covid-jobs-taxes /5920814002/.

68. "Gross Domestic Product, Third Quarter 2020 (Advance Estimate)," Bureau of Economic Analysis, October 29, 2020, https://www.bea.gov/news/2020/gross-do mestic-product-third-quarter-2020-advance-estimate.

69. Tyler Olson, "Bail Fund Backed by Kamala Harris and Joe Biden Staffers Bailed Out Alleged Child Abuser, Docs Indicate," Fox News, September 17, 2020, https:// www.foxnews.com/politics/bail-fund-backed-by-kamala-harris-and-biden-staf fers-bailed-out-alleged-child-abuser.

70. Ari Fleischer (@AriFleischer), "Page asked Qs re some of Pres. Trump's most controversial statements. Fair enough. But she didn't ask about Biden's you ain't black statement…," Twitter, October 7, 2020, 10:30 p.m., https://twitter.com/Ari Fleischer/status/1314030252193087488.

71. Caitlin O'Kane, "'Mr. Vice President, I'm Speaking': Kamala Harris Rebukes Pence's Interruptions during Debate," CBS News, October 7, 2020, https://www .cbsnews.com/news/kamala-harris-mr-vice-president-pence-interruptions/.

72. Rick Klein (@rickklein), "Unofficial speaking times—Pence: 35:22 Harris: 38:48 via @Kjwalsh_news," Twitter, October 7, 2020, https://twitter.com/rickklein/sta tus/1314032432769884160.

73. Jeremy W. Peters, "Who Won the Vice-Presidential Debate? Experts Weigh In," *New York Times*, October 8, 2020, https://www.nytimes.com/2020/10/08/us/po litics/who-won-the-debate.html.

74. Ibid.

75. Ibid.

76. Brooke Singman, "Trump Says He Won't Participate in Virtual Debate after CPD Announces Changes: 'Not Going to Waste My Time,'" Fox News, October 8, 2020, https://www.foxnews.com/politics/second-trump-biden-debate-will-be-vir tual-organizers-say.

77. Michael Moline, "Storm around Trump-Biden Debate Schedule Continues to Churn," Florida Phoenix, October 9, 2020, https://www.floridaphoenix.com/20 20/10/09/storm-around-trump-biden-debate-schedule-continues-to-churn/.

78. Mollie Hemingway (@MZHemingway), "Interesting tweet from debate moderator Steve Scully to Anthony Saramucci…," Twitter, October 8, 2020, https://twitter .com/MZHemingway/status/1314390761186775042.

79. Bob Dole (@SenatorDole), "The Commission on Presidential Debates is supposedly bipartisan w/ an equal number of Rs and Ds…," Twitter, October 9, 2020, 4:02 p.m., https://twitter.com/SenatorDole/status/1314657560994045952.

80. Newt Gingrich, "Abolish the Debate Commission," *Newsweek*, October 9, 2020, https://www.newsweek.com/abolish-debate-commission-opinion-1537931.

81. "Retire the Debate Commission," *Wall Street Journal*, October 16, 2020, https:// www.wsj.com/articles/retire-the-debate-commission-11602888751.

82. David Bauder, "C-SPAN Suspends Scully after He Admits to Lie about Hack," Associated Press, October 15, 2020, https://apnews.com/article/virus-outbreak-joe -biden-donald-trump-anthony-scaramucci-4657ccd8f5e51d1ce113290b9304f9d5.

83. Donald J. Trump (@realdonaldtrump), "I was right again! Steve Scully just admitted…," Twitter, October 15, 2020, 3:54 p.m. Account has since been suspended, tweet found at https://www.thetrumparchive.com.

84. David Rutz and Collin Anderson, "NBC News 'Undecided' Voters Previously Featured as Biden Supporters on MSNBC," Washington Free Beacon, October 6, 2020, https://freebeacon.com/media/undecided-voters-at-nbc-town-hall-previous ly-told-network-they-were-voting-biden/; Joseph A. Wulfsohn, "ABC Silent after Biden Town Hall Attendees Identified as Ex-Obama Speechwriter, Wife of Prominent Democrat," Fox News, October 16, 2020, https://www.foxnews.com /media/abc-silent-biden-town-hall-attendees-identified-dems.

85. "A Debate Downgrade for Foreign Policy," *Wall Street Journal*, October 20, 2020, https://www.wsj.com/articles/a-debate-downgrade-for-foreign-policy-1160323 6203.

86. "Campaign 2020: Trump-Biden Second Debate," C-SPAN, aired October 22, 2020, https://www.c-span.org/video/?475796-1/trump-biden-debate.

87. Ronna McDaniel, "RNC Statement on Letter to Commission on Presidential Debates," GOP, June 2, 2021, https://gop.com/rnc-statement-on-letter-to-commis sion-on-presidential-debates.

Chapter Seven: "Zuckerberg Should Be in Jail"

1. Allum Bokhari, "Leaked Video: Google Leadership's Dismayed Reaction to Trump Election," Breitbart, September 12, 2018, https://www.breitbart.com/tech/2018 /09/12/leaked-video-google-leaderships-dismayed-reaction-to-trump-election/.

2. Ibid.

3. Allum Bokhari, *#DELETED: Big Tech's Battle to Erase the Trump Movement and Steal the Election* (New York: Center Street, 2020), 29.

4. Ibid., 423.

5. Sheera Frenkel, "Renegade Facebook Employees Form Task Force to Battle Fake News," BuzzFeed, November 14, 2016, https://www.buzzfeednews.com/article /sheerafrenkel/renegade-facebook-employees-form-task-force-to-battle-fake-n.

6. Sam Levin, "Mark Zuckerberg: I Regret Ridiculing Fears over Facebook's Effect on Election," *The Guardian*, September 27, 2017, https://www.theguardian.com /technology/2017/sep/27/mark-zuckerberg-facebook-2016-election-fake-news.

7. Michael Nunez, "Former Facebook Workers: We Routinely Suppressed Conservative News," Gizmodo, May 9, 2016, https://gizmodo.com/former- facebook-workers-we-routinely-suppressed-conser-1775461006.

8. Laura Sydell, "On Its 7th Birthday, Is Twitter Still the 'Free Speech Party'?" National Public Radio, March 21, 2013, https://www.npr.org/sections/alltechcon sidered/2013/03/21/174858681/on-its-7th-birthday-is-twitter-still-the-free-speech -party.

9.   Kristen Purcell et al., "Search Engine Use 2012," Pew Research Center, March 9, 2012, https://www.pewresearch.org/internet/2012/03/09/search-engine-use-2012/.

10.   Allum Bokhari, "'The Good Censor': Leaked Google Briefing Admits Abandonment of Free Speech for 'Safety and Civility,'" Breitbart, October 9, 2018, https://www.breitbart.com/tech/2018/10/09/the-good-censor-leaked-google-briefing-admits-abandonment-of-free-speech-for-safety-and-civility/.

11.   Sarah Lai Stirland, "Obama Campaign Mocks McCain's Computer Illiteracy," *Wired*, September 12, 2008, https://www.wired.com/2008/09/obama-campaign-4/.

12.   Ed Pilkington and Amanda Michel, "Obama, Facebook and the Power of Friendship: The 2012 Data Election," *The Guardian*, February 17, 2012, https://www.theguardian.com/world/2012/feb/17/obama-digital-data-machine-facebook-election.

13.   Olivia Solon, "2016: The Year Facebook Became the Bad Guy," *The Guardian*, December 12, 2016, https://www.theguardian.com/technology/2016/dec/12/facebook-2016-problems-fake-news-censorship.

14.   Pilkington and Michel, "Obama, Facebook and the Power of Friendship."

15.   Laurie Segall, "Obama Campaign Opens Silicon Valley Field Office," CNN, February 17, 2012, https://money.cnn.com/2012/02/17/technology/obama_silicon_valley/index.htm.

16.   Hannah Parry and Chris Spargo, "'They Were on Our Side': Obama Campaign Director Reveals Facebook Allowed Them to Mine American Users' Profiles in 2012 because They Were Supportive of the Democrats," *Daily Mail*, March 19, 2018, https://www.dailymail.co.uk/news/article-5520303/Obama-campaign-director-reveals-Facebook-ALLOWED-data.html.

17.   Sasha Issenberg, *The Victory Lab: The Secret Science of Winning Campaigns* (New York: Broadway Books, 2012, 2013).

18.   Michael D. Shear, "Obama Campaign Releases iPhone App for Canvassing," *New York Times*, July 31, 2012, https://thecaucus.blogs.nytimes.com/2012/07/31/obama-campaign-releases-iphone-app-for-canvassing/.

19.   McKay Coppins, "The Billion-Dollar Disinformation Campaign to Reelect the President," *The Atlantic*, February 10, 2020, https://www.theatlantic.com/magazine/archive/2020/03/the-2020-disinformation-war/605530/.

20.   Barack Obama (@BarackObama), "Even if the methods are new, sowing the seeds of doubt, division, and discord to turn Americans against each other is an old trick…," Twitter, February 11, 2020, 4:05 p.m., https://twitter.com/BarackObama/status/1227337897692495873.

21.   Allum Bokhari, "Project Veritas Video Shows Former Twitter Employees Discussing 'Shadow Banning' Users," Breitbart, January 11, 2018, https://www.breitbart.com/tech/2018/01/11/project-veritas-video-shows-former-twitter-employees-discussing-shadow-banning-users/.

22.   "Twitter Terms of Service," Twitter, June 18, 2020, https://twitter.com/en/tos.

23.   Lucas Nolan, "Google CEO Sundar Pichai Can't Explain Why Trump Tops Image Search for 'Idiot,'" Breitbart, December 11, 2018, https://www.breitbart.com/te

ch/2018/12/11/google-ceo-sundar-pichai-cant-explain-why-trump-tops-image-se
arch-for-idiot/.

24. Allum Bokhari, "'The Smoking Gun': Google Manipulated YouTube Search
Results for Abortion, Maxine Waters, David Hogg," Breitbart, January 16, 2019,
https://www.breitbart.com/tech/2019/01/16/google-youtube-search-blacklist-sm
oking-gun/.

25. Alex Kantrowitz, "Silicon Valley's Right Wing Is Angry and Punching Back,"
BuzzFeed, July 15, 2019, https://www.buzzfeednews.com/article/alexkantrowitz/
how-silicon-valleys-angry-right-wing-sends-its-message-to.

26. Maxim Lott, "Google Pushes Conservative News Sites Far Down Search Lists,"
RealClearPolitics, September 20, 2020, https://www.realclearpolitics.com/articl
es/2020/09/20/google_pushes_conservative_news_sites_far_down_search_lists
_144246.html.

27. Ibid.

28. Peter Hasson, "Exclusive: Google Employees Debated Burying Conservative Media
in Search," The Daily Caller, November 29, 2018, https://dailycaller.com/2018/11
/29/google-censorship-conservative-media/.

29. Robert Epstein, Ronald E. Robertson, David Lazer, and Christo Wilson,
"Suppressing the Search Engine Manipulation Effect (SEME)," *PACM on Human-
Computer Interaction 1*, no. CSCW, article 42 (November 2017), https://dl.acm
.org/doi/pdf/10.1145/3134677.

30. *Why Google Poses a Serious Threat to Democracy, and How to End That Threat,
before the Senate Judiciary Subcommittee on the Constitution*, Testimony by
Robert Epstein before the U.S. Senate Judiciary Subcommittee on the Constitution,
June 16, 2019, https://www.judiciary.senate.gov/imo/media/doc/Epstein%20Testi
mony.pdf.

31. Allum Bokhari, "Robert Epstein: Google Shifted a 'Minimum' of 6 Million Votes
in 2020," Breitbart, November 24, 2020, https://www.breitbart.com/tech/2020
/11/24/robert-epstein-google-shifted-a-minimum-of-6-million-votes-in-2020/

32. Ibid.

33. Abby Ohlheiser and Hayley Tsukayama, "Reddit's CEO Regrets Trolling Trump
Supporters by Secretly Editing Their Posts," *Washington Post,* November 26, 2016,
https://www.washingtonpost.com/news/the-switch/wp/2016/11/26/reddits-ceo
-regrets-trolling-trump-supporters-by-secretly-editing-their-posts/.

34. Todd Spangler, "Twitter Permanently Bans Pro-Trump Meme Creator Carpe
Donktum for Repeated Copyright Violations," *Variety,* June 24, 2020, https://va
riety.com/2020/digital/news/twitter-bans-carpe-donktum-copyright-violations-tr
ump-1234647809/.

35. Ron Coleman (@RonColeman), "Today the New York Supreme Court dismissed
the 'toddlers meme' lawsuit for 'misappropriation' against our client Carpe
Donktum (Logan Cook)…," Twitter, July 9, 2021, 1:53 p.m., https://twitter.com
/RonColeman/status/1413556985144954891

36. James Walker, "Donald Trump Thanks 'My Keyboard Warriors' as His Army of
Trolls and Meme Makers Prepare for Battle in 2020 Election," *Newsweek,* May

15, 2020, https://www.newsweek.com/donald-trump-keyboard-warriors-election-1504290.

37. Gideon Resnick and Ben Collins, "Palmer Luckey: The Facebook Near-Billionaire Secretly Funding Trump's Meme Machine," Daily Beast, September 22, 2016, https://www.thedailybeast.com/palmer-luckey-the-facebook-near-billionaire-secretly-funding-trumps-meme-machine.

38. Kirsten Grind and Keach Hagey, "Why Did Facebook Fire a Top Executive? Hint: It Had Something to Do with Trump," *Wall Street Journal*, November 11, 2018, https://www.wsj.com/articles/why-did-facebook-fire-a-top-executive-hint-it-had-something-to-do-with-trump-1541965245.

39. "Transcript of Mark Zuckerberg's Senate Hearing," *Washington Post*, April 10, 2018, https://www.washingtonpost.com/news/the-switch/wp/2018/04/10/transcript-of-mark-zuckerbergs-senate-hearing/.

40. Grind and Hagey, "Why Did Facebook."

41. Dartunorro Clark, "Twitter Fact Checks Trump's Tweets for the First Time, Calls Mail-In Voting Claim 'Misleading,'" NBC News, May 26, 2020, https://www.nbcnews.com/politics/donald-trump/twitter-fact-checks-trump-s-misleading-tweet-mail-voting-n1215151.

42. Kate Conger and Davey Alba, "Twitter Refutes Inaccuracies in Trump's Tweets about Mail-In Voting," *New York Times*, May 26, 2020, https://www.nytimes.com/2020/05/26/technology/twitter-trump-mail-in-ballots.html.

43. "Trump Makes Unsubstantiated Claim That Mail-in Ballots Will Lead to Voter Fraud," Twitter, May 26, 2020, https://twitter.com/i/events/1265330601034256384?lang=en.

44. Conger and Alba, "Twitter Refutes Inaccuracies."

45. Gilad Edelman, "Twitter Finally Fact-Checked Trump. It's a Bit of a Mess," *Wired*, May 27, 2020, https://www.wired.com/story/twitter-fact-checked-trump-tweets-mail-in-ballots/.

46. Jordan Culver, "Trump Says Violent Minneapolis Protests Dishonor George Floyd's Memory, Twitter Labels 'Shooting' Tweet as 'Glorifying Violence,'" *USA Today*, May 29, 2020, https://www.usatoday.com/story/news/politics/2020/05/28/george-floyd-donald-trump-twitter-jacob-frey-thugs/5281374002/.

47. The White House 45 Archived (@WhiteHouse45), "Twitter, in an email to the White House moments ago, admitted that the very tweet they are censoring does not violate any Twitter rules…," Twitter, May 29, 2020, 3:31 p.m., https://twitter.com/WhiteHouse45/status/1266452015493906435.

48. Ibid.

49. Brett Samuels, "Trump: Any DC Autonomous Zone 'Will Be Met with Serious Force,'" *The Hill*, June 23, 2020, https://thehill.com/homenews/administration/504034-trump-any-dc-autonomous-zone-will-be-met-with-serious-force.

50. Ebony Bowden, "Twitter Defends Blocking Trump Tweets but Not Iran's Ayatollah Khamenei," *New York Post*, July 29, 2020, https://nypost.com/2020/07/29/twitter-defends-blocking-trump-tweets-but-not-irans-ayatollah-khamenei/.

51. Ali Khamenei (@khamenei_ir), "The elimination of the Zionist regime does not mean the massacre of the Jewish ppl...," Twitter, May 21, 2020, 3:26 p.m., https://twitter.com/khamenei_ir/status/1263551872872386562.

52. "World Leaders on Twitter: Principles & Approach," Twitter, October 15, 2019, https://blog.twitter.com/en_us/topics/company/2019/worldleaders2019.

53. Yoel Roth (@yoyoel), Twitter, https://twitter.com/yoyoel?ref_src=twsrc%5Egoogle%7Ctwcamp%5Eserp%7Ctwgr%5Eauthor.

54. Yoel Roth (@yoyoel), "I'm just saying, we fly over those states that voted for a racist tangerine for a reason," Twitter, November 8, 2016, 10:03 p.m., https://twitter.com/yoyoel/status/796186371408789505.

55. Steven Nelson and Natalie Musumeci, "Twitter Fact-Checker Has History of Politically Charged Posts," *New York Post*, May 27, 2020, https://nypost.com/2020/05/27/twitter-fact-checker-has-history-of-politically-charged-posts/.

56. Miranda Devine, "Project Veritas Uncovers 'Ballot Harvesting Fraud' in Minnesota: Devine," *New York Post*, September 27, 2020, https://nypost.com/2020/09/27/project-veritas-uncovers-ballot-harvesting-fraud-in-minnesota/.

57. Ibid.

58. Glenn R. Simpson and Evan Perez, "'Brokers' Exploit Absentee Voters; Elderly Are Top Targets for Fraud," *Wall Street Journal*, December 19, 2000, https://www.wsj.com/articles/SB97718372846852342.

59. Jonathan Dienst and Joe Valiquette, "Corruption Allegations Keep Growing in Paterson Vote-By-Mail Election," NBC News, May 13, 2020, https://www.nbcnewyork.com/news/local/corruption-allegations-keep-growing-in-paterson-vote-by-mail-election/2416111/.

60. Maggie Astor, "Project Veritas Video Was a 'Coordinated Disinformation Campaign,' Researchers Say," *New York Times*, September 29, 2020, https://www.nytimes.com/2020/09/29/us/politics/project-veritas-ilhan-omar.html.

61. Ibid.

62. Ibid.

63. Adam Goldman and Mark Mazzetti, "Ex-Spy Was Central to Project Veritas Hiring Effort, Testimony Shows," *New York Times*, October 21, 2020, https://www.nytimes.com/2020/10/21/us/politics/project-veritas-spy.html.

64. Camille Caldera, "Fact Check: No Proof of Alleged Voter Fraud Scheme or Connection to Rep. Ilhan Omar," *USA Today*, October 16, 2020, https://www.usatoday.com/story/news/factcheck/2020/10/16/fact-check-project-veritas-no-proof-voter-fraud-scheme-link-ilhan-omar/3584614001/.

65. Thomas Moore, "New York Times Defends Itself against Project Veritas Defamation Suit," *The Hill*, April 13, 2021, https://thehill.com/homenews/media/547995-new-york-times-defends-itself-against-project-veritas-defamation-suit.

66. Mark Hemingway, "NYT's Libel Defense: No Need for Opinion/Fact Labeling," RealClearPolitics, March 25, 2021, https://www.realclearpolitics.com/articles/2021/03/25/nyts_libel_defense_no_need_for_opinionfact_labeling_145476.html.

67. *Project Veritas v. The New York Times Company*, NY Slip Op. 31908 (U) (New York Supreme Court of Westchester County, 2021), https://assets.ctfassets.net/sy

q3snmxclc9/maEy58HDFCR7qdtFObWXx/46c075c522acef6a169b7ce051f895
5c/Order_denying_motion_to_dismiss.pdf.

68. Facebook (@Facebook), "Instead, we demote individual posts etc. that are reported by FB users and rated as false by fact checkers…," Twitter, July 12, 2018, 2:34 p.m., https://twitter.com/Facebook/status/1017477296943349760.

69. Ibid.

70. Molly Ball, "The Secret History of the Shadow Campaign That Saved the 2020 Election," *Time*, February 4, 2021, https://time.com/5936036/secret-2020-election-campaign/.

71. Barton Swaim, "'Pelosi' Review: The Speaker's Amanuensis," *Wall Street Journal*, May 4, 2020, https://www.wsj.com/articles/pelosi-review-the-speakers-amanuensis-11588630295.

72. Ball, "The Secret History."

73. Ibid.

74. Ibid.

75. "Ian Bassin," Influence Watch, n.d., https://www.influencewatch.org/person/ian-bassin/.

76. Ball, "The Secret History."

77. Ibid.

78. Ibid.

79. Ibid.

80. Ibid.

81. Ibid.

82. Ibid.

83. Ibid.

84. Ibid.

85. Issenberg, *Victory Lab*, 305.

86. Ball, "The Secret History."

87. Ibid.

88. Ibid.

89. Ibid.

90. "CEO Mark Zuckerberg on How Facebook Handled Election," ABC News Live on Facebook, November 17, 2020, https://www.facebook.com/ABCNewsLive/videos/383887209491187/.

91. Ball, "The Secret History."

92. Michael Scherer, "Mark Zuckerberg and Priscilla Chan Donate $100 Million More to Election Administrators, Despite Conservative Pushback," *Washington Post*, October 13, 2020, https://www.washingtonpost.com/politics/zuckerberg-chan-elections-facebook/2020/10/12/0e07de94-0cba-11eb-8074-0e943a91bf08_story.html.

93. "Center for Election Innovation & Research," Influence Watch, n.d., https://www.influencewatch.org/non-profit/center-for-election-innovation-research/.

94. David Plouffe, *A Citizen's Guide to Beating Donald Trump* (New York: Penguin Press, 2020), 111.

95. "Our Leadership" Chan Zuckerberg Initiative, n.d., https://chanzuckerberg.com/about/leaders/.

96. Brian Fung, "Inside the Democratic Party's Hogwarts for Digital Wizardry," *Washington Post*, July 8, 2014, https://www.washingtonpost.com/news/the-switch/wp/2014/07/08/inside-the-democratic-partys-hogwarts-for-digital-wizardry/.

97. "New Organization Institute (NOI)," Influence Watch, n.d., https://www.influencewatch.org/non-profit/new-organizing-institute/.

98. "COVID-19 Response Grants," Center for Tech and Civic Life, n.d., https://www.techandciviclife.org/our-work/election-officials/grants/.

99. Ibid.

100. Tom Scheck et al., "How Private Money from Facebook's CEO Saved the 2020 Election," National Public Radio, December 8, 2020, https://www.npr.org/2020/12/08/943242106/how-private-money-from-facebooks-ceo-saved-the-2020-election.

101. Nicholas Riccardi, "'Not Plan A': Charities Are Stepping Up to Pay for Elections," Associated Press, September 16, 2020, https://apnews.com/article/technology-elections-denver-mark-zuckerberg-election-2020-92257bbc1fefd9ed0e18861e5b5913f6.

102. Ibid.

103. Todd Shepherd, "Zuckerberg-Funded 2020 Election Grants Skewed Heavily toward PA's 'Blue' Counties," Broad and Liberty, April 13, 2021, https://broadandliberty.com/2021/04/13/zuckerberg-funded-grants-skewed-toward-blue-counties/.

104. Hayden Dublois and Tyler Lamensky, *Zuckerberg Went Down to Georgia: How Zuckerbucks Influenced the Georgia Elections* (Foundation for Government Integrity: May 24, 2021), https://thefga.org/wp-content/uploads/2021/05/How-Zuckerbucks-Influenced-the-Georgia-Elections.pdf, 4.

105. Ibid., 4.

106. Ibid., 7.

107. Ibid.

108. Ibid., 5.

109. Ibid.

110. Ibid., 6.

111. Ibid., 7.

112. Ibid.

113. "QuickFacts Florida," United States Census Bureau, n.d., https://www.census.gov/quickfacts/FL.

114. Hayden Dublois and Nic Horton, "How 'Zuckerbucks' Infiltrated & Influenced the 2020 Florida Election," Foundation for Government Accountability, February 25, 2021, https://thefga.org/wp-content/uploads/2021/02/Florida-Zuckerbucks_2020_election.pdf.

115. Scott Walter, "Zuckerberg's Return on Investment in Pennsylvania," Capital Research Center, May 20, 2021, https://capitalresearch.org/article/zuckerbergs-return-on-investment-in-pennsylvania/.

116. Ibid.

117. Ibid.

118. Ibid.

119. "Center for Tech and Civic Life," Influence Watch, n.d., https://www.influencewa tch.org/non-profit/center-for-tech-and-civic-life/.

120. "2010 Wisconsin Code Chapter 6. The Electors. 6. 84 Construction," Justia US Law, n.d., https://law.justia.com/codes/wisconsin/2010/6/6.84.html.

121. Celestine Jeffreys to Tiana Epps-Johnson, email, July 13, 2020, https://greenbay wi.gov/ArchiveCenter/ViewFile/Item/278, 221.

122. Tiana Epps-Johnson to Celestine Jeffreys, email, July 27, 2020, https://greenbay wi.gov/ArchiveCenter/ViewFile/Item/278, 8.

123. "The Behavioral Side of COVID-19," Ideas42, n.d., https://www.ideas42.org/.

124. Andrea Cordova McCadney, Derek Tisler, and Lawrence Norden, "2020's Lessons for Election Security," Brennan Center for Justice, December 16, 2020, https:// www.brennancenter.org/our-work/research-reports/2020s-lessons-election-secu rity.

125. "Center for Civic Design," Influence Watch, n.d., https://www.influencewatch.org /non-profit/center-for-civic-design/.

126. "Elections and Voting," U.S. Digital Response, n.d., https://www.usdigitalrespon se.org/our-projects/elections-and-voting/.

127. Ibid.

128. Ibid.

129. Ibid.

130. Ibid.

131. National Vote at Home Institute, n.d., https://voteathome.org/.

132. "Emails Show Likely Illegality in the Way Milwaukee Ran the Presidential Election," MacIver Institute, May 7, 2021, https://www.maciverinstitute.com/20 21/05/emails-show-likely-illegality-in-the-way-milwaukee-ran-the-presidential-elec tion/.

133. Ibid.

134. Ibid.

135. Ibid.

136. Ibid.

137. Ibid.

138. "The Verified Complaint of Richard Carlstedt, Sandra Duckett, James Fitzgerald, et al. to the Wisconsin Elections Commission against Meagan Wolfe, Eric Genrich, Celestine Jeffries, et al.," April 2021, https://legis.wisconsin.gov/assembly/22/bra ndtjen/media/1467/wisconsin-elections-commission-complaint-egk-signed.pdf.

139. Ibid.

140. Dan O' Donnell, "Green Bay's Handling of Presidential Election Violated at Least Five Laws," MacIver Institute, March 12, 2021, https://www.maciverinstitute.com /2021/03/green-bays-handling-of-presidential-election-violated-at-least-five-laws/.

141. M. D. Kittle, "Special Investigation: Infiltrating the Election," *Wisconsin Spotlight*, March 9, 2021, https://wisconsinspotlight.com/special-investigation-infiltrating -the-election/.

142. Ibid.

143. Ibid.

144. Declaration of Andrew Kloster, Scribd, n.d., https://www.scribd.com/document /498215405/Affidavit-Kloster.

145. Dan O' Donnell, "Wisconsin Clerks May Have Unlawfully Altered Thousands of Absentee Ballots," Newstalk 1130, November 7, 2020, https://newstalk1130.ihe art.com/featured/common-sense-central/content/2020-11-07-wisconsin-clerks -may-have-unlawfully-altered-thousands-of-absentee-ballots/.

146. Ben Krumholz, "Elections Chief Testifies in Second Hearing on Green Bay's Elections," Fox 11, March 31, 2021, https://fox11online.com/news/election/electi ons-chief-no-complaints-about-green-bay-consultant?src=link.

Chapter Eight: Burying Biden Corruption

1.   Katie Rogers, "At Cafe Milano, Politicians Are Served Dinner and Peace of Mind," *New York Times*, April 8, 2017, https://www.nytimes.com/2017/04/08/style/cafe -milano-donald-trump-washington.html.

2.   Roxanne Roberts, "Cafe Milano, Washington's Ultimate Gathering Hole, Turns 25 with VIP Party," *Washington Post*, November 12, 2017, https://www.washing tonpost.com/news/reliable-source/wp/2017/11/12/cafe-milano-washingtons-ul timate-gathering-hole-turns-25-with-vip-party/.

3.   Josh Boswell, "'Dad Will Be There but Keep That between Us for Now': Emails Reveal Joe Biden DID Meet with Hunter's Foreign Business Partners While He Was VP during a Dinner Organized by His Son to Introduce Potential Clients to His Powerful Father," *Daily Mail*, May 26, 2021, https://www.dailymail.co.uk/ne ws/article-9622767/Emails-reveal-Joe-Biden-DID-meet-Hunters-business-partne rs-VP.html.

4.   Emma-Jo Morris and Gabrielle Fonrouge, "Smoking-Gun Email Reveals How Hunter Biden Introduced Ukrainian Businessman to VP Dad," *New York Post*, October 14, 2020, https://nypost.com/2020/10/14/email-reveals-how-hunter-bi den-introduced-ukrainian-biz-man-to-dad/.

5.   Steven Nelson, Juliegrace Brufke, and Bruce Golding, "Joe Biden Was a 'Regular' at DC Hotspot Where He Met Hunter's Kazakh Associates," *New York Post*, May 28, 2021, https://nypost.com/2021/05/28/joe-biden-regular-at-dc-hotspot-where -he-met-hunters-associates/.

6.   Ebony Bowden, "Photo Shows Joe Biden Meeting Hunter's Alleged Business Partner From Kazakhstan," *New York Post*, October 20, 2020, https://nypost.com /2020/10/20/photo-biden-meets-hunters-alleged-partner-from-kazakhstan/.

7.   Mark Moore, "Joe and Hunter Biden Golfed with Ukraine Gas Executive in 2014," *New York Post*, October 1, 2019, https://nypost.com/2019/10/01/joe-and-hunter -biden-golfed-with-ukraine-gas-executive-in-2014/.

8. Morris and Fonrouge, "Smoking-Gun Emails"; Marshall Cohen et al., "US Authorities Investigate If Recently Published Emails Are Tied to Russian Disinformation Effort Targeting Biden," CNN, October 16, 2020, https://www.cnn.com/2020/10/16/politics/russian-disinformation-investigation/index.html.

9. Noah Manskar, "Twitter, Facebook Censor Post over Hunter Biden Expose," *New York Post*, October 14, 2020, https://nypost.com/2020/10/14/facebook-twitter-block-the-post-from-posting/.

10. "Fact: Big Media and Big Tech Stole the 2020 Election," NewsBusters, November 9, 2020, https://www.newsbusters.org/blogs/nb/nb-staff/2020/11/09/fact-big-media-and-big-tech-stole-2020-election.

11. Ibid.

12. Adam Entous, "Will Hunter Biden Jeopardize His Father's Campaign?," *New Yorker*, July 1, 2019, https://www.newyorker.com/magazine/2019/07/08/will-hunter-biden-jeopardize-his-fathers-campaign.

13. "Adam Entous," *New Yorker*, n.d., https://www.newyorker.com/contributors/adam-entous?source=search_google_dsa_paid&gclid=Cj0KCQjwxJqHBhC4ARIsAChq4avneP8G-22nkDd-m1rIIczdNasoeiLQ6lUgWvDflqwrSxorUxHiZxwaAo3-EALw_wcB.

14. Entous, "Will Hunter Biden Jeopardize His Father's Campaign?"

15. Colleen McCain Nelson and Julian E. Barnes, "Biden's Son Hunter Discharged from Navy Reserve after Failing Cocaine Test," *Wall Street Journal*, October 16, 2014, https://www.wsj.com/articles/bidens-son-hunter-discharged-from-navy-reserve-after-failing-cocaine-test-1413499657.

16. Randall Chase, "Estranged Wife: Biden Son Wasted Money on Drugs, Prostitutes," Associated Press, March 2, 2017, https://apnews.com/article/dover-joe-biden-us-news-dc-wire-71369b3f0f154fe0b8ec6db7dca57c42?utm_campaign=socialflow&utm_source=twitter&utm_medium=apsouthregion.

17. Bruce Golding, "Book Details How Hunter Biden's Wife Found Out about Affair with Beau's Widow," *New York Post*, March 30, 2021, https://nypost.com/2021/03/30/book-details-how-hunter-bidens-wife-found-out-about-affair-with-beaus-widow/.

18. Hunter Biden, *Beautiful Things* (New York: Gallery Books, 2021), 182.

19. Madison Dibble, "Arkansas Woman Impregnated by Hunter Biden Was Washington DC Stripper Called Dallas," *Washington Examiner*, November 27, 2019, https://www.washingtonexaminer.com/news/arkansas-woman-impregnated-by-hunter-biden-was-washington-dc-stripper-called-dallas.

20. Ibid.

21. Paul LeBlanc and Jessica Dean, "Hunter Biden Agrees to Pay Child Support in Paternity Case," CNN, January 27, 2020, https://www.cnn.com/2020/01/27/politics/hunter-biden-paternity-case-child-support/index.html.

22. Tim Hains, "Matt Gaetz: Why Would Burisma Hire Hunter Biden after History of Crack Cocaine Use?" RealClearPolitics, December 12, 2019, https://www.realclearpolitics.com/video/2019/12/12/matt_gaetz_why_would_burisma_hire_hunter_biden_after_history_of_crack_cocaine_use.html.

23. Ibid.
24. Entous, "Will Hunter Biden Jeopardize His Father's Campaign?"
25. Ibid.
26. Ibid.
27. Ibid.
28. Ibid.
29. Ibid.
30. Ibid.
31. Ibid.
32. Ibid.
33. "Allen Stanford Found Guilty in $7bn Ponzi Scheme," BBC, March 6, 2012, https://www.bbc.com/news/world-us-canada-17274724.
34. Jenny Strasburg and Thom Weidlich, "Biden's Son Sues Ex-Partner Lobbyist, with Senator's Brother, Alleges Fraud in Fund Buyout," *Washington Post*, February 21, 2007, https://www.washingtonpost.com/archive/business/2007/02/21/bidens-son -sues-ex-partner-span-classbankheadlobbyist-with-senators-brother-alleges-fraud -in-fund-buyoutspan/6e774f6d-b02d-4199-8664-7ebe44523563/.
35. Peter Schweizer, *Secret Empires: How the American Political Class Hides Corruption and Enriches Family and Friends* (New York: Harper, 2018), 396.
36. Ibid.
37. Daniel Hough, "China's Princelings Aren't Charming the New Middle Class," *The Conversation*, October 7, 2013, https://theconversation.com/chinas-prince lings-arent-charming-the-new-middle-class-18634.
38. Schweizer, *Secret Empires*, 376.
39. Ibid.
40. Lucien Bruggeman, "The Allegations about Hunter Biden's Business Dealings in China, Explained," ABC News, October 8, 2019, https://abcnews.go.com/Polit ics/allegations-hunter-bidens-business-dealings-china-explained/story?id=6611 1282.
41. "Bohai Harvest RST Shanghai Equity Investment Fund Management Co Ltd," Bloomberg, n.d., https://www.bloomberg.com/profile/company/1065971D:CH.
42. Ibid.
43. Tim Hains, "Schweizer: Obama Made Biden Pointman on Ukraine Two Months before Son Joined Burisma Board," RealClearPolitics, October 4, 2019, https:// www.realclearpolitics.com/video/2019/10/04/schweizer_obama_made_biden_po intman_on_ukraine_two_months_before_son_joined_burisma_board.html.
44. Mark Hemingway, "Hunter Biden's Burisma Post Had a Troubling Conflict, Watchdog Says," RealClearInvestigations, November 19, 2019, https://www.real clearinvestigations.com/articles/2019/11/19/hunter_bidens_burisma_post_had _a_troubling_conflict_watchdog_says_121260.html.
45. Ian Schwartz, "Joe Biden on Hunter: 'I Didn't Know He Was on the Board of That Company,'" RealClearPolitics, November 2, 2019, https://www.realclearpolitics .com/video/2019/11/02/joe_biden_on_hunter_i_didnt_know_he_was_on_the_bo ard_of_that_company.html.

46. Andrew Duehren and Dustin Volz, "Hunter Biden's Ukraine Work Raised Concerns with Obama Officials, GOP-Led Probe Confirms," *Wall Street Journal*, September 23, 2020, https://www.wsj.com/articles/republican-probe-finds-hunter-bidens-ukraine-work-raised-concerns-with-obama-officials-11600859178.

47. Javier E. David, "Ukraine Gas Producer Appoints Biden's Son to Board," CNBC, May 13, 2014, https://www.cnbc.com/2014/05/13/bidens-son-joins-ukraine-gas-companys-board-of-directors.html.

48. Michael Scherer, "Ukrainian Employer of Joe Biden's Son Hires a D.C. Lobbyist," *Time*, July 7, 2014, https://time.com/2964493/ukraine-joe-biden-son-hunter-burisma/.

49. Mark Hemingway, "Hunter Biden's Burisma Post Had a Troubling Conflict, Watchdog Says," RealClearInvestigations, November 19, 2019, https://www.realclearinvestigations.com/articles/2019/11/19/hunter_bidens_burisma_post_had_a_troubling_conflict_watchdog_says_121260.html.

50. Hemingway, "Hunter Biden's Burisma Post Had a Troubling Conflict."

51. James F. Reda and Arthur J. Gallagher & Co., "Board Pay—Not Just a Public Company Concern," Harvard Law School Forum on Corporate Governance, August 1, 2017, https://corpgov.law.harvard.edu/2017/08/01/board-pay-not-just-a-public-company-concern/.

52. Ibid.

53. Hemingway, "Hunter Biden's Burisma Post Had a Troubling Conflict."

54. Jessica Donati, "Firm Hired by Ukraine's Burisma Tried to Use Hunter Biden as Leverage, Documents Show," *Wall Street Journal*, November 5, 2019, https://www.wsj.com/articles/firm-hired-by-ukraines-burisma-tried-to-use-hunter-biden-as-leverage-documents-show-11573009615.

55. Ibid.

56. Camille Caldera, "Fact Check: Biden Leveraged $1B in Aid to Ukraine to Oust Corrupt Prosecutor, Not to Help His Son," *USA Today*, October 21, 2020, https://www.usatoday.com/story/news/factcheck/2020/10/21/fact-check-joe-biden-leveraged-ukraine-aid-oust-corrupt-prosecutor/5991434002/.

57. Ibid.

58. Edward J. Markey, Ron Wyden, Jeanne Shaheen, and Christopher S. Murphy to President Barack Obama, June 27, 2014, https://www.markey.senate.gov/imo/media/doc/2014-06-27_PresidentObama_Ukraine_energy.pdf.

59. Schweizer, *Secret Empires*, 70.

60. Ibid.

61. Kenneth P. Vogel and Iuliia Mendel, "Biden Faces Conflict of Interest Questions That Are Being Promoted by Trump and Allies," *New York Times*, May 1, 2019, https://www.nytimes.com/2019/05/01/us/politics/biden-son-ukraine.html.

62. U.S. Senate Committee on Homeland Security and Governmental Affairs and U.S. Senate Committee on Finance Majority Staff Report, *Hunter Biden, Burisma, and Corruption: The Impact on U.S. Government Policy and Related Concerns*, September 23, 2020, https://www.hsgac.senate.gov/imo/media/doc/HSGAC_Finance_Report_FINAL.pdf.

63. U.S. Senate Committee on Homeland Security and U.S. Senate Committee on Finance Majority Staff Report, 5.
64. Karoun Demirjian, Tom Hamburger, Paul Sonne, "GOP Senators' Report Calls Hunter Biden's Board Position with Ukraine Firm 'Problematic' but Doesn't Show It Changed U.S. Policy," *Washington Post*, September 23, 2020, https://www.washingtonpost.com/national-security/senate-gop-report-calls-hunter-bidens-board-position-problematic-but-offers-few-specific-examples-it-changed-obama-administration-policy/2020/09/23/4b66d41e-fd44-11ea-9ceb-061d646d9c67_story.html.
65. "Read The Full Transcript from the First Presidential Debate between Joe Biden and Donald Trump," *USA Today*, September 30, 2020, https://www.usatoday.com/story/news/politics/elections/2020/09/30/presidential-debate-read-full-transcript-first-debate/3587462001/.
66. Doug Stanglin, "Fact Check: Claims That Hunter Biden Received $3.5M from Russia Are Unproven, Lack Context," *USA Today*, October 1, 2020, https://www.usatoday.com/story/news/factcheck/2020/10/01/fact-check-unproven-claims-hunter-biden-got-3-5-m-russia/3586861001/.
67. Jon Greenberg, "Examining Trump Claim That Hunter Biden Got $3.5 Million from Wife of Moscow Ex-Mayor," PolitiFact, September 29, 2020, https://www.politifact.com/article/2020/sep/30/examining-trump-claim-hunter-biden-got-35-million-/.
68. Ibid.
69. Morris and Fonrouge, "Smoking-Gun Emails."
70. Ibid.
71. Emma-Jo Morris and Gabrielle Fonrouge, "Emails Reveal How Hunter Biden Tried to Cash in Big on Behalf of Family with Chinese Firm," *New York Post*, October 15, 2020, https://nypost.com/2020/10/15/emails-reveal-how-hunter-biden-tried-to-cash-in-big-with-chinese-firm/.
72. Ibid.
73. Ebony Bowden, "Hunter Biden Emailed Best Wishes from the 'Entire' Family in $10M Chinese Tycoon Ask," *New York Post*, December 16, 2020, https://nypost.com/2020/12/16/best-wishes-from-the-entire-biden-family-hunter-emailed-in-10m-chinese-request/.
74. Morris, "Emails Reveal How Hunter Biden Tried to Cash in Big."
75. Ibid.
76. Natasha Bertrand, "Hunter Biden Story Is Russian Disinfo, Dozens of Former Intel Officials Say," *Politico*, October 19, 2020, https://www.politico.com/news/2020/10/19/hunter-biden-story-russian-disinfo-430276.
77. Ibid.
78. Jim Clapper et al., "Public Statement on the Hunter Biden Emails," *Politico*, October 19, 2020, https://www.politico.com/f/?id=00000175-4393-d7aa-af77-579f9b330000.
79. Julian E. Barnes, Eric Schmitt, and Maggie Haberman, "Trump Said to Be Warned That Giuliani Was Conveying Russian Disinformation," *New York Times*,

October 15, 2020, https://www.nytimes.com/2020/10/15/us/politics/giuliani-rus
sian-disinformation.html.

80. Ibid.

81. Brian Flood, "NPR Slammed for Dismissing Coverage of Hunter Biden Laptop
Scandal as a 'Waste of Time,'" Fox News, October 22, 2020, https://www.foxne
ws.com/media/npr-slammed-dismissing-hunter-biden-laptop-scandal.

82. Jason Koebler, "We Are Collectively Losing Touch with Reality and It's Extremely
Obvious," *Vice*, October 15, 2020, https://www.vice.com/en/article/88a44v/new
-york-posts-hunter-biden-laptop-story-explained.

83. Anne Applebaum, "You're Not Supposed to Understand the Rumors about Biden,"
The Atlantic, October 23, 2020, https://www.theatlantic.com/ideas/archive/2020
/10/smears-against-biden-dont-need-make-any-sense/616824/.

84. Stephen L. Miller (@redsteeze), "Hang it in The Louvre," Twitter, December 10,
2020, 10:53 a.m., https://twitter.com/redsteeze/status/1337062913333399554/ph
oto/1.

85. Andy Stone (@andymstone), "While I will intentionally not link to the New York
Post, I want to be clear that this story is eligible to be fact checked…," Twitter,
October 14, 2020, 11:10 a.m., https://twitter.com/andymstone/status/131639590
2479872000.

86. Andy Stone (@andymstone), "This is part of our standard process to reduce the
spread of misinformation. We temporarily reduce distribution…," Twitter, October
14, 2020, 1:00 p.m., https://twitter.com/andymstone/status/1316423671314026496.

87. Jordan Davidson, "Twitter Blocks Users from Linking to the New York Post's
Bombshell Hunter Biden Report," The Federalist, October 14, 2020, https://the
federalist.com/2020/10/14/twitter-blocks-users-from-linking-to-the-new-york-po
sts-bombshell-hunter-biden-report/.

88. Brian Flood, "These Five People Are Allowed to Tweet but One of America's Oldest
Newspapers Can't," Fox News, October 21, 2020, https://www.foxnews.com
/media/twitter-allows-farrakhan-spencer-dictators-new-york-post-censored.

89. Joseph A. Wulfsohn, "ABC's George Stephanopoulos Avoids Explosive Hunter
Biden Report during Biden Town Hall," Fox News, October 15, 2020, https://
www.foxnews.com/media/abc-george-stephanopoulos-avoids-hunter-biden-joe
-biden-town-hall.

90. Joseph A. Wulfsohn, "CNN's Brian Stelter Says Twitter, Facebook Aren't Doing
Enough to Censor Right-wing 'Nastiness,'" Fox News, October 21, 2020, https://
www.foxnews.com/media/cnn-brian-stelter-twitter-facebook-censor-nastiness.

91. Ibid.

92. Ben Smith, "Trump Had One Last Story to Sell. The Wall Street Journal Wouldn't
Buy It," *New York Times*, October 25, 2020, https://www.nytimes.com/2020/10
/25/business/media/hunter-biden-wall-street-journal-trump.html.

93. "Tony Bobulinski Statement on Hunter Biden," C-SPAN, October 22, 2020, https://
www.c-span.org/video/?477307-1/tony-bobulinski-statement-hunter-biden.

94. Jerry Dunleavy, "Hunter Biden Falsely Claims Intelligence Community Concluded
Laptop Saga Was 'Russia Disinformation,'" *Washington Examiner*, April 9, 2021,

https://www.washingtonexaminer.com/news/hunter-biden-falsely-claims-intelli
gence-community-concluded-laptop-saga-russian-disinformation.

95. Andrew Duehren and James T. Areddy, "Hunter Biden's Ex-Business Partner
Alleges Father Knew about Venture," *Wall Street Journal*, October 23, 2020,
https://www.wsj.com/articles/hunter-bidens-ex-business-partner-alleges-father-kn
ew-about-venture-11603421247.

96. Ibid.

97. Charles Davis, "No Evidence for Trump Claim That Joe Biden Earned Money in
China, According to the Wall Street Journal, Contradicting Its Editorial Section,"
Business Insider, October 23, 2020, https://www.businessinsider.com/no-eviden
ce-trump-claim-joe-biden-earned-money-in-china-2020-10.

98. Jennifer Epstein (@jeneps), "This article will run in tomorrow's print WS...,"
Twitter, October 22, 2020, 11:07 p.m., https://twitter.com/jeneps/status/131947
5403002707968.

99. Caleb Ecarma, "The Wall Street Journal Cold War Explodes into the Limelight,"
Vanity Fair, October 23, 2020, https://www.vanityfair.com/news/2020/10/wall
-street-journal-cold-war-explodes-over-hunter-biden.

100. Jeffrey A. Trachtenberg, "WSJ Journalists Ask Publisher for Clearer Distinction
between News and Opinion Content," *Wall Street Journal*, July 21, 2020, https://
www.wsj.com/articles/wsj-journalists-ask-publisher-for-clearer-distinction-betwe
en-news-and-opinion-content-11595349198.

101. Kyle Cheney and Andrew Desiderio, "How 'Obamagate' and Hunter's 'Laptop
from Hell' Fizzled," *Politico*, November 8, 2020, https://www.politico.com/news
/2020/11/08/obamagate-hunter-biden-laptop-434984.

102. Sam Stein (@samstein), "According to Biden campaign metrics, online chatter
about the Hunter Biden story during the election's last week was greater...,"
Twitter, November 16, 2020, 11:34 p.m., https://twitter.com/samstein/status/132
8375805735481344.

103. Eric Tucker, Michael Balsamo, and Jonathan Lemire, "Hunter Biden Tax Problem
Examining Chinese Business Dealings," Associated Press, December 9, 2020,
https://apnews.com/article/hunter-biden-federal-tax-investigation-87c200c919aa
61396b5d43077bc5b0ff.

104. Erin Banco, Scott Bixby, and Sam Stein, "The Seeds of Hunter Biden's Current
Legal Woes Were Found on His Laptop," The Daily Beast, December 9, 2020,
https://www.thedailybeast.com/the-seeds-of-hunter-bidens-current-legal-woes-we
re-found-on-his-stolen-laptop.

105. Ibid.

106. Aaron Feis, "Tweet-a-Culpa: Twitter CEO Jack Dorsey Admits Post Lockout Was
'a Mistake,' *New York Post*, November 17, 2020, https://nypost.com/2020/11/17
/jack-dorsey-admits-lockout-of-the-post-was-a-mistake/.

107. Shane Goldmacher and Adam Nagourney, "Welcome to November. For Trump,
the October Surprise Never Came," *New York Times*, November 3, 2020, https://
www.nytimes.com/2020/11/01/us/politics/trump-october.html.

Chapter Nine: Fourteen Seconds Too Late

1. Anita Kumar, "Trump Readies Thousands of Attorneys for Election Fight," *Politico*, September 27, 2020, https://www.politico.com/news/2020/09/27/trump-legal-network-election-day-fight-422035.
2. John Kruzel, "Trump, Biden Build Legal Armies for Electoral Battlefield," *The Hill*, July 27, 2020, https://thehill.com/regulation/court-battles/508962-trump-biden-build-legal-armies-for-electoral-battlefield.
3. Annie Linskey, "Biden Predicts That Trump Will Try to 'Indirectly Steal' the Election," *Washington Post*, July 24, 2020, https://www.washingtonpost.com/politics/biden-predicts-that-trump-will-try-to-indirectly-steal-the-election/2020/07/23/cc55fe98-cd3c-11ea-91f1-28aca4d833a0_story.html.
4. Dianne Gallagher, "The Two Republican Members of the North Carolina State Board of Elections Abruptly Resign," CNN, September 24, 2020, https://www.cnn.com/2020/09/24/politics/north-carolina-board-of-elections/index.html.
5. Lindsay Marchello, "Election Lawsuit Challenges North Carolina's Absentee-by-Mail Requirements," *Carolina Journal*, May 8, 2020, https://www.carolinajournal.com/news-article/election-lawsuit-challenges-north-carolinas-absentee-by-mail-requirements/.
6. Tim Moore, "N.C. Voters and Lawmakers File Federal Suit to Stop 'Sue-and-Settle' Elections Scam by AG Stein and Cooper's Campaign Lawyer," Speaker Tim Moore North Carolina House of Representatives, September 26, 2020, http://speakertimmoore.com/n-c-voters-lawmakers-file-federal-suit-stop-sue-settle-elections-scam-ag-stein-coopers-campaign-lawyer/.
7. Mark Sherman and Jonathan Drew, "Supreme Court Leaves NC Absentee Ballot Deadline at Nov. 12," Associated Press, October 28, 2020, https://apnews.com/article/election-2020-samuel-alito-amy-coney-barrett-north-carolina-elections-4cb4c214446bcfadbd73dafca9353701.
8. "County Boards of Elections Now Contacting Voters with Absentee Ballot Deficiencies," North Carolina State Board of Elections, October 19, 2020, https://www.ncsbe.gov/news/press-releases/2020/10/19/county-boards-elections-now-contacting-voters-absentee-ballot.
9. A. P. Dillon, "Lawmakers Seek to End 'Sue and Settle' Agreements," *North State Journal*, March 31, 2021, https://nsjonline.com/article/2021/03/lawmakers-seek-to-end-sue-and-settle-agreements/.
10. "The First Presidential Debate," C-SPAN, September 29, 2020, https://www.c-span.org/debates/?debate=first.
11. Michael Decourcy Hinds, "Vote-Fraud Ruling Shifts Pennsylvania Senate," *New York Times*, February 19, 1994, https://www.nytimes.com/1994/02/19/us/vote-fraud-ruling-shifts-pennsylvania-senate.html.
12. "Philly Man Charged in ACORN Fraud Case," Trib Live, October 23, 2008, https://archive.triblive.com/news/philly-man-charged-in-acorn-fraud-case/.
13. Ibid.
14. Carrie Johnson, "Justice Dept. Finds No Malfeasance in Black Panther Voter Intimidation Case," National Public Radio, March 29, 2011, https://www.npr.org

/sections/thetwo-way/2011/03/29/134962673/justice-dept-finds-no-malfeasance
-in-black-panther-voter-intimidation-case.

15. Susan Cornwell, "Complaints about Voter IDs, Ballots, Long Lines in Election,"
    Reuters, November 6, 2012, https://www.reuters.com/article/us-usa-campaign-ir
    regularities-idUSBRE8A51E720121106.

16. Larry Mendte, "Did Dead People Vote in Philadelphia?," *Philadelphia Magazine*,
    November 16, 2012, http://www.phillymag.com/news/2012/11/16/election-dead
    -people-vote-philadelphia/.

17. Holly Otterbein, "Overheard at Philly Poling Place: No GOP Votes 'on My
    Machine!,'" *Philadelphia Inquirer*, January 24, 2018, https://www.inquirer.com
    /philly/news/politics/voter-fraud-philadelphia-197th-special-election-20180124
    .html.

18. "Ex-Elections Judge Admits Taking Bribes to Stuff Ballot Box," Associated Press,
    May 21, 2020, https://apnews.com/article/pa-state-wire-primary-elections-electi
    ons-philadelphia-4caee44c73736e54fdbf4ab052c52fe2.

19. Ellie Kaufman, "Expelled from House In 1980, Ex-Congressmen Now Charged
    with Bribery and Vote Manipulation from 2014 to 2016," CNN, July 23, 2020,
    https://www.cnn.com/2020/07/23/politics/michael-myers-charged-in-voting-scam
    /index.html.

20. Jeremy Roebuck, "A Former Pa. Congressman Caught in 1970s Abscam Sting Has
    Been Indicted Again—This Time for Election Fraud," *Philadelphia Inquirer*, July
    23, 2020, https://www.inquirer.com/news/ozzie-myers-indicted-voter-fraud-phila
    delphia-domenick-demuro-abscam-20200723.html.

21. "No. 01 of 2020, President Judge Administrative Order," Special Election Order,
    First Judicial District of Pennsylvania Court of Common Pleas of Philadelphia
    County, January 6, 2020, https://www.courts.phila.gov/pdf/regs/2020/01-of
    -2020-PJ-Order-Special-Election.pdf.

22. Ryan Briggs, "Lawyer behind Trump's Legal Campaign to Win PA Has a Long
    History in Philly," WHYY, November 13, 2020, https://whyy.org/articles/lawyer
    -behind-trumps-legal-campaign-to-win-pa-has-a-long-history-in-philly/.

23. Tony West, "How Linda Kearns Cleared the Ballot in the 197th," *Philadelphia
    Public Record*, March 23, 2017, http://www.phillyrecord.com/2017/03/how-lin
    da-kerns-cleared-the-ballot-in-the-197th/.

24. Ibid.

25. Ibid.

26. Ibid.

27. Ibid.

28. Ibid.

29. Nancy Phillips, "PollWatch: In Wissinoming, GOP Poll Watcher Says 2 Votes
    Logged before Polls Opened," *Philadelphia Inquirer*, November 8, 2016, https://
    www.inquirer.com/philly/news/GOP-poll-watcher-says-votes-recorded-before
    .html.

30. "Voting in Pennsylvania," Commonwealth of Pennsylvania, n.d., https://www.pa
    .gov/guides/voting-and-elections/.

31. "Pennsylvania Application for Emergency Absentee Ballot," Emergency Ballot Application, Votes PA, https://www.votespa.com/Resources/Documents/PADOS _EmergencyAbsenteeBallotApplication_English.pdf.

32. William Bender, "Nursing Home Resident's Son: 'That's Voter Fraud,'" *Philadelphia Inquirer*, November 3, 2017, https://www.inquirer.com/philly/news /vote-fraud-election-seniors-pennsylvania-20171103.html.

33. "Pennsylvania Election Code—Omnibus Amendments," No. 2019-77, Pennsylvania General Assembly, https://www.legis.state.pa.us/cfdocs/legis/li/uco nsCheck.cfm?yr=2019&sessInd=0&act=77.

34. Angela Couloumbis and Liz Navratil, "Pa. GOP Chairman Val DiGiorgio Resigns after Report about Interactions with Philly Council Candidate," *Pittsburgh Post-Gazette*, June 25, 2019, https://www.post-gazette.com/news/politics-state/2019 /06/25/Pa-GOP-chairman-Val-DiGiorgio-resigns-sexual-content-text-messages/st ories/201906250124.

35. Mark Hemingway, "Warning Signs in Pennsylvania of Mail Ballot Chaos in November," RealClearPolitics, September 25, 2020, https://www.realclearpolitics .com/articles/2020/09/25/warning_signs_in_pennsylvania_of_mail_ballot_cha os_in_november_144299.html.

36. Marie Albiges, "Mark Zuckerberg Helped Some Pennsylvania Counties Survive the 2020 Election. Right-Wing Lawmakers Say That Was Unfair," National Public Radio Pittsburgh, May 31, 2021, https://www.wesa.fm/politics-government/2021 -05-31/mark-zuckerberg-helped-some-pennsylvania-counties-survive-the-2020 -election-right-wing-lawmakers-say-that-was-unfair; "New Satellite Election Offices Open throughout Philadelphia," City of Philadelphia, September 29, 2020, https://www.phila.gov/2020-09-29-new-satellite-election-offices-open-througho ut-philadelphia/.

37. Trevor Carlsen and Hayden Dublois, "How 'Zuckerbucks' Infiltrated and Influenced the 2020 Pennsylvania Election," Foundation for Government Accountability, March 16, 2021, https://thefga.org/wp-content/uploads/2021/03 /Pennsylvania-Zuckerbucks-brief-3-16-21.pdf; "CEIR 2020 Voter Education Grant Program," Center for Election Innovation and Research, n.d., https://electioninno vation.org/research/ceir-2020-voter-education-grant-program/.

38. Danny Hakim and Nick Corasaniti, "Trump Campaign Draws Rebuke for Surveilling Philadelphia Voters," *New York Times*, October 22, 2020, https://www .nytimes.com/2020/10/22/us/politics/trump-campaign-voter-surveillance.html.

39. "Trump Campaign Loses Again in Suit Over Philly Voter Offices," Associated Press, October 23, 2020, https://apnews.com/article/donald-trump-pennsylvania -lawsuits-philadelphia-elections-bda443784ff186c0b4b661be5be2a65f.

40. *Donald J. Trump for President, Inc. v. Philadelphia County Board of Elections*, 02035 (2020).

41. *Donald J. Trump for President, Inc. v. Philadelphia County Board of Elections*, No. 983 C.D. (2020).

42. "Authorize a Designated Agent to Help You Obtain and/or Return Your Mail-In or Absentee Ballot," Pennsylvania Department of State, n.d., https://www.votespa

.com/Resources/Documents/Authorize-Designated-Agent-for-Mail-in-or-Absent ee-Ballot.pdf.

43. Linda A. Kerns, emailed letter to Philadelphia City Commissioners, October 16, 2020, https://drive.google.com/file/d/1q9AaCq5XLWtA47hacEaI7iS0OYxrSCXy /view.

44. Hakim and Corasaniti, "Trump Campaign Draws Rebuke."

45. Ibid.

46. Chris Brennan, "Trump Campaign Is Warned about Videotaping Philly Voters Dropping Off Mail Ballots," *Philadelphia Inquirer*, October 22, 2020, https:// www.inquirer.com/politics/election/trump-campaign-surveillance-philadelphia -mail-ballot-drop-boxes-20201022.html.

47. Ibid.

48. Todd Shepherd, "Exclusive: Trump Campaign Calls Out Mayor Kenney Over 'Two Ballots' Picture," Delaware Valley Journal, October 23, 2020, https://delaw arevalleyjournal.com/exclusive-trump-campaign-calls-out-mayor-kenney-over -two-ballots-picture/.

49. Ibid.

50. Ibid.

51. "Emergency Petition for Allowance of Appeal by Defendant the City of Philadelphia Board of Elections," Courthouse News, November 5, 2020, https://www.co urthousenews.com/wp-content/uploads/2020/11/dem-petition-pa.pdf.

52. Matt Miller, "Trump Wins Legal Fight as Pa. Court Says Watchers Must Be Allowed within 6 Feet of Philly Vote Counting," Penn Live Patriot-News, November 5, 2020, https://www.pennlive.com/elections/2020/11/trump-wins-le gal-fight-as-pa-court-says-his-watchers-must-be-allowed-within-6-feet-of-philly -vote-counting.html.

53. William Bender and Maddie Hanna, "GOP Judicial Candidate's Name Wrong on Philly Voting Machines," *Philadelphia Inquirer*, November 7, 2017, https://www .inquirer.com/philly/news/politics/city/election-philadelphia-voting-machines-re publican-judge-fizzano-cannon-20171107.html.

54. Ibid.

55. Victor Fiorillo, "Court Orders Philly to Allow Elections Watchers within 6 Feet of Vote Counters," *Philadelphia Magazine*, November 5, 2020, https://www.philly mag.com/news/2020/11/05/election-watchers-philadelphia-vote-count/.

56. Ibid.

57. Miller, "Trump Wins Legal Fight as Pa. Court."

58. Dylan Segelbaum, "Pa. Supreme Court Takes Appeal of Ruling Allowing Philadelphia Poll Watchers within 6 Feet," *York Daily Record*, November 9, 2020, https://www.ydr.com/story/news/politics/elections/2020/11/09/pennsylvania -supreme-court-to-hear-appeal-ruling-allowing-poll-watchers-within-6-feet-phila delphia/6226539002/.

59. Ibid.

60. *General Election Mail-In Ballot Guide for Philadelphia Voters*, City of Philadelphia, n.d., https://www.phila.gov/media/20200908090657/Mail-in-ballot-guide-single-page-ENGLISH.pdf.
61. "Voting by Mail-in or Absentee Ballot Is Safe, Secure, and Easy," Votes PA, n.d., https://www.votespa.com/Voting-in-PA/Pages/Mail-and-Absentee-Ballot.aspx.
62. Julian Routh, "Court Strikes Down Counting of 2,349 Ballots in Allegheny County," *Pittsburgh Post-Gazette*, November 19, 2020, https://www.post-gazet te.com/news/politics-state/2020/11/19/Nicole-Ziccarelli-PA-state-Senate-vs-Brew ster-election-ballots-Commonwealth-Court/stories/202011190151; Pete Williams and Nicole Via y Rada, "Trump's Election Fight Includes Almost 50 Lawsuits, It's Not Going Well," NBC News, November 23, 2020, https://www.nbcnews.com /politics/2020-election/trump-s-election-fight-includes-over-30-lawsuits-it-s-n12 48289.
63. Routh, "Court Strikes Down Counting."
64. Kim Lyons, "Ziccarelli Continues to Say Certain Mail-In Ballots Shouldn't Be Counted, Even after Courts Disagree," *Pennsylvania Capital-Star*, November 30, 2020, https://www.penncapital-star.com/election-2020/ziccarelli-continues-to -say-certain-mail-in-ballots-shouldnt-be-counted-even-after-courts-disagree/.
65. "Voting by Mail-In or Absentee Ballot Is Safe, Secure, and Easy," Votes PA.
66. "Guidance Concerning Civilian Absentee and Mail-In Ballot Procedures," Pennsylvania Department of State, September 28, 2020, https://www.dos.pa.gov /VotingElections/OtherServicesEvents/Documents/DOS%20Guidance%20Civil ian%20Absentee%20and%20Mail-In%20Ballot%20Procedures.pdf.
67. *Joseph B. SCARNATI, III, et al., Applicants, v. Kathy BOOCKVAR, in Her Official Capacity as Secretary of Pennsylvania, et al., Respondents; Republican Party of Pennsylvania, Applicant, v. Kathy Boockvar, In Her Official Capacity as Secretary of Pennsylvania, et al., Respondents*, 2020 WL 5912579 (U.S.), 16.
68. Appeal of Nicole Ziccarelli, "In Re: 2,349 Ballots in the 2020 General Election," Commonwealth Court of Pennsylvania, November 19, 2020, https://www .pacourts.us/Storage/media/pdfs/20210604/012152-file-10625.pdf
69. Ibid.
70. Ibid.
71. Julian Routh, "Pa. Supreme Court Allows Count of 2,000 Ballots Challenged by Nicole Ziccarelli," *Pittsburgh Post-Gazette*, November 23, 2020, https://www.po st-gazette.com/news/crime-courts/2020/11/23/Pa-Supreme-Court-allows-count -ballots-challenged-Nicole-Ziccarelli-jim-brewster/stories/202011230112.
72. Ivan Pentchoukov, "Pennsylvania Supreme Court Rejects Six Appeals Which Challenged 10,684 Ballots over Missing Info," *Epoch Times*, November 23, 2020, https://www.theepochtimes.com/mkt_app/pennsylvania-supreme-court-rejects -six-appeals-which-challenged-10684-ballots-over-missing-info_3591032.html.
73. Ibid.; Jonathan Lai, "Philly Will Count Undated Mail Ballots the Pa. Supreme Court Said Should Be Thrown Out," *Philadelphia Inquirer*, May 26, 2021, https:// www.inquirer.com/politics/election/philadelphia-undated-mail-ballots-pennsylva nia-supreme-court-20210526.html.

74. Katie Meyer, "In Last-Minute Reversal, Philly Commissioners Won't Count Undated Ballots," WITF, June 1, 2021, https://www.witf.org/2021/06/01/wolf-cl ashes-with-philly-commissioners-says-undated-primary-mail-ballots-shouldnt-co unt/.

75. "WD Pa Draft Complaint," U.S. District Court for the Western District of Pennsylvania, November 25, 2020, https://storage.courtlistener.com/recap /gov.uscourts.pawd.273768/gov.uscourts.pawd.273768.1.0.pdf.

76. Clarence Thomas, *Republican Party of Pennsylvania v. Veronica DeGraffenreid, Acting Secretary of Pennsylvania, et al.*, Supreme Court of the United States, February 22, 2021, https://www.supremecourt.gov/opinions/20pdf/20-542_2c83.pdf.

77. Ibid.

78. Ibid.

79. Ibid.

80. Marley Parish, "Trump Campaign Targets Centre Campaign in Lawsuit Alleging 'Fraudulent Votes' in Pa.," *Centre Daily Times*, November 10, 2020, https://www .centredaily.com/news/politics-government/election/article247090102.html.

81. Cynthia Fernandez and Jonathan Lai, "Talks Collapse on a Deal to Let Pennsylvania Counties Open Mail Ballots before Election Day," *Philadelphia Inquirer*, October 22, 2020,https://www.inquirer.com/politics/election/pennsylv ania-counting-mail-ballots-election-day-negotiations-stall-20201021.html.

82. "Cancelled Ballot Notification," Office of the Philadelphia City Commissioners, n.d., https://www.philadelphiavotes.com/en/home/item/1873-cancelled_ballot_no tification_info.

83. Deanna Paul, "Pennsylvania Lawsuit Challenges 1,200 Mail-In Ballots in Philadelphia Suburb," *Wall Street Journal*, November 3, 2020, https://www.wsj .com/livecoverage/trump-biden-election-day-2020/card/5EyBU9LbzlzGPbqo Rkwd.

84. Katherine Landergan and Josh Gerstein, "GOP Effort to Block 'Cured' Pennsylvania Ballots Gets Chilly Reception from Judge," *Politico*, November 4, 2020, https://www.politico.com/news/2020/11/04/gop-pennsylvania-blocking-bal lots-lawsuit-434045.

85. John Daniel Davidson, "In Nevada, a Corrupt Cash-for-Votes Scheme Is Hiding in Plain Sight," The Federalist, November 11, 2018, https://thefederalist.com/20 20/11/18/in-nevada-a-corrupt-cash-for-votes-scheme-is-hiding-in-plain-sight/.

86. Paul Bedard, "Pro-Biden Effort Offered Native Americans $25–$500 Visa Gift Cards and Jewelry to Vote," *Washington Examiner*, December 3, 2020, https:// www.washingtonexaminer.com/washington-secrets/pro-biden-effort-offered -native-americans-25-500-visa-gift-cards-jewelry-to-vote.

87. Amy Sherman, "Fact-Checking Trump's Statement That Native Americans Were Paid to Vote," PolitiFact, June 10, 2021, https://www.politifact.com/article/2021 /jun/10/fact-checking-trumps-statement-native-americans-we/.

88. U.S. Code, "18 U.S. Code § 597–Expenditures to Influence Voting," https://www .law.cornell.edu/uscode/text/18/597.

89. Jacques Billeaud, "Arizona Officials Seek Dismissal of Trump's Election Suit," Associated Press, November 12, 2020, https://apnews.com/article/election-2020 -joe-biden-arizona-phoenix-lawsuits-3b478ff1da58e748cf5ad249058a57e1.

90. Ibid.

91. Ibid.

92. Andrew Oxford, "Complaints against 9 Attorneys Involved in Election Lawsuits Dismissed by Arizona Bar; 12 Still Pending," Arizona Central, March 15, 2021, https://www.azcentral.com/story/news/politics/elections/2021/03/15/arizona-bar -dismisses-complaints-against-attorneys-election-lawsuits/4710871001/.

93. Jerod MacDonald-Evoy, "Katie Hobbs Is Being Dragged for a 2017 Tweet Criticizing Trump. She Won't Apologize," *Arizona Mirror*, November 13, 2020, https://www.azmirror.com/2020/11/13/katie-hobbs-is-being-dragged-for-a-2017 -tweet-criticizing-trump-she-wont-apologize/.

94. Katie Hobbs (@katiehobbs), "There are Trump t-shirts. And people not embarrassed to wear them. In airports," Twitter, September 30, 2015, 2:35 p.m., https://twitter.com/katiehobbs/status/649291518293970944.

95. Katie Hobbs (@katiehobbs), "At least the racist, sexist, homophobic campaign rhetoric didn't make it into actual policies. Oh, wait...," Twitter, October 6, 2017, 1:25 p.m., https://twitter.com/katiehobbs/status/916353710195843072.; Katie Hobbs (@katiehobbs), "If Trump wins we won't have a country to move out of," Twitter, August 3, 2016, 1:22 a.m., https://twitter.com/katiehobbs/status/760707 334029082624.

96. Katie Hobbs (@katiehobbs), "There is so much deplorable at Trump rallies it's hard to keep track," Twitter, October 22, 2016, 6:49 p.m., https://twitter.com/katieho bbs/status/789961890654859264.

97. Chuck Neubauer, "Soros and Liberal Groups Seeking Top Election Posts in Battleground States," *Washington Times*, June 23, 2011, https://www.washingt ontimes.com/news/2011/jun/23/section-527-works-to-seat-liberals-as-election -ove/.

98. Bob Christie, "Democrat Declares Victory in Arizona Secretary of State Race," Associated Press, November 16, 2018, https://apnews.com/article/7661ea46b45f 432db0e893137598b581; "Democrat Jocelyn Benson Wins Michigan Secretary of State Race, Defeating Republican Mary Treder Lang," Associated Press, November 7, 2018, https://apnews.com/article/fe7b2ce606554a5eab15d6b6b72e ac07.

99. Avi Zenilman, "Secretaries of State Give Dem Firewall," *Politico*, November 2, 2008, https://www.politico.com/story/2008/11/secretaries-of-state-give-dem-fire wall-015105.

100. Maryclaire Dale, "Appeals Court Rejects Trump Challenge of Pennsylvania Race," Associated Press, November 27, 2020, https://apnews.com/article/election-2020 -donald-trump-pennsylvania-elections-philadelphia-d9c96c4593ec278f3b1d4bc 564068df6.

101. "Highlights from the Transition: Biden Wins Georgia and Trump Wins North Carolina as Final States Are Called," *New York Times*, November 25, 2020,

https://www.nytimes.com/live/2020/11/13/us/joe-biden-trump#trump-puts-giuliani-in-charge-of-his-lawsuits-challenging-the-election-results.

102. Veronica Stracqualursi, "Trump Puts Guiliani in Charge of Post-Election Legal Fight after Series of Losses," CBS 58, November 16, 2020, https://www.cbs58.com/news/trump-puts-giuliani-in-charge-of-post-election-legal-fight-after-series-of-losses.

103. "2020-11-09 Complaint as Filed," U.S. District Court for the Middle District of Pennsylvania, n.d., https://cdn.donaldjtrump.com/public-files/press_assets/2020-11-09-complaint-as-filed.pdf.

104. Jacob Jarvis, "After Encouraging Harassment, Lincoln Project Puts Trump Lawsuit Supporters on Notice: 'We Are Going to Take a Look at You,'" *Newsweek*, November 11, 2020, https://www.newsweek.com/lincoln-project-trump-lawsuits-1546683.

105. Ibid.

106. "Code of Professional Conduct," United States District Court for the Middle District of Pennsylvania, n.d., https://www.pamd.uscourts.gov/sites/pamd/files/forms/conduct.pdf.

107. Debra Cassens Weiss, "Lawyer for Trump Campaign Complains of 'Abusive' Voicemail from Kirkland Associate, Asks to Withdraw," *ABA Journal*, November 17, 2020, https://www.abajournal.com/news/article/lawyer-for-trump-campaign-complains-of-abusive-voicemail-from-kirkland-associate-asks-to-withdraw.

108. Bruce Golding, "Trump 2020 Lawyer Accuses Pa. Secretary of State's Attorney of 'Harassment,'" *New York Post*, November 16, 2020, https://nypost.com/2020/11/16/trump-lawyer-accuses-penn-sec-of-state-attorney-of-harassment/.

109. Rachel Abrams, David Enrich, and Jessica Silver-Greenberg, "Once Loyal to Trump, Law Firm Pulls Back from His Election Fight," *New York Times*, November 13, 2020, https://www.nytimes.com/2020/11/13/business/porter-wright-trump-pennsylvania.html.

110. Matt Friedman, "Man Featured at Giuliani Press Conference Is Convicted Sex Offender," *Politico*, November 11, 2020, https://www.politico.com/states/new-jersey/story/2020/11/09/man-featured-at-giuliani-press-conference-is-a-sex-offender-1335241.

111. Ibid.

112. *Donald J. Trump for President, Inc. et al., Plaintiffs, v. Kathy Boockvar, et al., Defendants*, U.S. District Court for the Middle District of Pennsylvania, November 21, 2020, https://www.pamd.uscourts.gov/sites/pamd/files/20-2078_202.pdf.

113. Ibid.

114. Ryan Briggs, "Trump Campaign Lawyer in Philadelphia Withdraws from Federal Election Suit," WHYY, November 19, 2020, https://whyy.org/articles/trump-campaign-lawyer-in-philadelphia-withdraws-from-federal-election-suit/.

115. Jon Swaine, "In Scathing Opinion, Federal Judge Dismisses Trump Campaign Lawsuit in Pennsylvania," *Washington Post*, November 21, 2020, https://www.washingtonpost.com/politics/us-judge-dismisses-trump-campaign-lawsuit-in-pa/2020/11/21/cc097fbe-2c50-11eb-9b14-ad872157ebc9_story.html.

116. "PA Lawsuit: 21K Decreased on Voter Rolls, Evidence of Voting Activity after Death," Public Interest Legal Foundation, November 5, 2020, https://publicinterest legal.org/press/pa-lawsuit-21k-deceased-on-voter-rolls-evidence-of-voting-activity -after-death/.

117. Rudy Giuliani (@RudyGiuliani), "At least 21K Dead People on Pennsylvania Voter Rolls…," Twitter, November 6, 2020, 11:17 a.m., https://twitter.com/rudygiulia ni/status/1324747799641100288?lang=en.

118. Davey Alba, "No, 20,000 Dead People in Pennsylvania Did Not Vote," *New York Times*, November 6, 2020, https://www.nytimes.com/2020/11/06/technology/de ad-voters-pennsylvania.html.

119. David Mikkelson, "Debunking Trump Tweets: 20,000 Dead Voters in Pennsylvania," Snopes, November 19, 2020, https://www.snopes.com/fact-check /20000-dead-voters-in-pennsylvania/.

120. Ibid.; Robert Farley, "Thin Allegations of 'Dead People' Voting," FactCheck.org, November 9, 2020, https://www.factcheck.org/2020/11/thin-allegations-of-dead -people-voting/.

121. "Lawsuit to Remove Dead Voters in Pennsylvania Ends Win for Election Integrity," Public Interest Legal Foundation, April 7, 2021, https://publicinterestlegal.org/pre ss/lawsuit-to-remove-dead-voters-in-pennsylvania-ends-with-win-for-election-in tegrity/.

122. Scott Clement, Dan Balz, and Emily Guskin, "Post-ABC Polls: Biden Leads Trump Narrowly in Michigan, Significantly in Wisconsin," *Washington Post*, October 28, 2020, https://www.washingtonpost.com/politics/2020/10/28/wisconsin-mic higan-poll-post-abc/.

123. "Wisconsin: Trump vs. Biden," RealClearPolitics, n.d., https://www.realclearpoli tics.com/epolls/2020/president/wi/wisconsin_trump_vs_biden-6849.html.

124. Patrick Marley and Bruce Vielmetti, "Judge Orders 234,000 Purged from Wisconsin Voter Rolls," *USA Today*, December 13, 2019, https://www.usatoday .com/story/news/nation/2019/12/13/wisconsin-voter-registration-judge-orders-234 -000-purged-rolls/2643852001/.

125. "Guidance for Indefinitely Confined Electors COVID-19," Wisconsin Elections Commission, March 29, 2020, https://elections.wi.gov/node/6788; Eric Litke, "Voters, Not Clerks, Decided Who Was on 'Indefinitely Confined' List," PolitiFact, November 20, 2020, https://www.politifact.com/factchecks/2020/nov/21/joe-san felippo/voters-not-clerks-decided-who-was-indefinitely-con/.

126. Scott Bauer, "Wisconsin Supreme Court Rejects Green Bid for Ballot Access," Associated Press, September 14, 2020, https://apnews.com/article/wisconsin-hip -hop-and-rap-elections-election-2020-courts-5f112111c2e3601f8a6cd9987f8e 2b21.

127. Jason Zimmerman, "Kanye West Kept off Wisconsin Presidential Ballot," First Alert WBAY, August 20, 2020, https://www.wbay.com/2020/08/20/kanye-west -kept-of-wisconsin-presidential-ballot/.

128. "2016 Wisconsin Results," *New York Times*, November 8, 2016, https://www.ny times.com/elections/2016/results/wisconsin.

129. Ibid.
130. Ibid.
131. Ibid.
132. "Special Teleconference Meeting," Wisconsin Elections Commission, August 20, 2020, https://elections.wi.gov/node/7024.
133. Ibid.
134. Reid J. Epstein, "A Conservative Justice in Wisconsin Says He Followed the Law, Not the Politics," *New York Times*, December 20, 2020, https://www.nytimes.com/2020/12/20/us/politics/wisconsin-justice-brian-hagedorn.html.
135. Dan O'Donnell, "How the Wisconsin Elections Commission Illegally Disenfranchised the Green Party," MacIver Institute, September 16, 2020, https://www.maciverinstitute.com/2020/09/how-the-wisconsin-election-commission-illegally-disenfranchised-the-green-party/.
136. *Howie Hawkins and Angela Walker, Petitioners, v. Wisconsin Elections Commission*, Supreme Court of Wisconsin, September 14, 2020, https://www.wpr.org/sites/default/files/20ap1488-oa_hawkins_v._wis._elections_commission.pdf.
137. Ibid
138. Ibid.
139. Kevin Reed, "Democrats Engineer Removal of Green Party Presidential Candidates from Pennsylvania Ballot," World Socialist, September 18, 2020, https://www.wsws.org/en/articles/2020/09/18/penn-s18.html.
140. Ibid.
141. Ibid.
142. Ibid.
143. Ibid.
144. "Marshall Cohen, Katelyn Polantz, and Kelly Mena, "Pennsylvania Supreme Court Election Rulings Are Big Wins for Biden," CNN, September 17, 2020, https://edition.cnn.com/2020/09/17/politics/pennsylvania-supreme-court-green-party-presidential-ballot/index.html.
145. Zimmerman, "Kanye West Kept off Wisconsin Presidential Ballot."
146. Ibid.
147. *Kanye West, Michelle Tidball, and Fred Krumberger, Plaintiffs, v. Wisconsin Elections Commission, Defendant*, U.S. District Court of the Eastern District of Wisconsin, September 3, 2020, https://www.wied.uscourts.gov/sites/wied/files/documents/opinions/20-CV-1348%20West%20et%20al.%20v.%20Wisconsin%20Elections%20Commission%20%2831%29.pdf.
148. Gail Collins, "Presidentially, Two Parties Is Plenty," *New York Times*, September 16, 2020, https://www.nytimes.com/2020/09/16/opinion/third-parties-2020.html.
149. Maggie Haberman, "Evan McMullin, Anti-Trump Republican, Mounts Independent Presidential Bid," *New York Times*, August 16, 2016, https://www.nytimes.com/2016/08/09/us/politics/evan-mcmullin-independent-candidate.html.

150. Kenneth Lovett, "Smokes-for-Votes-Scandal Could Burn Nyer," *New York Post*, November 14, 2000, https://nypost.com/2000/11/14/smokes-for-votes-scandal-co uld-burn-nyer/.

151. Ibid.

152. Jim Burns, "Wisconsin Homeless Reportedly Given Free Cigarettes for Gore Votes," CNS News, July 7, 2008, https://cnsnews.com/news/article/wisconsin-ho meless-reportedly-given-free-cigarettes-gore-votes.

153. Jon Greenberg, "Carlson: Democrats Use Newports to Get Out the Homeless Vote," PolitiFact, October 28, 2014, https://www.politifact.com/factchecks/2014 /oct/28/tucker-carlson/carlson-democrats-use-newports-get-out-homeless-vo/.

154. Ibid.

155. Ibid.

156. John Fund, "Milwaukee Puts a Vote-Fraud Cop Out of Business," *Wall Street Journal*, November 4, 2008, https://www.wsj.com/articles/SB12257611348949 5571.

157. Ibid.

158. Dan O'Donnell, "Democrat Vote Fraud Has Been Rampant in Milwaukee for Decades," 1130 WISN, November 6, 2020, https://newstalk1130.iheart.com/fea tured/common-sense-central/content/2020-11-06-democrat-vote-fraud-has-been -rampant-in-milwaukee-for-decades/.

159. Ibid.

160. "ACORN Worker Sentenced to 10 Months for Election Fraud," CNN, November 18, 2010, http://www.cnn.com/2010/CRIME/11/18/election.worker.sentenced/in dex.html.

161. "Election Fraud Cases," Heritage Foundation, https://www.heritage.org/voterfra ud/search?state=WI&combine=&year=&case_type=All&fraud_type=All&pa ge=2.

162. Fund, "Milwaukee Puts a Vote-Fraud Cop Out of Business."

163. Ibid.

164. "City of Milwaukee Disregarded Ineligible Voter List on First Day of Early Voting," MacIver Institute, October 23, 2012, https://www.maciverinstitute.com/2012/10 /felonvotemke/.

165. Chris Rochester, "Almost 4,000 Cases of Likely Voter Fraud Recorded by Wisconsin Officials after 2016 Election," MacIver Institute, June 18, 2018, https:// www.maciverinstitute.com/2018/06/almost-4000-cases-of-voter-fraud-recorded -by-wisconsin-officials-after-2016-election/.

166. Mary Spicuzza, "City of Milwaukee Defends its Handling of Absentee Ballots amid Criticism from Scott Walker," *Milwaukee Journal Sentinel*, November 7, 2018, https://www.jsonline.com/story/news/politics/elections/2018/11/07/scott-wal ker-eyes-damaged-absentee-ballots-recount-decision/1918944002/.

167. Alison Dirr, "Milwaukee County Presidential Recount Wraps Up with Biden Adding to His Margin over Trump," *Milwaukee Journal Sentinel*, November 27, 2020, https://www.jsonline.com/story/news/politics/elections/2020/11/27/milwa ukee-county-recount-wraps-up-biden-adding-his-margin/6428186002/.

168. Dan O'Donnell, "How the Wisconsin Elections Commission Destroyed Fair Elections in Wisconsin," MacIver Institute, November 5, 2020, https://www.ma civerinstitute.com/2020/11/how-the-wisconsin-elections-commission-destroyed -fair-elections-in-wisconsin/.

169. Ibid.

170. Dan O'Donnell, "Wisconsin's Miraculous Vanishing Ballot Rejection Rate," MacIver Institute, February 3, 2021, https://www.maciverinstitute.com/2021/02 /wisconsins-miraculous-vanishing-ballot-rejection-rate/.

171. Eric Litke, "Fact Check: Wisconsin's November Absentee Rejection Rate Was in Line, Not an 'Anomaly,'" *USA Today*, February 12, 2021, https://www.usatoday .com/story/news/factcheck/2021/02/12/fact-check-wisconsins-absentee-ballot-re jection-rate-expected/6736935002/.

172. Cheyenne Haslett and Ashley Brown, "23,000 Absentee Ballots Were Rejected in Wisconsin's April Primary. That's More Than Trump Won the State by in 2016," ABC News, August 20, 2020, https://abcnews.go.com/Politics/23000-absentee -ballots-rejected-wisconsins-april-primaries/story?id=72472209.

173. Christina A. Cassidy, "Voter Outreach Led to Big Drop in Rejected Mail Ballots," Associated Press, March 16, 2021, https://apnews.com/article/politics-wisconsin -coronavirus-pandemic-elections-atlanta-25b5218ee92dadf78be274211bef6c6b.

174. Litke, "Fact Check: Wisconsin's November Absentee Rejection Rate Was in Line."

175. Nathaniel Rakich, "Why So Few Absentee Ballots Were Rejected in 2020," FiveThirtyEight, February 17, 2021, https://fivethirtyeight.com/features/why-so -few-absentee-ballots-were-rejected-in-2020/.

176. Ibid.

177. Ibid.

178. "Wisconsin Election Results," *New York Times*, March 8, 2021, https:// www.nytimes.com/interactive/2020/11/03/us/elections/results-wisconsin.html.

179. *Donald J. Trump, et al., Petitioners, v. Joseph R. Biden, et al., Respondents*, Supreme Court of the United States, December 29, 2020, https://www.supremec ourt.gov/DocketPDF/20/20-882/164938/20201229165341814_No.%2020-__P etitionForAWritOfCertiorari.pdf.

180. Ibid.

181. Ibid.

182. Ibid.

183. Ibid.

184. Todd Richmond, "GOP Warns Madison to Drop Plan to Collect Ballots in Parks," Associated Press, September 25, 2020, https://apnews.com/article/madison-wisco nsin-archive-voting-2020-1ac6842b8cb5bc014475070181259bf0.

185. Ibid.

186. "Wisconsin Justices Deny Vote Challenge," Press Reader, December 4, 2020, https://www.pressreader.com/usa/arkansas-democrat-gazette/20201204/281530 818593500.

187. Ibid.

188. Benjamin Yount, "Conservative Wisconsin Justices Blast Decision to Punt on President's Election Lawsuit," The Center Square, December 3, 2020, https://www .thecentersquare.com/wisconsin/conservative-wisconsin-justices-blast-decision-to -punt-on-president-s-election-lawsuit/article_62929f5a-3599-11eb-a72e-57caa0 edb413.html.

189. Ibid.

190. Ibid.

191. "Case No.: 2020AP2038," Supreme Court of Wisconsin, filed December 14, 2020, https://www.wicourts.gov/sc/opinion/DisplayDocument.pdf?content=pdf&seqN o=315395.

192. Ibid.

Chapter Ten: The Trouble with Fulton County

1.   Mitchell Harrison, "Sworn Affidavit," *Pearson v. Kemp*, 1:20-cv-04809-TCB.2, November 25, 2020, https://www.documentcloud.org/documents/20420331-mit chell-harrison-affidavit.

2.   Alivia Harris, "Some Ballots Will Not Be Counted until Wednesday in Georgia following Water Main Break," WLVT, November 4, 2020, https://www.wvlt.tv /2020/11/04/some-ballots-will-not-be-counted-until-wednesday-in-georgia-follo wing-water-main-break/.

3.   *Coreco Ja'Qan Peterson, et al. v. Brian Kemp, et al.*, 1:20-cv-4809-TCB.2, December 6, 2020, https://storage.courtlistener.com/recap/gov.uscourts.gand.28 4055/gov.uscourts.gand.284055.72.1.pdf.

4.   Michelle Branton, "Sworn Affidavit," *Pearson v. Kemp*, 1:20-cv-04809-TCB.1, November 25, 2020, https://www.courtlistener.com/docket/18694655/1/29/pear son-v-kemp/.

5.   Branton, "Sworn Affidavit," 2.

6.   Harrison, "Sworn Affidavit," 3.

7.   Associated Press, "Trump Campaign Sues Chatham County, Georgia Board of Elections," WRBL, November 4, 2020, https://www.wrbl.com/news/georgia-ne ws/trump-campaign-sues-chatham-county-georgia-board-of-elections/.

8.   David Shafer (@DavidShafer), "Let me repeat. Fulton County election officials told the media and our observers that they were shutting down the tabulation center at State Farm Arena at 10:30 p.m. on election night only to continue counting ballots in secret until 1:00 a.m.," Twitter, November 9, 2020, 7:22 p.m., https://twitter .com/DavidShafer/status/1325956840769859586.

9.   David Shafer (@DavidShafer), "No one disputes that Fulton County elections officials falsely announced that the counting of ballots would stop at 10:30 p.m.... " Twitter, November 9, 2020, 7:34 p.m., https://twitter.com/DavidShafer/status /1325960023902711813.

10.   David Shafer (@DavidShafer), "The @AJC is gaslighting you when they report that there is no evidence of irregularity in the election," Twitter, November 9, 2020, 7:43 p.m., https://twitter.com/DavidShafer/status/1325962296041103361.

11. Matt Johnson (@MattWSB), "We saw absentee ballot counting at State Farm Arena wrap up at 10:30. Workers will be back in the morning," Twitter, November 3, 2020, 11:20 p.m., https://twitter.com/MattWSB/status/1323842460217430016.

12. Ben Brasch, "Fulton County Election Results Delayed after Pipe Bursts in Room with Ballots," *Atlanta Journal-Constitution*, November 3, 2020, https://www.ajc.com/news/atlanta-news/fulton-election-results-delayed-after-pipe-bursts-in-room-with-b%20allots/4T3KPQV7PBEX3JVAIGJBNBSVJY/.

13. Joe Henke (@JoeHenke), "Fulton County spokeswoman tells me absentee ballot counters at State Farm Arena were sent home at 10:30, will be back at 8:30 a.m. to work on finishing processing absentee ballots. This is separate from counting of in-person ballots…," Twitter, November 3, 2020, 11:55 p.m., https://twitter.com/JoeHenke/status/1323851215118151682.

14. Nightline (@Nightline), "JUST IN: The Fulton County public affairs manager for elections tells @ABC News that the election department has sent State Farm Arena absentee ballot counters home despite earlier intentions to complete processing tonight," Twitter, November 3, 2020, 11:31 p.m., https://twitter.com/Nightline/status/1323845257142951937; ABC News Politics (@ABCPolitics), "NEW: The election department sent the ballot counters at the State Farm Arena in Atlanta home at 10:30 p.m., Regina Waller, the Fulton County public affairs manager for elections, tells ABC News," Twitter, November 3, 2020, 11:34 p.m., https://twitter.com/ABCPolitics/status/1323846118208376834; Emily Shapiro, "Pipe Bursts in Atlanta Arena Causing 4-Hour Delay in Processing Ballots," ABC News, November 3, 2020, https://abcnews.go.com/Politics/pipe-bursts-atlanta-arena-causing-hour-delay-processing/story?id=73981348; Elizabeth Nouryeh, "Fulton County Stopped Counting Absentee Ballots for the Night," *North Fulton Neighbor*, November 3, 2020, https://www.mdjonline.com/neighbor_newspapers/north_fulton/fulton-county-stopped-counting-absentee-ballots-for-the-night/article_91ee4c04-1e56-11eb-b8dd-ab745d920a95.html.

15. Richard Elliot, "Fulton County Broke the Law in Handling of Absentee Ballot Requests, State Investigation Finds," WSB-TV, August 27, 2020, https://www.wsbtv.com/news/local/fulton-county/fulton-county-broke-law-handling-absentee-ballot-requests-state-investigation-finds/XWE4XMFIRVHETHSI3LT7OJA36Y/.

16. Rosie Manins, "Atlanta Law Firms Deny Conflict in Georgia Election Suits," Law 360, November 12, 2020, https://www.law360.com/articles/1328184/atlanta-law-firms-deny-conflict-in-georgia-election-suits.

17. Tommy Beer, "Who's Cleta Mitchell, Trump's Lawyer on Georgia Call?" *Forbes*, January 5, 2021, https://www.forbes.com/sites/tommybeer/2021/01/05/whos-cleta-mitchell-trumps-lawyer-on-georgia-call/?sh=6ebe704747f5.

18. Steve Fennessy and Jess Mador, "Georgia Today: Behind Relentless Death Threats against Raffenspergers, Georgia Election Officials," Georgia Public Broadcasting, June 18, 2021, https://www.gpb.org/news/2021/06/18/georgia-today-behind-relentless-death-threats-against-raffenspergers-georgia.

19. "Four Seasons Total Landscaping Presser Was 'Chaotic, Confusing and a Bit Surreal,' Says Reporter," CBC Radio, November 9, 2020, https://www.cbc.ca/ra

dio/asithappens/as-it-happens-monday-edition-1.5795271/four-seasons-total-lan
dscaping-presser-was-chaotic-confusing-and-a-bit-surreal-says-reporter-1.579
5402; Joel Shannon, Jo Ciavaglia, and James McGinnis, "Giuliani Holds Press
Conference at Landscaping Business, Prompting Confusion," *USA Today*,
November 7, 2020, https://www.usatoday.com/story/news/nation/2020/11/07/gi
uliani-holds-press-conference-four-seasons-total-landscaping/6209235002/; David
Eggert, "Giuliani to Republicans: Pressure Legislature on Biden Win," Associated
Press, December 2, 2020, https://apnews.com/article/election-2020-joe-biden-do
nald-trump-legislature-constitutions-1d853c0a4cdf262ce45e2814b39731d2.

20. Fred Lucas, "4 Highlights from Georgia Senate's Election Fraud Hearing," Daily
Signal, December 3, 2020, https://www.dailysignal.com/2020/12/03/4-highlights
-from-georgia-senates-election-fraud-hearing/; Right Side Broadcasting Network,
"Live: Michigan State Senate Committee on Oversight Holds Hearing on Election
Issues 12/1/20," YouTube, December 1, 2020, https://www.youtube.com/watch
?v=X0-vyw9qbdw.

21. Andrew C. McCarthy, "As Time Is Running Out, Trump Campaign Files Stronger
Lawsuit in Georgia," *National Review*, December 7, 2020, https://www.national
review.com/2020/12/as-time-is-running-out-trump-campaign-files-stronger-law
suit-in-georgia/.

22. Adam Murphy, "Lawmakers Hear Bombshell Allegations of Georgia Election
Fraud," CBS 46 News, December 3, 2020, https://www.cbs46.com/news/lawma
kers-hear-bombshell-allegations-of-georgia-election-fraud/article_8404e930-35
e5-11eb-8ac3-1fc96e3b52d8.html.

23. Brendan Keefe, "Fact-Checking Claims about Fulton County's Election: These
'Suitcases' Are Actually Ballot Containers," First Coast News, December 4, 2020,
https://www.firstcoastnews.com/article/news/politics/elections/fact-checking-cla
ims-about-fulton-countys-election/85-89c150d2-c917-44b6-b7ab-a29dd9dcb888.

24. Erik Wemple, "Opinion: Bogus 'Suitcase' Story Rolls Away from Fox News,"
Washington Post, December 5, https://www.washingtonpost.com/opinions/2020
/12/05/bogus-suitcase-story-rolls-away-fox-news/.

25. Wemple, "Opinion: Bogus 'Suitcase' Story Rolls Away from Fox News."

26. Johnny Edwards, "Clash with GOP May Boost Elections Candidate," *Atlanta-
Journal Constitution*, May 12, 2013, https://www.ajc.com/news/local-govt-polit
ics/clash-with-gop-may-boost-elections-candidate/zHBfbuLOslijxHvDwWYzbJ/.

27. Tristan Justice, "China-Funded Facebook Fact-Checker Is Now Censoring
Criticism of Its Fake Fact Checks," The Federalist, December 7, 2020, https://the
federalist.com/2020/12/07/china-funded-facebook-fact-checker-is-now-censoring
-criticism-of-its-fake-fact-checks/.

28. Shapiro, "Pipe Burst in Atlanta Arena Causing 4-Hour Delay in Processing
Ballots."

29. Branton, "Sworn Affidavit," 3.

30. Regina Waller, email, "Fox News Crew Request," November 3, 2020, https://jus
tthenews.com/sites/default/files/2021-03/wallerem.pdf.

31. "Keisha Bottoms," Ballotpedia, n.d., https://ballotpedia.org/Keisha_Bottoms; Sophie Bushwick, "An Expert on Voting Machines Explains How They Work," *Scientific American*, November 3, 2020, https://www.scientificamerican.com/article/an-expert-on-voting-machines-explains-how-they-work/.

32. Stephen Deere, "Atlanta Mayor's Campaign Paid Firm Registered to Election Official," *Atlanta Journal-Constitution*, July 10, 2018, https://www.ajc.com/news/local-govt—politics/atlanta-mayor-campaign-paid-firm-registered-election-official/yhLLC8tSFuuYP0c4dWZ1yI/.

33. Cindy Morley, "Conflict of Interest in Fulton County Elections Office," InsiderAdvantage, December 28, 2020, https://insideradvantage.com/2020/12/28/conflict-of-interest-in-fulton-county-elections-office/.

34. Milo Godio, "Fox News Reporter Debunks Georgia Election Fraud Claims Made by Tucker Carlson and Sean Hannity," *Newsweek*, December 4, 2020, https://www.newsweek.com/fox-news-reporter-debunks-georgia-election-fraud-claims-made-tucker-carlson-sean-hannity-1552397.

35. Alan Duke and Hallie Golden, "Fact Check: Video from Georgia Does NOT Show Suitcases Filled with Ballots Suspiciously Pulled from under a Table; Poll Watchers Were Not Told to Leave," Lead Stories, December 3, 2020, https://leadstories.com/hoax-alert/2020/12/fact-check-video-from-ga-does-not-show-suitcases-filled-with-ballots-pulled-from-under-a-table-after-poll-workers-dismissed.html.

36. "State Election Board Report," Seven Hills Strategies, November 13, 2020, https://justthenews.com/sites/default/files/2021-06/Unabridged%20Notes.pdf.

37. "Georgia Official Raffensperger: 'We Had Safe, Secure, Honest Elections,'" CBS News, January 10, 2021, https://www.cbsnews.com/video/georgia-official-raffensperger-we-had-safe-secure-honest-elections/.

38. Brad Raffensperger (@GaSecofState), "Fulton County's continued failures have gone on long enough with no accountability…," Twitter, July 15, 2020, 11:18 a.m., https://twitter.com/GaSecofState/status/1415692351176052738.

39. "Chapter 13: Canvassing and Certifying an Election," U.S. Election Assistance Commission, n.d., https://www.eac.gov/sites/default/files/eac_assets/1/6/EMG_chapt_13_august_26_2010.pdf.

40. Stephen Fowler, "Fulton County Fires Elections Director after Best (and Worst) 2020," Georgia Public Broadcasting, February 16, 2021, https://www.gpb.org/news/2021/02/16/fulton-county-fires-elections-director-after-best-and-worst-2020.

41. Mark Niesse, "Georgia Election Investigation Looks into Fulton Ballot Drop Box Forms," *Atlanta Journal-Constitution*, June 14, 2021, https://www.ajc.com/politics/georgia-election-investigation-looks-into-fulton-ballot-drop-box-forms/5HN5HTQ4NJF3ZMDNY5DDUV3TBA/.

42. "A Warning on Georgia's Signature Match," *Wall Street Journal*, December 31, 2020, https://www.wsj.com/articles/a-warning-on-georgias-signature-match-11609460042.

43. Wes Cantrell (@wcantrell), "Signature Verification for Mail-In Ballots is a joke! Today confirmed it. I received notification that my ballot was accepted. The top signature is my official one on file. The 2nd is how I signed my application. The

3rd is how I signed the ballot envelope. We must fix this!" Twitter, December 22, 2020, 2:41 p.m., https://twitter.com/wcantrell/status/1341469034987057152.

44. Greg Dolezal, "I tested the signature match for absentee ballots in Georgia and it failed. I'm tired of the deniers saying there is 'no evidence' sig match doesn't work...," Twitter, December 15, 2020, 2:34 p.m., https://twitter.com/dolezal4senate/status /1338930333077696513.

45. "Voting and Registration in the Election of November 2016," U.S. Census Bureau, May 2017, https://www.census.gov/data/tables/time-series/demo/voting-and-regi stration/p20-580.html.

46. William H. Frey, "For the First Time on Record, Fewer than 10% of Americans Moved in a Year, Brookings Institution, November 22, 2019, https://www.broo kings.edu/blog/the-avenue/2019/11/22/for-the-first-time-on-record-fewer-than-10 -of-americans-moved-in-a-year/.

47. "Register to Vote," Office of Brad Raffensperger, n.d., https://sos.ga.gov/index.php /elections/register_to_vote.

48. Dale Russell, "Election Investigations of Absentee Ballots and Double Voting in Southeast Georgia Underway," Fox News, August 28, 2020, https://www.fox5at lanta.com/news/election-investigations-of-absentee-ballots-and-double-voting-in -southeast-georgia-underway.

49. Greg Bluestein, Jim Galloway, and Tia Mitchell, "The Jolt: What We Know, and Don't Know, about Double-Voting in Georgia," *Atlanta Journal-Constitution*, September 9, 2020, https://www.ajc.com/politics/politics-blog/the-jolt-what-we -know-and-dont-know-about-double-voting-in-georgia/M35VZZVRVVBURF OVCXLI7ER77M/.

50. Ibid.

51. Paul Sperry, "With U.S. Senate Runoffs Near, Georgia's Not Prosecuting Its Unprecedented Number of Double Voters," RealClearInvestigations, December 13, 2020, https://www.realclearinvestigations.com/articles/2020/12/13/with_runo ffs_near_georgias_not_prosecuting_its_unprecedented_number_of_double_vote rs_126356.html.

52. "Transcript: President Trump's Phone Call with Georgia Election Officials," *New York Times*, January 3, 2021, https://www.nytimes.com/2021/01/03/us/politics /trump-raffensperger-georgia-call-transcript.html.

53. David Wickert, "Trump Appeals Election Lawsuit to Georgia Supreme Court," *Atlanta Journal-Constitution*, December 12, 2020, https://www.ajc.com/politics /election/trump-appeals-election-lawsuit-to-georgia-supreme-court/YBVWPYG QGZBXBCXXM2N6AG3474/.

54. "Judge Denies Trump Motion to Decertify Georgia's Presidential Election Results," Fox 5, January 5, 2021, https://www.fox5atlanta.com/news/judge-denies-trump -motion-to-decertify-georgias-presidential-election-result.

55. Krista Monk, "President Trump's Legal Team Withdraws Ga. Election Challenges," WTOC, January 7, 2021, https://www.wtoc.com/2021/01/07/president-trumps -legal-team-withdraws-ga-election-challenges/.

56. "Transcript: President Trump's Phone Call with Georgia Election Officials."

57. Ibid.
58. Andrew Prokop, "The Past 48 Hours in Trump's Attempt to Steal the Election, Explained," Vox, January 4, 2021, https://www.vox.com/2021/1/4/22211984/tr ump-raffensperger-georgia-hawley-cruz-election.
59. *Trial Memorandum of the United States House of Representatives in the Impeachment Trial of President Donald J. Trump*, United States House of Representatives, February 2, 2021, 10, https://judiciary.house.gov/uploadedfiles /house_trial_brief_final.pdf?utm_campaign=5706-519.
60. Mollie Hemingway, "Media's Entire Georgia Narrative Is Fraudulent, Not Just the Fabricated Trump Quotes," The Federalist, March 17, 2021, https://thefedera list.com/2021/03/17/medias-entire-georgia-narrative-is-fraudulent-not-just-the-fab ricated-trump-quotes/.
61. Joel Pollak (@joelpollak), "Not only did Democrats use the false @washingtonpost 'find the fraud' story in the impeachment brief, but @RepDean also cited it in oral arguments at trial, complete with a slide highlighting the relevant (fake) quotes in the Post article…," Twitter, March 15, 2021, 8:24 p.m., https://twitter.com/joelpo llak/status/1371618421167718404; *Trial Memorandum of the United States House of Representatives in the Impeachment Trial of President Donald J. Trump*, 10.
62. Lindsey Ellefson, "Washington Post Now Says Trump Never Told Georgia Official to 'Find the Fraud,'" The Wrap, March 15, 2021, https://www.thewrap.com/was hington-post-donald-trump-find-the-fraud-correction/.
63. Mark Winnie, "New Recording Reveals Trump Called Georgia Investigator Leading Signature Match Audit," WSB-TV, March 11, 2021, https://www.wsbtv .com/news/local/new-recording-reveals-trump-called-georgia-investigator-leadi ng-signature-match-audit/WEIRQJXKOJFVDGBGATBZOAMSPA/?utm_cam paign=snd-autopilot.
64. Amy Gardner, "Recording Reveals Details of Trump Call to Georgia's Chief Elections Investigator," *Washington Post*, March 11, 2021, https://www.washing tonpost.com/politics/trump-call-georgia-investigator/2021/03/11/c532ea2e-827a -11eb-ac37-4383f7709abe_story.html.
65. Mark Hemingway, "Washington Post Accuses Trump of a Crime Based on Fabricated Quotes," The Federalist, March 16, 2021, https://thefederalist.com/2021/03/16/was hington-post-accuses-trump-of-a-crime-based-on-fabricated-quotes/.
66. David Shafer, "The Secretary of State's office secretly recorded the conversation, mischaracterized its content to the Washington Post and then attempted to delete the recording. It was recently discovered in a laptop 'trash' folder as part of an open records search," Twitter, March 15, 2021, 2:41 p.m., https://twitter.com/DavidS hafer/status/1371531925135953931.
67. Becket Adams, "Audio Shows the Media Got the Trump Georgia Story All Wrong," *Washington Examiner*, March 15, 2021, https://www.washingtonexaminer.com/opin ion/audio-shows-the-media-got-the-trump-georgia-story-all-wrong.
68. Sarah Westwood, "Trump-Georgia Phone Call Story Reopens Old Wounds: Everything You Need to Know," *Washington Examiner*, March 17, 2021, https://

www.washingtonexaminer.com/politics/trump-georgia-investigator-phone-call
-explained-everything-you-need-to-know.

69. Hemingway, "Media's Entire Georgia Narrative Is Fraudulent, Not Just the Fabricated Trump Quotes."

70. Quinn Scanlan, "County Election Officials Put Problem-Plagued Primary in Past, as Early Voting Starts in Georgia," ABC News, October 12, 2020, https://abcne ws.go.com/Politics/county-election-officials-put-problem-plagued-primary-past /story?id=73527020.

71. Brad Raffensperger, letter to Mona Harrington, April 15, 2020, https://www.eac .gov/sites/default/files/paymentgrants/cares/GA_CARES_Disbursement_Request Letter.pdf.

72. "CEIR 2020 Voter Education Grant Program," Center for Election Innovation and Research, n.d., https://electioninnovation.org/research/ceir-2020-voter-educ ation-grant-program/.

73. Wright Gazaway, "GA Sec. of State Mails Out Millions of Absentee Ballot Applications," WTOC, April 1, 2020, https://www.wtoc.com/2020/04/01/ga-sec -state-mails-out-millions-absentee-ballot-applications/.

74. Margot Cleveland, "New Evidence Indicates Enough Illegal Votes in Georgia to Tip 2020 Results," The Federalist, July 9, 2021, https://thefederalist.com/2021/07 /09/new-evidence-indicates-enough-illegal-votes-in-georgia-to-tip-2020-results/; Rich Welsh, "One Man Is About to Flip Georgia, Nullify Biden's Victory," Liberty One, n.d., https://libertyonenews.com/one-man-is-about-to-flip-georgia-nullify-bi dens-victory/; 11Alive, "Second Georgia Senate Election Hearing," YouTube, December 3, 2020, https://www.youtube.com/watch?v=hRCXUNOwOjw&t=1 5733s.

75. Kate Brumback, "Georgia Official Announces Investigations, Defends Election," Associated Press, November 30, 2020, https://apnews.com/article/election-2020 -georgia-state-elections-elections-voter-registration-0dda2f95b4cea6506be9fb65 55195a1c.

76. Rachel Tillman and Associated Press, "Georgia Investigating Groups Allegedly Registering Non-Residents to Vote," Spectrum News 1, November 30, 2020, https://spectrumlocalnews.com/nys/central-ny/news/2020/11/30/georgia-investi gating-illegal-voter-registration.

Epilogue: Consent of the Losers

1. Yoni Appelbaum, "How America Ends," *The Atlantic,* December 2019, https:// www.theatlantic.com/magazine/archive/2019/12/how-america-ends/600757/.

2. Leigh Ann Caldwell, "Despite Objections, Congress Certifies Trump's Election," NBC News, January 6, 2017, https://www.nbcnews.com/politics/congress/despi te-objections-congress-certifies-donald-trump-s-election-n704026.

3. "Presidential Election Results: Biden Wins," *New York Times,* n.d., https://www .nytimes.com/interactive/2020/11/03/us/elections/results-president.html.

4. Benjamin Swasey and Connie Hanzhang Jin, "Narrow Wins in These Key States Powered Biden to the Presidency," NPR, December 2, 2020, https://www.npr.org /2020/12/02/940689086/narrow-wins-in-these-key-states-powered-biden-to-the -presidency.

5. "Michigan Recount Stopped after Judge Says Jill Stein Has No Legal Standing," *The Guardian,* December 8, 2016, https://www.theguardian.com/us-news/2016 /dec/07/us-election-recount-halted-michigan-jill-stein; Byron Tau, "Jill Stein Supporters Drop Pennsylvania Recount Suit," *Wall Street Journal*, December 4, 2016, https://www.wsj.com/articles/jill-stein-supporters-drop-pennsylvania-reco unt-suit-1480810987; "Jill Stein's Election Recount Ends as Wisconsin Finds 131 More Trump Votes," *The Guardian*, December 12, 2016, https://www.theguardi an.com/us-news/2016/dec/12/pennsylvania-recount-jill-stein-request-denied.

6. Colby Itkowitz, "Hillary Clinton: Trump Is an 'Illegitimate President,'" *Washington Post*, September 26, 2019, https://www.washingtonpost.com/politics /hillary-clinton-trump-is-an-illegitimate-president/2019/09/26/29195d5a-e099-11 e9-b199-f638bf2c340f_story.html; William Cummings, "'You Can Have an Election Stolen from You,' Hillary Clinton Warns 2020 Democrats," *USA Today*, May 6, 2019, https://www.usatoday.com/story/news/politics/onpolitics/2019/05 /06/hillary-clinton-warns-2020-democratic-candidates-stolen-election/1116477 001/; Jordan Davidson, "Four Years Later, Bitter Hillary Clinton Claims 2016 Election Was 'Stolen' from Her," The Federalist, October 26, 2020, https://the federalist.com/2020/10/26/four-years-later-bitter-hillary-clinton-claims-2016-elec tion-was-stolen-from-her/.

7. Quinn Scanlan, "Here's How States Have Changed the Rules around Voting amid the Coronavirus Pandemic," ABC News, September 22, 2020, https://abcnews.go .com/Politics/states-changed-rules-voting-amid-coronavirus-pandemic/story?id= 72309089.

8. "COVID-Related Election Litigation Tracker," Stanford-MIT Healthy Elections Project, n.d., https://healthyelections-case-tracker.stanford.edu/.

9. Pat Beall et al., "2020 Election Could Hinge on Whose Votes Don't Count," PBS, October 8, 2020, https://www.pbs.org/wgbh/frontline/article/2020-election-could- hinge-on-whose-votes-dont-count/.

10. Samuel Alito, *Republican Party of Pennsylvania v. Kathy Boockvar, Secretary of Pennsylvania, et al.*, U.S. Supreme Court, October 28, 2020, https://www .supremecourt.gov/opinions/20pdf/20-542(1)_3e04.pdf.

11. Ibid.

12. Ibid.

13. Ibid.

14. Clarence Thomas, *Republican Party of Pennsylvania v. Veronica DeGraffenreid, Acting Secretary of Pennsylvania, et al.*, U.S. Supreme Court, decided February 22, 2021.

15. Brett Kavanaugh, *Democratic National Committee, et. al. v. Wisconsin State Legislature, et. al.*, October 26, 2020, https://www.courtlistener.com/opinion/48 01280/democratic-national-committee-v-wisconsin-state-legislature/.

16. Ibid.

17. Ibid.

18. "Senate Hearing on Election Security and Administration," C-SPAN, December 16, 2020, 01:22:34, https://www.c-span.org/video/?507292-1/senate-hearing-elec tion-security-administration.

19. Jenni Fink, "Trump Campaign Has Enough 'Provable, Illegal Ballots' to Overturn the Election, Giuliani Says," *Newsweek*, November 19, 2020, https://www.news week.com/trump-campaign-has-enough-provable-illegal-ballots-overturn-election -giuliani-says-1548778; Christiana Zhao, "Sidney Powell Suggest 2020 Election Can Be Overturned by Recalling Electors for Fraud," *Newsweek*, June 26, 2021, https://www.newsweek.com/sidney-powell-suggests-2020-election-can-overturn ed-recalling-electors-fraud-1604442.

20. Fergal Gallagher, "Why Millions Don't Trust the Election Results, Despite No Evidence of Widespread Fraud: Experts," ABC News, November 22, 2020, https:// abcnews.go.com/Technology/millions-trust-election-results-evidence-widespread -fraud-experts/story?id=74258192.

21. Miles O'Brien, "Will Georgia's New Voting Machines Solve Election Problems— or Make Them Worse?" *PBS NewsHour*, October 26, 2020, https://www.pbs.org /newshour/show/will-georgias-new-voting-machines-solve-election-problems-or -make-them-worse.

22. Ibid.

23. Ibid.

24. Ibid.

25. Ibid.

26. "Election Security," C-SPAN, June 12, 2018, 01:18:10, https://www.c-span.org/vi deo/?446920-1/justice-homeland-security-officials-testify-election-security.

27. *Kill Chain: The Cyber War on America's Elections*, HBO, 2020, https://www.hbo .com/documentaries/kill-chain-the-cyber-war-on-americas-elections.

28. "Election Security," C-SPAN, March 21, 2018, 1:17:48, https://www.c-span.org/vi deo/?442759-1/senate-intelligence-committee-hearing-focuses-election-security.

29. Ibid.

30. Associated Press, "How to Treat 'Election Deniers' and 'Big Lie' Adherents Is an Ongoing Challenge for Mainstream News Organizations," MarketWatch, June 24, 2021, https://www.marketwatch.com/story/how-to-treat-election-deniers-and -big-lie-adherents-is-an-ongoing-challenge-for-mainstream-news-organizations -01624570721.

31. Rowan Scarborough, "Obama DNI Clapper Leaked Dossier Story on Trump: House Intel Report," Associated Press, April 28, 2020, https://apnews.com/artic le/jake-tapper-barack-obama-archive-james-comey-russia-716b6449b87caf8bc5 996c4eb46ef766.

32. "American Voters Have Few Kind Words for Trump, Quinnipiac University National Poll Finds; Expel Moore If He Wins, Voters Say Almost 2–1," Quinnipiac University, December 12, 2017, https://poll.qu.edu/poll-release-legacy?releaseid= 2507; "Half of U.S. Voters Say Russians Have Something on Trump, Quinnipiac

University National Poll Finds; but Voters Say Both Sides at Fault for Bad Relations," Quinnipiac University, July 24, 20218, https://poll.qu.edu/poll-release -legacy?releaseid=2557;

33. Chris Khan, "Despite Report Findings, Almost Half of Americans Think Trump Colluded with Russia: Reuters/Ipsos Poll," Reuters, March 26, 2019, https://www .reuters.com/article/us-usa-trump-russia-poll/despite-report-findings-almost-half -of-americans-think-trump-colluded-with-russia-reuters-ipsos-poll-idUSKCN1R 72S0.

34. Christopher Mele and Annie Correal, "'Not Our President': Protests Spread after Donald Trump's Election," *New York Times*, November 9, 2016, https://www.ny times.com/2016/11/10/us/trump-election-protests.html.

35. Melanie Eversley, Aamer Madhani, and Rick Jervis, "Anti-Trump Protests, Some Violent, Erupt for 3rd Night Nationwide," *USA Today*, November 11, 2016, https://www.usatoday.com/story/news/nation/2016/11/11/anti-trump-protesters -pepper-sprayed-demonstrations-erupt-across-us/93633154/; Mele and Correal, "'Not Our President.'"

36. Ray Sanchez, "Weekend Brings More Anti-Trump Protests across the Nation," CNN, November 12, 2016, https://edition.cnn.com/2016/11/12/us/protests-electi ons-trump/index.html.

37. J. J. Gallagher, David Caplan, and Stephanie Ebbs, "Tens of Thousands Protest Trump Victory, 124 Arrested," ABC News, November 10, 2016, https://abcnews .go.com/Politics/thousands-us-protest-president-elect-donald-trump/story?id=43 427653.

38. Ibid.

39. Ibid.

40. Chelsea Bailey, "High School Students Stage Walkouts in Protests to Trump Presidential Win," NBC News, November 9, 2016, https://www.nbcnews.com/news /us-news/high-school-students-stage-walk-outs-protest-trump-victory-n681646.

41. Christopher Mele and Patrick Healy, "'Hamilton' Had Some Unscripted Lines for Pence. Trump Wasn't Happy," *New York Times*, November 19, 2016, https://www .nytimes.com/2016/11/19/us/mike-pence-hamilton.html.

42. Jonathan Landay and Scott Malone, "Violence Flares in Washington during Trump Inauguration," Reuters, January 20, 2017, https://www.reuters.com/artic le/us-usa-trump-inauguration-protests/violence-flares-in-washington-during-tru mp-inauguration-idUSKBN1540J7; Elise Viebeck, "Nearly 70 Democrat Lawmakers Now Skipping Trump's Inauguration," *Washington Post*, January 19, 2017, https://www.washingtonpost.com/news/powerpost/wp/2017/01/16/more -than-30-democratic-lawmakers-now-skipping-trumps-inauguration/.

43. Kyle Cheney and Gabriel Debenedetti, "Electors Demand Intelligence Briefing before Electoral College Vote," *Politico*, December 12, 2016, https://www.politico .com/story/2016/12/electors-intelligence-briefing-trump-russia-232498.

44. Mollie Hemingway, "Obama, Biden Oval Office Meeting on January 5 Was Key to Entire Anti-Trump Operation," The Federalist, May 8, 2020, https://thefedera

list.com/2020/05/08/obama-biden-oval-office-meeting-on-january-5-was-key-to
-entire-anti-trump-operation/.

45. Krystina Skurk, "How Michael Flynn Got Caught in the Crossfire between Two
Obama Agencies Looking to Get Trump," The Federalist, July 16, 2020, https://
thefederalist.com/2020/07/16/how-michael-flynn-got-caught-in-the-crossfire-bet
ween-two-obama-agencies-looking-to-get-trump/; "Why Jeff Sessions Recused,"
Wall Street Journal, July 27, 2017, https://www.wsj.com/articles/why-jeff-sessions
-recused-1501111108.

46. Ibid.

47. John Santucci et al., "Members of Trump Cabinet Discussing Invoking 25th
Amendment: Sources," ABC News, January 7, 2021, https://abcnews.go.com
/Politics/lawmakers-call-trumps-impeachment-wake-capitol-hill-violence/story
?id=75097032.

48. Jamie Ehrlich, "Maxine Waters Encourages Supporters to Harass Trump
Administration Officials," CNN, June 25, 2018, https://www.cnn.com/2018/06
/25/politics/maxine-waters-trump-officials/index.html.

49. Joel Pollak, *Neither Free Nor Fair* (self-published Amazon Kindle ebook, 2020).

50. Brittany De Lea, "Trump's Blue Collar Boom: Earnings Rising Fastest for Lowest-
Paid Workers, President Says," Fox Business, January 28, 2020, https://www.fox
business.com/money/trump-rally-wildwood-new-jersey-2020.

51. "Presidential Polls 2020," NBC News, n.d., https://www.nbcnews.com/politics
/2020-elections/presidential-polls.

52. Jennifer Graham, "Is Google Biased against Conservatives?," Deseret News,
August 14, 2020, https://www.deseret.com/indepth/2020/8/14/21362500/is-goog
le-biased-against-conservatives-breitbart-news-donald-trump-utah-mike-lee; Brad
Parscale, "Trump Is Right: More Than Facebook & Twitter, Google Threatens
Democracy, Online Freedom," *USA Today*, September 10, 2018, https://www.usa
today.com/story/opinion/2018/09/10/trump-google-youtube-search-results-biased
-against-republicans-conservatives-column/1248099002/.

53. David Ingram, "Facebook and Twitter Keep Fact-Checking Trump on Voting by
Mail. He's Undeterred," NBC News, September 29, 2020, https://www.nbcnews
.com/tech/tech-news/facebook-twitter-keep-fact-checking-trump-voting-mail-he
-s-n1241339; Peter Baker, "Trump Embraces Fringe Theories on Protests and
Coronavirus," *New York Times*, August 30, 2020, https://www.nytimes.com/20
20/08/30/us/politics/trump-protests-violence-coronavirus.html.

54. Nicquel Terry Ellis, "Guns, Lies, and Ballots Set on Fire: This is Voter Suppression
in 2020," *USA Today*, October 29, 2020, https://www.usatoday.com/story/news
/nation/2020/10/29/2020-election-voter-suppression-looks-like-guns-lies-and-fi
res/6044702002/.54.

Index